Love, War, and Classical Tradition
in the Early Modern Transatlantic World:
Alonso de Ercilla and Edmund Spenser

MEDIEVAL AND RENAISSANCE
TEXTS AND STUDIES

VOLUME 444

Love, War, and Classical Tradition in the Early Modern Transatlantic World: Alonso de Ercilla and Edmund Spenser

Cyrus Moore

ARIZONA CENTER FOR MEDIEVAL

ACMRS

AND RENAISSANCE STUDIES

Tempe, Arizona
2014

THE ARIZONA CENTER FOR
MEDIEVAL &
RENAISSANCE
STUDIES

Published by ACMRS (Arizona Center for Medieval and Renaissance Studies)
Tempe, Arizona
© 2014 Arizona Board of Regents for Arizona State University.
All Rights Reserved.

Library of Congress Cataloging-in-Publication Data

Moore, Cyrus (Professor)
  Love, war, and classical tradition in the early modern transatlantic world :
Alonso de Ercilla and Edmund Spenser / Cyrus Moore.
       pages cm. -- (Medieval and Renaissance Texts and Studies ; Volume 444)
  Includes bibliographical references and index.
  ISBN 978-0-86698-492-8 (acid-free paper)
  1. European literature--Renaissance, 1450-1600--History and criticism.
  2. Epic literature--History and criticism. 3. Ercilla y Zúñiga, Alonso
de, 1533-1594--Criticism and interpretation. 4. Spenser, Edmund,
1552?-1599--Criticism and interpretation. 5. Civilization, Classical--Influence.
  6. Classical literature--Influence. 7. Love in literature. 8. War in literature. I.
Title.
  PN721.M65 2014
  809'.031--dc23

                                                                                      2014034957

∞
This book is made to last. It is set in Adobe Caslon Pro,
smyth-sewn and printed on acid-free paper to library specifications.
Printed in the United States of America

In Memoriam

Larry Don Moore (1939-1969)
Allan S. Hoey (1907-1995)

Table of Contents

ACKNOWLEDGMENTS

It is a pleasure to thank the Arizona Center for Medieval and Renaissance Studies and Dr. Leslie MacCoull for their support. I also gratefully acknowledge the inspiration and assistance of two exemplary scholars throughout this project, Clare Carroll and the late Isaías Lerner, who originally proposed the juxtaposition of authors presented here.

Je parle espagnol à Dieu, italien aux femmes,
français aux hommes et allemand à mon cheval.

"I speak Spanish to God, Italian to women,
French to men, and German to my horse."

—*attributed to Charles V*

❧

Delicatus ille est adhuc cui patria dulcis est.
Fortis autem iam cui omne solum patria est,
perfectus vero cui mundus totus exilium est.

"The man who finds his homeland sweet is still a tender beginner;
he to whom every soil is as his native one is already strong;
but he is perfect to whom the entire world is as a foreign land."

—*Hugh of St. Victor,* Didascalicon *(trans. Marie and Edward Said)*

A reader is in a place, in a school or university, in a work place, or in a specific country at a particular time, situation, and so forth. But these are not passive frameworks. In the process of widening the humanistic horizon, its achievements of insight and understanding, the framework must be actively understood, constructed, and interpreted.

Edward Said,
Humanism and Democratic Criticism (75)

PREFACE

The Renaissance was once memorably described as an unparalleled expansion of space and recovery of time.[1] Our own age, by contrast, has reversed the dynamic, distance contracting to irrelevancy while time has slipped our grasp, any sense of a past beyond that of our parents as tenuous as the talk of imaginary worlds. A link to the early-modern transatlantic setting of the present study was suggested by the Chilean earthquake of March 2010, which drew wide-scale attention to a largely unknown part of the Southern Cone. Television news showed scenes of devastation in communities near Concepción, followed by civic unrest at the lack of government response, which quickly segued into images of the army patrolling streets and suppressing demonstrations. While the rapid militarization of the disaster may have surprised some viewers, it was only the most recent of a half-millennium of military interventions in a region long identified with conflict between Chile's foreign colonists and its indigenous population, who, following the example made of their counterparts in the United States, were relocated to reservations during the nineteenth century, so that German, Swiss, and Italian immigrants could settle their ancestral lands. While the effort to recover these lands continues today, the beginning of the conflict stretches back five hundred years, to when the Spanish first pushed south from Peru in a series of military campaigns to colonize the area, extract its mineral wealth, and put an end to the fierce resistance of its inhabitants, protagonists of Alonso de Ercilla's *La Araucana*. Their descendants, known today as the Mapuche, are those whose images briefly caught the world's attention in 2010.

The frisson of finding in those faces a momentary conduit between the present day and the poems discussed below is only one of many. Descendants of Spenser's Irish and English survive as well, of course, as does the memory of their often bloody conflict, the origins of which form part of the context of Spenser's poem and which was officially resolved only in 1998. Even more noteworthy is the perennial nature of key concerns to which both poems give voice:

---

[1] Perry Anderson, *Lineages of the Absolutist State* (London: NLB, 1974), 420–28, at 422.

the challenge of deploying traditional military force against an untraditional foe; the frequent inconclusiveness of military encounters despite the clear materiel superiority of one side over the other; the ramifications for dominant cultures of sustained attempts to subjugate subaltern ones, projects whose costs are moral as well as economic and whose motives expose a complex web of interests, public and private, principled and pecuniary, the unwieldy mix consolidated in the texts considered here under the guise of religion or humanism: Christianity for the Spanish, saving the souls of a continent; civility in the case of the English, root-ing out the Scythian barbarity of Ireland. Especially striking is a warning about the unexpected consequences of excessive violence, eloquently if ineffectively voiced by the Spanish commander, who counsels his troops that "el rigor excesivo en el castigo / justifica la causa al enemigo" ("excessively harsh punishment justi-fies the cause of the enemy") (21.56.6–8). Shortly thereafter, in a scene evocative of Spenser's Talus, Spanish soldiers amputate the hands of an Araucan fighter as an example to others, eliciting his taunt that "[. . .] quedan otras muchas esforza-das / que saben gobernar bien las espadas" ("there remain many others who can bravely and skillfully wield a sword") (22.47.7–8). The warning recurs much later, near the poem's close, when the Indian leader, Caupolicán, just before his double execution by impalement and arrows, warns of "otros mil Caupolicanos"—"a thousand other Caupolicanos"—in the years to come (34.10. 1–3). England and Spain both suffered the blow-back of such violence. The Spanish were ultimately unsuccessful in their counter-insurgency against the Araucans, who, confronted with the deadly novelties of horses and firearms, soon learned to lure their oppo-nents into marshes where horses were immobilized and narrow mountain passes susceptible to ambush, from which the attackers disappeared into the surround-ing countryside. If England was better at this type of warfare it was due largely to a surge of forces into Ireland in the second half of the sixteenth century that pursued a policy of mass starvation and civilian massacre—the "remedy of the sword" reluctantly advocated by Irenius in Spenser's *A View of the Present State of Ireland*. Ercilla's and Spenser's poems both address the relative merits of soft and hard power in a context of asymmetric warfare, with the moral foundation for intervention itself taking on surprising importance among the Spanish, culmi-nating in the Valladolid debates between Las Casas and Vitoria.

While these issues suggest correlatives with the world today, they resonate toward antiquity as well. Virgil's *Aeneid*, a text of unsurpassed importance for both Ercilla and Spenser, delves deeply into the cost of empire, examining the corrosive effects of avarice, ambition, and uncontrolled anger. While the price paid by the individual for public good is often cited as the poem's central insight, memorably enacted in the scenes between Aeneas and Dido, a less dramatic but more pervasive dis-ease infects the narrative as well, the sense that the Carthag-inian queen is only one of many left behind in Rome's imperial project, the "New World Order" envisioned by Augustus. A lofty vision drives Virgil's epic program, but as key scenes throughout the poem make clear, facts on the ground repeatedly interfere with heroic ideals. The caveat is as applicable to early modern as to ancient poets of empire, who elide the discrepancies as best they can. While considerations such as these, conjuring continuities with the past, threaten the veil between art and life, it is to art that the following pages turn, restoring the boundary between fiction and history that enables the insights the former alone brings to the latter.

New York
2012

To grasp the special nature of an epoch or a work, to perceive the nature of the relations between works of art and the time in which they were created, is an endless problem which each of us, exerting the utmost concentration, must endeavor to solve for himself and from his own point of view.

Erich Auerbach,
Literary Language and its Public in Late Latin Antiquity and the Middle Ages (12)

I. Texts and Contexts, Temporal and Territorial

1. Eyewitness Testimony and Twelve-Step Plans

Why read Alonso de Ercilla's *La Araucana* alongside Edmund Spenser's *The Faerie Queene*? What do these bulwarks of national literature, Spain's historical epic of conquest in Chile and England's heroic romance of knights and damsels, reveal in concert that they don't individually, justifying the crossing of so many geographical and cultural boundaries?

Comparisons of epic have traditionally remained within borders of close affiliation, early modern studies favoring Ariosto and Tasso, Spenser and Milton, or Ercilla and Camoens, the first four authors also read against each other and all in light of Homer, Virgil, and less prominent interlocutors. While studies of Iberian epic have a distinguished tradition within the Luso-Brazilian academy, these works are rarely studied in conjunction with their European counterparts. This stems on the one hand from the distinctiveness of American subject matter; it derives on the other from less tangible criteria, including the traditional isolation of the peninsula as well as the prerogatives of national language academies, whose specializations at times inhibit comparative projects. Readings of affiliated texts possess clear potential advantages, most notably in the cogency of their theses. The present study's contention, that the same key classical images appropriated by Ercilla and Spenser have dramatically different significance in different contexts and thus much to tell us about the societies and literary praxes in which they are embedded, is straightforward enough. What we learn, by contrast, is more diffuse. One key finding explored below concerns how thoroughly epos and eros, traditionally associated with the opposing genres of epic and romance, are in fact entwined from antiquity on, imagery assigned the one repeatedly discovered in service to the other, a rhetorical *contaminatio* resisting repeated efforts to sequester the two and suggesting, in the end, proto-psychological insight. Similarly noteworthy is how Ercilla and Spenser both incorporate not only the *elocutio* of key epic topoi but their *dispositio* as well, that is, their structural as well as expressive functions, revealing unexpected adherence to traditional narrative construction. More broadly, it soon becomes clear that it was not only the economic, military, and literary rivalries, both within and among these societies and their neighbors and set against the backdrop of increasing confessional strife, that shaped literary production and interpretation, but that both poets' personal experiences were equally formative of the process. Ultimately these factors illuminate not only what we would expect, that conceptions of the Old World helped shape understandings of the New, from the Atlantic archipelago of Ireland to the southern cone of the Americas, but also that the New propelled changing perceptions of the Old.

For the *Araucana*, published in three parts in 1569, 1578, and 1589, Ercilla announced the modest goal of an eyewitness account of the efforts made by the Spanish to suppress an Indian insurgency in one of the farthest outposts of their American empire. His opening lines emphatically rejected the scope of the sixteenth century's most famous narrative poem, Lodovico Ariosto's *Orlando Furioso*: "No las damas, amor, no gentilezas / de caballeros canto enamorados" ("Not of ladies, love, nor of the gallantries of enamored knights do I sing") (1.1.1–2) the *Araucana* begins, promising instead to adhere to the themes of "el valor, los hechos, [y] las proezas" ("valor, deeds, and prowess") (1.1.5) and to provide "[. . .] relación sin corromper sacada / de la verdad, cortada a su medida" ("an account taken from the truth without corrupting it and cut to its measure") (1.3.5–6) by one who was "[. . .] de parte dello buen testigo" ("a reliable witness to much of it") (1.5.8).[1] For thirteen cantos, more than 7500 lines and a third of the poem, Ercilla adhered to his plan. Then near the end of Part I he inserted a brief but highly-charged scene between the leading Araucan warrior and his beloved. The episode was set on the eve of a fateful battle, and its tragic eroticism provoked a breach of martial decorum from which the poem never recovered. Other encounters with Araucan women soon followed, now featuring the narrator himself. Other passages explored issues of love and erotic desire, and by the end of the work it was the counterpoint of these discourses with the enframing chronicle that left the deepest impression. Spenser's project, by contrast, was never modest. Having shown himself both innovative and ambitious years earlier in *The Shepherds' Calendar*, he laid out a grand scheme of twenty-four books for the *Faerie Queene*, the first twelve to treat twelve private moral virtues, the latter twelve public ones, his goal: "to fashion a gentleman or noble person in vertuous and gentle discipline."[2] As the vehicle for this endeavor, published in two parts in 1590 and 1596, Spenser created a "historicall fiction," an allegorized version of Franco-Burgundian

---

[1] Text for *La Araucana* is from Isaías Lerner's edition of the poem (Madrid: Catedra, 1993); all translations in the following pages are those of the author unless otherwise indicated.

[2] The phrase is from Spenser's "Letter to Ralegh"; text for the Letter and for Spenser's poem is from A. C. Hamilton's edition of *The Faerie Queene* (London: Longman, 1977).

legends of Arthur and the origins of Britain interwoven with elements of classical epic and popular romance. Structuring each book around a knight and a quest, Spenser's poem invoked by design what Ercilla's embraced mid-course, the confrontation of opposing forces, traditionally gendered, but not exclusively so: war and love, violence and nurturance, emotion and reason.

The *Araucana* and *Faerie Queene* share key contextual concerns. Both poems are dedicated to sovereigns-as-ideal-readers by authors whose relations with the court are a constant subtext to their narratives. Both narratives speak from the margins of power, literally and figuratively, reflecting competing concerns of court and colony, metropole and periphery. In the background of both poems are colonial projects in which both authors were actors, Ercilla as a *chapetón* or new arrival in the Americas in contrast to a previous generation of conquistadors, now settled *encomenderos*, whose conduct he frequently found repugnant; Spenser as one of Ireland's "New English," a recently landed gentleman thanks to the expropriations of the Munster plantation scheme, in contrast to the "Old English" inhabitants of the Pale, whose social and moral legitimacy he attacked both here and more directly in *A View of the Present State of Ireland*. Both poets experienced the tension between nobility and royalty characteristic of the period, Ercilla in an apparent breach of etiquette that threatened him with capital punishment and resulted in his precipitous departure from the New World; Spenser through his association with the Leicester and Essex factions, whose bitter disagreements with Elizabethan policy had such dire consequences for their leaders. Both poems inscribe providentialist history, Ercilla's a celebratory one of Spanish empire, Spenser's a confrontational one of militant Protestantism. In both cases the pride of imperial expansion emerges against a backdrop of anxiety over security at home, England with regard to domestic unrest (the Northern rebellion of 1569, the Ridolfi plot of 1570) as well as to Irish rebels, all potential beneficiaries of assistance from Spain and continental co-religionists; Spain with an eye to *morisco* uprisings (Granada, 1568–1570), revolt by the Low Countries (which began in 1568), and the ominous Turk, a potential co-conspirator with the former as well as a daunting competitor for Mediterranean and potentially world dominion during these years. The exposure to ostensibly barbaric cultures was formative for both poets and their cultures and became, for both, the site of competing visions of national identity pitting class-based economic interests against traditional political and religious ideologies and power structures. Finally, each author's grand project, Ercilla's discovered in the process of composition, Spenser's thoroughly premeditated, fell short of its intended goal, the *Araucana* coming to an unexpected halt halfway through Part III, the *Faerie Queene* falling silent with only six of its twenty-four quests completed, its ambitious moral program supplanted, in the poem's closing pages, by an escapist adventure story. Both curtailments are inextricably bound up with the intrusion of the poets into their narratives.

Differences in the texts and contexts of these works are equally stark. Just beneath its labyrinthine surface Spenser's work is frequently at odds with Tudor

policy and uneasy with female regency, infusing the poem with a sense of political urgency and driving its use of allegory. Supportive of Habsburg policy,
the *Araucana* is less topical, its political references typically epideictic. Ercilla's
criticism of the conduct of Spain's counterinsurgency in Chile, by contrast, is
trenchant, drawing the poet ineluctably beyond issues of just war and legitimate
conquest into an intensely personal examination of the conflicts between honor,
duty, and virtue more broadly considered. Ercilla's relationship with regency, in
contrast to Spenser's, is both more detached and more personal. The difference
is captured in a brief prefatory letter to Philip II that accompanied the 1569 *Araucana* (subsequent editions replaced it with a *pro forma* dedication), in which
it is clear that the poet viewed the king as more than the symbolic father of his
subjects. The letter opens with the words, "Como en los primeros años de mi ni-
ñez, yo comenzase a servir a vuesa Magestad," that is, "Since in the first years of
my childhood I began to serve your Majesty," then recalls how a young Ercilla
(thirteen at the time) had entered the king's service as a page after the death of
his natural father, a magistrate and advisor to the *Consejo Real*, and how he continued in this role when his mother, *dama mayor* to the empress Doña María,
died, "viéndome huérfano de padres, y tan mozo" ("seeing myself orphaned of
parents and such a young boy").[3] If the suggestion of monarch as adoptive parent
is wishful thinking, the young man's presence at court was highly privileged and
insured genuine if limited proximity. Once the poem is underway this proximity
to authority authorizes aesthetic legitimacy:

> Y haberme en vuestra casa yo criado,
> que crédito me da por otra parte,
> hará mi torpe estilo delicado,
> y lo que va sin orden, lleno de arte [. . .] (1.5.1–4)

> And having grown up in your household, which lends me further credit,
> will make my dull style delicate and that which has no order full of art.

Here and in numerous apostrophes to Philip Ercilla both recalls and reminds his
principal reader of their earlier association. While Spenser had no such personal
connection with the British monarch, unlike Ercilla he was an established poet
before beginning the *Faerie Queene* and remained close from his student days at
Cambridge to friends associated with the powerful earl of Leicester, whose pa-
tronage he enjoyed through much of his career. During the decades he worked on
the *Araucana*, Ercilla served intermittently as a royal emissary, but never regained

---

[3] Reproduced in Elizabeth B. Davis, *Myth and Identity in the Epic of Imperial Spain*
(Columbia: University of Missouri Press, 2000), 29; the translation is Davis's. For the
limited biographical data on Ercilla, see José Toribio Medina, *Vida de Ercilla* (México:
Fondo de Cultura Económica, 1948) and idem, "El preceptor de Ercilla," *Boletín de la
Academia Chilena* 2 (1919): 265–86.

his previous proximity to power. Made government inspector of books in 1577 (among his *aprobaciones* are those for Fernando de Herrera's 1580 edition of the works of Garcilaso de la Vega), he pursued the decidedly unaristocratic business of financial speculation to support his family. An additional difference between the poets and their poems: while Spenser lived the last twenty years of his life in Ireland, Ercilla spent no more than seven in or on his way to and from the New World, much of this consumed by travel and staging time in neighboring locations. He spent scarcely a year in what was then part of the Viceroyalty of Peru, now Chile, among the Araucans, today's Mapuche, who thereafter engaged so much of his imagination. Turning finally to a colonizing culture's relationship to language, a theme of special significance for the *Faerie Queene*, as will be seen, there was a fundamental difference between Spain's emphasis on and frequent thematization of the linguistic difference it encountered in the Americas and Elizabethan England's repression of the same phenomenon in Ireland, an ideologically driven occlusion affecting not only colonial policy and its associated texts, but the historical reception of related literary works, including Spenser's poem.[4]

2. Critical Trends, Persistent Questions

Recent readings of the *Araucana* and *Faerie Queene* appear in each case to have reached a similar juncture. While Ercilla's poem was a sixteenth-century best seller and has been widely admired by literati ever since for its style and descriptive power, its anomalies, which in addition to the aforementioned ones of theme and structure include the absence of a Spanish hero, an often admiring depiction of the native Amerindians, and frequently harsh denunciations of the Spanish, have generated perennial discussion about Ercilla's true sympathies and led to the paradox of the poem being taken on the one hand as the *Urtext* of anti-Spanish Chilean nationalism and on the other as the prototypical inscription of Habsburg imperial glory.[5] While the issue of the poet's attitude toward

---

[4] Patricia Palmer explores the Elizabethan marginalization of linguistic difference in Ireland and the ensuing "discourse of sameness," which she argues prepared the way for increasingly violent intervention: *Language and Conquest in Early Modern Ireland: English Renaissance Literature and Elizabethan Imperial Expansion* (Cambridge: Cambridge University Press, 2001), 39, 46, 74, 155.

[5] Among the best-known accolades for the *Araucana* are those of Cervantes, whose *Galatea* (1585) praises Ercilla for his exceptional grace and whose "inquisition of the books" in the 1605 *Quijote* identifies the *Araucana* as one of the three best works of Spanish heroic verse. In his *Discours sur le Poème Epique* (c. 1755), after characterizing Ercilla as "le plus raisonnable des anciens poètes espagnols" ("the most reasonable [i.e., less refined, more historically oriented] of the old Spanish poets"), Louis Racine condemned the episodes of the Araucan women as digressions inserted to break monotony (quoted

the events he describes is entirely legitimate, there was a period several decades
ago when the question began to be posed in the American academy primarily as
one of Ercilla's pro- or anti-imperialism per se. The fact that the majority of His-
panists regularly rejected the latter characterization didn't stop its periodic reappearance, returning to prominence most recently when the poem was featured
in a widely-read study that argued for a subversive secondary tradition of heroic
poetry or "epic of the losers," anti-imperialist in spirit, inaugurated by Lucan and
Ovid and eventually identified by the Cinquecento debates with Ariosto and
the genre of romance.[6] Given the *Araucana*'s celebration of Habsburg empire,
application of the thesis to the *Araucana* was always problematic. The misreading
stemmed in part from granting too much importance to Ariosto relative to other
literary influences on Ercilla and too little to culturally specific determinants of
genre. For despite Cinquecento pronouncements to the contrary, the *Furioso* was
read principally in Spain as dynastic epic and its author identified as a model
lyricist, as Ercilla notes early in the *Araucana*, as discussed below in Part 2. As
for Lucan, his significance for Golden Age Spain was overwhelmingly stylistic
rather than ideological, his verse a paradigm of historical rhetoric rather than re-
publican ideology.[7] The irony, if not inaccuracy, of enshrining the Araucans as a

---

in Frank Pierce, *La Poesía Epica del Siglo de Oro* [Madrid: Gredos, 1961], 53, still the primary reference for the *Araucana*'s reception); Voltaire offered an ambivalent assessment of
Ercilla in his *Essai sur la poésie épique* of 1726, arguing that the speech made by Colocolo
in Canto 2 excelled that of Nestor in the *Iliad*, but complaining a few pages later how
stunning it was to see the poet, having risen so high, fall so far (quoted in Pierce, *Poesía
Epica*, 42–43). A number of early Spanish texts on poetry, including those by Sánchez
de Lima (1580), Díaz Rengifo (1592), and Alfonso de Carvallo (1616), cite Ercilla as a
rhetorical model.

[6] David Quint, *Epic and Empire: Politics and Generic Form from Virgil to Milton*
(Princeton: Princeton University Press, 1993). For a pervasive critique of Quint's read-
ing of Ercilla see Davis, *Myth and Identity*, 12, 20, 43–45; Craig Kallendorf argues that
Quint recognizes but doesn't pursue grounds for Ercilla's sympathy for the Indians in the
Aeneid's own ambivalence ("Representing the Other: Ercilla's *La Araucana*, Virgil's *Aeneid*, and the New World Encounter," *Comparative Literature Studies* 40 [2003]: 394–414,
at 412 n. 20). Andrés I. Prieto offers a counter-reading to Quint's analysis of the Actium-
Lepanto association ("El Segundo Carlomagno: Las Visiones Proféticas de San Quintín
y Lepanto en *La Araucana* de Ercilla," *Hispanófila* 140 [2004]: 81–99, at 91–92). For recent commentary sympathetic to Quint's reading, see Barbara Simerka, whose analysis
of Siglo de Oro *indiano* dramas, history plays, and burlesque epic articulates a concept of
"counter-epic" more nuanced than Quint's: *Discourses of Empire: Counter-Epic Literature
in Early Modern Spain* (University Park: Pennsylvania State University Press, 2003), esp.
4, 36–37; cf. Barbara Fuchs, "Traveling Epic: Translating Ercilla's *La Araucana* in the
Old World," *Journal of Medieval and Early Modern Studies* 36 (2006): 379–95. The reception of the *Araucana* is discussed in greater detail below in Part II.

[7] Isaías Lerner, "Ercilla y Lucano," in *Hommage à Robert Jammes*, Anejos de Crit
icón 1 (Toulouse: Presses Universitaires du Mirail, 1994), 2: 683–91; idem, "Persistencia

paradigmatic defeated people might also be noted, since they denied the Spanish a victory in Chile for more than three hundred years, the briefly honored treaty of Quillén with Spain (1641) marking the first and only formal defeat of a European power on New World soil.[8] Perhaps most interesting about these twentieth-century claims regarding the *Araucana*'s "true" message is the degree to which they recall the poem's early reception, when Spain's enemies singled out Ercilla's scenes of Spanish cruelty to enhance their propagation of the notorious Black Legend. Recent commentary on the poem, enriched by a number of significant works, appears finally to have moved beyond this narrow question.

A similar trajectory might be seen to characterize commentary on the *Faerie Queene*, which following New Criticism's mid-century close readings became more openly politicized with post-structuralist developments in literary theory. New Historicism extended the critical context of the poem to Elizabethan court pageantry, sixteenth-century religious tensions, and England's troubled relationship with Ireland. Cultural studies, particularly feminist theory and gender studies, found fertile soil in female regency, while colonial theory focused new scrutiny on Spenser's long residence in Ireland and his participation in its government, exploring his role in the administration of empire alongside his creation of its imagery. The Irish question, much of it focused on the nature of Spenser's relationship to oppressive colonial policies, took a literary turn in the 1990s, when his indebtedness to Gaelic speech and literature received renewed attention. More recently a turn away from the contextuality of New Historicism to textuality more narrowly construed has occurred, most notably in studies pursuing detailed intertextual analyses of Spenser's poetry vis-á-vis Irish as well as classical traditions, Ovid most notable among the latter.[9] While overt politicization of literary studies may have declined since the 1970s and 80s, the study of Spenser and Ovid just mentioned offers a clear example of how the political persists, in this case arguing Spenser's hostility to imperial ambition by his purported rejection of the Augustan program put forward by Virgil, lodestar of the

---

de metáforas: Lucano, Ercilla, el romancero," in *Siglos Dorados: Homenaje a Augustin Redondo*, ed. Pierre Civil (Madrid: Castilla, 2004), 765–74.

[8] The treaty of Quillén was signed on 6 January 1641 and ratified by Philip III on 29 April 1643; the eighteenth-century *Diccionario geográfico-histórico de las Indias Occidentales ó América* (Madrid: B. Cano, 1786–1789) of Antonio de Alcedo still refers to the Araucans as "[. . .] enemigos implacables de los Españoles, que no han podido nunca reducirlos ni sujetarlos [. . .]" ("implacable enemies of the Spanish, who have never been able to reduce nor subject them") (1: 142). "Pacification" of the Araucanians became Chilean policy in the late nineteenth century; cultural autonomy remains contentious in the region to the present day: cf. Debra A. Castillo, "Impossible Indian," *Chasqui: Revista de Literatura Latinoamericana* 35 (2006): 42–57, at 47–48.

[9] Cf. Richard A. McCabe, *Spenser's Monstrous Regiment: Elizabethan Ireland and the Poetics of Difference* (Oxford: Oxford University Press, 2002); Syrithe Pugh, *Spenser and Ovid* (Aldershot: Ashgate, 2005); Palmer, *Language and Conquest*.

translatio studii and thus of pivotal importance for both our authors, in favor of the individualism, eroticism, and playful irony of Ovid.[10] Ercilla's relationship with Virgil is far from purely reverent, as his attack on the *Aeneid*'s treatment of Dido, one of the *Araucana*'s most revealing passages makes clear, but his disagreement with Virgil is not over empire per se. While Spenser's readings of Virgil are more complex, what is clear from the moment such questions are posed is how thoroughly an interpretation of either author's relationship to Virgil depends on how the *Aeneid* itself is read.

3. Re-reading Virgil

Attributions of pro- or anti-Virgilian sympathies are frequently made in the context of unacknowledged assumptions about the *Aeneid* and its author. Arguing that Spenser rejects Virgil's Augustan imperialism for Ovid's ironic individuality, for example, on the one hand conflates author and text and on the other assumes that the *Aeneid* endorses the political program it describes. The first, or "intentional fallacy," was long ago rejected by literary criticism and survives here only because of the *Aeneid*'s status as a "classic," which among non-classicists, at least, keeps it secure behind a facade of ostensibly transparent meaning where poet and poem are one. The second is belied not only by passages in Virgil's other works, but by two millennia of commentary on "problematic" passages of the *Aeneid* itself, especially those featuring Dido, the "loss" of Creusa, and the killing of Turnus, the dissonance of which was apparent even among the poet's contemporaries. Ovid himself is the best example, having drawn on these scenes for his own renditions of Dido in the *Heroides* and Creusa and Turnus in the *Metamorphoses*, activating oppositional readings latent in the model. The antithesis between Virgil and Ovid is itself a largely Ovidian creation, obscuring the degree to which both poets appropriated the same sophisticated language and ironic attitudes of Hellenism and the Alexandrian epyllion.[11] Ovid and others who wrote "against" Virgil, especially Lucan and Statius, had the effect of

---

[10] Pugh, *Spencer and Ovid*, esp. 1–3, 63–72, 121–36, 177–99, 272–73; McCabe argues, by contrast, that Spenser avoids choosing between the two authors, instead exploiting the ever-present possibility of doing so: *Monstrous Regiment*, xi; cf. John Watkins, who maintains that Spenser constantly revises his understanding of Virgilian identity: *The Specter of Dido: Spenser and Virgilian Epic* (New Haven: Yale University Press, 1995), 6–8. See also Philip Hardie, "Spenser's Vergil: *The Faerie Queene* and the *Aeneid*," in *A Companion to Vergil's* Aeneid *and its Tradition*, ed. Joseph Farrell and Michael C. J. Putnam (Oxford and Malden, MA: Wiley-Blackwell, 2010), 173–85.

[11] Cf. Richard F. Thomas on the failure of Virgilian criticism to distinguish between character voices and the voice of the poet; Thomas notes that the fact that Ovid's Dido was already present in Virgil's portrait of the queen gets lost in conflicts between Chris-

monumentalizing the *Aeneid* and identifying its author with an Augustan vision of imperial accomplishment and social order. Servius, Macrobius, and Donatus, along with many who followed in their footsteps, strove mightily to construct the same normative reading, glossing whatever didn't fit the Augustan project.[12] Following antiquity, as Christian allegoresis shifted attention from ideology to morality, enabling a reading like Augustine's, who bemoaned his entrapment in the wanderings of Aeneas and Dido's romantic tragedy,[13] secular opposition to the Augustan *Aeneid* emerged in autonomous narratives that told of Aeneas as a traitor to Troy and of Dido as the chaste and tragic queen of Carthage long before Aeneas ever lived, responses to the poem that were banished from learned commentary and thrived in vernacular romance traditions. While early humanists eschewed such popular legends, emphasizing a text-based philology that restored historical context, they were alert to a work's deeper meaning. In the case of Virgil this meant enshrining an Augustan *Aeneid* as a repository of moral and rhetorical exempla while sharing reservations about the poem's cardinal values, notably *pietas* and the control of anger. Petrarch was among those who accused the Virgilian hero of lapses of the former, and the latter became a topic in the Cinquecento debates, which while monumentalizing Virgil as epic saw Francesco Salviati arguing that Ariosto's work was preferable to Virgil's because the killing of Rodomonte was better justified than that of Turnus.[14] Tasso's *Gerusalemme Liberata* went so far as to rewrite Virgil's climactic scene not once but twice in order to leave no doubt as to its justification, drawing on a neo-Aristotelian critique of honor inspired by renewed interest in Aristotle's *Ethics*, which followed

---

tian and pagan readings and allegorical and pedagogical traditions: *Virgil and the Augustan Reception* (Cambridge: Cambridge University Press, 2001), 18–19, 79, 135, 155 ff.

[12] Peter E. Knox, "Savagery in the *Aeneid* and Virgil's Ancient Commentators," *Classical Journal* 92 (1997): 225–33, at 228–29; cf. Thomas, *Virgil*, 29. By contrast, Servius's reading of the *Eclogues* found ample criticism of the Augustan regime: Richard A. McCabe, "Annotating Anonymity, or Putting a Gloss on *The Shepheardes Calender*," in *Ma(r)king the Text: The Presentation of Meaning on the Literary Page*, ed. J. Bray et al. (Aldershot: Ashgate, 2000), 35–54, at 42–43.

[13] See Garry Wills, "Vergil and St. Augustine," in *Companion*, ed. Farrell and Putnam, 123–32; S. G. MacCormack, *The Shadows of Poetry: Vergil in the Mind of Augustine* (Berkeley: University of California Press, 1998).

[14] Joseph C. Sitterson Jr., "Allusive and Elusive Meanings: Reading Ariosto's Vergilian Ending," *Renaissance Quarterly* 45 (1992): 1–19, at 10 ff.; cf. Thomas, who notes that defenders of Aeneas are usually quick to point out that his characterization as having abandoned Troy is something that comes from Turnus (*Aen.* 12.15): *Virgil*, 157; cf. Kallendorf, "Philology, the Reader, and the *Nachleben* of Classical Texts," *Modern Philology* 91 (1994): 137–56, at 137–38; cf. idem, "Historicizing the 'Harvard School': Pessimistic Readings of the *Aeneid* in Italian Renaissance Scholarship," *Harvard Studies in Classical Philology* 99 (1999): 391–403, esp. 399–400. See also Dennis Looney, "Marvelous Vergil in the Ferrarese Renaissance," in *Companion*, ed. Farrell and Putnam, 158–72.

the rediscovery of the *Poetics*.[15] Tasso, in thrall to Counter-Reformation fervor, saw Aeneas' behavior as both a moral failure and a structural mistake. Ariosto, by contrast, would appear to have read the *Aeneid*'s climactic scene and its other fraught passages as manifestations of Virgil's nuanced approach to his subject and as a clear indicator of the poet's reservations regarding Augustan policies, an authorial distancing Ariosto himself developed into the full-blown comic irony of the *Furioso*. Christian and secular humanists largely continued their presentation of an Augustan *Aeneid*, turning increasingly to allegoresis to resolve its ambiguities.

The utilitarian humanism that migrated north from Italy in the early modern era focused on the *Aeneid* as a storehouse of independent moral and rhetorical models, relying on allegoresis and on vernacular translation to elide, distort, or simply ignore problematic passages. Virgil's covert hostility to Augustanism, as evidenced by the *Eclogues*, was widely recognized in Spenser's time, but increasingly the *Aeneid* itself was favorably or unfavorably received depending on the view of centralized authority, admired in Restoration England while by the eighteenth century it was considered the work of an Augustan apologist.[16] Romanticism decried Virgil as derivative of Homer, a view that persisted in German classicism, and it wasn't until the end of the nineteenth century that the interpretive complexity of the poem returned as a subject of serious attention. A monolithic, civilization-celebrating *Aeneid* continued to be the norm until after the Second World War and into the 1950s and 1960s, when more nuanced, i.e., pessimistic, interpretations of the poem began to appear.[17] New Criticism's focus on ambiguity, a trope that proved especially productive with regard to Virgil, helped propel the change, with a number of studies exploring what was conceived as a contrast between the poem's multiple voices, namely private ones of sacrifice and loss and public ones of celebration and achievement.[18] Following the 1970s the traditionally staid domain of classicists experienced a partial politicization somewhat similar to that affecting other areas of academia. New Histori-

---

[15] Cf. Lauren Scancarelli Seem, "The Limits of Chivalry: Tasso and the End of the *Aeneid*," *Comparative Literature* 42 (1990): 116–25, at 116.

[16] McCabe, "Annotating," 41–44; cf. Thomas, *Virgil*, 223. See also Henry Power, "The *Aeneid* in the Age of Milton," in *Companion*, ed. Farrell and Putnam, 186–202.

[17] Denis Feeney, "How Virgil Did It," review of Gian Carlo Conte, *The Poetry of Pathos: Studies in Virgilian Epic*, and of Randall T. Ganibann, *Statius and Virgil: The "Thebaid" and the Reinterpretation of the "Aeneid*," *TLS*, 15 February 2008: 26–27; cf. Kallendorf, "Historicizing," 391; and idem, "Vergil and Printed Books, 1500–1800," in *Companion*, ed. Farrell and Putnam, 234–50.

[18] Adam Parry, "The Two Voices of Virgil's *Aeneid*," *Arion* 2 (1963): 66–80; cf. Charles Martindale, "Descent into Hell: Reading Ambiguity, or Virgil and the Critics," *Proceedings of the Virgil Society* 21 (1998): 111–50, at 116–17; Thomas discusses the distinction between ambiguity in Virgil and concepts of polysemy, diphony, and polyphony (*Virgil*, xv).

cism's focus on how power relations determined meaning shifted attention from examinations of ambiguity, which tended toward open-ended readings, to more closed interpretations of the *Aeneid*.[19] An ancient "counter-classical" sensibility was identified in conjunction with a new appreciation for Sophocles and Euripides, a perspective emphasizing man's limitations and failures instead of his accomplishments and highlighting Virgil's inheritance from classical tragedy.[20] In contrast to Ercilla and Spenser studies, the controversy among some classicists became more politically explicit, with these darker readings of the poem, which became known as those of the "Harvard School," denigrated by opponents as expressions of opposition to the Vietnam war, while "Augustan" interpretations were linked conversely with the policies of Reagan and Thatcher.[21] As such overt politicization declined, as elsewhere in the academy, questions regarding the sensibility of the *Aeneid* persisted, generating numerous explorations of the textual origins of the poem's complexity and of the ambiguities attendant on its depiction of Augustus's new world order, a place not meant for characters as sympathetically portrayed as Tityrus, Dido, and even Turnus. Spenser, in particular, was aware of the need that Virgil felt to disguise his criticism of power in literary imagery, having followed his lead in *The Shepherds' Calendar*.[22] Working against

[19] Don C. Fowler, "First Thoughts on Closure: Problems and Prospects," *Materiali e Discussioni per l'Analisi dei Testi Classici* 22 (1989): 75–122; cf. idem, "Second Thoughts on Closure," in *Classical Closure: Reading the End in Greek and Latin Literature*, ed. D. H. Roberts et al. (Princeton: Princeton University Press, 1997), 3–22, in which Fowler also comments on the desirability of deconstructing Quint's overly schematic thesis in *Epic and Empire*, 8–9; and idem, *Roman Constructions: Readings in Postmodern Latin* (Oxford: Oxford University Press, 2000), 6 ff.

[20] W. R. Johnson, "The Problem of the Counter-Classical Sensibility and Its Critics," *California Studies in Classical Antiquity* 3 (1970): 123–51, esp. 125–35, 143; cf. Johnson's subsequent influential study, *Darkness Visible: A Study of Vergil's* Aeneid (Berkeley: University of California Press, 1976).

[21] John Henderson, "Exemploque Suo Mores Reget," *Hermathena* 164 (1998): 101–16, at 113–14; cf. Thomas, *Virgil*, 223; cf. Martindale on the association of New Criticism's tolerance of diversity and complexity of outlook with "soft liberalism" ("Descent," 119).

[22] Inter alia, see Knox on the use of *saevus* or "savage," long associated with Turnus and Mezentius, but also applied to Juno and to Aeneas himself: "Savagery," 228; cf. the discussion of Virgil's ironic use of *aurea condet saecula* in Johnson, "Problem," 138–43. With regard to Augustus's new world order: "aspice venturo laetantur ut omnia saeclo!" ("Behold, how all things exult in the age that is at hand!") (*Ecl.* 4.52), see Thomas, *Virgil*, 296; cf. idem, "The 'Sacrifice' at the End of the *Georgics*, Aristaeus, and Vergilian Closure," *Classical Philology* 86 (1991): 211–18, at 212; on ambiguity as intertextuality, see Martindale, "Descent," 122. McCabe explores the significance of the political ambivalence identified by Servius in Virgil's *Eclogues* for *The Shepherds' Calendar*, noting that Virgil's covert hostility to the policies of Augustus was generally accepted in Spenser's day ("Annotating," 43–44; cf. *Spenser's Monstrous Regiment*, 8). For recent discussion of the broader issues raised here, see Craig Kallendorf, *The Other Virgil: "Pessimistic" Readings of*

the exploration of ambiguity in heroic poetry has been an ongoing bias against complexity in epic per se, often conceived in contemporary literary theory as a foil for the novel and modernity rather than being read in its own historical context.[23] The reappearance of a monolithically Augustan *Aeneid* as late as the mid-1990s suggests that a basic divide in the way the *Aeneid* is read is inescapable, enabled, on the one hand, by a complex and subtle text and revealing, on the other, the fundamentally ideological activity of constructing meaning from texts, a process begun by authors but completed by readers whose perspective on the world is an indispensable resource they bring to the task whatever their purpose or level of sophistication.[24]

Because of its focus on texts rather than authorial intention, intertextual analysis has largely supplanted discussions of allusion and ambiguity. Intertextuality reveals how the dialogic quality of language, Bakhtin's image of words bringing with them traces of earlier enunciations, applies just as readily to texts, which exist within a system of texts, as *parole* to *langue*, from whose existence they derive their meaning. Intertexts run the gamut from extensive, advertised quotations to traces that exist only "under erasure," awaiting a strong reader to recognize and assign them significance. Since their function is not self-evident but ranges from respectful to parodic, questions of authorial intention persist, however, as do those related to ideology, since which intertexts are focused on

the Aeneid *in Early Modern Culture* (London: Oxford University Press, 2007), and idem, "Vergil in Printed Books."

[23] Thomas views the work of Mikhail Bakhtin as having contributed to this problem, ascribing to him the position that epic contains a single voice, the dominant one of a culture, in contrast to the novel (*Virgil*, 16). Bakhtin in fact asserts otherwise, noting that the "novelization" of literature occurred at several points in its history: "In the era of Hellenism a closer contact with the heroes of the Trojan epic cycle began to be felt; epic is already being transformed into novel," and "From the point of view of polyglossia, Rome was merely the concluding phase of Hellenism, a phase whose final gesture was to carry over into the barbarian world of Europe a radical polyglossia [. . .]": *The Dialogic Imagination*, trans. Caryl Emerson and Michael Holquist, ed. Michael Holquist (Austin: University of Texas Press, 1981), 15–63. Also citing Bakhtin as having contributed to the bias in literary studies in favor of modernity, Elizabeth Davis notes that Spanish imperial epic is broadly viewed as lacking literary merit by Golden Age specialists, who continue to focus on genres privileged by the nineteenth century, i.e., lyric, comedia, and the novel; the result, as Davis points out, is a canon that reflects our own interests, e.g., the late twentieth-century focus on Renaissance Petrarchism and global power, rather than those of early modern Spain (*Myth and Identity*, 2, 9–11).

[24] Karl Galinsky, *Augustan Culture: An Interpretive Introduction* (Princeton: Princeton University Press, 1996); cf. Thomas, "The 'Sacrifice' at the end of the *Georgics*," 212; and idem, *Virgil*, 135.

always comes at the expense of others left un- or under-acknowledged.[25] Such caveats notwithstanding, intertextual analysis comes closest not only to traditional philology, but also to the praxis of early modern humanists, whose new sense of the past drove efforts to read in an appropriately historical context, a task made possible by remaining acutely attuned to the traces of antiquity and, increasingly, of illustrious near-contemporaries.[26]

While the *Aeneid* presents an essential contextual issue for reading Ercilla and Spenser, other key topics include the impact of Ariosto, noted earlier, as well as that of Tasso, together with the literary debates over epic and romance that engulfed them and the associated attacks on romance that spread with the Counter-Reformation; the role of Castiglione's *Il Cortegiano* in both reflecting and helping shape an aesthetics of *cortegianía* that spread beyond social etiquette to literary production; the importance of Neoplatonism, and of the triad of the concupiscent, irascible, and rational faculties that comes to dominate both poems' treatment of the themes of love and war; and the political realities behind the *translatio imperii et studii*, manifest most notably in Spain in the literary projects of Garcilaso and Boscán and in England in those of Protestant intellectuals at Cambridge. These topics are briefly addressed in the following pages before introducing the imagery that will be the focus of the present study.

4. Debating Ariosto:
Fever Dreams and Judicious Delight

The Cinquecento debates, which occupied Italian literati throughout the lifetimes of Ercilla and Spenser, embroiled their participants in a mix of ethical, linguistic, and rhetorical concerns, many of which had a direct impact on issues

---

[25] R. O. A. M. Lyne explores the relationship between allusion and intertextuality: "Virgil's *Aeneid*: Subversion by Intertextuality. Catullus 66.39–40 and Other Examples," *Greece and Rome* 41 (1994): 187–204, at 187–89; on intertexts and "strong readers," see Fowler, *Roman Constructions*, 118–22, 128; on ambiguity as intertextuality, see Martindale, "Descents," 122.

[26] Kevin Krogh discusses the distinction between the Bakhtinian "other" and the colonial "Other" of more recent theory, arguing that the encounter with the latter becomes one of multiple "others" constituting the context to which Bakhtin's utterance responds: "Reading Spanish Colonial Literary Texts: The Example of *La Araucana*," *Journal of Iberian and Latin American Studies* 10 (2004): 35–43. Fowler discusses the bi-directionality of intertextual references and the way in which traces of contemporary theory are left in ancient texts as we read them (*Roman Constructions*, 129–30). Sitterson argues that in its range and sophistication sixteenth-century understanding of heroic poetry compares favorably with our own: "[. . .] an enduring hermeneutic typology crossing centuries and cultural differences to reveal enduring ways we come to terms with certainty and uncertainty of meaning" ("Allusive," 15).

addressed in the following pages. Arising between defenders and detractors of the *Furioso*, in final form by 1532, the initial question of the controversy as to whether Ariosto's work was epic or romance went through several distinct stages, with both positions being argued at different times by those who wanted to ennoble the poem.[27] Since chivalric romance had no ancient theoretical pedigree, an early approach to the problem was to minimize the differences between the two genres and stress the *Furioso*'s affinities with epic. This was done through moral allegories, which turned Ariosto's poem into a program of moral virtue, and by emphasizing any and all points of contact between the *Furioso* and the classics. Differences were minimized and problematic passages suppressed, part of the familiar procedure of intertextual analysis. As the case for the *Furioso* as epic became less tenable, due in part to a growing familiarity with Ovid's *Metamorphoses*, whose decidedly un-epic digressions and multiple storylines helped spur the recognition of the ancient "counter-classicism" noted earlier, Ariostan partisans changed tack. Now they argued for the prestige of chivalric romance, citing Ovid as its illustrious progenitor and proclaiming it the modern equivalent of epic, with the *Furioso* its finest exemplar.[28] The disputes were fueled by the immense popularity of Ariosto's work and frequently reflected extra-textual topics, including the tastes of popular readers versus learned ones and the prestige of the vernacular, itself recently subject to debate in Italy. Various critical issues were at stake, among them the delineation of literary genres, left incomplete by antiquity; the formation of the humanist canon, which by the end of the century would include the *Furioso* as one of its first vernacular entries; and the validity of modern culture with its new style of poetry, or *maniera ariotesca*, in the face of ancient authority daily enhanced by humanist scholarship. Not to be underestimated was the impact of substantial profits to be made by early publishers, who adapted their proficiency at marketing humanist editions of the classics to Ariosto's work, the success of which then led, *volte versa*, to a demand for *ottava rima* versions of the classics, including the *Metamorphoses*. Aristotle's *Poetics*, rediscovered at the close of the fifteenth century but not more broadly known until vernacular translations and commentaries were disseminated around the middle of the next, signaled another stage of the debates, which now coalesced around

---

[27] Bernard Weinberg, *A History of Literary Criticism in the Italian Renaissance*, 2 vols. (Chicago: University of Chicago Press, 1961); cf. Daniel Javitch, *Proclaiming a Classic* (Princeton: Princeton University Press, 1991); Lawrence Rhu, *The Genesis of Tasso's Narrative Theory* (Detroit: Wayne State University Press, 1993); Margaret W. Ferguson, *Trials of Desire: Renaissance Defenses of Poetry* (New Haven: Yale University Press, 1983).

[28] Cf. Charles Segal, "Narrative Art in the *Metamorphoses*," *Classical Journal* 66 (1971): 331–37; and idem, "Ovid's Orpheus and Augustan Ideology," *Transactions and Proceedings of the American Philological Association* 103 (1972): 473–94. W. R. Johnson notes that the counter-classical vision of man's tragic weakness and of the futility of his culture constitutes a "ferocious rejection of all that humanists cherish": "Problems," 135.

the concept of narrative unity, in contrast to which the variety and *entrelacement* of romance stood in sharp relief.[29] With the appearance of Tasso's *Gerusalemme Liberata* in 1581 and *Discorsi dell'arte poetica* in 1587, the debate changed course once more as attention shifted to the differences between Ariosto's work and Tasso's and to the latter's conjoining of Tridentine doctrine with Aristotelian theory to link the wandering plot of romance with moral turpitude.[30] The association, made in antiquity, gained new potency with the Counter-Reformation's emphasis on obedience to authority, and thus the debates wound down with the century and their impact migrated to other countries, having moved from largely formal and secular issues at their start to decidedly religious and moral ones at their close.

If romance, unlike epic, had no illustrious pedigree, its condemnation did, continuing a long tradition of attacks on *fabulae licentiosae* or *milesiae* which ran through Augustine, Dante, and Petrarch to Vives and Agrippa, attacks which accused such narratives of at best wasting time and at worst corrupting morals. Appearing regularly in these denunciations was Horace's *aegri somnia, vanae*, the idle imaginings or dreams of someone ill, originally employed as part of a structural critique of narratives lacking Aristotelian unity, which Horace famously compared to a painting that joined the head of a human to the body of a horse and the tail of a fish. An early seventeenth-century critique of the *Araucana* as *acephalo*, or headless, due to its lack of a hero, still carried this connotation, whereas most uses of the image had long since acquired moral overtones, as in Petrarch's reference to human life as "sogno d'infermi e' fola di romanzi" ("an ill dream, a tale of vain romance").[31] Frequently in the background of condemna-

---

[29] Aristotle's *Poetics* was translated into Latin in 1498 by Giorgio Valla; Aldus published the first Renaissance Greek edition of the text in 1508; increased familiarity with the work came with Robortello's vernacular commentary on it, published in 1548; Bernardo Segni's vernacular translation, the first, followed in 1549. Barbara Fuchs discusses the growing obsession with the specifications of the *Poetics* during this period with the Tridentine Church's deepening suspicions of the links between humanism and Protestantism: *Mimesis and Empire* (Cambridge: Cambridge University Press, 2001), 24.

[30] The *Discorsi* were begun in 1565 but not published until 1587; they were substantially revised and republished as *Discorsi del poema heroico* in 1594/5. The *errare-errore* association is made by Petrarch throughout the *Rime Sparse*; Minturno linked romance *errare* with moral *errore* in his *Arte poetica* (1564); the terms had been compared in antiquity by Horace (*Satires* 2.3.48–51).

[31] From Horace's *Ars poetica*: "[. . .] isti tabulae fore librum / persimilem, cuius, velut *aegri somnia, vanae / fingentur species* [. . .]" ("a book may be like just such a picture if it portray *idle imaginings* shaped like *the dreams of a sick man*") (6–8, emphasis added) (English translation by Walter Jackson Bate, in *Critical Theory Since Plato*, ed. Hazard Adams [New York: Harcourt Brace Jovanovich, 1992], 68); cf. Petrarch in the *Triumphus Cupidinis*: "Ben è 'l viver mortal, che si n' aggrada, / *sogno d'infermi e fola di romanzi!*" (4.69) (emphasis added) ("This mortal life, that we do cherish so, / Is an ill dream, a tale of vain

tions of romance was the rhetorical triad of *delectare, docere,* and *movere* (to please, to teach, and to move), adduced in order to accuse such tales of devoting themselves to the first term alone.[32] Never far from these issues were the ancient enmities between philosophy and poetry on the one hand and dialectic and rhetoric on the other. Not surprisingly, defenses of romance often echoed those of poetry, ranging from the simple appeal to a refreshing pause from serious pursuits, the contrast of *otium* and *negotium,* to elaborately constructed arguments, the best known of the early modern period being Philip Sidney's *Apologie for Poetrie,* which claimed for its art the *summum bonum* of inspiring virtue.

The endlessly proliferating *Amadís* novels, especially popular in France and Spain during this period, were prime targets of anti-romance opprobrium, which threatened any author who indulged in the fantastic. Ercilla notes the problem near the end of the *Araucana,* when he states that "Quien muchas tierras vee, vee muchas cosas / que las juzga por fábulas la gente" (36.1.1–2) ("Whoever sees many lands sees many things that people consider to be fictions"). Spenser voices the anxiety more pointedly in the proem to Book 2 (his concern all too justified given Lord Burghley's response to the poem), where he worries, "That all this famous antique history, / Of some th'aboundance of an idle braine / Will iudged be" (2.1.1–3).[33] Spenser mounts a proleptic defense against such criticism in the "Letter to Ralegh," part of the paratextual apparatus of the 1590 *Faerie Queene,* where he promotes his "historicall fiction" as "plausible and pleasing," turning a integral attribute of romance to his favor by asserting that readers enjoy such narratives "rather for *variety* of matter, then for *profite* of the ensample" (737). A few lines later he stresses the traditional contrast between history's examples and philosophy's arguments, pointing out "[. . .] how much more profitable and gratious is doctrine by ensample, then by rule" (737). The "Letter" goes on to differentiate the method of the historian proper, who "discourseth of affayres orderly as they were donne" (738), from Spenser's own procedure, which "thrusteth into the middest [. . .] and there recoursing to the thinges forepaste, and divining of

---

romance") (*The Triumphs of Petrarch,* trans. Ernest Hatch Wilkins [Chicago: University of Chicago Press, 1962]). The criticism of the *Araucana* as *acephalo* is made by Cristóbal Suárez de Figueroa (*Hechos de Don García Hurtado de Mendoza, Quarto Marqués de Cañete,* 1613); such complaints were often voiced by supporters of Ercilla's commander in Chile, García Hurtado de Mendoza, with whom the poet had serious disagreements and whom the poem largely ignores; see 100 n. 73, infra.

[32] Cf. Cicero, *Orator,* 69, and Quintilian, *Institutio Oratoria,* 4.482.

[33] In Ercilla's case the passage is a close imitation of the *Orlando Furioso*'s exordium to Canto 7, which in quintessential Ariostan fashion is followed by precisely the type of fabulous romance invention the statement is meant to exclude: the palace of Alcina. Spenser alludes to Burghley's criticism in the Proem to Book 4 (1–3) and in the final stanza of Book 6 (6). Burghley is known to have been critical of Spenser's work: see *The Spenser Encyclopedia* (Toronto: University of Toronto Press, 1997), 122.

things to come, maketh a pleasing Analysis of all" (738), an approach he associates, in another instance of the early modern malleability of genre, with "all
the antique Poetes historicall," identified as Homer, Virgil, Ariosto, and Tasso.
Spenser's brief discussion is especially notable for its elision of history and poetry, each traditionally contrasted with philosophy; its references to profit and
graciousness, terms not usually associated with the topic; and its invocation of
the *ab ovo / in medias res* opposition, accompanied by a brief explanation of how
the poet exploits this device.[34] Rarely noted are significant similarities between
these aspects of Spenser's discussion and another early modern paratext, Jacques
Amyot's foreword to his 1547 translation of Heliodorus's *Aethiopica* into French,
a work championed by Scaliger, which had a substantial impact on romances
for the next half-century, including Sidney's *Arcadia*. Amyot's Heliodorus, the
first in a vernacular, was translated into Spanish in 1554 and became popular in
Spain, best known for its impact on Cervantes's *Persiles y Sigismunda*, and by all
appearances familiar to Ercilla as well, as will be seen.[35] Thomas Underdowne
translated Amyot's text into English, minus the crucial foreword, circa 1569, as
An Aethiopian Historie. Amyot went on to translate Plutarch's *Lives* in 1559, later
Englished by Sir Thomas North, and essential concepts in his preface to this
later work were utilized by Sidney in his *Apologie*, discussed in Part 4, below. As
one of the few scholars of the period with a knowledge of Greek and as a clerical figure (emissary of Francis I to Trent and later royal tutor) who translated
both history and Greek romance, Amyot was uniquely situated to comment on
the structural and moral issues involved in their comparison and contrast. His
remarks on Heliodorus, which adeptly elide a number of romance attributes with
the function of history, have the added interest of appearing in the context of an
indirect exchange in France among translators of history and translators of the
Amadís novels, a protracted dialogue inscribed in the prefaces to their works over
several decades contemporaneous with the early Cinquecento debates, offering a
less systematic but nonetheless influential response to a number of the same key
issues. The exchange began in 1527 with Jacques Colin, an early benefactor of

---

[34] Cf. Horace, *Ars poetica*, 147–148.87
[35] Further discussion of Heliodorus and Spenser is found below, 115 n. 57. Cf. Mar-
cel Bataillon, *Erasmo y España* (Mexico: Fondo de Cultura Económica, 1950), 622; on
Heliodorus and Cervantes, see Isabel Lozano Renieblas, *Cervantes y el mundo de Persiles*
(Alcalá de Henares: CEC, 1998), 81, 125–26, 189–92; cf. Alban K. Forcione, *Cervantes,
Aristotle, and the* Persiles (Princeton: Princeton University Press, 1970), esp. 49–50. Don
C. Fowler identifies the *Aethiopica* as thematizing the issue of open versus closed endings
("Second Thoughts," 17); see 11 n. 19, supra. See J. R. Morgan, "Heliodoros," G. Sandy,
"The Heritage of the Ancient Greek Novel in France and Britain," and M. Futre Pinhei-
ro, "The *Nachleben* of the Ancient Novel in Iberian Literature of the Sixteenth Century,"
in *The Novel in the Ancient World*, ed. Gareth Schmeling (Leiden: Brill, 1996), 417–56,
735–73, 775–99 respectively.

Amyot and later the translator of Castiglione's *Courtier* (1537), who in a prefatory letter to his translation of Thucydides invokes Petrarch's *sogno d'infermi* in criticizing those who waste their time reading romances rather than history. Over the next twenty years the *Amadís* translators, facing increasing censure, offered a series of justifications in their forewords ranging from the *otium* topos to the value of reading per se because it circumvents idleness, to the claim that the tales of chivalry contain hidden wisdom.[36] The sophistication of the discussion increased dramatically with Amyot's "Le proême du Traducteur" to the *Aethiopica*, which begins by identifying history as best suited for providing refreshment from more serious work "[. . .] à cause de la *diversité* des choses que y sont comprises [. . .] entendu en même temps que le *profit* est conjoint avec le plaisir" ("because of the diversity of things comprised there [. . .] [its being] understood at the same time that profit is combined with pleasure").[37] The *proême* then notes that some readers consider the structure of history, in contrast to its subject matter, to be too austere to be sufficiently pleasing, "[. . .] à cause qu'elle doit réciter les choses nettement & simplement, ainsi comme elles sont avenues, & non pas en la sorte qu'elles seraient plus plaisantes à lire" ("due to its having to recite things neatly and simply as they have occurred [*ab ovo*], and not in a way that would be more pleasing to read [*in medias res*]"). Narratives which enjoy such freedom, by contrast, are fictitious stories or *contes fabuleux*, and Amyot's ensuing proposal is for *contes fabuleux en forme d'histoire*, the best of which "[. . .] sont les moins eloignées de nature, & où il y a plus de *vérisimilitude*" ("are the least distanced from nature, and where there is more verisimilitude"), a quality for which "il faut *entrelacer* si dextrement du vrai parmi du faux, en retenant toujours *semblance de vérité*" ("it is necessary to interweave the real and the false so cleverly, always retaining the semblance of truth").[38] With regard to recent *contes fabuleux*, i.e., the *Amadís* novels, Amyot complains that, "ce soient plutôt songes de quelque malade rêvant en fièvre chaude, qu'inventions d'aucun *homme d'ésprit & de jugement*" ("they are rather the dreams of someone ill with a high fever rather than the inventions of a person of spirit and judgement"), adding that, "qu'ils ne sauroient avoir *la grâce*, ni la force de *délecter* le loisir d'un *bon entendement*" ("they would be capable neither of the grace nor the power to delight the leisure of someone of sound understanding"). The *Aethiopica*, by contrast, exemplifies the hybrid narrative he is championing, not only because it rewards virtue and punishes vice, but also be-

---

[36] The principal works and translators referred to here are Nicolas Herberay des Essarts, *Le Premier Liure de Amadis de Gaule*, 1540; Claude Colet, *Neufiesme livre d'Amadis de Gaule*, 1553; and Jacques Gohorry, *Le quatorzieme livre d'Amadis de Gaule*, 1547.

[37] Text for Amyot's "Proême" to the *L'Histoire Aethiopique d'Heliodore* is that of the New York Public Library's 1553 manuscript edition of the poem, transcribed in Appendix B, below; translations are those of the author.

[38] Cf. Horace: "[   ] atque ita mentitur, sic veris falsa remiscet" ("[. . .] and he invents, mixing fiction with truth"), *Ars poetica*, 151 (see 16 n. 31, for translation).

cause "[. . .] la *disposition* en est si singulière" ("its organization is so singular"), namely, "[. . .] car il commence au milieu de son histoire, comme font les Poëtes Héroiques" (" because it starts in the middle of its story, as do the heroic poets"), a procedure whose benefit, he goes on to explain, is "la force d'atraer & retenir la lecteur" ("the power to attract and retain the reader"), who keeps reading to find out about both the beginning and the end. As for those who would still reject such a morally and structurally superior narrative (readers like Lord Burghley or Plato one suspects), Amyot turns the traditional attack on romance against them, accusing them of "une fièvre d'austerité intraitable" ("an intractable fever of austerity") (5).[39]

5. The Courtly Alternative

The frequent references in Amyot's discussion to judgement, sensibility, and graciousness are evidence of the primary force that militated against excessive emphasis on moral and structural regulation during this period, the program of *cortegianía* or courtiership most memorably inscribed in Castiglione's *Il Cortegiano*, first published in 1528 but probably completed by 1516. Courtliness was everything the fevered denunciations of romance and the Cinquecento debates were not: not too moralistic, not too scholarly, not too insistent, its proponents opposing good taste to rules, decorum to moralizing, and broadly speaking a Neoplatonically inspired aestheticization to Neoaristotelian neoclassicism.[40] Castiglione had a substantive impact on both Ercilla and Spenser, yet the central elements of his program acquired fundamentally different connotations between

---

[39] Amyot begins the tradition of seventeenth-century French bishops, most notably Pierre-Daniel Huet (*Traité des l'origine des romans*, 1670), legislating on rules of the humanist-Christian novel; cf. Mark Fumaroli, "Jacques Amyot and the Clerical Polemic Against the Chivalric Novel," *Renaissance Quarterly* 38 (1985): 22–40; Sergio Capello argues that Amyot shares Castiglione's project of shaping the moral and civic man and was probably influenced by Castiglione's ideas about the value of fiction, or *discorso faceto* ("Histoire fabuleuse e poetica del romanzo in Jacques Amyot," unpublished paper, Università di Udine, 1997, 11–12).

[40] Cf. Peter Burke, *The Fortunes of the Courtier: The European Reception of Castiglione's Cortegiano* (Cambridge: Polity Press, 1995), 10–12. Castiglione's emphasis on taste appears in various guises, from the emphasis on "una certa grazia" ("a certain grace") (1.14) and "un certo bon giudicio e grazia" ("a certain good judgement and grace") (1.21) to references to "omini che hanno *ingegno*" ("men who have *ingenuity*") (1.35) and who recognize what is proper by "un certo *giudicio naturale*, e non per arte o regula alcuna" ("a certain *natural judgement*, and not through any art or rule") (1.35). Citations from *Il Cortegiano* indicate book and section in the Arnoldo Mondadori edition (ed. Carlo Cordié [Milan: Mondadori, 1991]); English translation is based on that of George Bull (New York: Penguin, 1967).

their inclusion in the *Araucana*, where they largely reflect their original context, and the *Faerie Queene*. These changes are among the most vivid indicators of the shift in "psychological chorography" between the cultures, geographies, and time periods associated with the two poems. *Sprezzatura*, the master trope, is introduced in the Urbino salon by Lodovico da Canossa, papal diplomat and friend of Erasmus, whom Francis I made bishop of Bayeux and who very probably would have known Amyot. It is Da Canossa who encourages the courtier "[. . .] usar in ogni cosa una certa sprezzatura che nasconda l'arte" ("to use in everything a certain *sprezzatura* that conceals art") (1.26). In contrast to such studied spontaneity, desirable in any situation, two additional terms are directed more narrowly to maintaining affability in the face of potential disagreement: *dissimulazione* accomplishes this by artful indirection, by drawing attention away from while simultaneously focusing on an issue; *mediocrità* skirts antagonism through a balancing of viewpoints, artful compromise, and amiable demurral. Pervading all aspects of the courtly milieu is *grazia*, the elegant ease of proper social interaction.[41] The *Courtier*'s emphasis on affability reflects what Norbert Elias termed the "courtization of the warrior," a monopolizing of force by the early modern absolutist state, mirrored locally by stricter control of the emotions and increased self-restraint. *Cortegianía* is ultimately identified with an additional concept that Elias focused on, *civiltà*, another key term whose meanings shift dramatically over the sixteenth century, from politeness or civility to civilized life and civilization itself.[42]

---

[41] "Psychological chorography" is McCabe's phrase (*Spenser's Monstrous Regiment*, 1). Noting that *sprezzatura* was an old term meaning "setting no price on," Burke identifies the elision of aesthetic and ethical concerns that eventually inform *cortegianía* with the concepts of *phronesis* and *sophrosyne*, which Aristotle referred to the prudence and temperance of Odysseus in contrast to Achilles; Xenophon developed this into *sophrosyne*, or discretion, and *eukosmia*, or decorum; Cicero drew on these ideas to articulate concepts of *decorum* and *neglegentia diligens*, or studied negligence; following Cicero, Ovid is associated with concepts of *ars casum simulat*, or of art producing the illusion of spontaneity, and, more explicitly, with *ars est celare artem*, or with the point of art being to conceal art (*Fortunes*, 10–12).

[42] Norbert Elias, *On Civilization, Power, and Knowledge: Selected Writings*, ed. Stephen Mennell and Johan Goudsblom (Chicago: University of Chicago Press, 1998), 71–72, 75. Elias's best-known study, *The Civilizing Process*, was originally published in Germany in 1939, but not translated into English until 1978 (vol. 1) and 1982 (vol. 2). Elias notes that *civilité* took on a specific meaning with the publication in 1530 of Erasmus's *De civilitate morum puerilium*; for discussion that takes issue with Elias's thesis, see Dilwyn Knox, "*Disciplina*: The Monastic and Clerical Origins of European Civility," in *Renaissance Society and Culture*, ed. John Monfasani and Ronald G. Musto (New York: Italica Press, 1991), 107–35. Cf. Peter Burke's examination of the warrior's lack of self-control as countered by concepts of *curialitas*, in which the inclusion of literacy represented a precursor to the ideal of arms and letters: early Renaissance humanists rejected the linkage; the

While Castiglione's program is inherently political, deriving its emphasis on indirection from the behavior required in the presence of a powerful ruler, its goal is not to stifle opinion as much as to control it within domestically political, or polite, limits. As such, it marks one point in the perpetual oscillation between two poles of rhetorical praxis that cycle through the history of oratory beginning in antiquity: deliberative during periods of political pluralism, epideictic when power is centralized. Classical rhetoric's *in utramque partem* exercises, which developed a speaker's ability to argue either side of a proposition, were exploited by both. The basis of literary dialogue and a practice that worked to identify ambiguity and complexity, this skill, which ironically scholasticism's *disputationes* did a better job of preserving than more dogmatic varieties of humanism, lay at the heart of the ancient enmity between rhetoric and philosophy, which condemned such flexibility as sophism, insisting instead on absolute truth.[43] The ancient quarrel between appearance and reality, opinion and truth, resurfaces at numerous points in the discussion of Ercilla and Spenser. It is especially prominent in the world of the *Faerie Queene*, where truth is typically identified with reformed religion and appearance with the threat of moral contamination. As the sixteenth century progressed and the atmosphere of religious and political discourse grew increasingly polarized, deliberative rhetoric declined and the early humanist dialogue was increasingly supplanted by treatises, *apologiae*, diatribes, and by treatises-masquerading-as-dialogues, the dialogicity of which rarely extended beyond the name. It is not that all early cinquecento dialogues were truly dialogic, as Virginia Cox makes clear, but rather that, "even where it does not evince a 'dialogical conception of the truth,' the humanist dialogue *does* express a 'dialogic conception of the cognitive process.'"[44] As Cox goes on to explain:

> With the collapse of humanist ideals, discussion is no longer conceived of as a means for exploring the truth, and written dialogue has relinquished its corresponding role as a *provocatio*. Truth now appears as an absolute,

---

courtier helped reestablish it (*Fortunes*, 15). Anthony Cascardi argues that the subversion of violent instincts within increasingly restricted court circles encouraged poets to substitute pastoral for heroic verse, although he notes that Spain's prestige as an imperial power worked against this tendency: *Ideologies of History in the Spanish Golden Age* (University Park: Pennsylvania State University Press, 1997), 251, 267.

[43] Stephen Greenblatt explores the importance of the *in utramque partem* concept for English Renaissance culture in *Renaissance Self-Fashioning: From More to Shakespeare* (Chicago: University of Chicago Press, 1980), 231 ff.

[44] V. Cox, *The Renaissance Dialogue: Literary Dialogue in its Social and Political Contexts, Castiglione to Galileo* (Cambridge: Cambridge University Press: 1992), 62; also cf. Eva Kushner, "Renaissance Dialogue and Subjectivity," in *Printed Voices: The Renaissance Culture of Dialogue*, ed. Dorothea Heitsch and Jean-François Vallée (Toronto: University of Toronto Press, 2004), 229–41.

hallowed by authority and defined by political interest: a commodity to be meted out by an omniscient *princeps sermonis* (68).[45]

The development is exemplified by two works of special significance to Spenser: Stefano Guazzo's *La Civil Conversazione* and Lodowick Bryskett's *A Discourse of Civill Life*, discussed below in Part 3, as well as by Spenser's own *View*.

6. Garcilaso, Boscán, and the Spanish *Translatio*

Elias argued that a crucial aspect of courtization, which he traced across a diversity of nationalities, was the use of a common language, initially Italian and then French, which functioned as Latin had earlier, manifesting the unity of Europe and the new social formation at its core, court society, embodied in the concept of *civilité*.[46] Subsequent development of these ideas by others identified the unifying language with Petrarchism, whose revolutionary prosody and new sense of subjectivity became a hallmark of modernity as well as an inescapable challenge for sixteenth-century poets, who through its mastery displayed their own coming-of-age together with that of their cultures, the latter in a *translatio studii* which each envisioned as passing from Greece to Rome to Italy and thence respectively and exclusively to themselves.[47] Not surprisingly, the dynamic manifested itself

---

[45] Cox argues that the single most important factor in the shift from dialogue to monologue was the Counter-Reformation, with the advent of print technology leading to increased public impatience with erudition and demand for more informative rather than philosophical enquiry: *Renaissance Dialogue*, 63. For an introduction to the diversity, development, and critical reception of the dialogue form in early modern Spain, see Lía Schwartz, "El diálogo en la cultura áurea: de los textos al género," *Insula: Revista de Letras y Ciencias Humanas* 542 (1992): 1–28; Walter J. Ong explores the sixteenth-century shift from Socratic dialogue to monologue in the context of Ramus's commodification of knowledge, in *Ramus, Method, and the Decay of Dialogue: From the Art of Discourse to the Art of Reason* (Chicago: University of Chicago Press, 1958), esp. 151–52.

[46] Cascardi notes that Petrarchan lyric acted as a common language even in Spain, where it wasn't the principal poetic language for many years; he argues that Elias's concept of "courtization" is supported by Anthony Grafton's and Lisa Jardine's description of humanist training as fostering docility toward political authority (*Ideologies*, 153, 251, 285); cf. Anthony Grafton and Lisa Jardine, *From Humanism to the Humanities* (Cambridge, MA: Harvard University Press, 1986), xiv, 22–25. James Nicolopulos's study of the reception of *La Araucana* among Peruvian criollos offers an illuminating example of Cascardi's thesis: "Reading and Responding to the Amorous Episodes of the *Araucana* in Colonial Peru," in *Ésta de Nuestra América Pupila: Estudios de Poesía Colonial*, ed. Georgina Sabat-Rivers (Houston: Society for Renaissance and Baroque Hispanic Poetry, 1999), 227–43, at 232.

[47] Cf. John Freccero, "The Fig Tree and the Laurel: Petrarch's Poetics," in *Literary Theory and Renaissance Texts*, ed. Patricia Parker and David Quint (Baltimore: Johns

differently in different localities depending on Petrarch's identity prior to the integration of his poetics, the status of the target country's vernacular, and the geopolitical context into which the new prosody was introduced. In Spain the influence of the *Trionfi* and *Canzoniere* was apparent as early as the 1400s, while integration of *Rime Sparse* metrics awaited Juan Boscán and Garcilaso de la Vega, who began experimenting with Italian verse forms in the late 1520s.[48] England had potent ties to Petrarch through his association with Chaucer and the medieval, proto-Protestant tradition. Both Ercilla and Spenser embed Petrarchan imagery in pastoral, Ercilla employing the combination in a critique of brutality, Spenser using pastoral allegory and satire to comment on Tudor politics and culture. Intimately related to epic's erotic opposition, pastoral has a natural affinity with both poems, one set in the midst of what is often an idealized, rural society in the New World, the other frequently evoking a bucolic setting threatened by demonic recidivism. In the wake of classical literary theory's complex association of pastoral and epic, the epicurean innocence of Theocritan shepherds and Greek romance's exploration of the birth of erotic awareness held special appeal for early modern authors. When pastoral appears in other genres, often announced by a *locus amoenus*, it typically signals a temporary retirement from worldly concerns and stands in sharp contrast to history. Its contrast with epic is even sharper, the bucolic world celebrating renunciation and insularity; epic, aspiration and expansion.[49]

Hopkins University Press, 1986), 20–33; Linda Gregerson, *The Reformation of the Subject: Spenser, Milton, and the English Protestant Epic* (Cambridge: Cambridge University Press, 1995), 6. On Petrarchism and the New World, see Roland Greene, *Post-Petrarchism: Origins and Innovations of the Western Lyric Sequence* (Princeton: Princeton University Press, 1991); cf. Alicia de Colombí-Monguió, *Petrarquismo peruano: Diego Dávalos y la "Miscelánea Austral"* (London: Tamesis, 1995).

[48] Early examples of Petrarchan influence in Spain are associated with the works of Juan de Mena and the Marqués de Santillana, the latter of whom composed "sonetos fechos al itálico modo" as well as allegorical "decires" and "visiones" closely related to the *Trionfi*; for Mena, see the fundamental work of María Rosa Lida de Malkiel, *Juan de Mena, poeta del prerrenacimiento español* (México: El Colegio de México, 1984 [orig. 1950]); cf. Giovanni Caravaggi, "Petrarch in Castile in the Fifteenth Century: The *Triumphete de Amor* by the Marquis of Santillana," in *Petrarch's "Triumphs": Allegory and Spectacle*, ed. Konrad Eisenbichler and Amilcare A. Iannucci (Toronto: Dovehouse Editions, 1990), 291–306, and Roxana Recio, *Petrarca en la Península Ibérica* (Madrid: Universidad de Alcalá de Henares, 1996); also see Anne J. Cruz, "The *Trionfi* in Spain: Petrarchist Poetics, Translation Theory, and the Castilian Vernacular in the Sixteenth Century," in *Petrarch's "Triumphs,"* ed. Eisenbichler and Iannucci, 307–24; cf. Francisco Rico, "El Destierro del Verso Agudo," in *Homenaje a José Manuel Blecua* (Madrid: Gredos, 1983), 525–51.

[49] Cf. Renato Poggioli, *The Oaten Flute: Essays on Pastoral Poetry and the Pastoral Idea* (Boston: Harvard University Press, 1975), 4; cf. David Quint, *Origin and Originality in Renaissance Literature: Versions of the Source* (New Haven: Yale University Press, 1983), 45–46.

The period of Spanish experimentation with Italian verse was ripe with opportunities for cultural exchange. In 1524 Castiglione became papal nuncio at the court of Charles V; it was here that Boscán, tutor in etiquette to the future duke of Alba, came to know the Venetian ambassador, Andrea Navagero, who in a legendary conversation in 1526 in the Generalife gardens at the Alhambra encouraged Boscán to adopt Italian metrics. Equally important, Garcilaso, who had often traveled to Italy as part of the king's guard and as a royal courier, resided in Naples from 1532 until his death in 1536, becoming a highly regarded participant in the literary life of the city, which centered around the Accademia Pontaniana and such luminaries as Jacopo Sannazaro, Antonio Minturno, Bernardo Tasso, and Pietro Bembo. Playing a formative role in Boscán's and Garcilaso's adaptation of the new poetry was Boscán's translation of Castiglione's *Cortegiano*, undertaken during the same period the two were experimenting with the sonnet and canzone and an additional sign of their cultural estrangement. The result was a prosody thoroughly mediated by *cortegianía*, with *sprezzatura* affecting every aspect of its development, beginning with Boscán's translation and extending to the absence of a systematic Spanish poetics until later in the century.[50] Da Canossa's advice regarding *sprezzatura*, which Boscán translated as "desprecio o descuido," i.e., disdain or carelessness, the first term aptly conveying the coincidence of social and aesthetic concerns, followed his exhortation to avoid *la affettazione* or affectation. The term caught Boscán's attention, since into an otherwise faithful translation of the passage he inserted a paraphrase explaining that "[. . .] nosotros, aunque en esto no tenemos vocablo proprio, podíemos llamarle curiosidad o demasiada diligencia y *codicia* de parecer mejor que todos" ("we, while not having our own word for this, can call it curiosity or excessive diligence and *greed* to appear better than everyone else") (*Cortesano*, 73).[51] The association with *codicia* in particular is revealing, since it lends a distinctly moralistic cast to Castiglione's aesthetics, an attitude characteristic of early modern Spain that Ercilla fully embodies, frequently invoking the same transgression.

[50] Cf. Richard Helgerson, *A Sonnet from Carthage: Garcilaso de la Vega and the New Poetry of Sixteenth-Century Europe* (Philadelphia: University of Pennsylvania Press, 2007), 32; cf. Ignacio Navarrete, *Orphans of Petrarch: Poetry and Theory in the Spanish Renaissance* (Berkeley: University of California Press, 1994), 32, 38. Boscán's translation was published in 1534, two years before that of Jacques Colin, mentioned earlier (18, supra); cf. Alicia de Colombí-Monguió, "Boscán frente a Navagero: el nacimiento de la conciencia humanista en la poesía española," *Nueva Revista de Filología Hispánica* 40 (1992): 143–68.

[51] Citations from Boscán's *Los Cuatro Libros del Cortesano* are taken from the Libros de Antaño edition (Madrid: Imprenta de M. Rivadeneyra, 1873). The most substantial study of Boscán and Castiglione is that of Margherita Morreale, *Castiglione y Boscán: El Ideal Cortesano en el Renacimiento Español*, 2 vols. (Madrid: Anejos del Boletín de la Real Academia Española, 1959).

Sprezzatura manifests itself in the Spanish *translatio studii* via *imitatio*, Castiglione's syncretic version of which contrasts sharply with Bembo's meticulous Ciceronianism. Inspired by the imitative praxis of Petrarch, Canossa recommends that the fledgling courtier observe a variety of models, using *bon giudicio* or good judgement to choose from among them, advice he illustrates with the famous apian simile from Horace and Seneca. Offered in the context of refining courtly manners, the advice is repeated with only slight variation shortly thereafter when the discussion turns to the subject of writing, which is framed by the Count's observation that "la scrittura non è altro che una forma de parlare che resta ancor poi che l'omo ha parlato" ("writing is nothing else than a form of speaking that remains even after a man has spoken") (1.29), a statement with profound implications for cultures that embrace *cortegianía*. At this point Federico Fregoso voices the conservative, Bembian position on the developing vernacular, arguing for the restriction of vocabulary to words "approvato dal tempo" ("approved by time") (1.30), i.e., the lexicon of Petrarch and Boccaccio. The sense of threat associated with *consuetudine* or current usage is one that surfaces a generation later in England.[52] Canossa's expansive rejoinder culminates with a simile comparing the natural life of languages to the progression of seasons, the image suggesting a Platonic transmigration of souls, with throngs of world-weary words rather than ghostly spirits now crowding a Lethean shore:

> Come le stagioni dell'anno spogliano de' fiori e de' frutti la terra, e poi di novo d'altri la rivestono, così il tempo quelle prime parole fa cadere, e l'uso altre di novo fa rinascere e dà lor grazia e dignità fin che, dall' invidioso morso del tempo a poco a poco consumate, giungono poi esse ancora alla lor morte; perciocché, al fine, e noi ed ogni nostra cosa è mortale. (1.36)

> Just as the seasons of the year despoil the earth of its flowers and fruits and then reclothe it anew with others, so time causes those first words to fall, and usage causes others to be reborn anew and gives them grace and dignity until, consumed little by little through the gnawing of time, even they then arrive at their death; since, finally, we and all our possessions are mortal.[53]

The same organic, historicist perspective informs Canossa's advice regarding literary imitation. When Boscán's translation was finally completed, an introductory letter by Garcilaso accompanied it, praising the work in Castiglione's own terms for having achieved the goal "[. . .] que fué huir del afetacion" ("which was to flee from affectation") while using language "[. . .] muy cortesanos y muy admitidos de

---

[52] See 121, infra. The other key proponent of eclectic imitation during this period is Erasmus, whose *Dialogus Ciceronianus* appeared in the same year as *Il Cortegiano*, 1528.

[53] Castiglione's simile is an elaboration of a briefer one by Horace: "As the forest changes its leaves at the decline of the year, so, among words, the oldest die; and like all things young, the new ones grow and flourish" (*Ars poetica*, 46–48).

los buenos oidos, y no nuevos ni al parecer desusados de la gente" ("quite courtly
and well accepted by those with a good ear, and not words either new or unused
by people") (13).[54] The prestige of Spain's vernacular, so different from the situation in Italy and later in England, had much to do with Boscán's and Garcilaso's
conservative attitude toward neologisms. *Cancionero* verse forms, by contrast, were
clearly deficient, in part, as Boscán says, because of their lack of a clear genealogy compared to the Italian canzone and sonnet, traceable from the Greeks and
Romans to the Catalan poets, Provencal troubadours, and thence to Dante and
Petrarch, a heritage insuring nobility and appropriateness.[55] A generation after
Boscán and Garcilaso, Ercilla, a direct beneficiary of their courtly aesthetics but
faced with articulating New World novelty, introduced many new terms, a significant number of which were absorbed into the language.[56]

Two brief paratexts by Boscán provide important insight into the reality of
the *translatio* in which he and Garcilaso were engaged: the *Prólogo* to his 1534
Cortesano and a dedication to the duchess of Soma that appeared fourteen years
later in the first edition of his and Garcilaso's collected works. In the first text
Boscán characterizes translation from Latin to the vernacular as inaccurate and
misleading, a "vanidad baxa y de hombres de pocas letras" ("a base vanity of
men of few letters") who "andar *romanzando* libros" ("go about making romance

---

[54] Citations from Garcilaso's *Epistola*, which follows Boscán's *Prólogo*, are from the
edition of the *Cortesano* noted above (n. 51). On *cortegianía* disguising literary criticism
as conversation, see Erika Rummel, *The Humanist-Scholastic Debate in the Renaissance and
Reformation* (Cambridge, MA: Harvard University Press, 1995), 2–3.

[55] Boscán discusses the issue in his introductory paratext *A la duquesa* (86–87),
which appears in his and Garcilaso's *Obras Completas*, citations of which are taken from
the Turner edition (Madrid: Turner, 1995). The prestige of the Spanish vernacular is
often identified with Antonio de Nebrija's association of language and empire in his
Gramática castellana of 1492; the linkage is predated by that of García de Santa María,
who proclaims the function of *castellano* as an instrument of political unification in the
prologue to his *Vitae patrum* of c.1490; cf. Domingo Yndurain, "La invención de una
lengua clásica," *Edad de Oro* 1 (1982): 13–34. For additional discussion of the conflict
between Castiglionian poetics and the Spanish *Cancionero* tradition, see Navarrete, *Orphans*, 17–22, 38 ff.

[56] See Isaías Lerner, "Garcilaso en Ercilla," *Lexis* 2 (1978): 201–21, at 215 n. 24
for a compilation of Ercilla's most important neologisms; cf. idem, "America y la poesía
épica áurea: la versión de Ercilla," *Edad de Oro* 10 (1991): 125–39, esp. 135, which discusses the tension in the *Araucana* between historical accuracy and literary innovation in
terms of heteroglossia; also see idem, "Ercilla y la formación del discurso poético áureo,"
in *Busquemos Otros Montes y Otros Ríos*, ed. Elias L. Rivers (Madrid: Castalia, 1992),
155–66, which considers the broader context of Ercilla's contributions to Siglo de Oro
poetic discourse.

versions of books") (6).[57] He distinguishes his own work in terms of *traducir* or *mudar*, by which he signifies translation from one romance language into another that is "quiza tan buena" ("perhaps just as good") (6). The implication is double and also ambivalent: on the one hand his work is superior to texts made for those without facility in the classical languages; on the other, his attitude is courtly rather than scholarly, its emphasis on *sprezzatura* disdaining (*desprecio o descuido*) the intensity of scholarly work altogether. Boscán stresses that his experiments were governed by *jüizio* or judgement (83), his own as well as Garcilaso's (86), and, anticipating the distinction between amateur and professional that Elizabethan poets will later emphasize to justify their writing, he denies that he actually worked at the new forms (84), a claim he repeats a few lines later in conjunction with the *otium-negotium* topos utilized by defenders of romance (85). Boscán's translation of Castiglione and his and Garcilaso's project of *translatio* more broadly foreground a lack of scholarly attitude, which, based on rules rather than judgement, was fundamentally at odds with *sprezzatura*.

The resistance the new poetry encountered in Spain is acknowledged by Boscán in his *A la duqesa de Soma* of 1548, where he notes that many readers, deprived of the medieval *Cancionero*'s use of rhyme, alliteration, and oxytones, complained that they didn't know if they were reading poetry or prose (83–84).[58] Boscán's famous answer to these complaints was the rhetorical question: "¿Y quién se ha de poner en pláticas con gente que no sabe qué cosa es verso, sino aquel que calçado y vestido con el consonante os entra de un golpe por el un oído y os sale por el otro?" ("And who has to get involved in discussions with people who don't know what poetry is except for that which, clothed and shod in

---

[57] Citations from Boscán's *Prólogo* are from the cited edition of the *Cortesano* (n. 51, supra); cf. Juan de Mena's comment in the *Proemio* to his translation of the *Ilias Latina*, discussed in greater detail below (56 n. 20, infra): "Así esta obra reçibirá dos agravios: el uno en la traduçion latina, e el más dañoso y mayor en la interpretaçión del romançe, que presumo y tiento de le dar" ("Thus this work [Homer's *Iliad*] will receive two insults: one in its Latin translation, and the more damaging and greater in its translation into the vernacular, which I presume and attempt to provide for it") (103). Boscán's and Garcilaso's collected works were first published by Boscán's widow in 1543.

[58] The situation is captured succinctly by Cristóbal de Castillejo's contemporaneous "Reprehensión Contra Los Poetas Españoles Que Escriben En Verso Italiano," or "Reprimand Against Spanish Poets who Write in Italian Verse," which calls for an inquisition against the new versifiers:

Bien se pueden castigar
a cuenta de anabaptistas,
pues por la ley particular
se tornan a baptizar
y se llaman petrarquistas.

They may well be punished as Anabaptists, since by their own law they baptize again and call themselves Petrarchists.

consonants, enters one of your ears with a clap and then exits the other?") (84).[59]
The dispute highlights the degree to which the new poetry and process of *translatio* infused with *sprezzatura* encouraged a form of poetry that was closer to prose.
The result was ultimately two distinct conceptions of poetry: the first, associated
with the *cancionero* tradition, which saw it as fundamentally different from daily
speech and part of an Aristotelian province of art where technical rules were
more important than language; the second, which conceived of the membrane
between life and art as porous and of poetic diction and rhythm as appropriately
natural, a Platonically inspired poetics of speech embraced by Garcilaso and exemplified in the Renaissance mantra of "arms and letters," an aestheticization of
life that Ercilla himself would famously embrace in his reference to living with
"la pluma ora en la mano, ora la lanza" ("now with my pen in hand, now with my
lance") (20.24.8).[60]

In broader terms, Spain's cultural appropriation from Italy during this period reveals the conjoining of overwhelming military and political dominance
with an acute sense of cultural inferiority, a disjunction of *translatio imperii* and
studii, combining cultural estrangement and continuity, that fueled a desire not
simply to embrace the new poetry, but to replicate for Spain the *renovatio* of literary expression that Bembo, Castiglione, and their colleagues had accomplished

---

[59] Nebrija had already condemned the use of rhyme and had characterized the oxytone
as a medieval holdover in his *De artis Rhetorica* of 1529; cf. Elias L. Rivers, "El problema de
los géneros neoclásicos y la poesía de Garcilaso," in *Garcilaso: Actas de la IV Academia Literaria Renacentista* (Salamanca: Ediciones Universidad de Salamanca, 1986), 49–60.

[60] Anne J. Cruz explores how the conceit of arms and letters, predicated in the Middle Ages on the class distinction between soldier and noble, shifted to complementarity
in the Siglo de Oro when the aristocracy finally relinquished its prejudice against education, due in part to the influence of Castiglione (the Marqués de Santillana, Iñigo López
de Mendoza, was an earlier, notable exception). Cruz questions the characterization of
Garcilaso as one of the first to balance the two, arguing that he repeatedly undermines
military accomplishment in favor of the vanquished and the vulnerable; she sees Ercilla as
more accurately articulating the moment when such a balance materialized: "Arms Versus Letters: The Poetics of War and the Career of the Poet in Early Modern Spain," in
European Literary Careers: The Author from Antiquity to the Renaissance (Toronto: University of Toronto Press, 2002), 186–205, esp. 188–89, 192–97. Richard Helgerson makes a
similar argument regarding Garcilaso: *A Sonnet from Carthage*, 8, 36–38. On the implicit
treatment of arms and letters in Juan de Encina's *Arte de Poesia Castellana* (1496), and on
the explicit approximation of verse to prose in the *Dialogo de la lingua* (1535) by Juan de
Valdés, heavily influenced by Castiglione, see Navarrete, *Orphans*, 24–26, 48; Navarrete
notes that Boscán avoids the *otium/negotium* dichotomy, opposed to the courtly aestheticization of life, by describing the time he spends on the translation as *sosiego* rather than
ocio: *Orphans*, 48. The discussion here and below of Plato's poetics of speech as contrasted
to Aristotle's poetics of imitated action is indebted to Don H. Bialostosky, *Making Tales*
(Chicago: University of Chicago Press, 1984), esp. 11–26.

with regard to Italian. For its part, Italy, possessing nothing of empire beyond a longing for its ancient one now lost, experienced the obverse inferiority of *imperii*, which Vives and Valla symbolically assuaged with an empire of language, Ciceronian Latin, long before Spenser's evocation of a less grandiose vernacular domain. While the sixteenth-century's "new poetry" was driven by Petrarchan introspection and the intimacy of lyric, therefore, it evolved in a context saturated with empire, real and recollected, and frequently associated, at least nominally, with the "old poetry" of epic. The result was a contrast of dynamics, modernizing and vernacular and driven by Petrarchism and vernacular humanism, on the one hand, but also classicizing and Romanizing, inspired by the daily experience of those who conquered new worlds and supported by classical humanism, on the other. As they were in Petrarch, both aspects are present in Garcilaso, who in addition to sonnets and *canciones* wrote Latin odes and vernacular Horatian epistles; like his predecessor, Garcilaso also thematized the opposition, contrasting images of empire and martial endeavor to private longing and loss. A similarly bifurcated spirit, modernizing, private, and vernacular, as well as classicizing, engrandizing, and Romanizing, pervades the *Araucana*. In contrast to Garcilaso, a lyric poet figuring empire, however, Ercilla's epic employs lyric to inscribe the genre's traditional erotic challenge while simultaneously marking the author's proficiency in the new poetry and new culture of *civilité*. This aspect of the *Araucana* is manifest most noticeably in the Araucan women episodes, while a classicizing spirit informs the poem's Stoic perspective, its overall gravitas, and its erotic as well as martial imagery. These contrasting dynamics were reflected in distinctly different senses of lived experience in sixteenth-century Spain and Italy, with many citizens of the former participating in what they felt to be epic enterprises in both the New World and the Old, a heroic age of military and political expansion that drove the production of some seventy literary epics in the century following 1550.[61] Were the study of Siglo de Oro literature to reflect the dynamics of the period, epic would demand much more attention than lyric or the *comedia*, beneficiaries of modern literary biases that also characterize other European vernaculars.[62]

The end of this intense century of *translatio studii*, Italy to Spain and then Italy to England, is sharply delineated by the different receptions offered courtiership, from Ercilla's largely intact transmission of it to the 1580s and 90s in England, where, after decades of tension between the monarch and opposing factions at what was perceived to be an increasingly corrupt court, Castiglione's primary values had been largely inverted. In this altered context, *sprezzatura*, the graceful lack of concern disguising the effort of courtly pursuits, and *dissimulazi-*

---

[61] See Andrew Laird, "The *Aeneid* from the Aztecs to the Dark Virgin," in *Companion*, ed. Farrell and Putnam, 217–33, esp. 224.

[62] Cf. Maxime Chevalier, *Lectura y lectores en la España del Siglo XVI y XVII* (Madrid: Turner, 1976), 105; cf. 12 n.23, supra.

one, its handmaiden, were denigrated as dissimulation and deceit; *mediocrità*, the capacity for multiple perspectives and the pinnacle of cordial disagreement, was reduced to the meaning it still holds today; and *grazia*, or grace, once the apex of sophisticated elasticity, was more likely the basis of Calvinist salvation than a mark of courtly comportment. By this point *civiltà*, the epitome of Castiglione and Erasmus, had relinquished its idealism as well, now less a matter of social grace than at best a bulwark and at worst a battering ram of civilization, with the *conversazione civile* of Guazzo, Bryskett, and other Castiglionian epigones less a program for culture than a guide to career advancement.

7. Imaging Eros and Epic:
The Abandoned Woman and the Night Raid

Over the course of the sixteenth century similar if less drastic shifts in valence played out in the venerable imagery of confrontation between love and strife, images that the discussion below will show to be pivotal to both Ercilla and Spenser. The contrast is an ancient one, surfacing in the relationship of Ares and Aphrodite.[63] Homer pursued the opposition, launching a tradition of heroic narrative in which the erotic repeatedly plays an unsettling role, figuring internal conflicts that became characteristic of the genre.[64] While neither the *Iliad* nor the *Odyssey* explores the conflict between eros and epos that characterizes heroic poetry beginning with Apollonius' *Argonautica*, Homer is an important source for two key images emblematic of the opposition: the abandoned woman, enacted by Nausikaa in the episode of Odysseus among the Phaeacians (*Od.* 8.460 ff.), and the night raid, conducted by Odysseus and Diomedes during the Trojan war (*Il.* 10.252 ff.).[65] Subsequent epics embellished these images through allusions to lyric, pastoral, and tragedy. According to Lawrence Lipking's 1988 study of the abandoned woman, the image's career in heroic poetry is defined by an act that's equally constitutive of the hero who leaves her behind. Not long a maiden whose hopes and disappointments are only suggested, she soon becomes identified with Sappho's irrational passion. Once eroticized, she is frequently situated in a *locus amoenus* where she enacts a Theocritan distinction between sexual dalliance and troubled passion, the latter eventually spiraling into a rejection-based hatred in-

---

[63] See H. David Brumble, *Classical Myths and Legends in the Middle Ages and the Renaissance* (Westport, CT: Greenwood Press, 1998), 205–10.

[64] Davis argues that epic has inherent contradictions and ideological divisions it cannot entirely suppress, resulting in a certain characteristic dualism: *Myth and Identity*, 11–12; cf. Helgerson, who argues that a "profound self-division" characterizes the poetry of empire beginning with Virgil: *Sonnet from Carthage*, 14.

[65] Barbara Pavlock, *Eros, Imitation, and the Epic Tradition* (Ithaca: Cornell University Press, 1990), 4.

spired by Euripides' Medea.[66] The *Argonautica*, which represents the most significant transformation of epic in antiquity, elaborates each of these characteristics
in its exploration of the sensations of love and of the effect of private passion on
the public sphere, its Medea conjoining Homer's civilized maiden with Euripides'
barbarian queen in a sensitive depiction of first love gradually supplanted by passionate rage. Other poets elaborated the figure in other directions. Catullus' verses on Peleus and Thetis emphasize Ariadne's fidelity, focusing on a quality found
earlier in Homer's Penelope and accentuated by Ovid, whose Ariadne in *Heroides*
10 provides the model for Ariosto's Olimpia. By the time the *Heroides* transforms
her into a vision of heroinism, the abandoned woman has come to embody the
dual principles of opposition per se: her earliest manifestation as subversive inertia
and passive endurance challenging epic's Aristotelian fixation on action; her subsequent angry persona actively contesting epic teleology, both incarnations forces
of resistance to literary standards and to the canon itself. At her most evocative an
analogue of ageless keening and of the archetypal poet attempting to articulate
what is lost, the abandoned woman is indispensable to epic and its hero, a negative
model that balances, however briefly, the teleology of the former; a foil for the latter, who if he were only self-aware might see in her not only what he gives up, but
also what frequently drives him on, the shame of helplessness which once identified with becomes the engine of his perseverance and at times his rage.[67] Lipking

---

[66] Cf. Lawrence Lipking, *Abandoned Women and Poetic Tradition* (Chicago: University of Chicago Press, 1988). Sappho's famous Second Ode (L. P. 31) survived antiquity
through its inclusion in Longinus's *Peri Hypsous*, which presented it as an example of sub-
lime lyric; the text and poem were rediscovered by Robortello and published in 1554:

> ἀλλ' ἄκαν μὲν γλῶσσα ἔαγε, λέπτον
> δ' αὔτικα χρῶι πῦρ ὑπαδεδρόμηκεν,
> ὀππάτεσσι δ' οὐδ' ἓν ὄρημμ', ἐπιρρόμ-
> βεισι δ' ἄκουαι,
> κὰδ δέ μ' ἴδρως ψῦχρος ἔχει, τρόμος δὲ
> παῖσαν ἄγρει, χλωροτέρα δὲ ποίας
> ἔμμι, τεθνάκην δ' ὀλίγω 'πιδεύης
> φαίνομαι

my tongue falters, a thin / flame runs quickly under my skin / my eyes see nothing,
thunder / spins through my ears // cold sweat pours down on me and trembling / rushes
over me and greener than / grass and on the brink of dying I / seem to myself
Text and translation are from Lipking (*Abandoned Women*, 59).

[67] Cf. Lipking, *Abandoned Women*, 3, 134; Lipking notes that Ovid's Sappho (*Heroides* 15), who having lost her *pudor* assumes her "second career" as poet-whore, is subsequently often preferred to the poet herself (68); Gail Holst-Warhaft explores the role of
the lamenting woman in social structures such figures simultaneously threaten and reinforce: *Dangerous Voices: Women's Laments and Greek Literature* (London: Routledge, 1992);
see also Margaret Alexiou, *The Ritual Lament in Greek Tradition* (Cambridge: Cambridge
University Press, 1974). Cf. Walter Cohen, who argues that women drive the masculinist

argues that while the male poet and men in general need the abandoned woman to articulate their own sense of abandonment and associated darker passions, men and women both fear the figure not so much for her Otherness as for the familiarity with which she threatens a return of the repressed (*Abandoned Women*, 19). For the epic hero, his brief identification with the figure ends by reinforcing sexual difference, her pity confirming his strength. The potency of the process stems directly from the transgressive quality of the transgendering identification, sure to enact a cost. The result is a division of virginal maiden or virtuous matron on one side, courtesan-whore on the other, conjuring a genealogy of schizoid heroines: the two Sapphos, two Helens (i.e., Stesichorus' *eidolon*), two Venuses (*Coelestis* and *Vulgaris*), and two Didos. The phenomenon is particularly notable in the *Faerie Queene*, where Spenser, acutely sensitive to such shifts in register, employs them side by side. Ercilla, by contrast, whose appropriation of the figure stays closer to the epic model (although in repeatedly adopting her perspective he enacts his own Ovidian move), ultimately performs a more enigmatic maneuver, his defense of Dido fiercely denying the possible transformation of the abandoned woman into anything other than a paragon of chastity and virtue, suppressing her alter ego in the creation of his own.[68]

Virgil's version of this central figure is the most complex of the ancient tradition, his Dido exhibiting vital traits of each of her models.[69] The *Aeneid* also presents an essential variation on the night raid, Virgil's version of the episode, in contrast to Homer's brief excursion into the brutality of the heroic ethos, now linking four types of desire. Three of these, the lust for blood, for wealth, and for fame, latent in Homer, had been explicitly juxtaposed by Euripides in the *Rhesus*, named for the sleeping warrior whom Diomedes kills for his champion horses (*Il.* 10.474). Virgil adopts the triad, then complicates it by suggesting the potential for sexual lust as well, exchanging the hapless spy of Homer's narrative, Dolon, for Nisus and Euryalus, a pair whose homoerotic bond echoes that of Achilles and Patroclus.[70]

---

discourse of empire even in their absence: "The Discourse of Empire in the Renaissance," in *Cultural Authority in Golden Age Spain*, ed. Marina S. Brownlee and Hans Ulrich Gumbrecht (Baltimore: Johns Hopkins University Press, 1995), 270–76.

[68] Robortello's publication of Sappho was instrumental in reviving the ancient theory of the two Sapphos, enabling early modern writers to bypass intermediaries such as Ovid and return directly to an unblemished, ennobling version of the poet and her verses.

[69] See Brumble, *Myths*, 101–3.

[70] In a final variation on the Doloneia in antiquity, Statius' *Thebaid* inverts Virgilian values by presenting the fight for Thebes as madness and the night raid, now carried out by two luckless comrades, Hopleus and Dymas, for the sole purpose of burying their leaders, as one of the epic's few examples of *pietas*. Statius' combination of the night raid with the search for the corpse of a beloved inspires Ariosto's episode of Cloridano and Medoro (*O.F.* 18.165 ff.). This conjunction links the night raid and abandoned woman

8. Classical Imagery in Early Modern Contexts

The reading of the *Araucana* and *Faerie Queene* that follows pays particular attention to these and related images, a number of which, as just noted, are Homeric in origin. Two, the abandoned woman and the night raid, inscribe epic's eternal conflict with eros. Three additional figures, an extended simile for the dawn that is consistently juxtaposed to depictions of violence, the *antiqua silva* or ancient forest, a site that mingles foreboding with transformative purification and prophetic insight, and the catalogue of trees, an image that following Homer was often employed in conjunction with the forest, are prime components in epic's structural logic. That these images from pagan antiquity figure prominently in Ercilla's chronicle or Spenser's romance epic is unexpected. That they play important roles in both not only reveals unexpected homologies between the two works, but the variations of their applications expose critical differences as well, while reminding us of the capacity of literary images to figure differently in different contexts, their core identities possessing excess significance available for local purposes. In core respects these images are liminal, either literally, as in the *Araucana*, invoked at points where attention shifts from the traditionally masculine world of conflict and violence to the ostensibly feminine concerns of beauty and chastity, or figuratively, more often the case in the *Faerie Queene*, where conflict is as often psychomachic as physical and the distinctions between opposing forces more likely to blur into unsettling similarities between the virtues and their opposites.

Another set of equally venerable images discussed below is associated with the attention both poems devote to erotic passion and its aftermath: love as a fire, a wound, and as poison. Derived from epic, lyric, and tragedy, by the early modern era many of these figures were as worn as the Petrarchan cliches with which they were often combined and were similarly ripe for rejuvenation or parody. Ercilla and Spenser faced deeper conflicts regarding such conceits, which in the context of religious reformation, Catholic and Protestant, they often found offensive and frequently rejected or revised. Ercilla's treatment of desire, framed by a Virgilian opposition to duty and informed by Petrarchan idealization, is focused on private conduct. Spenser envisions desire as the site of a contest between temperance and its absence, but also enshrines it as the source of the quest and of civil society. The object of erotic passion and a principal subject for both authors is ideal feminine beauty, for Ercilla a transcendental vision, for Spenser a present danger or potential benefit. Notwithstanding their different trajectories, the dangers of desire lead Ercilla and Spenser to the same three elements of what in the former's case is a Platonic paradigm and in latter's an Aristotelian one:

---

motifs previously combined by Sophocles' Antigone and Xenophon's Panthea; see 68 n. 30, infra.

chastity or continence, shamefastness or self-respect, and the force behind these
two, symbolized in the bridle or halter of self-control. For Ercilla the struggle
is an individual one, first manifest in *aidos*, or shame, and *kleos*, or honor, pagan
epic values associated with the Araucan warriors, then transposed in the course
of the Araucan women episodes into their internalized, Christian versions based
on Plato: continence or *sophrosyne*, and personal honor or *timeis*. Emphasis on the
latter is even greater in Spenser where these issues take on implications for public
policy, and as passages in the *View* make clear, eventually pose a threat to which
the bridle of self-control is no longer equal, leaving the sword of conquest as the
only alternative.[71]

As the foregoing suggests, the significance of this imagery is often quite different in Ercilla and Spenser. A crucial factor in this difference was the increasing stridency of religious discourse as the sixteenth century progressed, raising
the stakes for the English poet, for whom the failure of virtue became not only
dishonorable, as in the ancient world, but fraught with the possibility of damnation in the modern, Protestant one. In such a context the abandoned woman
became a potential seductress and demonic double and the night raid a hotbed of
erotic perversity. As for the loss of shame and continence, the consequences were
now no longer limited to self-destruction but threatened civil society. The Reformation's heightened sensitivity to Christianity's conflict of interest with classical antiquity aggravated these tensions, since, unlike patristic efforts to concili-
ate the two, it accentuated their differences. The conflict, a fundamental one for
Protestant authors, is manifest on multiple levels in the *Faerie Queene*. Thematically, encounters both implied and explicit occur between Christian and classical figures and values. A structural analogue emerges in the variations and near-
repetitions of characters, events, and images in settings affiliated now with one
world view, now with the other. This parodic principle of intratextual echoing in
Spenser's text has a linguistic analogue in the poet's punning wordplay, which on
the one hand draws attention to etymology and the cultural context of signification, while on the other, via unremitting emphasis on the slippage between the
literal and the figurative, it poses a threat to signification. These two dangers,
the first, that of pagan, epic values to Christianity, the second, that of linguistic anarchy to signification, are related by the anxiety that both reflect regarding
a loss of control, in one case, over man's relationship to God, in the other, over
human speech to meaning. In both the *Araucana* and *Faerie Queene* the concern
with control is fundamental. In both poems it has a literary, and in Spenser's case

---

[71] Referring to the use of the *View* as "a sort of prose 'gloss'" to Spenser's poetry, a practice indulged in here and elsewhere in the present study, McCabe notes that
"[. . .] their relationship is far more intricate. It is often forgotten that the prose is, in so
many respects, just as 'fictive' as the verse. Indeed the verse seems to 'gloss' the prose by
entertaining disquieting possibilities that neither Irenius nor Eudoxus may be allowed to
broach" (*Spenser's Monstrous Regiment*, 4).

a linguistic correlative. In the *Araucana* the issue manifests itself most sharply in the competition between Virgil's version of Dido and earlier narratives of the heroine that by Ercilla's time were identified as popular and medieval. The conflict exposes a principal function of humanism, which worked to establish a homogenized version of the past. Spenser's struggle with control manifests itself most directly in his rejection of courtly discourse for an archaic dialect associated with apocalyptic Protestantism and representing the linguistic embodiment of religious and national purity. For both Ercilla and Spenser these conflicts reveal an effort to articulate identity in the present and future by controlling the identity of the past. A more immediate goal of the process was the control of popular culture: in the case of humanism, a popular, medieval past; for the reformers, Protestant and Catholic, unauthorized ritual and religious practice; within the *Faerie Queene* itself, the irrepressible polyvalency of speech.

Gender, implied or explicit, pervades every aspect of Ercilla's and Spenser's narratives, from issues of structure, theme, and imagery to many of the tensions and conflicts just enumerated. Genre itself is subject to the distinction, from the opposition of history and lyric in the *Araucana*, the former male and associated with the evidentiary and verifiable, the latter female and focused on emotion and the literary, to a corresponding but more complex contrast in the *Faerie Queene* between the epic and hortatory on the one hand and romance on the other, the former extroverted, purposeful, and superficially masculine, the latter perpetually susceptible to the distractions of emotion. These associations are reflected in the theory and interpretation referred to earlier, closed endings identified with the masculine, open-ended ones with the feminine, the latter indelibly associated with Circe and Juno, the first of whom works to retard the conclusion of the story through erotic attachment, the second by inciting unending strife.[72] Numerous corollary issues have gender affiliations in the early modern period, from the association of the vernaculars with the female (mother tongues and the imbibing of language with mother's milk), in contrast to the masculine character of Latin and Greek, to the feminine world of courtiership compared to the predominantly masculine character of humanism. As will be seen upon further investigation by characters, commentators, and the poets themselves, many of these dramatic distinctions are only apparent, a fact that imbues the poems and their commentary with much of their complexity and texture.

---

[72] See Brumble, *Myths*, 73–75, 190–92.

9. Selected Readings, Key Conceits

The discussion of the *Araucana* in Part 2 focuses on six key passages that most clearly expose the poem's structuring contrast between love and war and the associated modes of lyric and epic. Four of these feature encounters with Araucan women: Guacolda, Tegualda, Glaura, and Lauca. While long the objects of study, here these episodes are examined alongside two additional passages closely related in theme and function: the first, a prophetic display of Spanish imperial majesty that segues abruptly into a hallucinatory vision of Spanish beauty; the second, Ercilla's impassioned defense of Dido, in many ways the poem's thematic and emotional zenith. Each of these episodes is framed by similar issues, beginning with the structural one of how such material, which varies from lyric elegy to Boccaccian tales to Greek romance, can be integrated into the surrounding chronicle in a way that marks their literary identity while sustaining a claim to historical realism. Each of the episodes is distinct in character and tone, often by dint of generic affiliation, while many of the same key themes are emphasized throughout. Foremost among these themes are the instability of fate and a requisite Stoic response, the dangers of passion, wrathful as well as erotic, and the ideal of a Neoplatonic hierarchy in which the rational rules over the irascible and concupiscent. Each episode articulates a defense of women while inscribing an Erasmian vision of love as conjugal, chaste, and freely given. Consistently significant is a concept of Christian courtliness combining the best of classical and modern virtues: Virgilian *piedad* emanating from "el *pío* Felipe," *clemencia*, decorum, and a deep sense of personal honor. All six episodes fulfill some of the same key functions, beginning with the erotic critique of epic violence, a critique that, filtered through *cortegianía* and the intimacy of lyric, expands into a revision of imagery of Virgil, Petrarch, Ariosto, and Garcilaso. Most important, in Ercilla's encounters with the Araucan women an unknowable Amerindian Other is supplanted by literary topoi that project an incipient subjectivity closely related to the author's own self-revelation, resulting in a series of unexpected and unprecedented correspondences between natives of the Old World and the New and between the poet and his characters. The effect is that of a multi-layered Conquest, symbolic as well as territorial, the former, ultimately most important, driven by rationality rather than greed and less about the expansion of empire than self-control and self-creation. Ercilla's encounter with the Araucan women is first and foremost an encounter with himself, captured most succinctly, as will be seen, in the *razón de mí* of his defense of Dido.

In Part 3 the discussion shifts to issues raised by the transition from a transatlantic world of violent conflict between clearly identified foes to the intensely internal, *chiaroscuro* world of the *Faerie Queene*. One of the chief dynamics in Spenser's poem is a competition among discourses of the courtier, the humanist, and the reformer. Around mid-century a brief *convivencia* flourished in England among these three, with *cortegianía* offering a link between the reformers and

Italian humanists, while humanism bridged the courtly and reforming worlds, all three united in a struggle against popular culture. In an increasingly strident atmosphere, with fears of Italian immorality vexing Puritan observers of early-modern English drama and a growing disgust with what was felt to be the worsening corruption of Elizabeth's court, the courtier's fall from grace was not long in coming.[73] In the wake of Castiglionian aesthetics pressure grew for a Protestant theory of art, and Sidney's *Apologie* obliged, its Neoplatonic vision of universal reason in human affairs conflating poetic virtuosity with virtue itself. For Spenser, the reform of poetics, religion, and politics were inextricably entwined. Threats to his program were many, the most tenacious embedded in what came to be seen, in contrast to the benign vision he and Gabriel Harvey shared when younger, as a treacherous kingdom of language he struggled to contain through his rejection of the courtly *patois*. Fatally undermining this effort and the ostensible purity of his archaic alternative were its inescapable links to the speech of the Old English citizenry of his principal target, Elizabethan Ireland, exacerbating what was seen already as the courtly duplicity of language and a broader struggle between appearance and reality. This struggle eventually engulfs not only the poem's characters but its readers, both faced with a series of doublings, substitutions, and repetitions inscribing the threat of linguistic polysemy. As the poem progresses these dangers begin to meld with those of mistaking enemies for friends, and good Irish for bad, foregrounding a threat of contamination and assimilation, all of which is projected in fears of civil disorder. Spenser attempts to limit the impact of these forces on narrative structure by the use of etymology and allegoresis.[74] Often rejected by classical humanists, the return of the latter reflects a distrust of *dissimulazione* that had spread from the lexicon of art to its very structure, with reformed art, in direct contravention of *cortegianía*, now based on strategies that called attention to themselves at every opportunity. The ultimate goal of these efforts, the transition from a cult of manners to the colonial project of Christian civility, reaches its calamitous conclusion against the backdrop of Ireland.

---

[73] Deteriorating economic conditions in early mid-century England intensified opposition to popular culture, with regulations enacted to suppress promiscuity, ale houses (with which prostitution was associated), and folk rituals; during this period the latter were frequently conflated with Catholic ceremony, resulting in an alliance between religious reformers and conservatives generally: John Guy, *Tudor England* (Oxford: Oxford University Press, 1988), 220–21.

[74] Cf. Michael Murrin, "Renaissance Allegory from Petrarch to Spenser," in *The Cambridge Companion to Allegory*, ed. Rita Copeland and Peter T. Struck (Cambridge: Cambridge University Press, 2010), 162–76; Kenneth Borris, "Allegory, Emblem, and Symbol," in *The Oxford Handbook of Edmund Spenser*, ed. Richard A. McCabe (Oxford: Oxford University Press, 2010), 473–61.

The exploration of the *Faerie Queene* in Part 4 begins by examining the intertextual forests of the Legends of Holiness and Temperance, in which the abandoned woman, the night raid, the ancient wood, the catalogue of trees, and the extended simile of the dawn all feature prominently. The confluence of epic and romance affiliations in these images emphasizes the polyvocality of Spenser's text. As the poem progresses, the density of allusion reveals a depth of literary self-consciousness suggesting a *tertiary* degree of epic, one so infused with echoes of both the oral and written traditions that its characters constantly verge on ironic self-awareness. In shifting from temperance to chastity Book 3 moves from a predominantly male to a female world. The result is a gendering of continence that emphasizes shame and the sexualization of self-control, eventually focusing on the distinction among the concupiscent, irascible, and rational parts of the soul. The movement from forest paths of the early parts of the poem to images of interweaving, tapestry, and *entrelacement* both here and in the Legend of Friendship introduces an ultimately unsuccessful attempt to differentiate between good and bad types of erotic passion while championing conjugal love. The accumulation of images and intertexts by this point in the poem invokes an intratextuality that threatens to upstage Spenser's lessons. The cultural process of *translatio*, it becomes clear, is never as straightforward as it seems; a remainder always persists, threatening recidivism and requiring revision. In the Legend of Justice the use of allegory undergoes a fundamental change from a richly evocative, moral-anagogical version of the device reminiscent of Dante to a simpler historical mode, resulting in a relative transparency of meaning highlighting the importance of Ireland as a context for the narrative. This intrusion of the mundane reflects a growing loss of confidence by the poet in his initially ambitious moral program, a decline the Legend of Courtesy exaggerates not only by focusing on the courtliness so roundly rejected heretofore, but also by turning from the struggle for virtue that defines the earlier quests to tales of miraculous escape and the improbable revelation of hidden identities. Here the ultimate breakdown of relations among courtliness, humanism, and the reformers is not so much enacted as ignored, and, the *rota Virgilii* reversed, grand concerns are eclipsed by melodramatic ones.

Several noteworthy tropes both shape and help elucidate the discussion that follows. The theme and variations of quest, conquest, and reconquest/*Reconquista* echo repeatedly in these pages, spanning the early transatlantic world from the romance forests of Spenser's England and English troops in Ireland, to Ercilla's epic struggles in the Southern Cone and Spain's territorial recovery of the Iberian peninsula. Conquest in these poems is not only militaristic and territorial, but also political, religious, moral, and erotic. A similar inflection pertains to empire and imperial aspiration, figured additionally in Spenser's linguistic kingdom and the establishing of literary canons. Reconquest is likewise polysemous, naming what both poets pursue as they associate themselves and their texts with the ideals and images of earlier eras, ancient and medieval, asserting control of the past in literary visions designed to influence the present and shape the future. The filiation and affiliation in which they engage are additional key figures, with the hybrid product that often results from the associations they discover or assert noteworthy as well. Early transatlantic contact has been seen as an originary moment for hybridity in Western culture, from fanciful illustrations of New World inhabitants to the equally imaginative explanations of scholars in both the Old World and the New attempting to reconcile Scriptural history with what they actually encountered. A related effort engages Ercilla and Spenser with regard to literary tradition, generating the generic hybrids discussed below.[75]

All of these issues are subsumed, to a significant degree, in the conceit of translation/*translatio*. The concept of the remainder is only one of numerous insights from contemporary translation theory that recommend the process as the master trope of the present study, from textual transpositions at one end of the spectrum to the cultural project of *translatio* at the other, which often relied on the physical translation of natives and settlers. Recent work in this area emphasizes the fragility of the literal-figural distinction, arguing that no translation is merely linguistic or neutral, but rather that each inscribes a violent cultural-political process reflecting hierarchies of dominance and marginality, Bakhtin's world of agonistic speech writ large. The conflict has both intra- and interlingual dimensions, the former manifest in the major and minor variants associated with the "semiotic regimes" of cultural constituencies, the latter in the role of domestic agendas within translation itself, which inevitably engages in the validation or revision of cultural values. The goal of the praxis as traditionally pursued: a transcending of the linguistic and cultural differences that required translation to begin with, resulting in a domestication of the foreign and presentation of the cultural Other as the same, the recognizable, and the familiar. Traditional approaches to the topic often focused on the distinction between *ad verbum* and *ad sensum*, the first characterized as literal or faithful, the second given latitude for a paraphrase or gloss, potentially more accurate at capturing meaning. Contemporary discussion has moved beyond this dichotomy to the inescapable result of either approach, a "domestic remainder" and overtones of earlier identities revealing the inherent hybridity of a never-final product. The goal of those who articulate these insights: translation that resists the craft's traditional ethnocentricity, acknowledging rather than eliding difference, and the encouragement of "foreignizing" or "minoritizing" versions of texts.[76] While much of this work has

---

[75] See Homi Bhabha, *The Location of Culture* (London: Routledge, 1994), 37, 162–64; on the hybrid quality of American-matter epics in early modern Spain, see Isaías Lerner, "Épica y lírica: un diálogo de géneros," in *El Canon poético en el siglo XVI* (Seville: Universidad de Sevilla—Grupo PASO, 2008), 298–320.

[76] See Lawrence Venuti, *The Translator's Invisibility: A History of Translation* (London: Routledge, 1995), 17–19; cf. the same author's exploration of translation's simultaneous construction of a domesticized foreign text and domestic subject, "a position

been developed in the context of colonial theory, the conditions for which post-date the sixteenth century, the fundamental tensions identified and built on so productively are often present in the early modern period. "Semiotic regimes" are at the heart of the *questione della lingua*, Boscán's and Garcilaso's rejection of the *Cancionero* in favor of a properly elevated but unpretentious Castilian, and, especially, Spenser's efforts to restore an English redolent of Protestant purity. When it comes to translation per se, the competition for cultural identity is manifest at every level of the process, from vernacular versions of Latin and Greek to renditions from one vernacular to another. The former impels the conflicts of Virgilian reception, the latter Boscán's work on the *Cortesano*, from his selection of the text to his lexical choices. Similar tensions will be noted below in early modern versions of the *Aeneid* in Spanish and English and in numerous translations from Italian and Spanish, among them translations of the *Araucana* itself into English and Dutch within twenty years of its publication. The hybrid quality of such works has often been noted, their "domestic remainders" frequently identified as points where textual interrogation proceeds most productively.

As for the *translatio imperii et studii* more broadly, a transfer of power, authority, and knowledge conjoined with their conversion from one set of cultural signifiers to another, the underlying forces are as clear as ever, from the translation of pagan antiquity via Christian allegoresis and the programs of individual cultures to construct identity through affiliation and suppression, to the efforts by humanism to transmit a coherent canon of ancient learning, an achievement possible only through the suppression of competing traditions, especially medieval ones. In recent years early modern literary studies have turned their attention to secondary aspects of the *translatio*, from the alienation at its core to the after-effect of the process when projected abroad. The first manifests itself not only on the level of a culture that abandons aspects of its praxis to identify with an illustrious predecessor, but also has an impact on the protagonists of such a project, a role repeatedly played by poets from antiquity on. Exacerbated in the case of Ercilla and Spenser by the geographic and cultural dis-placement/dis-location of travel on the one hand and self-imposed exile on the other, alienation becomes an essential component of both authors' narratives, reflected, in turn, in their appropriation of and identification with the abandoned woman. When cultural identity is projected elsewhere, by contrast, as it was both in the Americas and in Ireland, a process of reverse-*translatio*, of the New World's impact on the Old,

---

of intelligibility that is also an ideological position informed by the codes and canons, the interests and agendas of certain domestic social groups," in *The Scandals of Translation: Towards an Ethics of Difference* (London: Routledge, 1998), 68; cf. 93, 178. See also Susanna Morton Braund, "Mind the Gap: On Foreignizing Translations of the *Aeneid*," in *Companion*, ed. Farrell and Putnam, 449–64. Cf. Raymond Williams's concept of the "residual" effects of cultural change in *Marxism and Literature* (Oxford: Oxford University Press, 1977), 121 ff.

also occurs, a defamiliarizing of the familiar that alters fundamental categories of identity and understanding at home.[77]

---

[77] Cf. Helgerson, *Sonnet from Carthage*, 53 ff.; cf. David A. Lupher, *Romans in a New World: Classical Models in Sixteenth-Century Spanish America* (Ann Arbor: University of Michigan Press, 2003), 321.

[. . .] when the "other" is interpreted and "domesticated" by appeal to the familiar, there is always the risk that the current will be reversed and that the familiar will be "defamiliarized" by the conceptually unruly "other."

David A. Lupher,
Romans in the New World: Classical Models in Sixteenth-Century Spanish America
(321)

II. Love, War, and Ercilla's *razón de mí*

1. The Heroines of Arauco

Twentieth-century commentary on Ercilla's Araucan women began by viewing them as largely authentic, continuing a tradition, extending to the poem's early reception, of reading the *Araucana* as largely historical and of judging these episodes, however anomalous, as realistic. Once the passages were deemed literary strategies, however successful, attention turned to questions of their provenance and function, and while consensus regarding the former gradually coalesced, disagreements over the latter persisted. The majority of these studies have focused on the contrast between the episodes and the framing narrative, a disjunction they characterize in terms ranging from "pluralistic vision" to "fractured subjectivity," the former describing a narrative whose structural and ideological fissures may deconstruct but do not disable it, the latter designating a project that falls apart.[1] Other commentary has identified Ercilla's work as a wellspring of

---

[1] The claim of authenticity is associated in particular with Medina, *La Araucana*; cf. idem, "Las Mujeres en *La Araucana* de Ercilla," *Hispania* 2 (1928): 1–12; for the literary provenance of Ercilla's heroines, the still essential work is that of Lía Schwartz, "Tradición Literaria y Heroínas Indias en *La Araucana*," *Revista Iberoamericana* 38 (1972): 615–25; for Ariosto and Ercilla, Maxime Chevalier's masterful *L'Arioste en Espagne* (Bordeaux: Institut d'Etudes Ibériques et Ibéro-Américaines de l'Université de Bordeaux, 1966); for other source studies, see the works of Isaías Lerner, inter alia "Garcilaso" and "Ercilla y Lucano," and James Nicolopulos's insightful analysis of the poem in terms of Renaissance strategies of imitation, which focuses on the prophetic episodes and their intertexts with Virgil, Lucan, and Juan de Mena: *The Poetics of Empire in the Indies: Prophecy and Imitation in* La Araucana *and* Os Lusíadas (University Park: Pennsylvania State University Press, 2000); cf. idem, "Reading and Responding," 227–43.

Among commentaries that reference the Araucan women episodes in the terms noted here, see William Melczer, who describes Ercilla as struggling to balance a Virgilian conflict between ideological commitment and moral imperative, resulting in the poem's pluralistic vision: "Ercilla's Divided Heroic Vision: A Reevaluation of the Epic Hero in *La Araucana*," *Hispania* 56 (1973): 218–20; Ramona Lagos explores what she sees as an anti-heroic contest between loyalty and disloyalty, the former that of the Araucan women

Chilean nationalism, locating within the narrative disjunction a cultural one driving the emergence of Hispanoamerican consciousness conceived in terms of life-as-alienated-experience and a profound sense of marginality.[2] While the same disjunction has driven the tendency to approach the poem as either pro-Araucan or pro-Spanish, in moving beyond this basic dichotomy more recent criticism has referenced the Araucan women in more theoretical terms, exploring a juxtaposition of gender and the discourse of imperial geography, offering a subaltern perspective on what it identifies as a semantics of oppression, and arguing that they present a meditation on the ontological status of literature.[3]

---

to their husbands, the latter that of Spanish soldiers to fundamental Christian values: "El incumplimiento de la programmación épica en *La Araucana,*" *Cuadernos Americanos* 238 (1981): 157–91; cf. Jaime Concha, "El Otro Nuevo Mundo," in *Homenaje a Ercilla* (Concepción: Universidad de Concepción, 1969) 31–82, and idem, "*La Araucana,* epopea della controconquista," *Materiali Critici* 2 (1981): 93–128.

    For recent studies that question the *Araucana*'s functionality as epic, see Barbara Fuchs, who suggests that "[. . .] Ercilla's text leads the reader to the verge of epic time and time again, only to suggest that it might be a dead end where America is concerned": *Mimesis and Empire,* 48; cf. eadem, on the way the *Araucana* "comes undone" through the pressure of romance on epic: "Traveling Epic: Translating Ercilla's *La Araucana* in the Old World," *Journal of Medieval and Early Modern Studies* 36 (2006): 379–95, at 381; Michael Murrin, *History and Warfare in Renaissance Epic* (Chicago: University of Chicago Press, 1994), 214 ff.; Castillo, "Impossible Indian," and Davis, *Myth and Identity.* On "profound self-division" as characteristic of early modern imperial epic, see Helgerson, *A Sonnet from Carthage,* 14 ff.

    [2] Appropriation of the *Araucana* as Chile's foundational text is closely associated with Medina, *La Araucana*; José Promis explores what he describes as the poem's unstable point of view and "mannerist" vision of life-as-alienated-experience in relation to a Hispanoamerican sense of marginality in *The Identity of Hispanoamerica: An Interpretation of Colonial Literature,* trans. Alita Kelley and Alec E. Kelley (Tucson: University of Arizona Press, 1991), 53–54; Gilberto Triviños explores this phenomenon in terms of colonial theory, the myth of modernity, and an encounter with the Other: "Revisitando la Literatura Chilena: 'Sigue Diciendo: Cayeron / Di Más: Volverán Mañana'," *Atenea* 487 (2003): 113–33; Castillo discusses contemporary Chilean political jargon involving the "autonomous" regions of the Mapuche, examining its relationship to literary texts, including the *Araucana*: e.g., "el indio manso" (the poor, victimized Indian), "el indio heróico" (laudatory but safely dead), "el indio permitido" (bearing limited rights), and "el indio falso" (acculturated or assimilated): "Impossible Indian," 43 ff.

    [3] Ricardo Padrón explores the *Araucana*'s contrasting discourses of masculinist conquest and feminized geography: "Love American Style: The Virgin Land and the Sodomitic Body in Ercilla's *Araucana,*" *Revista de Estudios Hispánicos* 34 (2000): 561–84; Raúl Marrero-Fente examines Ercilla's literary ontology: "Épica, fantasma, y lamento: la retórica del duelo en *La Araucana,*" *Revista Ibero-Americana* 73 (2007): 15–30, at 22; as noted earlier, Krogh discusses the Colonial "other" and Bakhtinian "other" in the *Araucana* (13 n. 26, supra). For an earlier influential study that argued for Ercilla's anti-

The six passages discussed below are examined in narrative order, beginning with Guacolda, then moving to the vision of Spanish beauty, the encounters with Tegualda, Glaura, and Lauca, and ending with the defense of Dido. While these scenes share many themes and functions, important differences distinguish them. Guacolda's story occurs in the course of Part I's description of the early stages of the Araucan insurgency, prior to Ercilla's arrival on the scene in Part II. Although the narrator pointedly asserts the accuracy of his account, the details of the story are by their nature not verifiable. Additionally, the third-person narration and absence of the narrator's participation allow for a structural and thematic simplicity the other passages lack, endowing the scene with a paradigmatic quality to which each of the remaining episodes responds. The vision or dream of Spanish beauty inverts this structure, featuring no Araucan women but transposing key themes from the Guacolda episode into terms of the narra-

---

imperialism, see Beatriz Pastor, who located a pervasive critique of Spain in the opposition between Spanish behavior and the Araucan women's attributes of fidelity, honor, and chastity; Pastor resurrected the spirit if not the letter of the poem's earlier nationalization by Chileans in asserting that its divided sensibility embodies the emergence of Hispanoamerican consciousness: *Discursos narrativos de la conquista: mitificación y emergencia* (Hanover, NH: Ediciones del Norte, 1988), 377, 436.

For studies that argue against an "anti-imperialist" reading of the poem, see inter alia Agustín Cueva's early, influential work, "El espejismo heroico de la conquista: ensayo de interpretación de *La Araucana*," *Casa de las Américas* 110 (1978): 29–40; Francisco Javier Cevallos, who discusses the poem's early reception: "Don Alonso de Ercilla and the American Indian: History and Myth," *Revista de Estudios Hispánicos* 23 (1989): 1–20; Janik Dieter, "La valoración múltiple del indio en *La Araucana* de Alonso de Ercilla," in *La imagen del indio en la Europa moderna* (Seville: CSIC, 1990), 237–88; Bernal Herrera, "*La Araucana*: conflicto y unidad," *Criticón* 53 (1991): 57–69; Wilfredo Casanova, "*La Araucana*: epopeya de las manos," *Bulletin Hispanique* 95 (1993): 99–117; Roberto Castillo Sandoval, "'¿Una misma cosa con la vuestra?': Ercilla, Pedro de Oña y la apropiación post-colonial de la patria araucana," *Revista Iberoamericana* 61 (1995): 231–47; Georgina Sabat-Rivers, "*La Araucana* bajo el lente actual: el noble bárbaro humilado," in *La cultura literaria en la América virreinal: concurrencias y diferencias*, ed. José Pascual Buxó (México: UNAM, 1996), 107–23; Gilberto Triviños, "El mito del tiempo de los héroes de Valdivia, Vivar y Ercilla," *Revista Chilena de Literatura* 49 (1996): 5–26; Gregory Shepherd, "Ercilla's Creative and Critical Conflicts: Balancing Oppositions in *La Araucana*," *Latin American Literary Review* 26 (1998): 120–33; Lara Vila i Tomás, "La Épica española del Renacimiento (1450–1605): propuestas para una revisión," *Boletín de la Real Academia Española* 83 (2003): 137–50.

Davis proposes discourse analysis as a way of moving beyond opposing readings of the poem: *Myth and Identity*, 17–18; Kallendorf endorses a similar goal, proposing controlled studies of intertextual environment that read the classics through a filter of postcolonial theory: "Representing," 395–96.

For Virgil in Ercilla, see S. G. MacCormack, *On the Wings of Time: Rome, the Incas, Spain, and Peru* (Princeton: Princeton University Press, 2007), 216–18.

tor's own experience, adumbrating an association between the poet and his characters that the other passages elaborate. In the defense of Dido, which follows the encounters with Tegualda, Glaura, and Lauca, earlier themes and theses are reprised in terms of an archetypal literary heroine, a structure whose ostensible distance from the enframing chronicle is undermined by similarly unexpected intimacy.

Among the recurring themes of these passages are the importance of Stoic perseverance in the face of inconstant fate; the dangers of lust and anger, ideally controlled within a hierarchy of the rational, irascible, and concupiscent; and the virtues of love as freely given, conjugal, and chaste, conditions that typically frame it in the context of marriage, reflecting contemporary Tridentine sensibilities. The narrator's role as a perfect Christian courtier is emphasized throughout the encounters. The importance of class emerges in the representation of the heroines as daughters of native nobility and in the narrator's differentiation of himself from the *vulgo* soldiers with whom he serves.[4] Key theses work to unify the episodes, most notably the erotic critique of epos, gradually elaborated by Ercilla to encompass a *renovatio* of ancient, medieval, and contemporary literary models.[5] The process begins with a shift from the documentary verse of chronicle into lyric and erotic elegy, distinguishing the passages from the surrounding narrative and fulfilling a number of crucial functions. Most prominently, lyric establishes Ercilla's competency in the new poetry, an inescapable challenge for an Iberian court poet in the generation succeeding Garcilaso, allowing him to establish his homage to and independence from not only his celebrated countryman but also Petrarch, Ariosto, and Sannazaro. Most importantly, lyric provides the poet with a way of figuring, and figuring out, the Amerindian Other. A century after contact between the Spanish and the New World, Ercilla's representation of this Other continues via literary topoi and the familiar epithets of courage, cleverness, and ferocity. Articulating these traits for men results in the heroic harangues of the leading Araucan warriors so admired by Voltaire. When

---

[4] José Durand identifies two class-based groups of Spanish arrivals in the New World, those who have come in hopes of making their fortune and those whose freedom from financial need permits them, in some instances, to take moral stands, particularly regarding the treatment of the indigenous population; Durand examines how the predominance of nobility among the troops who traveled to Peru with García Hurtado de Mendoza, Ercilla among them, affected relations with the commander, Pedro de Valdivia, and his soldiers: "El Chapetón Ercilla y la honra Araucana," *Filología* 10 (1964): 113–34.

[5] The orientation outlined here has similarities to the work of Juan M. Corominas, who conceives of a dialectic in Ercilla's poem between "la acción y la palabra—*epos*—por una parte, y el *logos líricos* y el eros platónico por otra" ("action and the word—*epos*—on the one hand, and the lyrical *logos* and platonic eros on the other"): *Castiglione y "La Araucana": Estudio de una influencia* (Madrid: José Porrúa Terranzas, 1980), 43.

it comes to the doubly estranged Araucan women, the poet embellishes their stories with a mix of tragedy, elegy, and adventure genres, largely displacing them with figures enacting a variety of literary, philosophical, and theological topoi.[6] While such displacement is far from unique for the period, when New World cultures still functioned as a *tabula rasa* for projections of the Old, Ercilla's pursuit of the process is distinctive for the degree to which it becomes interwoven with his own self-fashioning. Most simply, his efforts produce a narrator-participant imbued with *pietas, cortesía*, and *clemencia*, the same key attributes the poem associates with Philip II and thus a crucial component of the poet's *imitatio* of and affiliation with the king. Before long the process takes on an even more intimate cast, revealing the narrator to be as vulnerable to the vicissitudes of fate and desire as are his unfortunate heroines, whose experiences his own simultaneously reflect and revise. Initially this elision is limited to reasserting the proper relation between reason and the emotions; eventually, after many admiring references to the Araucans, it unequivocally asserts the differences between them and himself, repudiating the pagan epic values of public shame and honor at the heart of Araucan society in favor of private, Christian virtues. The juxtaposition of graphic violence and idealized encounters suggests a retreat from trauma, not surprising in light of the brutality the poet both witnessed and participated in. More broadly, the lyrical expression of emotion, whether of erotic desire or the longing for someone or something now lost, a quality of the past or vision of the future, creates a liminal space in the poem, a common ground where Araucan, Spaniard, and, ideally, the poem's reader all meet. Whether briefly interrupting the narrative, as does the appearance of Lauca, or developed into self-contained interpolations, as are the stories of Guacolda, Tegualda, and Glaura, these passages, through their contrast with depictions of the long counter-insurgency campaign, offer an alternative vision of human contact with an Other, figured as female, and of a Conquest, now one of virtue and honor, the latter quality unexpectedly personal, as the narrator's claim of *razón de mí* in his defense of Dido makes clear.

---

[6] The *Araucana*'s first reference to native women is in fact documentary, coming in the Prologue, where the poet notes that when the Araucan army suffers heavy losses the women serve as soldiers, at which time "[. . .] peleando algunos como varones, se entreguen con grande ánimo a la muerte" ("some of them fighting like men, they give themselves up with great bravery to death") (70). A similar observation accompanies the first appearance of women, in Canto 10, where they are described as joining the Araucan warriors to chase down fleeing Spaniards, exhibiting "varonil esfuerzo" ("manly spirit") (10.3.4).

2. Guacolda and the Erotic Bower at Penco

The Guacolda episode introduces a number of features that soon become familiar, among them the imagery of erotic passion derived from multiple ancient and
modern sources: Sappho, Euripides, Catullus, Callimachus, Virgil, Ovid, and
Apollonius; Petrarch, Dante, Ariosto, and Garcilaso. The revision of this imagery is particularly striking in the case of Ariosto, the most popular narrative
poet of the period whose transposition into Ercillan terms is marked by the elision of irony by earnestness. The scenes with Guacolda also introduce Ercilla's
unexpectedly systematic appropriation of other models, namely Virgil, where the
imitatio extends beyond particular imagery to the relationship between this imagery and its original context, that is, to the *dispositio* as well as *inventio* and *elocutio* of the archetype.

Guacolda makes her appearance at the end of Canto 13 in conjunction with
the climactic death of Lautaro, a formidable Araucan leader responsible for a series of bloody Spanish defeats that have dominated the narrative up to this point.
Having originally pushed south into Chile, or *Nueva Toledo*, for a brief period
in 1536, the Spanish returned to found Santiago in 1541, exploiting local tensions between the Indians in the north, who often fought alongside them in the
thousands, and the aggressive Araucans in the south. Despite such alliances and
the fearsome efficiency of firearms and horses, terrifying novelties the *Araucana*
memorably describes (e.g., 1.64.1–8), native uprisings were a frequent phenomenon, and Santiago was destroyed only eight months after its founding. The town
was quickly rebuilt by the Spanish commander of the region, Pedro de Valdivia,
who by 1550 had established numerous additional settlements, including Concepción, almost halfway down the coast. Within a year La Imperial and a fortification at Tucapel had also been built, both of these south of the formidable
Biobío river at Concepción that marked the boundary of the Araucan homeland
or *estado*. Although the Spanish had known for years about modest Indian gold
mines in the north of this territory, a fundamental change came to the region in
1552, when large deposits of placer gold were discovered near Concepción. By
early 1553 a mine using the forced labor of natives was operational, and before
the year was out the Araucans had met in council and decided to revolt.[7] While
the larger engagements in the ensuing hostilities involved thousands of men,

---

[7] On the context of the Spanish discovery of gold and the Araucan revolt, see
Lupher, who notes the contrast between the empire- and city-building Aztecs and Incas and the "primitive" Araucans on Spain's colonial frontier in Chile (*Romans*, 295–98);
Spain's income from American silver dropped by half from 1544 to 1550, due primarily
to the troubles in Peru; see John Lynch, *Spain under the Habsburgs*, 2 vols. (New York:
New York University Press, 1981), 1: 61; citing Ricardo F. Keun (*Y así nació la frontera*,
1986), Simerka notes that in addition to forced labor, the Araucan revolt was motivated
by Valdivia's destruction of their crops and general mistreatment (*Discourses*, 22).

rarely did the Spanish number more than five hundred, cavalry and *arcabuceros* combined, and many encounters were much smaller, often the result of highly effective guerilla tactics employed by the Araucans, including fighting in lowland marshes impenetrable by horses and using treacherous mountain passes to ambush their enemies, hobbled by heavy armor and lack of maneuverability. The latter occurs with devastating effect near the start of the poem, following a surprise attack on the Tucapel fort that destroyed it, forcing its Spanish defenders to run for their lives.[8] Learning of this dramatic escalation in violence, Valdivia quickly mounted a punitive raid, but was trapped in an ambush that he and his men narrowly fought their way out of and turned into a rout, only to have a temerarious Araucan youth rally his fleeing companions and reverse yet again, eventually chasing down and killing all the Spanish, including the commander. The loss of Valdivia and ascension of the daring young Indian leader, Lautaro, was traumatic, and shortly thereafter the Spanish were driven with significant losses from another fortification in the area and forced to flee back across the Biobío to Concepción. Here panic spread among the residents, who abandoned it for Santiago some thirty miles to the north. As feared, Lautaro, now second-in-command to Caupolicán, the Araucan chief, soon led a force that sacked Concepción, but at this point the Araucan momentum was broken by a series of meteorological portents that frightened them into returning to the *Estado*.[9] Regrouping several months later, the Indians resumed their attacks, overrunning the Spanish fort at Penco, near the remains of Concepción, and once again drawing near Santiago. With tension building for a confrontation that threatened to decide the Spanish effort to penetrate the area once and for all, Ercilla indulges in a strategic digression to describe how the recently appointed viceroy in Peru, having put down

---

[8] Ercilla attributes the overrunning of Tucapel to the greed of Valdivia, who detoured on the way to reinforce the fort in order to collect tribute from the Indians (2.92.1–8); for earlier references to Spanish avarice as a root cause of the Araucan uprising, a sentiment Ercilla voices on numerous occasions, see 1.69.1–8 and 2.6.1–4; on the Spanish being outnumbered 100 to 1, see 2.82.6; a later reference notes the difference as 60 to 2000 (3.57.1–3.58.2); cf. the reference to 3000 Indians at 3.69.2; Lerner notes that such numbers should be viewed as suggestive: *Araucana*, 158 n. 101.

[9] Lautaro's effectiveness as a leader was enhanced by his having been friendly with the Spanish, even serving as page to Pedro de Valdivia (3.67.5–8; 3.34.14). Cf. Lupher's overview of the Spanish counter-insurgency against the Araucans: *Romans*, 297 ff. Kevin Krogh provides a succinct overview of Ercilla's whereabouts between 1555 and 1563, including the Chilean campaigns: *Reading*, 40–41. Contemporary sources for events during this period include Gerónimo de Vivar, *Crónica y Relación copiosa y verdadera de los Reinos de Chile* (1558); Alonso de Góngora Marmolejo, *Historia de Chile desde su descubrimiento hasta el año 1575* (1536–1575); Pedro Mariño de Lobera, *Crónica del Reino de Chile* (1593); and Valdivia's own letters, *Cartas de Pedro de Valdivia que tratan del descubrimiento y conquista del Reino de Chile*; all of these texts are available online at the *Biblioteca Virtual Miguel de Cervantes*: http://www.cervantesvirtual.com/.

the military rebellion there that Ercilla originally left home to help suppress, learned of the Araucan revolt and sent some ten ships of men and supplies, the poet among them, under the command of his son, Don García Hurtado de Mendoza. Once this small armada is underway in difficult autumn seas, the narrative resumes in Chile near the main Araucan stronghold, which the Spanish have just discovered with the help of their Indian allies and are surrounding in darkness for a surprise dawn attack. It is here that Lautaro, impelled by "duro hado" or harsh fate (13.44.3), removes his armor for the first time in many weeks to be with his beloved, Guacolda, and after falling asleep has a nightmare in which he is overcome by "un soberbio español" ("an arrogant Spaniard") (13.45.3). Awakened by "la rabia y pena junto" ("a combination of rage and anguish") (13.45.8), he awakens Guacolda, who, learning of the dream, becomes distraught on realizing she has had a similar one and, convinced that his death is near, tearfully entreats him to re-arm and send his men to guard the wall. Lautaro does his best to calm her, reminding her of his reputation and gently chiding her for her lack of confidence, but she remains inconsolable. After a tension-heightening break between cantos, the Spanish attack, Lautaro is killed, and the first of a series of Araucan defeats takes place.[10]

The scenes with Guacolda have long been identified with Ariosto's depiction of Doralice, who does her best to dissuade Mandricardo from fighting Ruggiero (*O.F.* 30.36). Mandricardo attempts to console her by emphasizing his prowess while noting, in a couplet that Ercilla imitates quite closely, how little she must think of him if she is so afraid: "Ben mi mostrate in poco conto avere, / se per me un Ruggier sol vi fa temere" ("How very little you must think of me if a Ruggier all by himself can make you anxious") (30.38.7–8), reprised sardonically in Spanish as "¡Buen crédito con vos tengo, por cierto / pues me lloráis de miedo ya por muerto!" ("I certainly have a good reputation with you, since you weep with fear for me as already dead") (13.54.7–8).[11] Mandricardo goes on to fight Ruggiero and is killed. Despite such clear imitation, differences in tone between the Ariostan and Ercillan scenes reveal that the appropriation is entirely formal. Ariosto's scene is characteristically ironic, for while Doralice's grief may be quite genuine, she is an energetically fickle partner who would have given her love to Ruggiero rather than be alone (*O.F.* 30.72.5–30.73.4). Ercilla's episode, by contrast, is purely tragic: a heroic warrior lets down his guard at the prompting of desire, and

---

[10] The use of a canto break to heighten narrative tension is a technique Ercilla learns from Ariosto; see Daniel Javitch, *"Cantus Interruptus* in the *Orlando Furioso," MLN* 95 (1980): 66–80; cf. Nicolopulos's analysis of the storm encountered by the Spanish on their voyage south as an essential epic device: *Poetics,* 21 ff.; Nicolopulos briefly discusses the Guacolda episode, which, in contrast to the reading presented here, he regards as a seamless part of the narration of martial events (31).

[11] English translation of Ariosto is by Guido Waldman, *Orlando Furioso* (Oxford: Oxford University Press, 1974).

disaster follows. Any suggestion of chivalric dalliance is entirely absent, and as is true throughout these episodes, the quality of amorous attachment is conjugal and chaste. While the immediate reference and staging of the scene is indebted to Ariosto, the more powerful affiliation is with Andromache, who, convinced of Hector's imminent death, longs for her own and remains inconsolable in spite of his reassurances, accusing him of feeling no pity and urging him to put the army on guard outside the walls (*Il.* 6.407–413; 433–434). While moved to pity (*Il.* 6.484), as is Lautaro, Hector is driven by the chief concern of classical heroes, a desire for glory or *kleos* and the fear of *aidos* or shame (*Il.* 6.440–446), two classical pagan values that Ercilla frequently associates with the foremost Araucan warriors. Differentiating these from Christian integrity and honor, a process recalling E. R. Dodds's distinction between shame and guilt cultures (a parallel whose full import is reached with not Ercilla but Spenser), is an essential theme of the Araucan women episodes, beginning with Tegualda's Neoplatonic approach to the issue.[12] An additional allusion in these scenes is to the epic garden of delight, the erotic bower where the hero is beguiled into abandoning his martial project, a seduction frequently associated with the removal of his armor. More prevalent in the *Faerie Queene*, the presence of the erotic bower in the *Araucana* is transformed, as are other topoi, by historical realities, on the one hand, and by poem's earnestness, on the other, the traditional dalliance that temporarily delays the epic project figured here as fatal gesture.

The rhetoric of the Guacolda scene is characteristic of passages of intense emotion in Ercilla's poem: highly stylized, with intricate syntax and an emphasis on rhetorical devices of repetition. Such language has been employed earlier in the poem, most notably in descriptions of fighting, and its use here clearly marks the scene as literary rather than documentary. The physical description of the female protagonist, as in later episodes, is abstract, limited in this case to the single cliche of beauty. Guacolda's emotions, on the other hand, as well as Lautaro's, are the focus of the passage from its opening lines:

> Aquella noche el bárbaro dormía
> con la bella Guacolda enamorada,
> a quien él de *encendido amor* amaba
> y ella por él no menos *se abrasaba*. (13.43.5–8)

That night the barbarian slept with his beautiful beloved, Guacolda, whom he cherished with a *burning passion* and who *burned* no less ardently for him.[13]

---

[12] Murrin notes the model offered by Andromache, referencing the critical tradition that saw Homeric allusions in Ercilla's poem: *History and Warfare*, 167 and 313 n. 33; Dodds's discussion is found in *The Greeks and the Irrational* (Berkeley: University of California Press, 1951), esp. chap. 2.

[13] In addition to the use here of assonance, consonance, and polyptoton, Ercilla also favors the use of antithesis (13.46.4), anaphora (13.53.4–8; 14.12.3–6), paradox (13.49.4),

The image of love as fire, recurrent throughout these episodes, associates the heroine most directly with Virgil's descriptions of Dido, as do subsequent references to *la llaga de amor* ("the wound of love") (13.49.3) and to love as *dulce veneno* ("sweet poison") (14.3.4).[14] Such images also recall the lyrics of Petrarch and Garcilaso, the latter the object of a more direct imitation a few lines later in Guacolda's description of love as "el áspero camino de mi suerte" ("the difficult

---

and chiasmus (14.5.7–8). For analysis of the poet's rhetoric see Isaías Lerner, "Ercilla y la formación del discurso poético áureo," in *Busquemos Otros Montes y Otros Ríos*, ed. Elias L. Rivers (Madrid: Castalia, 1992), 155–66. An especially vivid description of fighting appears at C. 22.31.1–8; the use of *bárbaro* with regard to the Araucans signifies their lack of belief in God.

[14] Cf. Venus's wish that Cupid "[. . .] donisque furentem / incendat reginam atque ossibus implicet ignem" ("inflame the queen to madness with his gifts and implant the fire into her very bones") (1.659–660) and, a few lines later, that "occultum inspires ignem fallasque veneno" ("breathe a hidden fire into her and infuse poison into her undetected") (1.688); cf. the banquet scene, where it is said of Dido "ardescitque tuendo" ("and gazing [at Aeneas] she takes fire") (1.713); also see "At regina gravi iamdudum saucia cura / volnus alit venis et caeco carpitur igni" ("But the queen, long since injured by grave disquiet, feeds the wound with her life-blood and is consumed by hidden fire") (4.1–2); cf. "ardet amans Dido traxitque per ossa furorem" ("Dido burns with love and draws the madness through her bones") (4.101), and "est mollis flamma medullas / interea et tacitum vivit sub pectore volnus. / uritur infelix Dido totaque vagatur / urbe furens, qualis coniecta cerva sagitta" ("meanwhile the tender flame consumes her marrow and the secret wound lives near her heart. Unhappy Dido burns and wanders through all the city in a frenzy—even as a hind, smitten by an arrow") (*Aen.* 4.66–69); English translations of Virgil are based on those of H. R. Fairclough in the Loeb edition, *Aeneid* (Cambridge, MA: Harvard University Press, 1935). Virgil's adaptations of Apollonius in such imagery are particularly striking; see Damien P. Nelis, "Apollonius and Virgil," in *A Companion to Apollonius Rhodius*, ed. T. D. Papanghelis and A. Rengakos (Leiden: Brill, 2001), 237–59. Cf. Cupid's first arrow shot at Medea: "βέλος δ' ἐνεδαίετο κούρῃ / νέρθεν ὑπὸ κραδίῃ, φλογὶ εἴκελον·" ("and the bolt burnt deep down in the maiden's heart, like a flame") (*Argo.* 3.286–287); and esp.: "τοῖος ὑπὸ κραδίῃ εἰλυμένος αἴθετο λάθρῃ / οὖλος Ἔρως" ("so coiling round her heart, burnt secretly Love the destroyer (3.296–297); also see "κῆρ ἄχεϊ σμύχουσα" ("her heart smouldering with pain) (3.446) and "σμύχουσα διὰ χροός" ("a smouldering fire through her frame") (3.762); χροός is the same term used by Sappho in the earlier example (χρῶι) and means, more literally, *skin*; see 31 n. 66, supra. Catullus' Poem 64 represents an intermediary, thus with regard to Ariadne's first seeing Theseus: "non prius ex illo *flagrantia* declinavit / lumina quam cuncto concepit corpore *flammam* / funditus atque imis *exarsit* tota medullis" ("no sooner did she lower from him her incandescent eyes / than she conceived throughout her body a flame, / and totally, to the center of her bones, she burned") (91–93); cf. later references to "*incensam* [. . .] mente puellam" ("her mind aflame") (97) and "*ardenti* cordi furentem" ("the madness of her burning heart") (124); English translations of Catullus are based on those of Thomas Banks, "Catullus, Poem 64: The Wedding of Peleus and Thetis," http://www.stoa.org/diotima/anthology/cat64.shtml.

road of my fate") (13.46.8), and in her reference to "el preciso hado y dura suerte" ("inescapable fate and cruel fortune") (13.56.10).[15] By voicing her stoic desire to join Lautaro in death, Guacolda associates herself with heroines of antiquity:

> aunque el golpe que espero es insufrible,
> podré con otro luego remediarme,
> que no caerá tu cuerpo en tierra frío
> cuando estará en el suelo muerto el mío. (13.47.5–8)

> although the blow I await is insufferable, I can soon save myself with another, for before your body falls cold to the earth mine will be dead on the ground.

Lautaro expresses his love predominantly in terms of power relations: "*libre* en estos brazos os *poseo*" ("*freely* in these arms I *possess* you") (13.48.8); "Mi vida está *sujeta* a vuestras manos / y no a todo *el poder* de los humanos" ("My life is *subject* to your hands and not to any human *power*") (13.49.8). Boasting that he alone has freed the Araucans from Spanish oppression (13.50.3–6), this legalistic vocabulary expands to include *domado* ("dominated"), *sometía* ("submitted"), *dominio* ("dominion"), and *tiranía* ("tyranny"), the first of these recalling the narrator's famous opening description of the Araucans as "el fiero pueblo no *domado*" ("the fierce, *indomitable* people") (1.11.5).[16] Employed in the course of his expressions of love for Guacolda, such terminology suggests a contrast between forced and free relations that will eventually implicate the Conquest itself, a contrast the encounter with Tegualda will make more explicit. Here Guacolda echoes the mix of amorous and legal vocabulary, beseeching Lautaro to rearm himself in the name of "aquella voluntad pura, amorosa, / que *libre* os di cuando más *libre* estaba" ("that pure, loving affection that I *freely* gave you when I was more *free*")

---

[15] For the "áspero camino" image, see Garcilaso's *Sonnet 6* (1) and *Canción 4* (20); for "el preciso hado," see the apostrophe in *Elegía 1* (76–78).

[16] The central octave of Lautaro's speech:

> ¿Quién el pueblo araucano ha restaurado
> en su reputación que se perdía,
> pues el soberbio cuello no *domado*
> ya doméstico al yugo *sometía*?
> Yo soy quien de los hombros le ha quitado
> el español *dominio* y *tiranía*:
> mi nombre basta solo en esta tierra,
> sin levantar espada, a hacer la guerra. (13.50.1–8)

Who was it restored their lost reputation to the Araucans when their proud, *indomitable* necks were tamely *subjected* to the yoke? I'm the one who cast Spanish *domination* and *tyranny* from their shoulders, and in this land my name alone is enough to wage war without ever raising a sword.

(13.52.5–6). Unable to incite him to action, she can only repeat her intention of dying beside him (13.55.7–8). The narrator ends the canto with a retreat from his emotional description of the scene:

> Pero ya *la turbada pluma mía*
> que en las cosas de amor nueva se halla,
> *confusa, tarda, y con temor* se mueve
> y a pasar adelante no se atreve. (13.57.5–8)

> But now *my troubled pen*, finding itself newly amidst matters of love, is *confused* and *fearful*, and moving *sluggishly*, dares go no further.

These lines are the first indication of a complex interaction that will develop among the narrator, his characters, and the stories they tell, expressing a trepidation that applies not only to the matter of love but also to the imminent demise of his Araucan protagonist. Subsequent episodes reveal this allusion to the poet's own feelings to be far from solely rhetorical. Canto 14 opens with one of the poem's numerous articulations of the traditional defense of women, illustrated here by the example of Guacolda's "puro amor" ("pure love") (14.1.6). The denouement, in which Guacolda's worst fears come true and Lautaro is killed, follows a brief glimpses of the couple that recapitulates key imagery in a virtuosic display of alliteration, polyptoton, antithesis, and hyperbaton:

> Así los dos unidos corazones
> conformes en amor desconformaban
> y dando dello allí demostraciones
> más el dulce veneno alimentaban. (14.3.1–4)

> Thus these two united hearts, agreeing in love, disagreed, and their demonstrations of it fed the sweet poison even more.

While three of the elements just noted, Guacolda's stoic fortitude in the face of calamity, the imagery of mutual, passionate love, and the poet's use of elevated diction, distance the episode from chivalric literature, four additional passages link it directly to heroic poetry, establishing Ercilla's deliberate evocation of the erotic critique of epic. None of these intertexts has been emphasized in previous commentary, the first pair most likely because of their obscurity, the last perhaps for the opposite reason. The first, briefest passage comes near the beginning of the episode, just after Guacolda asserts her freely given love, adding: "y dello el alto cielo es buen testigo" ("and of which high heaven is my witness") (13.52.5–7), words that recall heaven's witnessing of the encounter between Dido and Aeneas ("[. . .] conscius Aether conubiis") ("Heaven, the witness to their bridal") (*Aen.* 4.167–168). In contrast to subsequent episodes, there is no mention here of marriage or references to the characters as anything other than a loving couple, only this clear evocation of Virgil, an association reinforced a few lines earlier by a reference to the *tálamo* or wedding bed she shares with Lautaro (13.47.2).

The second passage, equally subtle if more complex, comes near the episode's conclusion and features both a general allusion to the night raid based on the time of day and a specific intertext based on the Spanish slaughter of sleeping Indians, a detail of epic versions of the topos that describe the killing of sleeping soldiers. Homer's text details how Odysseus and Diomedes, after killing the Trojan spy, Dolon, go on to slaughter sleeping Thracians in order to steal the chariot and horses of their captain, Rhesus. [17] The best-known ancient variation of the motif, which Ercilla imitates, is Virgil's, whose tale of Nisus and Euryalus begins with Nisus's description of the enemy: "lumina rara micant, *somno vinoque soluti* / procubere [. . .]" ("Few are their gleaming lights; *relaxed with wine and slumber,* they lie prone") (9.189–190). Virgil repeats the phrase twice within the next few lines, once, exactly, when the pair are proposing their plan to their comrades (9.236), and then once the raid is underway, with slight variation: "passim *somno vinoque* per herbam / corpora *fusa* vident," that is, "everywhere they see bodies *stretched with wine and slumber* along the grass" (9.316–317). [18] Ercilla's appropriation of the phrase comes in his description of the moments just after daybreak when mistakenly confident Araucan guards leave their posts to join their sleeping comrades:

> Cuando ya las tinieblas y aire escuro
> con las esperada luz se adelgazaban,
> las centinelas puestas por el muro
> al nuevo día de lejos saludaban,
> y pensando tener campo seguro
> también a descansar se retiraban,
> quedando mudo el fuerte y los soldados
> *en vino y dulce sueño sepultados.* (14.6.1–8)

> When the gloom and darkness began to disperse the longed-for light, the sentinels posted on the wall greeted the new day from afar, and believing the camp secure, they also retired to rest, the entire fort remaining silent and the soldiers *buried in wine and sweet sleep.*

Ercilla's version of the phrase exhibits several small but significant deviations. Virgil does not qualify *sleep,* although its epithet in Homer is frequently "sweet"

---

[17] Cf.: "Now these were slumbering, worn out with toil, and their fair battle gear lay by them on the ground, all in good order, in three rows, and by each man was his yoke of horses. But Rhesus slept in their midst [. . .]" (*Il.* 10.471–474) (English translation of the *Iliad,* unless otherwise indicated, is by A. T. Murray, revised by William F. Wyatt, in the 1999 Loeb edition).

[18] Fairclough's translation ("everywhere they see bodies stretched along the grass in drunken sleep") has been altered here to emphasize Virgil's parallel construction.

(e.g., *Il.* 2.2; 10.4, 24.3, 24.636). More significant is the inversion of Virgil's hen-diadys, Ercilla writing *vino y dulce sueño* rather than *somno vinoque*, and his use of the emphatic *sepultados* instead of a correlate for *soluti* or *fusa*, a variation, it turns out, associated with Virgil's earlier use of the phrase in a description of the treachery by which Troy was betrayed to the Greeks. This story, told by Aeneas at Dido's banquet, focuses on the Pelasgian guile (*Aen.* 2.106, 152) of the Greek decoy, Sinon, who tricked the Trojans into drawing the wooden horse within the city, after which the Argives emerge and "invadunt urbem *somno vinoque sepul-tam*" ("they storm the city, *buried in sleep and wine*") (2.265). While the echo may be intentional on Ercilla's part, suggesting the deviousness of the Spanish attack as well as its devastating effectiveness, his use of the phrase, both its reversal of *sleep* and *wine* and incorporation of *sepultados*, is most likely explained by his fa-miliarity with the most popular translation of the *Aeneid* in Spain at that time, completed by Gregorio Hernández de Velasco in 1555.[19] Hernández de Velasco transposes the phrase from Troy's fall to the night raid's second use of the image: "Do ya llegados, veen a cada passo / Cuerpos *en vino y sueño sepultados*," or, "hav-ing arrived at which [the Rutulian camp], at every step they see bodies *buried in wine and sleep*" (9.319–320). Both Hernández de Velasco and Ercilla employ the *endecasílabo* line; *dulce* aptly completes the latter's.[20]

---

[19] Davis argues that the problem of fraud, especially as manifest in betrayal, is a central concern of Ercilla's poem that critics have underrated (*Myth and Identity*, 46–47); cf. Murrin, *History and Warfare*, 145–46. The issue returns below in the poem's defense of Dido, 96–113, infra. Although he doesn't discuss the *somno vinoque* phrase, Kallen-dorf notes that while Ercilla's Virgilian allusions regularly associate the Spanish with Trojans, "further voices" in the *Araucana* link the Trojans to the Indians and the Spanish to Trojan adversaries. Kallendorf argues on the one hand that this constitutes an imita-tion of the *Aeneid*, where ambiguity is manifest as "additional" voices (see 11 supra); on the other he sees it as a vital complicating of Ercilla's sympathies in the *Araucana*, which he characterizes as profoundly Virgilian ("Representing," 397–409). Kallendorf argues against the tendency of earlier studies to assume that Ercilla's lack of facility with Latin required his use of translations, such as the work of Hernández de Velasco discussed here ("Representing," 412 n. 23). Nicolopulos, who takes the same position, doesn't mention Hernández de Velasco's translation and doubts Ercilla's close familiarity with the *Iliad* (*Poetics*, 273 n. 3).

[20] Text of Hernández de Velasco, modernized from the 1557 manuscript at the His-panic Society of America Library, is reprinted in Appendix A. The potential for a third related intertext also exists, Juan de Mena's mid-1400s translation of the *Ilias latina*, or *Homerus latinus*, an anonymous first-century epitome of Homer's work that is part of the complex afterlife of the Trojan epic cycle. Based on secondary traditions that combine echoes of Virgil, Ovid, and the erotic elegy of Propertius into a hybrid of classical epic and Greek romance, the *Ilias latina* gradually lost influence in the Middle Ages to the narratives of Dictys and Dares, discussed below (103 ff.). Its version of the crucial scene in the Doloneia is distinctly Virgilian, stating that: "intrant atque ipsum *somno vinoque*

The third important intertext in the Guacolda episode follows immediately upon the second, describing the dawn preceding the Spanish attack:

Era llegada al mundo aquella hora
que la escura tiniebla, no pudiendo
sufrir la clara vista de la Aurora,
se va en el ocidente retrayendo;
cuando la mustia Clicie se mejora
el rostro al rojo oriente revolviendo,
mirando tras las sombras ir la estrella
y al rubio Apolo Délfico tras ella. (14.7.1–8)

That hour had arrived in the world when gloomy darkness, unable to with-stand the bright sight of Aurora, retreats to the west, and when sad Cly-tie revives, turning her face toward the reddening east as she watches the morning star trail after the shadows, followed by blond Delphic Apollo.

This description, together with similar ones earlier in the poem, recalls various epic models, beginning with Homer's well-known formulation: "Now Dawn rose from her bed beside lordly Tithonus, to bring light to immortals and to mortal men" (*Il.* 11.1–2). Ercilla's version, with its reference to Aurora, references Vir-gil's rendition of the topos: "Et iam prima novo spargebat lumine terras / Tithoni croceum linquens Aurora cubile" ("And now early dawn, Aurora, was sprinkling fresh rays upon the earth as she left the saffron bed of Tithonus") (*Aen.* 4.584–585 and 9.459–460). Ercilla's skillfully elaborates Virgil's couplet into an oc-tave by referencing Ovid's story of heartbroken Clytie, transformed into a helio-trope after being abandoned by Apollo (*Met.* 4.204–273), particularly apt since

---

sepultum / obtruncant [. . .]" ("they entered and slaughtered him [Rhesus], buried in sleep and wine") (729–730), a phrase Mena construes as "entraron calladamente en las tien-das de Reso y mataron y despedaçaron a éste, al qual *en sueño e vino* fallaron *sepultado*" ("they quietly entered the tents of Rhesus and cut him to pieces and killed him, whom they found buried in sleep and wine") (50–54). Hernández de Velasco's overall use of the phrase may thus reflect Mena's and the transposition of the *Ilias latinus*, although his re-versal of the hendiadys clearly signals his appropriation by Ercilla. Although Nicolopulos doesn't mention Mena's translation, his demonstration of Ercilla's indebtedness to other works of this illustrious predecessor would suggest his familiarity with it (*Poetics*, 85–88). The phrase comes close to taking on a reality of its own in at least one history of the Arau-can wars, a nineteenth-century text in which an Araucan traitor, Andresillo (Ercilla tells the story in Canto 30), is described as attempting to lure the Indians into an attack on the Spanish fort, which he assures them will be easy, "[. . .] porque los españoles dormian con el calor la siesta desnudos y desarmados" ("because the Spanish were taking their siesta unclothed and unarmed in the heat"): Diego de Rosales, *Historia General de el Reyno de Chile, Flandes Indiano*, 3 vols. (Valparaiso: Mercurio, 1877–1878), 2: 76.

it suggests Guacolda's impending bereavement by Lautaro.[21] Just as important as the language in Ercilla's appropriation of the dawn simile is its location within the enframing narrative, which reveals an additional significant homology with its model. In the *Iliad* the simile is bracketed on one side by the conclusion of the Doloneia, which ends Book 10, and on the other by Zeus's sending of Eris, the goddess of strife, among the Achaeans, precipitating some of the fiercest fighting in the poem (*Il.* 11.3–4 ff.). Virgil's descriptive couplet appears twice in the *Aeneid*: first, as dawn reveals the departing ships of Aeneas (4.584–585), precipitating Dido's suicide (4.663); then, in imitation of Homer, immediately after the killing of Nisus and Euryalus that ends the night raid (9.459–460) and just before scenes of renewed savagery as Turnus wreaks havoc outside the walls of the Trojan camp. The *dispositio* or structural positioning of the dawn set-piece fulfills several functions in classical epic. Most important, it juxtaposes mimetic tranquility to mayhem, accentuating the differences between the two and, in Virgil's case at least, suggesting a critique of the violence while heightening its attendant pathos. It also offers respite, distancing both narrator and reader from the circumambient carnage. Notably, this respite is only temporary, as the suspended brutality of war returns with a vengeance shortly afterwards. Ercilla's octave reveals a process of imitation that references not only the *elocutio* of Virgil's Latin but also the *dispositio* of both Homer and Virgil, his simile following the *somno vinoque* associated with the night raid while preceding the devastating Spanish attack on the Araucan camp in which Lautaro is killed. The complex appropriation is enriched by the Ovidian allusion.

A final intertext with the *Aeneid* appears in the closing octave of the Guacolda episode. At this point the shouts of the attacking Spanish have broken the silence, and the Araucans, still half asleep, struggle to defend themselves. With no time to don either arms or clothing Lautaro takes his sword and, wrapping his arm in a blanket, rushes into the fighting. Just as he appears the Spaniards' Indian allies release a volley of arrows, one of which pierces his heart. The succinct description of his death concludes: "los ojos tuerce y con rabiosa pena / la alma, del mortal cuerpo desatada, / bajó furiosa a la infernal morada" ("his eyes rolled back, and with raging grief his soul, detached from its mortal body, sank furiously to the infernal dwelling") (14.18.6–8). The Virgilian allusion is to the

---

[21] Ercilla's prior use of this imagery, in Canto 2, mentions Aurora (2.50.1), the wife of Tithonus (2.54.2), Phaethon's chariot (2.55.1), and Apollo (2.57.5); on the distribution of these references over eight octaves to convey the duration of time associated with the appearance of dawn, see Lerner, *Araucana*, 120 n. 61; two subsequent passages in the *Araucana* also reference the topos: *la clara aurora* (17.33.8) and *la rosada Aurora* (18.75.8), both of which recall the simpler Homeric formula of "rosy-fingered dawn" found both in the *Iliad* (e.g., 1.477, 6.175, 9.707, 23.109, 24.788) and *Odyssey* (e.g., 2.1, 9.152, 13.18). On Ercilla's introduction of Clytie and other details of the lines, see Lerner, *Araucana*, 413 n. 13.

death of Turnus, of course, of which the poet says: "[. . .] ast illi solvuntur fri-
gore membra / vitaque cum gemitu fugit indignata sub umbras" ("but his limbs
are loosed by the chill of death and his soul with a moan flees indignantly to
the shades below") (12.951–952), the winged soul based on the earlier Homeric
formula describing the death of both Patroclus and Hector: "ψυχὴ δ' ἐκ ῥεθέων
πταμένη Ἀϊδόσδε βεβήκει, / ὅν πότμον γοόωσα [. . .]" ("his soul [free] of his limbs
went flying to Hades bemoaning his fate") (*Il.* 16.856–857 and 22.362–363), a
conceit taken up later, as will be seen, by Petrarch and Neoplatonism in the image of the lover's soul flying after the beloved.[22] Also present at this point in the
narrative is a subtle intratextual echo of Lautaro's nightmare with its "*rabia y
pena junto*" (13.45.8), a repetition emphasizing the dream's impending accuracy.[23] Lautaro's affiliation with Turnus is complex and revealing. Turnus is heroic,
with epic energy and stature and a certain appeal associated with the underdog.
He is also arrogant, violent, and, finally, among the poem's defeated. By contrast,
the association of Turnus with Patroclus and Hector, the tragic death of the first
a symbol of pathos, that of the second an example of implacable fate, is indicative of Virgil's transformation of what in Homer are discrete, contrasting emotions regarding violence and death into ambivalence toward the epic enterprise.
Such misgivings are even more pronounced in the *Araucana*, where Lautaro, like
Turnus, is not only heroic, imperious, brutal, and doomed to defeat, but also, by
virtue of his scene with Guacolda, part of an erotic perspective on the violence
he himself perpetuates elsewhere. His association with Virgil's flawed hero is one
of many indications of Ercilla's ultimate sympathies, which, while frequently ex-

---

[22] For a contrasting reading of this episode, which sees Lautaro's death as the culmi-
nation of a steady decline in character, see Nicolopulos, *Poetics*, 31; see Lyne's insightful
analysis of the subtle differences between two types of death in Virgil: one, Homeric in
origin and envisioning an afterlife, seen here, in which the soul goes beneath the earth
"with a shrill cry," e.g., that of Turnus (*Aen.* 12.951–952), echoing those of Patroclus and
Hector (*Il.* 16.857–858 and 22.363); the other, Lucretian, in which death is final and the
soul "slips away into the winds," e.g., that of Dido (*Aen.* 4.704) ("Virgil's *Aeneid*: Subversion by Intertextuality," 195–96).

[23] The translation of Homer is that of R. D. Williams, which more accurately pre-
serves the flying of the soul than does A. T. Murray's use of "fleeting" (see n. 17, supra).
The verb used by Homer, πέτομαι (to fly, be on the wing), used earlier by Odysseus's
mother during their encounter in the underworld, is the same as that used by Apollonius
in describing the lover's soul as flying after the beloved, imagery taken up by Petrarch and
discussed below, 71 ff. The Doloneia also refers to a nightmare, that of Rhesus, of whom
it is said that, "[. . .] an evil dream stood over his head that night, the son of Oeneus' son,
by the device of Athene") (*Il.* 10.496–497).

tended to the bravery and suffering of the Araucans, are finally and unquestion-
ably with the imperial project of the Habsburgs.[24]

Through its intertexts with classical epic the Guacolda episode fulfills several key functions. In juxtaposing the tenderness between two lovers to a murderous ambush of sleeping Indians it implicitly questions the latter, participating
in the traditional critique of epic by eros. In establishing similarities between its
heroine and Dido and in explicitly alluding to the Doloneia, it effectively combines the motifs of the night raid and the abandoned woman, a conjunction the
next encounter with an Araucan heroine, Tegualda, will pursue even further. The
lyrical component of these scenes provides the poet with a means of figuring the
Araucan Other while also enabling him, for the first time in the narrative, to exhibit his skill in the new poetry. Intertexts with Petrarch, Ariosto, and Garcilaso,
which dominate the first half of the episode, allow Ercilla both to pay homage
to and to distinguish himself from these predecessors, dissimulating some aspects of their influence and emphasizing others, all the while claiming his place
among them. The allusions to classical epic, which characterize the episode's remainder, not only affiliate it with epic rather than chivalric romance, but also reveal a deliberate linking between the climax of Part I of the *Araucana* and two of
the most pathetic passages in classical epic, the story of Dido, a topic Ercilla will
allude to repeatedly before his full-fledged defense of her in Cantos 32 and 33,
and the night raid as envisioned by Homer, imitated by Virgil, and translated by
Hernández de Velasco. The evocation of Turnus reinforces the genealogy of such
references while emphasizing the complexity of the poet's attitude toward this
heritage, itself complex, and helping clarify his sympathies. Ercilla's appropriation of the dawn simile suggests a keen awareness not only of the image's poetic
construction but also of its structural function in classical epic as well, capturing
not only the canonical contrast of formal beauty to death and destruction, but
the more specific positioning of the interlude with respect to a highly-charged
death scene and a resurgence of martial ferocity. Finally, the passing reference
made by the narrator to his own confusion regarding love, which appears near
the episode's midpoint, begins a new phase in the construction of his own persona, one that receives its fullest treatment in the visionary experience that follows soon thereafter.

---

[24] On Lautaro's brutal disciplining of his own soldiers, see 7.41.2; his arrogance climaxes in his demand of annual tribute from the Spanish in return for not pursuing them
all the way back to Spain (12.13.1–12.15.8).

3. Peak Experience: The Vision of Spanish Beauty

Important plot developments occur between the Guacolda episode and the next appearance of women in the narrative. The battle of Mataquito in which Lautaro is killed and the Araucan troops defeated rages on into Canto 15, the last of Part I, which concludes with a description of the Spanish reinforcements, Ercilla among them, in danger of shipwreck as they arrive from Peru. Part II of the poem, published in 1578, takes up where the narrative left off nine years earlier with the harrowing storm. When the ships are finally able to land on a small island in the bay of Concepción, the natives began massing for an attack, serendipitously averted by the appearance of a comet, which is interpreted as an omen of their ruin and sends them fleeing to the mainland (16.23.1–8).[25] Some weeks later a duplicitous Araucan embassy arrives with pledges of peace and cooperation. Undeceived, the Spanish contingent of some hundred and thirty cavalry and artillery remain on the island through two difficult winter months, then finally come ashore under cover of darkness and quickly construct a stronghold on a nearby hill. It isn't long before the Araucans, taken by surprise, begin gathering their forces again, and it is in this atmosphere of heightened anxiety regarding an imminent assault that the poet, writing late at night when the camp is quiet, suffers a momentary seizure or fit, after which he falls asleep and experiences a quasi-lucid dream dominated by two female figures: Bellona, the goddess of war, and Reason, a figure clad in white (C.17–18). The episode, which exposes an underlying tension between pastoral and history that is shared with other episodes, has been studied most notably as Ercilla's appropriation of epic prophecy, based closely on Juan de Mena's *Laberinto de Fortuna* and employed to link the relatively insignificant campaign in Chile with Spain's metropolitan center and broader imperial program.[26] The present discussion explores how much more than this traditional prophetic function is accomplished by the unexpected appearance of these figures and the scenes they narrate, whose differences from the Araucan women episodes is less dramatic than first appears. Most important, by the end of the episode Bellona and Reason are thoroughly implicated in the erotic, adumbrating for the first time in the poem the essential relationship among the irascible, rational, and concupiscent that dominates so much of the remaining treatment of love and war. As the scene develops, the suggestion at the end of

---

[25] The Spanish made landfall on what is today known as Quiriquina Island, in the Bay of Concepción. On the reality, or lack thereof, of the meteorological event, see Lerner, *Araucana*, 473 n. 53.

[26] Both these allegorical figures, as well as numerous other details, are found in Mena's poem; see Nicolopulos, *Poetics*, 28, 85–97; cf. Fuchs, "Traveling Epic," 380. Andrés I. Prieto argues the *Araucana*'s deployment of prophetic devices should be considered in the context of an intense struggle between the Papist and the Castellanista factions that dominated Philip II's court during the 1570s ("Visiones," 87–89).

the Guacolda episode of the narrator's personal experience of these issues is made explicit and his self-fashioning begins in earnest. The process draws unexpected correspondences with his characters yet also marks clearly-drawn differences with them, notably his implicit rejection of Stoic *apatheia*, which often lingers as a subliminal lesson of their tragic stories.

Briefly summarized, Bellona's appearance in the dream begins with lavish praise for the young poet's devotion to his bellicose subject conjoined with a call to deeper commitment: "ensancha el corazón y la esperanza; / y aspira a más de aquello que pretendes [. . .]" ("extend your hopes and heart, and aspire to more than what you're striving for") (17.40.6–7). Assuring him of her assistance, she promises to take him to a location providing material related not only to famous wars, but also to feminine beauty and love:

> Es campo fértil, lleno de mil flores,
> en el cual hallarás materia llena
> de guerras más famosas y mayores,
> donde podrá alimentar la vena.
> Y si quieres de damas y de amores
> en verso celebrar la dulce pena,
> tendrás mayor sujeto y hermosura
> que en la pasada edad y en la futura. (17.42.1–8)

> It's a fertile field, teeming with thousands of flowers, where you'll find abundant material of greater and more famous wars with which to nourish your inspiration. And if you want to celebrate the sweet pain of ladies and love in your verse, you'll find more subjects and greater beauty there than in any previous or future age.

After finding himself in the middle of this eroticized *locus amoenus*, an idealized storehouse of literary inspiration or *inventio*, the poet is abruptly precipitated to the peak of a pyramidal mountain, where he is given a dizzying view of Philip II's attack on the French at San Quentin, which Bellona begins by narrating, then unceremoniously breaks off in order to join, precipitating its victorious climax. In her absence the figure of Reason takes over as guide, narrating additional aspects of Spanish history before closing with a panorama of beautiful Spanish women that includes a prophetic introduction to the poet's future wife. The vision is violently interrupted by the expected Araucan attack.[27]

The introduction of erotic matter at this point in the narrative responds to accumulating protests by the narrator about the monotony of his subject. The complaint first appears at the start of Canto 15, a few octaves after the death of Lautaro. a retrospective justification for having spoken of his love for Guacolda.

---

[27] Nicolopulos notes the medieval allegorical tradition of the mountain vantage point, which he terms "an Andean Parnassus" (*Poetics*, 94, 279 n. 30).

Here the poet ponders how it will be possible to compose a poem worth reading without writing of love, recalling the self-imposed injunction against love stories with which the *Araucana* began and presaging key language in Bellona's introductory harangue:

> ¿Qué cosa puede haber sin amor buena?
> ¿Qué verso sin amor dará contento?
> ¿Dónde jamás se ha visto rica vena
> que no tenga de amor el nacimiento?
> No se puede llamar materia llena
> la que de amor no tiene el fundamento;
> los contentos, los gustos, los cuidados,
> son, si no son de amor, como pintados. (15.1.1–8)

> What good can there be without love? What verse without love will bring delight? Where has one ever seen a rich poetic vein not born of love? A subject that does not have love as its foundation cannot be called complete, for contentment, pleasures, and concerns, if not about love, are as illusory.

Love is necessary for the full treatment of any subject, he decides, citing Dante, Ariosto, Petrarch, and Garcilaso as examples of poets whom love has incited to greater accomplishments (15.2.5). A few pages later in the foreword to Part II the theme is explored in terms of maintaining reader interest as well as textual authority:

> [. . .] haber de caminar siempre por el rigor de una verdad y camino tan desierto y estéril , paréceme que no habrá gusto que no se canse de seguirme. Así temeroso desto, quisiera mil veces mezclar algunas cosas diferentes; pero acordé de no mudar estilo, porque lo que digo se me tomase en descuento de las faltas que el libro lleva [. . .]

> always having to walk according to the rigor of one truth, along a road so deserted and sterile, it seems to me there will be no taste that does not tire of following me. Fearing this, there were a thousand times I would have liked to intermix some different material, but I resolved not to change styles, so that what I speak of might offset the book's faults (463)

Following Bellona's departure and the whirlwind tour of Spanish imperial history, Reason remarks that if the poet wants to mix such harsh material with gentler he should turn his gaze to "[. . .] la belleza de las damas de España, que admirada / estoy, según el bien que allí se encierra, / cómo no *abrasa* Amor toda la tierra" ("the beautiful ladies of Spain, for considering the goodness contained therein I'm amazed Love doesn't inflame the entire earth") (18.64.6–8). True to her persona, she warns him to be on his guard against the sight of such beauty, lest his "ojos faciles" ("fickle eyes") (18.65.2) get him into difficulties she may be unable to resolve, i.e., lest he fall prey to erotic desire: "ni en tu fuerza y mi ayuda te confíes, / que aunque quiera después contraponerme, / tú cerrarás los ojos por no verme" ("nor count either on your own strength or my assistance, for even though I may later want to help you, you will close your eyes in order not to see me") (18.65.6–8). The warning only inflames the poet's desire, and the language of erotic passion reappears, this time in the narrator's own voice:

¡Oh condición humana!, que al instante
que me privó que el rostro no volviese,
sólo aquel impedirme fue bastante
a que *el prompto apetito se encendiese* [. . .] (18.66.1–4)

Oh human condition! The moment she warned me not to turn my head, her effort to stop me was itself enough *inflame the ready appetite.*

Ignoring her advice, he turns to see a panorama of Spanish beauties, not alone it should be noted, but accompanied by their enraptured consorts "al regalado y blando amor rendidos" ("surrendered to delicate and tender love") (18.69.3). Before he can get a closer look, Reason, "algo medroso y con turbado gesto / de haberme en tanto riesgo y trance puesto" ("somewhat fearful and with a troubled expression at having exposed me to such a dangerous risk") (18.70.7–8), abruptly propels him from the mountaintop back down to the *locus amoenus* that surrounds it.[28] This sardonic enactment of Neoplatonic love theory, with its emphasis on the role of vision in awakening desire, continues as the poet, spirited away too late and transformed by what he has seen, realizes he is free "del torpe y del grosero velo / que la vista hasta allí me iba ocupando" ("of the dull, crude veil that had covered my vision till then") (18.71.3–4) and experiences true love, which he describes in imagery echoing that used by Guacolda and Lautaro, now structured in the paradoxical cliches of Petrarchan emotion:

un *amoroso fuego* y *blando hielo*
se me fue *por las venas regalando*
y *el brío rebelde* y *pecho endurecido*
quedó al amor *sujeto* y *sometido*. (18.71.5–8)

an *amorous flame* and *tender chill* began to *thaw my veins*, and my *rebellious spirit* and *hardened heart* were *conquered* and *subdued* by love.

---

[28] The language of the passage emphasizes the contrast between eros and violence, the presence of *blando* echoing its earlier usage in one of the most disturbing descriptions of fighting between the Spanish and the Araucans, who experience the results of war unequally: "mas salen los efetos desiguales; / que los unos topaban duro acero, / los otros al desnudo y *blando* cuero" ("but the effects are unequal, since some were striking hard steel [i.e., Spanish armor], the others naked and tender flesh") (14.34.6–8).

The narrator wants to know more about the paradise he has just visited and in particular about one of the figures, "que vi a sus pies rendida mi fortuna" ("at whose feet I saw my fortune surrendered") (18.72.8), a woman whose name identifies her as the poet's future wife, Doña María de Bazán, whom he will marry in 1570, seven years after returning from the New World. But at this point where epic prophecy threatens to succumb to biography, his "dulce sueño" (18.74.5) or sweet dream is terrifyingly interrupted by the long-feared Araucan attack, and "en esta confusión, medio dormido" ("in this confusion, half-asleep") (18.75.1) he rushes to arm himself and take his position in the defense of the fort as "la rosada Aurora" (18.75.8) appears in the East.

There are numerous parallels here to the Guacolda episode as well as a series of inversions, structural patterns that drive the narrative. Among the latter: the Araucan couple both have nightmares of defeat and death; Lautaro assures Guacolda that dreams are false (13.51.4) and boasts that he is used to putting his fortune at risk and to achieving great martial success (13.51.5–8); the dream turns out to be true, however, and Lautaro is killed. Ercilla has a "dulce sueño," paradoxically among the poem's most factual passages since it uses epic prophecy to rehearse Philip II's military triumphs and identify the poet's future wife. Unlike Lautaro, who boasts of controlling fortune, Ercilla describes his own as subject to his beloved, and he survives the Araucan assault. Among the parallels: the imagery of love as fire (13.43.7, 13.48.4, 18.71.5), and the description of devotion in terms of subjection, the narrator maintaining that he is "al amor sujeto y sometido" ("conquered and subdued by love") (18.71.8), echoing Lautaro's "mi vida es sujeta a vuestros manos" ("my life is subject to your hands") (13.49.7). Finally, the narrator's confusion upon being awakened enacts his earlier confusion at the end of the Guacolda episode, where he spoke of "la turbada pluma mía" which "confusa, tarda y con temor se mueve" (13.57.5–7). These emotions are now made real while echoing the confusion of the Araucans, attacked when they, in turn, were sleeping (1.14.11.1), just as the narrator, like Lautaro earlier, struggles to awake and defend himself.

Such intratextual allusions in the *Araucana* serve several strategic functions. Structurally, the repetition of descriptive phrases strengthens narrative coherence while emphasizing key themes. The imagery associated with erotic passion, developed in such dramatically different contexts, creates new themes, not only focusing on love in contrast to war, but hinting at a fundamental correspondence between the two forces. This correspondence, manifest in the tension between epos and eros, is first suggested by Bellona's offering to act as a guide to the matter of love, fresh from narrating the military accomplishments of Philip II. The correlation is strengthened by similarities in the experience of the erotic and bellicose passions, notably in the confusion and fear evinced by each. Here, for the first time, the poem presents a symbolic ordering of these contrasting emotions and their titulary guide according to a Neoplatonic conception of the concupiscent, irascible, and rational, a hierarchical relationship the remaining episodes each clarify and reinforce. Additionally, these internal echoes create unexpected correspondences between cultures and characters, not only between Araucans and Europeans, citizens of the New World and the Old, but between genders and, most importantly, between the narrator and the protagonists. In this relation of sympathetic parody the former assumes the roles and shares the emotions of the latter, continuing a complex process of self-revelation while simultaneously invoking his empathy for and humanization of the Other, however literary the process remains. The attribution of amorous passion first described in terms of Guacolda and Lautaro to the poet continues his own humanization as well, inscribing what will soon be confirmed as his characteristic *renovatio* of epic through personal experience. The process of self-fashioning begins as early as Canto 13, with the synedoche of the narrator's confusion and fear. It continues here with his succumbing, like the rest of humanity, to the "prompto apetito" (18.66.4) of erotic attraction and with his clumsy performance in the lesson of Neoplatonic love, subverting expected assertions of clear-cut differences between the poet and the Amerindian Other and imbuing the poem with a hybrid quality that will only increase. The setting of these experiences contrasts an ideal world with the real one while thoroughly confusing the two. The site of the former is a pastoral paradise announced by a *locus amoenus*. While the restorative *otium* associated with such locales has its appeal, the vision offered by Bellona and Reason requires the poet to rise above such concerns to a higher realm, where, suspended on a panoptical peak between heaven and earth, he is shown a region not simply of beauty and truth but of historical inevitability and all-too-human loveliness. When the attractions of such beauty prove too great the narrator is spirited back to the pastoral world at its base, where, like the incarnated soul remembering its transmigratory glimpse of the heavenly spheres, he seeks to learn more about his ethereal experience. The harsh historical present intervenes, however, and the vision is dispersed. What began as a conventional contrast of ideal and real ends with their co-mingling, a conceptual *contaminatio* that rejects the disengagement of Stoic *apatheia* for the perturbations of eros at the very moment of an attempted escape from the surrounding reality. The Tegualda episode confirms the choice.

4. Tegualda: The Battle of Love and Detachment

Tegualda's story, which begins in a *novelesco* or Boccaccian mode and ends in tragedy, is as notable for the new issues it raises as for the familiar ones it deploys. Among the latter is the focus on erotic passion, now developed from the archetypal brevity of Guacolda and Lautaro into a sustained account blending elements of Ariosto's Isabella and Zerbino with a psychologically astute account of a young woman's falling in love, adeptly transposing the canonical male gaze into terms of female erotic desire. Here the imagery of such experience is further affiliated with classical sources, especially Virgil, which once again dominate the

Ariostan ones, and the Platonic quality of much of the underlying rationale is further articulated, now via Castiglione, on the one hand, with the heroine embodying qualities of *honestidad* and *vergüenza* while the narrator enacts the perfect courtier, and through allusions to the *Phaedrus*, on the other, in a powerful evocation of the soul as charioteer and horses. The terminology of the episode suggests new topics, from themes of justice and *civilité* to issues of just war and proper governance, all part of the poem's meta-discourses. The desideratum of conjugal love is manifest here in a symbolic exchange of rings, and the emphasis on honor shifts clearly from an epic focus on *kleos* to a more intimate vision of personal integrity. The distinction between arms and letters continues to be explored, while that between the narrator and his characters continues to erode, an ongoing process illustrated most vividly by Tegualda's unsuccessful attempt to remain free of emotional attachment and by her bittersweet conversion to passionate, chaste love.

Once awakened from his sweet dream into the nightmare of the Araucan attack, the poet abruptly ends the eighteenth canto, saving for the following two his account of the ensuing battle with its multiple, advertised allusions to Virgil, Lucan, and Ariosto. Before the fighting gets underway, however, Canto 19 opens with a two-octave reprise of the theme of female beauty, with the poet emphasizing his desire to honor women by writing of amorous subjects. The canto is filled with fighting and once again ends at a moment of suspense in the battle. Canto 20 begins by repeating the poet's complaint regarding the harshness of his martial theme, then shifts to the dilemma of keeping his word in light of his commitment to write only of military matters, a problem raised earlier in the prologue to Part II. This meditation on the importance of personal honor, which occupies three full octaves and is cast in *beatus ille* terms of how little significance a man's word has in the present age, suggests the importance to the poet of personal integrity, a quality central to both the Tegualda episode and the defense of Dido, which may also have special resonance in light of Ercilla's dramatic encounter with military justice during his brief sojourn in the New World. The fourth octave resumes the poet's query over why he must write about violence when he's capable of so much more (20.4), and the rumination is characteristically cut short by the resumption of battle, which lasts until the Araucans, after grievous losses, are forced to retreat (20.17).

In the ensuing interlude darkness falls, and the Spanish waste no time repairing their fortifications. Ercilla is assigned the night's first watch and goes to it pondering the hardships of military life and of having to write in intervals between fighting: "la pluma ora en la mano, ora la lanza" ("now with my pen in hand, now with my lance") (20.24.8), enacting his own elision of arms and letters. It is in such melancholy spirits, on a night "tan lóbrega y escura / que divisar lo cierto no podía" ("so dark and dismal it was not possible to discern things clearly") (20.27.1), that he sees what he believes at first to be a wild animal prowling among the dead. After some moments of hesitation, "[. . .] de aquella visión mal satisfecho, / con un temor, que agora aun no le niego" ("far from satisfied with that vision and with a fear that even now I do not deny") (20.28.1–2), he screws up his courage to investigate, and as he draws near realizes the creature is an Araucan woman. The mystery of Tegualda's presence is quickly solved as she begs to be allowed to search for the corpse of her husband. Characteristically foregrounding his own sensations, the narrator at first suspects some sort of treachery, but decides that Tegualda's lack of fear and "gran sosiego" ("great calm") (20.34.3) lends her credibility, concluding that there is only one explanation for such courage: "[. . .] que el pérfido amor, ingrato y ciego, / en busca del marido la traía" ("that perfidious love, ungrateful and blind, was leading her in search of her husband") (20.34.5–6). Filled with compassion and responding with courtly decorum, he assures Tegualda that he will help her, but persuades her to wait until morning, requesting in the meantime "[. . .] que su querella / [. . .] / desde el principio al cabo me contase" ("to tell me patiently and in all security of her grievances, from first to last") (20.35.5–7). She reluctantly agrees.[29]

The Tegualda episode, at 65 octaves the most elaborate of the Araucan women, is thus a *mise-en-abîme* structure, the framing narrative one in which the narrator tells of encountering a widow searching for the corpse of her husband, the widow's tale a tragic one of how she and her beloved, Crepino, met and fell in love. This construction distinguishes the Tegualda episode from Guacolda's, while linking it to the subsequent stories told by Glaura and Lauca. It also links it to the genre of *novelesco* or Boccaccian tale, the type of digression Cinquecento theorists discussed in terms of unity and variety and eventually identified with the genre of romance. While similarities between this episode and Ariosto's story of Isabella and Zerbino have routinely been emphasized by critics to emphasize this affiliation, once again such associations cannot be considered in isolation but must be taken in the context of the episode's many other references, an idiosyncratic mix of epic and pastoral motifs, Neoplatonic love theory, and allusions to Castiglione's ideal courtier, the combination of which suggests an atmosphere very different from romance, Ariostan or otherwise.

Tegualda's search for the body of her husband recalls ancient models, the most frequently cited being Xenophon's Panthea and Statius's Argia. These two figures, in turn, combine two older themes, the right to burial, found in Priam's embassy to Achilles and Antigone's defiance of Creon, and the loyal wife, exemplified by Homer's Penelope, an important presence in subsequent defenses of women, including Ercilla's (21.3). Deprived of their husbands, Panthea and Argia also evoke the motif of the abandoned woman.[30] Tegualda's determination to

---

[29] Lerner notes the topos of the request for an account that renews for the teller the sorrow related, associated most notably with Dido's request to Aeneas (*Aen.* 2.12–13): *Araucana*, 573 n. 65.

[30] Panthea retrieves her husband's body from the battlefield and despite Cyrus's attempts at consolation takes her own life after preparing the body for burial (*Cyropaedia*

join Crepino in death (20.32.5–8), like Guacolda's (13.46.5–8), is Stoic in nature, as Glaura's and Lauca's will be (28.40.5–8; 32.38.4–8). The primary themes of this classically-inspired framing story—justice, *civilité*, and true love—are the themes of Tegualda's own story as well. All are introduced within the first four octaves of her appearance:

> [. . .] Señor, señor, *merced* te pido,
> que soy mujer y nunca te he *ofendido*.
> Si mi dolor y desventura estraña
> a lástima y *piedad* no te inclinaren
> y tu sangrienta espada y *fiera saña*
> de *los términos lícitos* pasaren,
> ¿qué gloria adquirirás de tal hazaña,
> cuando *los justos cielos* publicaren
> que se empleó en una mujer tu espada,
> viuda, mísera, triste y desdichada?
> Ruégote pues, señor, si por ventura
> o desventura, como fue la mía,
> con *amor verdadero* y con *fe pura*
> *amaste tiernamente* en algún día,
> me dejes dar a un cuerpo sepultura,
> que yace entre esta muerta compañía.
> Mira que aquel que niega lo que es *justo*
> lo malo aprueba ya y se hace *injusto*.
> No quieras impedir obra tan *pía*,
> que aun en *bárbara* guerra se concede,
> que es especie y señal de *tiranía*
> usar de todo aquello que se puede.
> Deja buscar *su cuerpo a esta alma mía*,
> después furioso con rigor procede,
> que ya el dolor me ha puesto en tal estremo
> que más la vida que la muerte temo (20.28.7–20.31.8)

Sir, sir, I ask for *mercy*, since I am a woman and have never *offended* you. / If my grief and strange misfortune do not move you to *pity* and compassion, and your bloody sword and *fierce rage* pass beyond *permitted limits*, what glory will you win from such a deed, when *just heaven* makes it known you raised your sword against a woman, a wretched widow, unfortunate and grieving? / I beseech you then, sir, if ever there was a day when by chance or mischance, as with me, *you were tenderly in love*, with *true love* and *pure faithfulness*, that you allow me to bury a body lying among this dead company. Consider that he who denies what is *just* sanctions evil and himself

---

7.3.3–16). Statius's treatment of the theme is characteristically more complex, enacted on the same corpse-strewn landscape that a short time earlier saw his version of the Doloneia, the purpose of which Argia now reenacts, this time successfully; see 32–33 n. 70, *supra*.

becomes *unjust*. / You should not wish to hinder such a *pious* task, conceded even in *barbarous* war, for it is a sign and type of *tyranny* to use all the power at one's command. Allow this *soul of mine* to seek *its body* and afterwards proceed with bitter fury, for my grief has pushed me to such extremes that, more than death, I now fear life.

Tegualda's opening lines implicitly condemn the behavior of other Spanish soldiers while recalling the defense-of-women theme the narrator has addressed before, most explicitly at the opening of Canto 14, and will address again at the close of the present scene (21.3) and in the subsequent defense of Dido. Repeated references in these lines to justice, together with the legalistic overtones of such terms as *merced, ofendido, términos lícitos, justo*, and *injusto*, associate her speech with the themes of just war and proper governance.[31] Closely related is her appeal to the narrator's *piedad*, echoed in the reference to her *pía* task, since this is a trait that not only distinguishes a Christian monarch from a tyrant, but is also conceded to apply to certain aspects of "barbarous war" (20.31.2). Expounded here with considerable irony by a barbarian woman, piety was celebrated two cantos earlier at the victory of San Quentin, where Ercilla contrasted the Spanish troops who began to sack the city "sin *piedad*" (18.21.5) to their commander, Philip II, "el *pío* Felipe" (18.23.1), who restrained them, ordering that they protect the women and houses of worship (18.17–21). It is "del *piadoso* Rey la gran *clemencia*" ("the great *clemency* of the *pious* king") (18.28.1) that finally ensures Spain an honorable victory over the French, curbing illegitimate violence while establishing firm control. Ercilla's terminology has long been recognized as referencing Virgil's "pius Aeneas," an association the narrator himself makes an implicit claim to in his *compasión* toward Tegualda (20.35.1 and 21.6.5) and other Araucans, the evocation bringing with it some of the complexity of the *Aeneid*'s portrayal of the violence necessary for human society. The theme of love arises indirectly here in a question to the narrator about his own amatory experience (20.30.3–4), linking him with his characters in a manner reminiscent of earlier

---

[31] Ercilla's views on just war and proper governance, articulated most notably at 21.56.1–8, 23.12.4–23.13.8, and 37.13.1 ff., have frequently been discussed in relation to Bartolomé de Las Casas and Francisco de Vitoria, whose Valladolid debates took place in 1550 and 1551. A seventeen- or eighteen-year-old Ercilla was in the city with the court at the time. William Mejías-Lopez has explored the potential impact on Ercilla of Fray Gil González de San Nicolás, a former student of Vitoria's and friend of Las Casas who became Vicar General of Chile and whose outspoken defense of the Indians resulted in his being sent back to Peru by García Hurtado de Mendoza, Ercilla's commanding officer; González de San Nicolás and Ercilla became acquainted on the difficult voyage from Lima to Santiago. Mejías-Lopez also explores the fact that Ercilla's juris-consult father wrote on these topics: "Alonso de Ercilla y los problemas de los indios chilenos: algunas prerrogativas legales presentes en *La Araucana*," *Bulletin of Hispanic Studies* 69 (1992): 1–10.

passages. Tegualda describes her own love as true and pure, epithets the narrator echoes in his acknowledgment of her "casto y amoroso intento" ("chaste and amorous intent") (20.35.2). Her allusion to the beloved as the soul of the lover (20.31.5) repeats the popular Petrarchan cliche, made famous in Spain by Garcilaso's nineteenth sonnet. Ercilla's version is notable for its poignant inversion of gender and thrust, now no longer the canonical male search for completion in the female, but a woman whose soul seeks the body of her beloved husband, now deceased. Garcilaso also inspires Ercilla's adaptation of the conceit of fearing life more than death (20.31.8).[32]

Tegualda tells the story of a happy young woman, who as she nears marriageable age resists the attentions of all who would court her, naively content in her self-absorption. Her loving father, an Araucan chief, encourages his daughter to choose from among her many suitors, but she resists, describing how "De muchos fui pedida en casamiento / y a todos igualmente *despreciaba*" ("I was asked by many to marry and *disdained* all equally") (20.38.1–2), the echo of Boscán's translation for *sprezzatura*, *desprecio*, deftly suggesting the courtly aura that will soon envelop the proceedings. Undeterred, the young men stage a series of athletic contests and other festivities in Tegualda's honor, an event she describes as "[. . .] el postrero día / desta mi *libertad y señorío*" ("the last day of this my *liberty and sovereignty* arrived") (20.40.1–2), and the celebrations end with her falling abruptly in love with and marrying the winner of the competitions. While the story shares numerous details with Ariosto's tale of Isabella (*O.F.* 13.3–8), the similarities, as in the case of Guacolda and Doralice, are formal ones, as evidenced once again by the utter lack of sarcasm in these scenes, characterized instead by a fundamental earnestness.[33] Isabella says nothing of love

---

[32] For Petrarch's image of the beloved as the soul of the lover, see poem 37: "[. . .] il giorno ch' io / lassai di me la miglio parte a dietro" ("the day I left behind the better part of me") (51–52) (Petrarch translation is by Robert Durling, *Petrarch's Lyric Poems: The Rime Sparse and Other Lyrics*, trans. and ed. Robert M. Durling [Boston: Harvard University Press, 1967]); cf. Garcilaso's version of the conceit in Sonnet 19: "y dejé de mi alma aquella parte / que al cuerpo vida y fuerza 'staba dando" ("and I left that part of my heart that was giving life and strength to my body") (3–4); cf. Castiglione's use of the image in Emilia Pia's response to Bembo's inspired oration on love, where she warns him to be careful that his soul doesn't separate from his body (4.71). For Garcilaso's conceit of fearing life more than death, see Salicio's complaint in the First Eclogue (57–60), which also features the canonical erotic imagery discussed earlier; on Ercilla's inversion of the Petrarchan motif, with the female now the active subject, see Marrero-Fente, "Épica," 20.

[33] Isabella, whom Orlando finds captive, recounts how her father, the king, held a tournament to select a husband for her, during which she fell in love with the most gallant contender, Zerbino, the son of the king of Scotland. She blames *la nequizia* ("the spitefulness") (*O.F.* 13.4.6) of love for her troubles, much as Tegualda blames "el pérfido amor" ("perfidious love") (20.34.5); cf. Chevalier, *Arioste*, 152, and Schwartz, "Tradición," 620–23.

beyond naming it as the condition from which she suffers. Tegualda, by contrast, offers a thoroughly Platonic description of how she falls prey to erotic passion, an account that occupies twenty-eight octaves of the episode and is clearly its focus. She begins by employing the same sort of political terminology used by Guacolda and Lautaro, noting how, rather than paying attention to which of the young competitors were *vencedores* ("victors") or *vencidos* ("vanquished") (20.44.5–6), she was absorbed in the beauty of the woodland setting, which she observed "con un *ocioso* y *libre* pensamiento" ("with an *idle* and *free* mind") (20.44.8). The former epithet suggests a contrast between the *otium* of erotic innocence and the *negotium* of love; the latter recurs a few lines later when she compares her earlier state of innocence to what came afterwards: "*libre* a mi parecer y muy segura / de cuidado, de amor y desventura" ("*free*, it seemed to me, and entirely safe from care, love, and misfortune") (20.45.7–8). In the course of the suitors' games a shout erupts from the crowd, and Tegualda asks what is happening. She is told that one of the contenders, "aquel gallardo mozo bien dispuesto" ("that gallant and athletic young man") (20.48.1), has upset the hometown favorite, who is complaining of bad luck and demanding a rematch while "el *fácil* y *liviano* pueblo" ("the *capricious* and *volatile* public") (20.48.5) acclaims the new winner. The rules of the games do not allow a rematch, nor will the judges entertain such a *pedimiento* or petition from either contender unless Tegualda herself allows it (20.49–50). The two young men approach her, and with "una humilde y baja *cortesía*" ("an humble and meek *courtesy*") (20.51.6) the stranger offers himself as Tegualda's *siervo natural* ("natural slave") (20.52.3), willing to live and die in her service, anticipating the importance that Platonic imagery will assume in these lines.[34] He asks her *una merced* ("a favor") (20.51.7) of permitting a rematch: "Danos *licencia*, rompe *el estatuto* con *tu poder sin límite absoluto*" ("Grant us *permission*; suspend the *rules* with your *absolute, limitless power*") (20.53.7–8). This allusion to the power of the beloved is only the most explicit of numerous references here to freedom and servitude, judicial procedure and justice. Two additional themes that will shortly become important, loyalty and courtliness, are also introduced, the first contrasted to the *fácil* crowd and recalling Reason's warning about the poet's *ojos fáciles* (18.65.2), the second embodied in the decorum of the exchanges between Tegualda and the stranger.

Contact having been established between the protagonists, the vocabulary of the episode now shifts from an emphasis on legalisms to the language of erotic passion characteristic of earlier scenes. In contrast to earlier passages, such imagery is now subordinated to a strongly Neoplatonic emphasis on *honestidad* and *vergüenza,* or virtue and shame, especially as these are mediated by Castiglione, whose influence is increasingly evident as the episode proceeds. Tegualda recounts that with the young man awaiting with *baja reverencia* ("humble

---

[34] Cf. Plato's reference in the *Phaedrus*. "Therefore the soul [. . .] is ready to be a slave and to sleep wherever it is allowed, as near as possible to the beloved [. . .]" (252A).

reverence") (20.54.1) her reply to his petition, she watched him "sin *recato* y *advertencia*" ("without *caution* and *concern*") (20.54.3), indulging in the very behavior that Reason had earlier warned the narrator to avoid (18.65.2), not only granting him the rematch "*libre* y graciosamente" ("*freely* and graciously") (20.54.8) but also secretly wishing him the victory of it. When he goes on to win and the crowd brings him back to be presented with the victory wreath, she reveals that "[. . .] comencé a temblar y un *fuego ardiendo / fue por todos mis huesos discurriendo*" ("I began to tremble and a *burning fire went running through all my bones*") (20.58.7–8), a sensation that leaves her "[. . .] tan *confusa* y alterada / de aquella nueva *causa* y acidente / que estuve un rato atónita y *turbada*" ("so *confused* and agitated by this novel circumstance that for a moment I remained in *troubled shock*") (20.59.1–3). Recovering her composure she bestows the wreath "en todo dignamente" ("in total dignity") (20.59.6), then lowers her eyes, "de la *honesta vergüenza* reprimidos" ("constrained by *honorable shame*") (20.60.2). As the young man rejoins the festivities her internal struggle continues:

> Sentí una novedad que me apremiaba
> la *libre fuerza* y *el rebelde brío*,
> a la cual *sometida* se entregaba
> la *razón, libertad* y *el albedrío*. (20.61.1–4)

> I felt something new oppressing my *independence* and *rebellious vitality*, and *reason*, *liberty*, and *free will*, all now subdued, surrendered to it.

As Crepino keeps winning contests, Tegualda keeps losing her struggle for detachment. She briefly recovers, only to find "*ardiendo* en *vivo fuego* el *pecho frío*" ("my *cold breast burning* with an *intense fire*") (20.61.6), at which point she raises her eyes, "que la *vergüenza* allí tenía abajados" ("which *shame* had kept lowered until then") (20.61.8), and in a richly evocative octave describes the total collapse of what remains of her resistance, the canonical articulation of erotic desire now transcribed from male to female:

> Roto con *fuerza* súbita y furiosa
> de la *vergüenza* y *continencia el freno,*
> le seguí con *la vista* deseosa,
> cebando más *la llaga* y *el veneno.*
> Que sólo allí *mirarle* y no otra cosa
> para mi mal hallaba que era bueno,
> así que adonde quiera que pasaba
> tras sí *los ojos* y *alma* me llevaba. (20.62.1–8)

> With a sudden and furious *force* the *bridle* of *shame* and *continence* burst, and I followed him with a longing *gaze*, aggravating the *wound* and *poison* even more. I found that *looking at him* there was the only thing that eased my ill, and thus wherever he went he bore my *eyes and soul* in his wake.

The atmosphere throughout the earlier part of Tegualda's story is strongly Virgilian as a result of the repeated allusions to Dido in the imagery of love as a fire, a
wound, and as poison.[35] These images recall the love of Guacolda and Lautaro,
as well as the narrator's emotions during his vision of Spanish beauty (18.71.5–6).
Vivo fuego or living fire, which appears earlier in the canto describing the anger of the Araucan champion, Tucapelo (20.11.3), establishes one of the poem's
many implicit correspondences between love and war, a elision of the wrathful
and concupiscent that will feature much more prominently in Spenser. The reappearance of the epithets *confusa* and *turbada* (20.59.1–3), the same terms used by
the narrator to describe his discomfort in writing about the love of Guacolda and
Lautaro (13.57.5–7), foregrounds the correspondence being established between
his own experience and that of his characters, as does Tegualda's reference to "la
libre fuerza y *rebelde brío*" ("my independence and *rebellious vitality*") (20.61.2),
which echoes the poet's description of his own initial indifference to erotic attraction (18.71.7). The structuring of Tegualda's eventual defeat in her contest with
erotic desire as a series of struggles during which she momentarily recovers only
to finally succumb, her surrender marked by the loss of her shame, is reminiscent
of Apollonius' scene of the struggle between shame and desire in the young Medea first attracted to Jason, where her sense of shame is mentioned three times
in five lines to signify the force opposing her desire.[36] In contrast to the imagery
of irrational passion, Tegualda's repeated references to her eyes, mentioned three
times in three octaves (20.60–62), draw attention to the scene's Neoplatonic register, a countervailing force more fully articulated as she describes her struggle to
use reason to control her longing. This Neoplatonic language reaches its climax
in the striking image of the breaking of the restraint—literally, the bridle—of
shame and continence, offering the most concise construction yet of the relationship among the three terms that recur with stubborn insistence in references both
to love and war.[37]

---

[35] See 52 n. 14, supra.

[36] Cf.: "And for long she stayed there at the entrance of her chamber, held back by
shame (*aidos*); and she turned back once more; and again she came forth from within, and
again stole back; and idly did her feet bear her this way and that; yea, as oft as she went
straight on, *shame* held her within the chamber, and though held back by *shame*, bold desire kept urging her on. Thrice she made the attempt and thrice she checked herself, the
fourth time she fell on her bed face downward writhing in pain") (3.647–655). Ercilla
mentions Medea by name in a later scene where the sorcerer Fitón shows the narrator a
magical image of the world, including the isle of Colchis (28.12.5–8).

[37] Virgil notes the role of the eyes as Dido falls in love with Aeneas: "ardescitque tuendo" ("[she] takes fire as she gazes") (1.713); Apollonius again provides a model for such
imagery, with Medea stealing glances of Jason (3.444–445). The Neoplatonic emphasis
on the eyes as the pathway of love is emphasized in the *Courtier*, where it is stated that
"Però ben dir si po che gli occhi siano guida in amore [. . .]" ("So one can truly say that
the eyes are the guides of love") (3.61).

These terms *vergüenza* or shame, *continencia* or continence, and *el freno* or bridle, captured in the single anastrophic line "de la *vergüenza y continencia el freno*" or "the bridle of shame and continence" (20.62.2), most powerfully evoke the *Phaedrus*, where envisioning the soul as a charioteer and pair of horses Socrates says of the good horse: "τιμῆς ἐραστὴς μετὰ σωφροσύνης τε καὶ αἰδοῦς, καὶ ἀληθινῆς δόξης ἑταῖρος, ἄπληκτος, κελεύματι μόνον καὶ λόγῳ ἡνιοχεῖται·[. . .]" ("he is a lover of *honor* joined with *temperance* and *modesty*, and a companion of *true glory*; he needs no whip, but is commanded and guided by *reason* alone") (253D).[38] The two principal terms in this trio have a range of meanings in Plato, αἰδώς linking shame, modesty, and self-respect, σωφροσύνη associating temperance and moderation with chastity.[39] Prior to Plato, Homer's epithet for Penelope emphasized prudence, but she is also a model of chastity and directly associated with the concept of self-respect.[40] As seen in the *Argonautica*'s portrait of the young Medea, self-respect or shame is paramount to Apollonius. Virgil has Dido invoke a personified *Pudor*, which has the same connotations ranging from modesty to shame, as she struggles with her love for Aeneas (4.27), and of her sister Anna's successful encouragement of Dido's desire he says: "solvitque pudorem" ("and [it] loosed the bonds of shame") (4.55).[41] In Petrarch an additional distinction becomes apparent, shame and self-respect still linked in *verecundia* or *vergogna*, and temperance, modesty, and a general sense of virtue in *honestate*, while *castità* or *pudicitia* suggests a more sexualized chastity.[42] The *Trionfi del Castità* dramatizes the close relation among the three concepts, with *vergogno* and *honestate* leading off the procession while the rear is brought up by a pair of virtues recapitulating the two: "Timor-d'infamia" ("fear of infamy") and "Desio-sol-d'onore" ("desire for honor") (l. 87). Petrarch also employs the

---

[38] English translation of Plato is based on that by Harold North Fowler in the Loeb *Phaedrus* (Cambridge, MA: Harvard University Press, 1914), with the following variations: I construe ἐραστής as "lover" rather than "friend" because of the former's significance in the dialogue as a whole, a rationale applied as well to "companion" rather than "follower" for ἑταῖρος; my translation of the concluding phrase is more literal than Fowler's. Ercilla also employs *el freno* in its conventional sense of bridle, e.g., at 22.11.5.

[39] By contrast, feeling shame (i.e., being ashamed) and having a sense of shame (or not, as in shameless) are clearly distinguished in English, resulting in awkward translations such as *shamefast* or in periphrasis; cf. the use of σωφροσύνη at 254B; regarding αἰδώς, cf. 254A and ἀναιδείας as *shameless* at 254E; χαλινός as *bit* appears in 254C and 254D.

[40] Penelope's customary epithet is περίφρων ("very thoughtful, very careful") (*Od.* 19.53, 19.89, 19.103, 19.123); cf. Telemachus's allusion to αἰδώς in his description of her as "εὐνήν τ᾽ αἰδομένη" ("respecting the marriage bed") (16.75).

[41] Cf.: "sed mihi vel tellus optem prius ima dehiscat / [. . .] / ante, Pudor, quam te violo aut tua iura resolvo" ("But rather, I would pray, may earth yawn for me to its depths [. . .] before, O Shame, I violate thee or break thy laws!") (*Aen.* 4.24–27).

[42] This development is roughly coincident with the introduction of *pudenda* in English, which the OED cites as 1398.

image of the bridle or *il freno* with its full Platonic significance.[43] In the *Courtier*, *vergogna*, *pudicitia*, and *onestà* retain their Petrarchan distinctions, but now *continenzia* (3.5), the cognate of which will be adopted by Ercilla, is employed to signify self-control in the sexual sense. Castiglione's focus on these terms comes in the discussion of the virtues desirable in the lady of the court, which, reprising Petrarch in its emphasis on the "rarissima virtù" of *vergogna*: "[. . .] che in fine non è altro che *timor d'infamia*" ("which is finally nothing else than a *fear of disgrace*") (3.40), along with "[. . .] quella *onestà* che sempre ha da componer tutte le suè azioni" ("that *virtue* that must always accompany all her behavior") (3.5) focuses on "una certa *mediocrità* difficile" ("a certain difficult *compromise*") (3.5) between affability and virtue, succinctly distilling the *sprezzatura* of virtue the *Courtier* envisions. If Ercilla's earlier use of *despreciar* suggested Boscán's translation, the Spanish text's departure from the original when it comes to the terms discussed here suggests otherwise. Boscán begins faithfully enough, construing *vergogno* as *vergüenza* and *onestà* as *honesta*, but then renders *pudica* as *prudente* and substitutes the image of the bridle with a reference to the action it implies. Echoing Plato, Castiglione had Giuliano de' Medici observe, with regard to controlling the early stages of erotic desire: "[. . .] chi non ha perduto *il fren della ragione* si governa cautamente ed osserva i tempi, i lochi e quando bisogna s'astien da quel così intento mirare [. . .]" ("he who has not lost *the bridle of reason* governs himself cautiously and observes time and place and, when necessary, abstains from gazing intently like that [i.e., at the object his attraction]") (3.61). Boscán transcribes this as "quien no está del todo *desatinado* tiene en esto gran *tiento*, y considera el tiempo y el lugar; y, cuando es necesario, *refrena* el mirar muy ahincado [. . .]" ("he who isn't completely *reckless* uses great *caution* in this and considers the time and place and, when necessary, *refrains* from gazing very intently") (390). The use of *desatinado* (imprudent, reckless, from *tino* or good judgment, skillfulness) conveys the end of Castiglione's advice while ignoring the means by which it is achieved, i.e., the faculty of *reason*. Substituting the

---

[43] Citations to the *Trionfi* are from *Trionfi, Rime Estravaganti, Codice Degli Abbozzi* (Milan: Mondadori Editore, 1996); cf. Aristotle's *Ethics*, which notes that true courage "[. . .] is due to shame and to desire of a noble object (i.e. honor) and avoidance of disgrace, which is ignoble" (3.7.1116a) (translation is that of W. D. Ross in *The Basic Works of Aristotle*, ed. Richard McKeon [New York: Random House, 1970]). On the lover's desire for honor and virtue, cf. Petrarch's poem 154 (12–13); on the lover's shame upon recollecting less than virtuous behavior, cf. poem 1 (11–12), adapted by Garcilaso in the *First Eclogue* (63–66); for the image of the bridle, cf.: "largae 'l desio che i' teng' or molto a *freno*" ("I let loose my desire, which I now hold tightly *reined in*") (poem 47, 5), and poem 6, where speaking of "'l folle me' desio" ("my mad desire") (1), the poet says: "et poi che 'l *fren* per forza a sé raccoglie, / i' mi rimango in signoria di lui, / che mal mio grado a morte mi trasporta" ("and when he takes the *bit* forcefully to himself, I remain in his power, as against my will he carries me off to death") (9–11).

image of the bridle for the cognate verb, *refrenar* (*rein in*, but more generally *restrain*), further weakens both the force and Platonic identity of the passage, imbuing it with a more courtly and less humanist quality characteristic of Boscán's translation. Garcilaso employs *desatino* in the *Second Eclogue*, which dramatizes a sorcerer's cure of the madness of unrequited love (820), but later in the poem provides a precise rendition of the Platonic remedy, which "convierte'n odio aquel amor insano, / y restituye'l alma a su natura" ("converts that insane love into hate and restores the soul to its nature") (1093–94). The cure is achieved, in effect, by changing desire into a hatred of its consequence, emotional slavery and unhappiness, thus subordinating the concupiscent to the irascible, ideally allied, in this scenario, with the rational.[44] While Garcilaso's verses recall Plato's discussion of the rational, appetitive, and high-spirited aspects of the soul in the *Republic*, Tegualda's emphasis on the image of the bridle and her story's careful description of the process by which she finally loses control of her emotions and falls in love, precisely by failing "to abstain from gazing intently like that," as Castiglione put it, suggests that Ercilla's inspiration comes directly from the *Cortegiano*, a conclusion reinforced by his use of *continencia* (20.62.2) and *honesta* (20.60.2), key terms employed by Castiglione.[45]

Crepino eventually wins the competition and is brought before Tegualda to be awarded the prize of an emerald ring. Describing herself as "un medroso temblor *disimulando* / (que atentamente todos me miraron), / del *empacho y temor* pasado el punto" ("*hiding* a nervous trembling — for everyone was watching me closely — and having now passed the point of *embarrassment* and *fear*") (20.66.5–7), Tegualda now struggles to disguise her passion and behave with decorum, hiding her feelings for three weeks, "siempre creciendo el daño y *fuego ardiente*" ("the pain and *ardent fire* always growing") (20.69.3–4), until "por señas y rodeo" ("indirectly and by signs") (20.69.7), she leads her father to believe that she is finally submitting to his wishes regarding marriage, never revealing the passion that actually consumes her. Tegualda's dissimulation enacts a key aspect of

---

[44] Echoing this imagery, Nemoroso, once cured, realizes "la vileza / de lo que antes *ardiendo* deseaba" ("the vileness of that which before I, *burning*, desired") (1123–24). Garcilaso is considered to have composed the Second Eclogue between late 1533 and early 1534, roughly coincident with his assisting Boscán in polishing the *Cortesano*; cf. Bienvenido Morros, ed., *Garcilaso de la Vega: Obra poética y textos en prosa* (Barcelona: Crítica, 1995), xxxvi; 141. Albanio's story and the sorcerer Severo are based on Carino and the sorcerer Enareto in Sannazaro's *Arcadia* (*Prose*, 8–10), an additional source of Neoplatonic concepts during this period. Nicolopulos discusses the Second *Eclogue* as a conjoining of poetics and empire and explores the influence of Severo on Ercilla's sorcerer Fitón in "Pedro de Oña and Bernardo de Balbuena Read Ercilla's Fitón," *Latin American Literary Review* 26 (1998): 100–19.

[45] Cf. *Republic* 4.439d–439e. The discussion at this point in the *Republic* is central to Tasso and Spenser, as seen below.

courtliness articulated by Giuliano de' Medici, who states that "Però voglio che la mia donna di palazzo non con modi disonesti paia quasi che s'offerisca a chi la vole [. . .]" ("Thus I want my Court lady not to appear to offer herself to whoever wants her") (3.57). Courtliness has been explicitly invoked already, first in Crepino's "humilde y baja *cortesía*" ("humble and meek *courtesy*") (20.51.6) when he first approaches her, and then in Tegualda's reciprocal "de toda *cortesía*" ("complete *courtesy*") (20.68.1), behavior identified, in a phrase strongly reminiscent of Castiglione, as "lo que a las mujeres perficiona" ("that which makes women perfect") (20.68.2). Crepino's perfect courtliness, already contrasted to the coarseness of his rivals, continues with his giving the ring back to Tegualda with the gallantry: "con este favor quedaré *rico*" ("with this favor [i.e., her attention] I will remain *rich*") (20.67.5) (suggesting a virtuous form of wealth in contrast to the *codicioso* or avaricious spirit condemned elsewhere in the poem) and is summarized by her as a matter of "valor, suerte y linaje conocido, / junto con ser *discreto*, *honesto*, afable" ("valor, good fortune, and known lineage, together with his being *discreet*, *upright*, affable") (20.70.6–7). Finally, with both *honor y deseo* (20.72.2) satisfied, their marriage, however "*infelice* y triste" ("*unhappy* and sorrowful") (20.72.5), evoking Dido, is celebrated, and the operatic recitation comes to an end, all that remains a brief description of how "la sangrienta y rigurosa muerte / todo lo ha derribado por el suelo" ("bloody and rigorous death has brought everything to the ground") (20.73.3–4). The legalisms of these lines echo the vocabulary with which the episode began, the heroine asking rhetorically, "¿qué *recompensa* puede darme el cielo [. . .]?" ("what *recompense* can heaven offer me?") (20.73.6), and concluding:

> Éste es, pues, el *proceso*; ésta es la *historia*
> y el fin tan cierto de la dulce vida;
> he aquí mi *libertad* y breve gloria
> en eterna amargura convertida. (20.74.1–4)

> This, then, is the *process* and this the *history*, as well as sweet life's certain end. Here my *liberty* and brief glory are transformed into eternal bitterness.

The abstract quality of the initial couplet suggests that *historia* is employed as *history* rather than *story*, appropriate since history traditionally intrudes upon pastoral, bringing it to a close. One octave later, after Tegualda has reminded the narrator of the worthiness of her request to bury Crepino's body, "tan justa y *razonable*" ("so just and *reasonable*") (20.75.6), *historia* is repeated with its alternate meaning, Ercilla telling the reader that: "Aquí acabó su *historia*, y comenzaba / un llanto tal que el monte entercecía" ("with this she finished her *story* and began a lament that would have moved the mountain itself to compassion") (20.76.1–2). Back in the gloom of the Andean night, the narrator convinces Tegualda to wait until daylight to continue her search, arranging that she be placed "en *honesta* guarda y compañia / de mujeres casadas [. . .]" ("in *virtuous* custody and company of married women") (20.79.1–2). Canto 20 ends, leaving until the following one the conclusion of the episode. The narrative break allows the narrator to reflect on what he has just experienced, and Canto 21 opens with a tribute to the *piadosa* ("pious") (21.1.2) Tegualda, an "infelice bárbara hermosa" ("unfortunate, beautiful barbarian woman") (21.1.4) whose example belies those who would attack "las mujeres virtuosas" ("virtuous women") (21.2.4), condemning them to "duro *freno y vergonzosa* pena" ("harsh *restraint* and *shameful* suffering") (21.2.8). Ercilla's most elaborate defense of women follows, with a list of famous paragons of female chastity, including Dido, "a quien Virgilio injustamente infama" ("whom Virgil unjustly defames") (21.3.4), and Penelope, women in whose company Tegualda, we are assured, will rightfully take her place. The remainder of the episode, during which the heroine finds the corpse of her husband, grieves over it, and is accompanied with it away from the fighting, concludes with a final echo of earlier themes, her "piadoso amor" ("pious love") (21.4.4) and Ercilla's "gran *compasión*" ("great *compassion*") (21.6.5).[46]

The Tegualda episode emphasizes familiar themes and patterns while expanding the scope of the *Araucana* in important new directions. The variability of Fate and need for Stoic fortitude persist here as underlying issues, as do the defense of women and an emphasis on the conjugal, chaste nature of true love. The use of intertexts continues to affiliate the poem with ancient models, notably Virgil, on the one hand, and contemporary ones, especially Ariosto and Garcilaso, on the other, Ercilla's appropriations simultaneously revising fundamental aspects of these sources. An increasingly complex web of intratexts emphasizes key concerns while eroding any clear distinction between the narrator and his characters, an elision of arms and letters and ultimately of art and life. The inversion of familiar stereotypes this process enacts persists here, particularly in the Petrarchan cliches of longing and despair, now articulated from the perspective of the female rather than the male gaze, part of the poem's larger project of *renovatio*. Among new elements encountered in these octaves is an emphasis on the themes of justice, *civilité*, and loyalty. The first two link the episode with the poem's meta-discourse on just war and governance, succinctly identified with *piedad*, Aeneas' titulary virtue embodied by Philip II and Tegualda

---

[46] Ercilla's list of virtuous women, assembled from ancient and patristic sources, includes Judith, Camilla, Dido, Penelope, Lucretia, Hippo, Tuccia, Virginia, Fulvia, Cloelia, Portia, Sulpicia, Alcestis, and Cornelia. While scholars have noted these figures in Boccaccio's *De claris mulieribus* in particular (cf. Schwartz, "Tradición," 623; Lerner, *Araucana*, 588 n. 5), many of them were also accessible through Petrarch's *Trionfo d'Amore* and *Trionfo del Castitá*, which mention all but Fulvia, Cloelia, and Alcestis. For her part, Fulvia is mentioned in *Il Cortegiano* (237), and Cloelia and Alcestis are both noted in Diego de San Pedro's *Cárcel de Amor*, a work Corominas mentions as a potential influence on Ercilla's portrait of Glaura (*Castiglione*, 25).

and aspired to by the poet. For its part, loyalty is an issue not only for lovers and royal subjects, but for Ercilla to his martial theme. *Cortegianía* first emerges as a significant virtue in the *Araucana* in this episode, enacted in the courtly decorum of the protagonists, including the narrator. Platonic imagery makes its first sustained appearance here as well, initially in Tegualda's description of falling in love, with its emphasis on the role played by eyes, and then in the bridle of shame and continence, *honestidad* and *vergüenza*, envisioned as ideally controlling the emotional entropy that love entails through the proper configuration of the rational, concupiscent, and irascible. The exploration of desire is renewed in these verses, with an effort begun to distinguish between stages of the experience and articulate its broader context. While the value of resisting erotic passion receives periodic acknowledgment, usually by the Araucan heroines at the start of their tragic stories, such references are largely formulaic, and the depiction of love between couples is so positive that any sense of Stoic *apatheia* is clearly rejected. In any event, passion, once instilled, is irresistible. Tegualda's naive self-complacency succumbs in one dramatic collapse; the narrator's earlier fall, while literally and figuratively cushioned by Reason (18.71.8), was equally stark. Once subject to carnal desire, attention shifts to the corralling of its attendant emotions and behavior into conventional forms, principally that of matrimony. The repeated declarations by the Araucan heroines regarding the love freely given their spouses, together with the impromptu wedding ceremony symbolically enacted in Tegualda's and Crepino's exchange of rings, suggests the influence of contemporaneous Tridentine decrees on marriage.[47] The emphatically decorous quality of their love, in contrast to the carnality of Guacolda and Lautaro of Part I, some nine years earlier, may also reflect Counter-Reformation sobriety, increasingly influential as the century progressed. On a parallel plane, the process of distinguishing the classical epic virtue of *kleos* from an eventually Christian version of personal integrity continues here, the Platonic formulation evoked by Tegualda linking honor (τιμή) with temperance (σωφροσύνη) and modesty (αἰδώς), i.e., a temperate approach to honor in contrast to the ruthless pursuit of *kleos* by Homer's heroes (a modesty reiterated in the reference to δόξα ἀληθινή or *true* reputation or glory).[48] Shame, whose internalization as guilt has long been associated with the shift from pagan to Christian culture, is mentioned repeatedly here, yet any allusion to religion at this point in the poem is studiously avoided for an

---

[47] A large part of the twenty-fourth session of Trent in 1563 was dedicated to the issue of marriage; while embedding the ceremony in numerous restrictions and responsibilities, Chapter IX of the proceedings emphasizes that "[. . .] it is something singularly execrable to violate the freedom of matrimony" (*The Canons and Decrees of the Council of Trent*, trans. Rev. H. J. Schroeder, O. P. [Rockford, IL: Tan Books and Publishers, 1978], 189); note that the focus of the Fourth Session in 1546 had been to control the "unbridled spirits" of scriptural interpretation (18).

[48] (*Phaedrus*, 253D); see 75, supra.

emphasis on courtliness, a quality embodied by the narrator, with its "mediocrità difficile" or difficult compromise between affability and virtue, which like
courtliness in general rejects anything too strict or doctrinaire or, in this case, too
religious. Shortly after the passage in the *Courtier* that features this phrase, the
group at Urbino discuss *vergogna* or shame as the gift of Jove, sent to mankind
along with *giustizia* or justice to address the lack of "virtù civile" or civic virtue
(4.11). While the last of the encounters with Araucan women, featuring Lauca,
will unequivocally differentiate the Christian culture of Ercilla from the pagan
one of his characters, it remains for Spenser and the stricter views of religious
reformers to articulate the concept of guilt more fully.

5. The Adventure of Glaura and Cariolán

In contrast to the passages discussed thus far, which cluster within the first eight
cantos of Part II, six cantos devoted solely to military matters now intervene.
With the retreat of the Araucans and Tegualda's departure, attention turns to
preparations for the next engagement with the enemy. The Spanish are heart-
ened to learn of reinforcements of men and horses en route from Santiago in the
north and from La Imperial in the south. A corresponding epic catalogue lists
Araucan fighters and their allies arriving for what apparently will be a major
confrontation, and Canto 21 concludes with a speech by Don García praising his
troops and inciting them to greater glory while warning in language that echoes
pío Felipe at San Quentin that excessive violence forfeits moral superiority.[49] The
commander's harangue, which offers one of the poem's most explicit statements
regarding the divine right of Spanish conquest, adroitly transfers key terms just
discussed with regard to love to the matter of war, articulating with courtly decorum that the bridle of Platonic rationality applies not only to the concupiscent
component of the soul exemplified by Tegualda, but to the irascible as well:

> Lo que yo os pido de mi parte y digo
> es que en estas batallas y revueltas,
> aunque os haya ofendido el enemigo,
> jamás vos le ofendáis a espaldas vueltas;
> antes le defended como al amigo
> si, volviéndose a vos las armas sueltas,
> rehuyere el morir en la batalla,
> pues es más dar la vida que quitalla.
>
> Poned a todo en la *razón* la mira,
> por quien las armas siempre habéis tomado,
> que pasando los términos la ira

---

[49] See 70, supra.

pierde fuerza el derecho ya violado.
Pues cuando la *razón* no *frena* y tira
el ímpetu y *furor* demasiado,
el rigor excesivo en el castigo
justifica la causa al enemigo. (21.55.1–21.56.8)

All I ask of you now and say to you is that in these battles and skirmish-
es, even if the enemy has wounded you, never attack him when his back
is turned. Instead, defend him like a friend if he surrenders his arms and
hands them over to you, fleeing from death in battle, for it is greater to
grant a life than take it. / Think carefully about the *reasons* that have always
led you to take up arms, for when wrath passes beyond its proper limits,
right is violated and loses its force. And when *reason* no longer *restrains* excessive violence and *rage*, excessively harsh punishment justifies the cause
of the enemy.

Canto 22, devoted to the bloody battle of Lagunillas, opens with a five-octave
apostrophe to *pérfido amor tirano* ("perfidious, tyrannical love") (22.1.1), beginning with a variation on the narrator's by now familiar complaint about his
promise to write of war overriding his desire to write of love. In contrast such
earlier expressions, the lament is now couched in personal terms that simultaneously echo the cliches of erotic passion, especially those already employed by the
poem's heroines, most recently Tegualda (at 20.58.7–8 and 20.61.6):

¡Ay!, que ya siento en mi cuidoso pecho
labrarme poco a poco *un vivo fuego*
y desde allí con *movimiento blando*
ir por las venas y huesos penetrando. (22.1.5–8)

Alas! Already I feel *a lively fire* working little by little in my *anxious* heart
and *gently spreading from there through my veins and bones.*[50]

---

[50] Cf. 72–73, supra; as noted earlier, *vivo fuego* is also applied to the anger of the Araucan fighter, Tucapelo (20.11.3) (74, supra). While the image of fire penetrating bones
and veins recalls passages in Virgil and Apollonius citing each symptom independently
(52 n. 14, supra), their conjunction here in one phrase may once again reflect the impact
of Hernández de Velasco's *Aeneid*, which renders the key Virgilian couplet "[. . .] donisque
furentem / *incendat* reginam atque ossibus implicet *ignem*" ("*inflame* the queen to madness with his gifts and implant the *fire* into her very bones") (1.659–660) as "Y dentro
delos hueſſos y en las venas / Vn venenoſo y fiero ardor le emprēda ("and within her *veins
and bones* implant a poisonous and raging fire") (see Appendix A). The same conjunction
of fire, bones, and veins is also found in Petrarch: "come nell'ossa il suo foco si pasce, / e
ne le vene vive occulta piaga" ("as in my marrow his [Love's] fire sustains itself and lives
in my veins like a hidden sore") (*Triumphus Cupidinis* 3.181–182).

In elaborately rhetorical and increasingly ironic language, the narrator goes on to accuse Love of troubling him with memories (22.2.4) and to issue a subtly humorous and self-mocking warning: " Déjame ya, que no quieras que se diga / que porque nadie quiere celebrarte, / al último rincón vas a buscarme [. . .]" ("Let me be, for you do not want it said that having no one to celebrate you, you sought me out at the ends of the earth and used all your power to torment me") (22.2.5–7). The following octave, hovering between irony and earnestness, notes that more famous poets can be found to write of Love, then complains of still being bothered by recollections of a dream, perhaps the earlier vision of Spanish beauty, which the narrator now characterizes as "quizá vano" ("vain perhaps") (22.3.7). Hearing the noise of the approaching enemy, the poet repeats his "Déjame ya" (22.4.1), then reclaims some self-opinion with the observation that the circumstances in which he finds himself wouldn't provide much opportunity for even the most gifted imagination. The apostrophe's combination of ironic detachment and genuine melancholy suggest frustration at having to interrupt what has become the poem's parallel narrative of love stories, material which had proven popular with readers soon after the publication of Part I. Apparent here as well may be a decision to apportion this material more methodically to enhance its appeal.[51]

The battle of Lagunillas, which begins when Don García, having finished his rousing speech, leads the Spanish across the Biobío into the *Estado*, goes on for some forty octaves of grotesque realism featuring the aristeia of named soldiers on both sides. As is often the case in the poem, the greatly outnumbered Spanish are frequently on the verge of defeat, their carefully ordered squadrons scattered over the most difficult terrain into smaller groups engaged in hours of desperate hand-to-hand combat, situations which Ercilla quickly became known for describing with great flair.[52] Most of the fighting here is evenly pitched, "sin

---

[51] The story of Guacolda and Lautaro, possibly circulated prior to 1569, was adopted by writers of historical romances within thirteen years of the publication of Part I; cf. Lerner, *Araucana*, 48.

[52] Cf. the description of fighting in a swamp:

> Quién, el húmido cieno a la cintura,
> con dos y tres a veces peleaba;
> quién, por mostrar mayor desenvoltura,
> queriéndose mover más atascaba.
> Quién, probando las fuerzas y ventura,
> al vecino enemigo se aferraba
> mordiéndole y cegándole con lodo,
> buscando de vencer cualquiera modo. (22.31.1–8)

One, the wet muck up to his waist, was fighting with two or three at a time; another, wanting to move in order to have greater facility, became further enmired. Another still, testing both strength and luck, fastened onto his nearby enemy, biting and blinding him with mud, seeking to win however he could.

muestra ni señal de declararse / mínima de ventaja en parte alguna" ("without
any sign indicating the slightest advantage on either side") (22.32.3–4). Eventually the Araucans, realizing they will not be able to win outright, begin a retreat,
killing anyone they catch without mercy, "sin clemencia alguna" (22.15.4), vio-
lating the guidelines emphasized earlier. The Spanish then commit a much more
egregious violation, cutting off the hands of one of their prisoners as exemplary
punishment (22.46.1–5). Canto 23 opens with the often-noted harangue to a
gathering of Araucan leaders by the victim of that cruelty, Galbarino, who claims
that the Spanish are motivated by greed rather than by Christianity (23.12.4–
23.13.4). The Spanish, meanwhile, are moving further south into the neighboring valley when the narrator catches his first glimpse of an ancient Indian, whom
Reason had foretold would lead him to an Araucan sorcerer, Fitón. Reason's
preview of this encounter had emphasized having to first pass through a "selva escura" ("dark forest") (18.61.4), and after losing his way the narrator is led
through "una selva espesa" ("a thick forest") (23.30.5) into "[. . .] una selva de
árboles horrenda, / que los rayos del sol y claro cielo / nunca allí vieron el um-
broso suelo" ("a forest of horrendous trees, where the rays of the sun and blue sky
never saw the shady ground") (23.46.6–8). The repeated references are to the epic
motif of the *antiqua silva* or ancient forest, site of the entrance to the underworld

---

A few particularly dramatic situations are marked by Homeric similes, as in the
present scene:

> Como el airado viento repentino
> que en lóbrego turbión con gran estruendo
> el polveroso campo y el camino
> va con violencia indómita barriendo,
> y en ancho y presuroso remolino
> todo lo coge, lleva y va esparciendo,
> y arranca aquel furioso moviemiento
> los arraigados troncos de su asiento,
>
> con tal facilidad, arrebatados
> de aquel furor y bárbara violencia,
> iban los españoles fatigados,
> sin poderse poner en resistencia.
> Algunos, del honor avergonzados,
> vuelven haciendo rostro y aparencia
> mas otra ola de gente llegaba
> con más presteza y daño los llevaba. (22.13.1–22.14.8)

Like a rapid, raging wind that goes sweeping across the road and dusty plain in a
sudden, roaring storm, its indomitable violence catching up and scattering everything in
a great, surging whirlwind whose furious motion uproots trees from the earth, / with just
such facility the weary Spanish were seized by that violent barbarian fury and unable to
resist it. Some, ashamed for their honor, turn to face them and make a stand, but another
wave of men arrives and carries them off with even greater injury and speed.

in the *Aeneid* (6.179) and thus associated with foreboding as well as with the transformative insight of the prophecy that unfolds here. Regularly associated by Ercilla with Fitón (the narrator encounters him for a second time a few cantos later, after passing through "un bosque espeso" ("a thick wood") (26.40.6), it now leads to the sorcerer's cave, where in clear appropriation of epic tradition the narrator is shown a prophetic view of the Battle of Lepanto in 1571 via a crystal sphere. The vision, which like that overseen by Bellona and Reason functions to link the action of the *Araucana* with Spain's imperial project in Europe, occupies the remainder of this canto and all of the twenty-fourth, continuing the juxtaposition of supernatural and historical and paradoxically insuring, in the words of Fitón, "que podrás, como digo, ser de vista / testigo y verdadero coronista" ("that you will be able, as I claim, to be an eyewitness and truthful chronicler") (23.75.7–8).[53]

Several weeks pass as the Spanish proceed further into Araucan territory facing eerily little resistance. A solitary messenger appears at their camp to relay a challenge of single combat to end the conflict (25.7.1–25.12.8), but the Spanish suspect a ruse and prepare for an attack, which comes shortly thereafter (25.18.1). The ensuing battle of Millarapué is another major one and once again foregrounds a mix of memorable bravery and repulsive brutality. Caupolicán and Tucapelo distinguish themselves, supporting an Araucan advantage through many octaves. The Indians' luck begins to change as the canto closes, however, and as the following one opens they are finally routed. The Spanish are again excessively cruel, chasing down and killing all who attempt to flee, as their opponents had earlier. Once again they exact exemplary punishment, giving lengths of rope to each of twelve caciques—the eternally defiant Galbarino among them—who are forced to hang themselves, the cruelty of the scene indelibly accentuated by the lyrical couplet with which it concludes: "y los robustos robles desta prueba / llevaron aquel año fruta nueva" ("the mighty oaks bearing new fruit that year of the ordeal") (26.37.7–8).[54] In one of several passages in which the narrator emphasizes his own sense of clemency in contrast to those around him, he tries

---

[53] The prophetic episodes centered on Fitón are analyzed at length by Nicolopulos in *Poetics of Empire*; see 93 n. 1, supra.

[54] The use of forced self-hanging by the Spanish is also described by Gaspar Peréz de Villagrá in his account of the fall of the Acoma pueblo in the *Historia de Nueva Mexico* (1610); Lerner discusses the appropriation of Ercilla's use of the motif in Billie Holiday's song "Strange Fruit": "Persistencia de metáforas: Lucano, Ercilla, el romancero," in *Siglos Dorados: Homenaje a Augustin Redondo*, ed. Pierre Civil (Madrid: Castilla, 2004), 2: 765–74. Galbarino's defiant condemnation of the Spanish before his death: "Oh gentes fementidas, detestables, indignas de la gloria deste día!" ("Oh treacherous, detestable people, unworthy of this day's glory!") (26.25.1–2) is another Ercillan tour de force; its threat of unending war: "muertos podremos ser, mas no vencidos" ("dead we may be, but not defeated") (26.25.7), is discussed by Quint (*Epic*, 101 ff.).

unsuccessfully to have the life of Galbarino spared. The sequence of events that
followed the excessive cruelty of the Spanish a few cantos earlier now plays out
again, with attention shifted as far as possible from the bloody reality of the war
to another encounter with the supernatural Fitón. Once more the magus's crystal sphere offers a prophetic vision, this one a fifty-canto tour of the early modern world, a *mappamundi* that concludes with a preview of the unknown area
south of the *estado* whose exploration will feature in Part III of Ercilla's poem
(26.40.1–27.54.8). A few weeks later, as the Spanish move deeper into Araucan
territory, the narrator is scouting ahead of the troops when he catches sight of an
Araucan woman and gives chase. The woman is Glaura, whose story is told in
the following canto.

The exordium to Canto 28 echoes earlier warnings on the changeability of
fate, notable here for the degree to which the narrator now personalizes such sentiments in verses that could be spoken by any of his heroines, further linking his
experience with theirs:

> y pues sabemos ya por cosa cierta,
> que nunca hay bien a quien un mal no siga,
> roguemos que no venga y si viniere,
> que sea pequeño el mal que le siguiere.
>
> Que yo, de acuchillado en esto, siento
> que es de temer en parte la ventura;
> el tiempo alegre pasa en un momento
> y el triste hasta la muerte siempre dura. (28.2.5–28.3.1–4)
>
> And since we know for certain that there's never a good thing not followed by
> bad, we pray it doesn't come and that if it does, the bad that follows be small.
> // Being so experienced in this I feel that good luck is partly to be feared;
> happy times pass in a moment, and sad ones always last until death.[55]

As conventional as this attitude is within the poem, the emphasis here on the
narrator's own experience has led to speculation regarding potential causes of
such sentiments, among them Ercilla's judicial trouble in Chile, his later frustration regarding Philip II's tepid sponsorship, and the possibility of an early, unhappy love affair. By the time Part III was published in 1589 the poet had also
experienced the loss of his son and only child in the Armada of the previous year.
Whatever its source, the sense of personal melancholy will persist in spite of and

---

[55] Cf. Tegualda's "¡Ay de mí!, que es imposible / tener jamás descanso hasta la
muerte" ("Ah me, for it's impossible to find rest until death") (20.36.1–2).

in contrast to the continued success of the Spanish military campaign, its aura coloring events and ultimately precipitating the poem's premature end.[56]

Glaura's story echoes many of the themes of previous episodes, emphasizing the virtues of *piedad*, *clemencia*, and *cortesía*, the benefits of a loving relationship between father and daughter, the dangers of erotic passion uncontrolled by reason, and efforts at channeling such passion into chaste, conjugal love. In contrast to the episodes of Guacolda and Tegualda, however, these by now familiar concerns and the expected account of a love affair interrupted by war are couched in Boccaccian terms echoing Ariosto but derived from Greek romance, a formulaic genre that, rather than dwell on personal emotions, focuses on a plot-driven happy ending. Contrasting sharply with such conventionality is the facility with which Ercilla mixes such literary cliches with New World settings and his own experiences, creating the generic hybrids increasingly characteristic of his poem. In the Glaura episode this process is marked by a dramatic shift in the role of the narrator-soldier, now not simply a sympathetic listener but a co-conspirator with a tale of his own to tell. The story that he and the heroine jointly recount, in which Aristotelian *peripeteia* and *anagnorisis* are crucial, is one where the narrator plays the role of the era's most famous romance hero, *cortesía* domesticates the previously *indómito* savage, and the surprising denouement suggests an alternative to violent New World conquest.

The episode begins familiarly enough. In addition to being beautiful, like Guacolda, Glaura possesses "natural donaire y apostura" ("natural grace and elegance") (28.4.8) and "rara gentileza" ("rare gentility") (28.5.4), like Tegualda, marks of innate nobility reflecting her status as the daughter of a wealthy Araucan chief; like Tegualda, Glaura also agrees to recount her experience even though it pains her. Her account starts as a tale of domestic sexual abuse narrowly escaped, then segues into Greek romance adventure, a genre described by Bakhtin as involving two beautiful, chaste youths, often of mysterious lineage, who meet unexpectedly and suddenly fall in love, after which they are separated, experience a series of adventures, and are finally reunited and married, frequently after the revelation of noble parentage.[57] In brief, Glaura tells of having the happiness

---

[56] On Ercilla's judicial trouble while in Chile, see 100 n. 73, infra. Medina's study cites one of the only other verse outside the *Araucana* ascribed to Ercilla, a highly stylized *glosa* that Medina read biographically, using it to speculate on the possibility of an early unhappy love affair resulting in the poet's volunteering for military service in the New World (*Vida*, 21–23). The poem is notable for similar emotions expressed in many of the same images discussed here. Gregory Shepherd discusses Ercilla's growing disillusionment in the poem in terms of the widespread disappointment among the Spanish during this period with economic, military, and moral failures ("Balancing," 130–31).

[57] Bakhtin specifies that the Greek romance or "adventure novel of ordeal" is dominated by the logic of random contingency operating in a chronotope of reversible time and interchangeable space. Its events leave no trace on the protagonists, who are the same at

of a mutually respectful and loving relationship with her father disrupted by "el invidioso amor tirano" ("jealous, tyrannical love") (28.9.1), a characterization recalling the narrator's apostrophe to *pérfido amor tirano* ("perfidious, tyrannical love") (22.1.1) a few cantos earlier. For Glaura the trouble arises in the guise of a visiting uncle, who, driven by "mal deseo" ("evil desire") (28.12.3), expresses sexual interest in her. The uncle's eventual breaking of "los honestos límites" ("honorable limits") (28.12.4) rehearses key terms noted previously: the absence of *tino* or judgement (28.10.7) and his resulting *desatiento* or recklessness (28.14.4); efforts by the heroine to restrain or *refrenar* his daring (28.13.7); the failure of his *razón* or reason to control desire (28.14.6). In spite of all she can do to resist, the uncle is on the point of assaulting her when the household is attacked by Spanish soldiers and both uncle and father are killed. Glaura flees into the mountains to hide, but is accosted by two African slaves, part of those who accompanied the Spanish to the New World, who attempt to rape her (28.23.6–8).[58] Concerned more for "el honor y castidad preciada" ("honor and precious chastity") (28.24.5) than for her life, she is on the point of losing both when an Araucan youth comes to her rescue. Much like his earlier counterparts, Cariolán behaves with courtly propriety, and Glaura, charmed by his behavior as well as concerned for appearances, quickly accepts his offer of marriage, "por evitar al fin murmuraciones / y no mostrarme ingrata al beneficio" ("to avoid rumors finally and to not prove ungrateful for his help") (28.29.5–6). The marriage is only a few days old when the happy couple are surprised by Spanish troops, and Cariolán, like Glaura earlier, fearing for her honor rather than his life (28.31.6), encourages her to flee while he resists. Glaura hides in the trunk of a tree, and when she emerges Cariolán is nowhere to be found. Filled with remorse at having deserted him, she struggles with thoughts of suicide (28.37.5–6) and finally decides to disguise herself and approach a Spanish encampment in the hope of discovering Cariolán's fate. This is the point at which the narrator has encountered her, and here her story and the framing narrative merge (28.41). As her recitation concludes, however, the Spanish soldiers and Glaura are caught in an Araucan ambush, and a wild fight breaks out. In the melee an Araucan servant of Ercilla's comes to his defense, only to be recognized by Glaura as no other than Cariolán. The narrator,

---

the plot's conclusion as they were at its start and who experience the period between falling in love and getting married as an "extratemporal hiatus" to be suffered through rather than as a period influencing development ("Forms of Time and the Chronotope in the Novel," in idem, *The Dialogic Imagination*, trans. Emerson and Holquist, 86 ff.). As noted earlier, the best-known example of such ancient literature, the *Aethiopica* of Heliodorus, was widely available in Spain by the late 1550s (17, supra). On the possible influence of Heliodorus on the Glaura episode, see Charles Aubrun, "Poesía Epica y Novela: El Episodio de Glaura en *La Araucana* de Ercilla," *Revista Iberoamericana* 21 (1956): 261–73.

[58] Although slaves to the Spanish, Africans generally considered themselves superior to New World natives, who typically dislike them; cf. Lerner, *Araucana*, 766 n. 36.

as surprised and delighted as they, instantly releases them from any obligation, and the two quickly disappear in the surrounding chaos (28.44). Rather than describe what happens to the badly outnumbered Spanish, himself among them, the narrator interrupts the action to tell his part of the back-story, explaining in an apostrophe addressed to his royal reader how Cariolán came to be in his service in the first place. The digression functions on several levels, heightening suspense, as was seen in earlier interruptions, but also helping establish the verisimilitude of such an improbable *anagnorisis*. Most important, it reinforces the narrator's own moral character, particularly his *piedad* and *clemencia*, since it reveals that as one of the soldiers who came upon Glaura and Cariolán earlier, he had managed to save the young man's life, telling the soldiers who would have killed him that "[. . .] no es bien que el valiente mozo muera, / antes merece ser remunerado, / y darle así la muerte ya sería / no esfuerzo ni valor, mas villanía" ("it isn't good that the brave young man die, rather he deserves to be rewarded, and to kill him thus would be neither strength nor courage, but villainy") (28.49. 5–8). Cariolán, in turn, acknowledges Ercilla's magnanimity in a courtly speech, becoming another barbarian spokesperson on the attribute of piety, as was Tegualda earlier, as well as a mouthpiece for intricate lyrical constructions, notable here for assonance and consonance, antithesis and paradox and polyptoton:

> ¿Qué te importa
> que sea mi vida larga o que sea corta?
>
> Pero de mí será reconocida
> la obra pía y voluntad humana:
> pía por la intención, pero entendida
> se puede decir impía y inhumana,
> que a quien ha de vivir mísera vida
> no le puede estar mal muerte temprana,
> así que en no matarme, como digo,
> cruel misercordia usas conmigo. (28.50.7–28.51.8)

> What does it matter to you whether my life be long or short? / Nonetheless I acknowledge your humane motive and the piety of your deed: pious in intention, although one could say impious and in fact inhumane, for to one who must live a miserable life an early death can't be bad. Thus by not killing me, as I say, you treat me with cruel compassion.

While the rhetorical performance climaxes in the closing oxymoron, the deeper significance of the scene is captured in the following octave's description of Cariolán as "doméstico el que *indómito* había sido" ("docile he who had earlier been *indomitable*") (28.52.6), the notorious Araucan ferocity assuaged not by force but courtesy.

In terms of plot, Glaura's story models that of Ariosto's Isabella even more closely than did Tegualda's, since both here and in the *Furioso* the heroines are separated from their lovers, become victims of attempted rape, are saved by the unexpected approach of someone who rescues them, and are eventually rejoined with their partners in a dramatic recognition scene. The emphasis on the heroine's trials is typical of chivalric romance, as is the hero's gallant behavior and the descriptions of Glaura as running "acá y allá" ("here and there") (28.21.1) and "aquí y allí y acá y allá" ("here and there and now this way now that") (28.23.3), phrases that echo Ariosto's "di qua di là" ("here and there") and "di su di giù" ("now this way now that").[59] The focus on the heroine's chastity, by contrast, an obsession of Greek romance corresponding to Siglo de Oro sensibilities, aligns the episode more closely with the *novela de aventuras*, popular in the sixteenth and seventeenth centuries and inspiration for the Baroque novel in the seventeenth and eighteenth.[60] Cinquecento theorists regularly contrasted the multiple plots and repeated digressions of such narratives with the unity of epic, and while the gravity of Ercilla's heroines clearly distinguishes them from those of Ariosto, Glaura's story comes closest to inscribing a romance sensibility, its happy ending a uniquely complacent moment in the poem.[61] While the focus on events driven by *peripeteia* and *anagnorisis* is also unique, the intercalation of such a narrative in contrast to scenes of bloody combat recalls earlier episodes, and just as Greek romance represented a Hellenistic ironizing of classical values, the adventure story that Ercilla derives from it obliquely interrogates the military campaign the account of which it interrupts. Alongside these differences are many similarities that associate these passages with those previously discussed. Glaura's tale continues to emphasize the virtues of *cortesía*, *clemencia*, and *piedad*, the importance of courtly decorum, and the desirability of chaste, conjugal love. Developing these themes in contrast to uncontrolled "mal deseo," the passage continues to explicate the hierarchy of the rational, irascible, and concupiscent. A number of the episode's functions are also familiar. Once again Ercilla demonstrates his skill at a popular literary convention and indulges in the varied subject matter he so frequently yearns for, here paying homage to Boccaccio and Ariosto while correcting them both, the former's lustful male summarily punished, the latter's carefree irony entirely expunged in favor of earnestness. This plot-driven genre, unlike the previous episodes' focus on classical allusions, bridges popular and erudite culture and, in the hands of Ercilla, mingles an abstract, literary formula with factual detail: Glaura is a thoroughly literary figure; Cariolán, while embellished with courtly refinement, is from all indications a historical one. Their

---

[59] Cf. *Orlando Furioso* (27.61–28.50), whose intertexts are identified by Schwartz, "Tradición," 623. D. S. Carne Ross identifies "di qua di là" and "di su di giù" as quintessential descriptors of Ariostan romance wandering: "The One and the Many: A Reading of the *Orlando Furioso*, Cantos 1 and 8," *Arion* 5 (1966): 195–234.

[60] Cf. Futre Pinheiro, "*Nachleben* of the Ancient Novel in Iberian Literature."

[61] Cf. Daniel Javitch, *Proclaiming a Classic* (Princeton: Princeton University Press, 1991), 86 ff.; Nicolopulos offers further discussion of Ercilla's rejection of chivalric models for his Araucan women ("Reading," 227–30).

joining with the narrator in a seamless blend of story time and lived experience, which culminates in the narrator now casting himself, as has long been noted, as a brave and magnanimous Orlando to Glaura's Isabella and Cariolán's Zerbino, continues the poet's self-portrayal in conjunction with his characters.[62] The climax of their interaction offers a momentary glimpse of an alternative conquest in which Araucan resistance is tamed by courtly clemency. The narrator's growing melancholy, on the other hand, apparent in the exordium, persists, becoming increasingly important as the poem proceeds.

6. Lauca: The Enshrinement of Christian *piedad*

Araucan women make two appearances in the poem after Glaura. Both are brief, and only one, that by Lauca, will be considered here. The other, by the wife of Caupolicán, a few cantos later, has nothing in common with the episodes considered thus far, reflecting instead the documentary impulse of the poem's earliest references to Indian women as fierce fighters.[63] As Glaura and Cariolán disappear in the confusion of the Araucan ambush, the fighting around Ercilla intensifies. Trapped in a mountain pass, the Spanish escape certain death only when the Araucans become distracted by the spoils of their baggage train, their greed mirroring earlier descriptions of Spanish *codicia*.[64] Several weeks later, increasingly on the defensive, the Araucans convene a senate notable for the violent confrontation that erupts between Tucapelo and Rengo, their foremost champions, forestalling efforts to reach consensus on how resistance should be pursued. The fight is famously interrupted at the end of the canto just as a sword is raised for

---

[62] Cf. Schwartz, "Tradición," 624; cf. the earlier suggestion of the narrator's association with "pious Aeneas," 70, supra. Fuchs discusses the Glaura episode in relation to the anonymous sixteenth-century romance *El Abencerraje*, where a Christian warrior frees a Moor and his beloved ("Traveling Epic," 383 ff.).

[63] Fresia's appearance with her infant son follows the capture of Caupolicán, whom she mocks with having avoided "una breve muerte honrada" ("an early honorable death") (33.80.3–4) and tries to give the child, since "[. . .] ese membrudo / cuerpo en sexo de hembra se ha trocado" ("that muscular body of yours has changed into a female one") (33.81.5–6). On Fresia as a literary figure in her own right, her genealogy that of the severe Roman matron or implacable Spartan mother, see Schwartz, "Tradición," 625; for analysis of the gender reversal of the scene and additional sexual imagery of the poem, see Ricardo Padrón, "Love American Style," 574 ff.; cf. 47 n. 6, supra.

[64] Cf.: "Cuál con hambre y codicia deshonesta / por sólo llevar más se detenía, / costando a más de diez allí la vida / la carga y la codicia desmedida" ("Some were detained by indecent greed and the longing to take more, the booty and excessive greed costing more than ten their lives") (28.69.5–8); cf. earlier condemnations of Spanish greed, including Valdivia's at 2.92.7, and later ones, esp. Galbarino's at 23.12.4–23.13.4 and then later at 36.13–14.

a decisive blow (C. 29.15.1–29.53.8), inspiring Cervantes's well-known adaptation of the device between Books 8 and 9 of the 1605 *Quijote*. Ercilla's model is especially daring, the blow suspended for eleven years between Canto 29, which ends Part II of the poem, and Canto 30, which begins Part III.[65]

The third and final installment of the poem, in which the Spanish penetrate ever deeper into Araucan territory, opens with an eight-octave exordium on the illegitimacy of duels like the one in progress, a harangue that echoes Don García's earlier one on reason and violence, with the first of these qualities now mentioned five times as that which controls the second, "[. . .] sujeta al *freno* y señorio / de la *razón*" ("subjected to the *restraint* and control of *reason*") (30.2.5–6). Once again reason is identified as that which assures that "los términos justos" ("just limits") (30.2.8) are not exceeded, and when Caupolicán steps in to stop the fight between his warriors, it is "a la *razón doméstica*" ("to *domesticizing reason*") (30.22.8) the men are brought, the epithet echoing Cariolan's recent "domestication."[66] The narrative resumes at this point to describe how an elaborate Araucan plan to infiltrate the Spanish garrison at Concepción goes terribly awry, with their spy double-crossed and their two-thousand-man force led into a devastating trap prefiguring their ultimate subjection (31.48.7). The set-up is notable for the tragic irony with which it hints at a potential reversal of the battle at Mataquito in which Lautaro was killed, the double agent assuring Caupolicán that the Spanish fort will be unguarded during the midday siesta, when its soldiers will be found precisely as the Indians were during that earlier encounter: "en vino y dulce sueño sepultados" ("buried in wine and sweet sleep") (31.23.6).[67] The narrator's growing repugnance at the bloody events he describes is also emphasized, this final large-scale battle of the poem being preceded by a reflection on the inner conflict he feels at such times, a struggle between justifiable hatred of the enemy and human compassion that threatens to immobilize him (31.49.1–8). There's also a suggestion here in the use of *alejarse*, typically used to signify a physical withdrawal or retreat, of a link between such emotions and the extended digressions he regularly pursues:

> Si del asalto y ocasión me alejo,
> dentro della y del fuerte estoy metido;

---

[65] Parts I and II were bridged by a similar device involving the storm at sea (60–61, supra); in the present instance the narrator remarks: "Mas quien el fin deste combate aguarda / me perdone si dejo destroncada / la historia en este punto, porque creo / que así me esperará con más deseo" ("But whoever awaits the outcome of this combat, forgive me if I leave the story interrupted at this point, since I believe that thus you will await me with greater desire") (30.53.5–8). The device, as noted earlier, is an Ariostan one.

[66] Cf. 21.56.3 and 117, supra.

[67] The episode is a notable instance of the fraud with which Ercilla identifies the Araucans; see 72 n. 19, supra.

si en este punto y término lo dejo,
hago y cumplo muy mal lo prometido;
así dudoso el ánimo y perplejo,
destos juntos contrarios combatido,
lo dejo al otro canto reservado,
que de consejo estoy necesitado. (31.50.1–8)

If I distance myself from the situation and from the attack, abandoning it
at this point and juncture, I comply only poorly with what I have promised
[an historical account], for I was inside the fort and a part of it. Thus with a
perplexed and hesitant spirit, fighting these opposing thoughts and in need
of counsel, I leave them for the next canto.

The exordium to Canto 32 reinforces such misgivings with its focus on the quality of clemency, with the poet now claiming that, "por ella Roma fue tan podero-
sa, / y más gentes venció que por la espada" ("through this was Rome so powerful
and vanquished more people than by the sword") (32.1.5–6).[68] Similar thoughts
on the differences between justifiable fury during the heat of battle and cold-
blooded cruelty lead into the poem's most explicit condemnation of the Chilean
campaign:

La mucha sangre derramada ha sido
(si mi juicio y parecer no yerra)
la que de todo en todo ha destruido
el esperado fruto desta tierra;
pues con modo inhumano han excedido
de las leyes y términos de guerra,
haciendo en las entradas y conquistas
crueldades inormes nunca vistas. (32.4.1–8)

Unless my judgement and opinion is mistaken, it is the spilling of so much
blood that has so completely destroyed the hoped-for benefits of this land:
for here the laws and limits of war have been exceeded to an inhuman degree, our occupation and conquest committing enormous and heretofore
unseen cruelties.

The statement is confirmed by the battle and its aftermath, when once again
the Spanish exact exemplary punishment, summarily executing thirteen *caciques*
(32.20.1–8). Caupolicán manages to escape, and it is in the course of the Spanish
search for him over the next few days that Ercilla happens upon Lauca, a teenage
Araucan girl whom he finds bleeding from a head wound.

---

[68] David A. Lupher explores the classical tradition, and the model of Rome in particular, in Spanish New World settings from Mexico to Peru, with particular attention to
Ercilla and the *Araucana*: *Romans*, 296 ff.

The similarities between the Lauca episode and the passages already discussed are both structural and thematic. Her introduction into the narrative replays the narrator's accidental finding of Glaura, which also occurs shortly after a major battle and, more specifically, after the Spanish resort to group executions. Like the earlier women, Lauca possesses idealized attributes of beauty and nobility, and at the narrator's request she tells a story of how she arrived at her present predicament. The primary themes of her account—desire, true love, loyalty, and the fragility of happiness—echo the stories of her predecessors, as do secondary themes regarding enlightened parental attitudes toward marriage and loving relations between spouses, positions for which the figure of the abandoned woman in Ercilla has become, ironically, a champion. Lauca's narrative also presents yet another variation on the theme of piety, allowing the narrator to further elaborate upon his own persona while distancing himself unequivocally from the pagan values of epic heroism the *Araucana* frequently celebrates. Lauca collapses a life story very similar to Tegualda's into a few octaves: her father, with whom she enjoys a special closeness, marries her to the man of her choosing, who becomes both "esposo y dulce amigo" ("husband and sweet friend") (32.39.2). This unnamed man, whose attractions are such that Lauca believes "que en él hallara término el deseo" ("that in him desire would find its goal") (32.34.8), is gifted with "esfuerzo raro y valentía" ("rare strength and valor") (32.35.1), qualities that result in his early death as he attempts to protect her during a Spanish attack. A Spanish soldier, finding her agonizing over her husband's body and "*en parte* condolido de mi suerte" ("*partly* sympathizing with my ill-fortune") (32.36.4), strikes her in the head with his sword, "con brazo aunque *piadoso* no tan fuerte" ("with an arm that, while *compassionate*, was not forceful enough") (32.36.6), leaving her for dead. After voicing familiar topoi on the tiresomeness of life without her companion and on the impropriety of remaining alive now that he's dead (32.39.1–4), she begs the narrator to help her, appealing to his *piedad* to finish what the other soldier began (32.29.6–8). The narrator's first response is to associate himself with Lauca's predicament. Discerning that her injury is not fatal, he realizes that "[. . .] era / más cruel el amor que la herida" ("love was more cruel than the wound") (32.40.7) and recalls a similar experience of his own at a time when "[. . .] aquel rabioso fuego / labró en mi inculto pecho" ("that ravenous fire worked in my own unschooled breast") (32.40.5–6). His fleeting recollection, expressed in the amatory imagery employed by other characters, echoes the earlier reference to an unidentified love affair.[69] He acknowledges that Lauca's plea for death is so pitiful that "algún simple" ("a simpleminded man") (32.40.3) might accede to it, but quickly stipulates that such a response would represent a barbarous piety or pity ("bárbara piedad") (32.40.4), the term now shading into its secondary meaning, in contrast to the Christian pity of his own course of ac-

---

[69] Cf. 86, n.56, supra.

tion, which consists of comforting her while stressing the sinfulness of suicide as well as the irrelevance of her own death to that of her husband (32.41.1–4). The catechism completed, he dresses her wound and has her escorted out of danger.

While fulfilling a number of the functions associated with previous Araucan heroines, the narrator's brief encounter with Lauca develops into one of the poem's key scenes. Variations are offered on the themes of enlightened relations between parents and children and on the virtues of loyal, conjugal love, the passing references to both offset by the synecdochic power they derive from earlier, extensive treatments. Lauca began by believing that desire could be satisfied, finding its fulfillment in the figure of the beloved. Like the narrator and readers of the poem, she comes to realize such fulfillment is at best uncertain. The ambiguous characterization of the Spanish is doubly reinforced in these scenes, first by the heroine, who describes the soldier who strikes her as physically weak and as only partly sympathetic, implying less noble reasons for his action, then by the narrator, who condemns the soldier's behavior as simpleminded and barbarous. The narrator's response to the heroine focuses and defines the passage, not only distancing himself from the soldiers with whom he serves by distinguishing his genuinely Christian pity from theirs, but differentiating his values once and for all from those of the pagan world of epic heroism, from the *pietas* of Virgil as well as Homeric *kleos*. It is the Araucans who most frequently embody the latter with their combination of martial bravery, personal pride, and fierce independence. Aspects of this code, which persists in early modern Europe in vestiges of the nobility as a warrior class, appeal to the narrator, who associates brutal behavior, on the other hand, with moral perversion, whether that of the *vulgo* soldiery or of vicious Indians. The dutiful rectitude of Virgilian piety, by contrast, which inspires the portraits of Philip II and the narrator himself and which the poem so frequently emphasizes, is here refined to encompass the devotional component of its Christian correlate, while marital loyalty, so often emphasized by the protagonists of previous episodes, is similarly restricted by the religious injunction against taking one's life. The fact that the *Araucana's* distinction between proper and improper behavior does not coincide with that between barbarians and Christians complicates the poem, accentuating its hybrid quality and encouraging conflicting interpretations of the author's sympathies. At their worst both Indians and Spaniards are brutal and opportunistic, as are the latter in the lines just discussed. At their best both groups display bravery, fortitude, and integrity, as do the Araucan heroines and their spouses. In Lauca's request that the narrator help her die, the conflicting values of the ancient and modern worlds, dispersed throughout the narrative, collide in a single scene, and Christian compassion wins out over the glory of pagan conjugal loyalty that ends in death.

7. Andean Dido: Setting the Record Straight

With Lauca's departure the Spanish soldiers who had been searching for Caupolicán begin a long walk back to their camp. Having nothing more pressing to
discuss ("sin hallar otra cosa de importancia") (32.43.2), the narrator muses with
them over the loyalty shown by the Araucan women toward their spouses, ven-
turing the opinion that "no guardó la casta Elissa Dido / la fe con más rigor a
su marido" ("the chaste Elissa Dido did not guard her faith to her husband with
greater rigor") (32.43.7–8). One of the young soldiers quips:

> [. . .] que no tenía
> a Dido por tan casta y recogida,
> pues en la Eneyda de Marón vería
> que del amor libídino encendida,
> siguiendo el torpe fin de su deseo
> rompió la fe y promesa a su Sicheo. (32.44.3–8).

> [. . .] that he did not take Dido for so chaste and retiring, since in the *Aeneid*
> of Virgil he saw that consumed by libidinous love and following the infa-
> mous goal of her desire, she broke her faith and promise to Sychaeus.

Offended by what he considers a grave insult ("agravio tan notable") (32.45.1)
to "the chaste Phoenician" ("la casta fenisa") (32.45.4), the narrator decides it
reasonable ("cosa razonable") (32.45.5) to demonstrate to the young man that
he's mistaken, literally, that he was "walking erroneously" or "andaba errado"
(32.45.6) (suggesting the *errare-errore* conceit of romance). So he explains that
Virgil has misled him and others of his opinion, having defamed Dido in order
to embellish his portrayal of Aeneas and flatter Augustus, and he points out that
the two protagonists were separated by more than a century. The soldier and his
companions are astonished and ask the narrator to tell them her story, thus introducing, as the apparent result of an offhand remark, the *Araucana*'s longest sustained interpolation, a hundred-octave defense of Dido. The episode begins as a
digression but develops into what is arguably the heart of the poem as well as an
opportunity for the narrator, after recording the stories of so many others, to tell
his own, albeit obliquely, in a mix of the literary and real that captures like nothing else the spirit of Ercilla's revivification of classical tradition.

A complex web of structural, thematic, and functional correspondences links
these verses with the rest of the *Araucana*. The two accounts the narrator will implicitly compare, one an emblem of marital chastity, dear to ecclesiastical and didactic traditions, the other an image of tragic passion, canonized by literary ones,
each constitute a love story featuring female loyalty and chastity confronted by
uncontrolled male desire. Once again a heroine must protect herself against male
passion, maintaining her honor in the face of public scrutiny. The corrupting
force of greed, highlighted throughout the *Aeneid* (e.g. 3.56–57) as an evil that

undermines good intentions, plays a key role here, as do other familiar themes that acquire new significance in the process: the sanctity of justice and family, the importance of private honor, now contrasted with public reputation, and private interest, now weighed against the public good; once again the ignorance and coarseness of the *vulgo* is contrasted to the refinements of *culto*, specifically courtly, sensibility. Many of these issues operate on multiple levels, with analogues to earlier passages in the poem, to the narrator's personal experience, and to the experience of the Spanish in the New World generally. The result is a passage rich in supplementarity in which the goal of setting the record straight with regard to Dido takes on much broader implications.

In correcting Dido's story to conform with its pre-Virgilian plot and significance, Ercilla contrasts the *Aeneid*'s version of events with that found in the third-century historian Justin, juxtaposing what came to be associated with an eclectic Christian medievalism to a recently recovered, increasingly homogenized classicism. Rather than embrace Justin exclusively, however, Ercilla retains key elements from Virgil, notably those reflecting Dido's strength of character, intelligence, and leadership skills, all elements the Latin poet had elaborated upon. Virgil's Dido is a complex character, exposing less than admirable qualities in Aeneas, unfavorably portraying the private sacrifices ostensibly required of public life, and undercutting the heroic platitudes of the epic enterprise. While distinctly different, she is equally complex for Ercilla, initially and principally an archetype of virtue unjustly defamed, but by the end of the story, as others have noted, an ideal colonizer, implicitly contrasted with the Spanish. Justin, an early 'Orientalist' playing on the racism of sources that first refer to Dido in the context of the encounter between Hellenistic Greece and barbaric Tyre, had emphasized her exceptional beauty and cleverness: her "Tyrian guile."[70] In having his Araucan heroines mirror what he claims to be Dido's virtues, Ercilla rejects the negative stereotype even as he inaugurates its reverse in an image of the native American as noble savage. A variety of framing issues encountered earlier in the poem gain new prominence here. The narrator continues to emphasize the accuracy of history over fiction, with his often-stated desire for variety in a narrative devoted to war, related to the *otium-negotium* opposition, now addressed through the Horatian desideratum of pleasure-plus-instruction, *delectare* and *docere*. The eclectic *imitatio* of literary models, simultaneously appropriating and revisionary, continues as well, exposing a period prior to the homogenization of the humanist canon when a vibrant polyvalency of literary traditions still reigned, particularly in Spain, with its strong connections to the medieval past.[71] A number of the functions associated with the episodes discussed earlier continue here, among

---

[70] Cf. Brumble, *Myths*, 101.

[71] On the sense of continuity with the medieval past in early modern Spain, which in contrast to Italy did not view it as a Dark Age, see Octavio Di Camillo, *El Humanismo Castellano del Siglo XV* (Valencia: Fernando Torres, 1976), 65–66, 75–80.

them the erotic critique of epic, the defense of women, and the articulation of the proper relationship among the rational, concupiscent, and irascible. These verses also break new ground, their engagement with the complexity of literary history drawing attention to textual sources of ambiguity and ambivalence, qualities manifest in the multiple versions of literary characters that flourished for many centuries beginning in antiquity. This is true not only of Dido, available in chaste or libidinous variants, and other similarly bifurcated female figures noted earlier: the two Sapphos, two Helens, and two Venuses, but also of Aeneas, depending on the source alternately the savior or betrayer of Troy.[72] While often ideological in the recounting, these multiple personalities also represent an adumbration of psychological complexity and a recognition that no story is ever as simple as it appears. Manifest here as well is the perennial appeal of alternate endings to well-known stories, now reflected in the eagerness of the soldiers to hear the narrator's version of events they've previously known only through Virgil: "haciendo instancia todos en pedirme / que su vida y discurso les contase" ("everyone insisting that I tell them of her life and deeds") (32.47.3–4). These and other issues are adroitly introduced, meanwhile, in keeping with the strictures of courtly discourse, which is to say not too seriously. And once underway the poet's ongoing self-fashioning, oriented first and foremost, as usual, toward Philip II, achieves its sharpest delineation yet. The process begins with a focus on *fama* and the loss of public honor, which sounds like nothing so much as the anxiety associated with Spenser's Blatant Beast, offering an unexpected homology between the two poems. The image becomes more distinct in the defense as a whole, the intensity of which suggests that the stakes are more than purely literary. The self-portrait culminates in a play on the multiple meanings of two key terms, setting the stage for what is ultimately a re-envisioning of history both personal and global.

Dido's defense is preceded by ten octaves mixing nonchalance and earnestness, an exaggerated *sprezzatura* interspersed with allusions to the poem's cardinal values. The former is stressed repeatedly, from the characterization of the "digresión" (32.51.7) as no more than a welcome distraction from the fatiguing walk (32.47.5–6), to its offering relief from the poem's military matter, the familiar complaint about "el áspero sujeto" or harsh subject (32.50.1) that leads the poet once again, in an echo of Bellona's earlier invitation (17.42.1), to seek the refreshment of "anchura y campo descubierto" or "breadth and open country" (32.50.6). These assertions regarding a topic that "[. . .] a caso vino / cortada a la medida del camino" or "by chance came just made for the long road ahead" (32.51.8) (literally, "cut to the measure of the road," echoing the poem's initial lines that described the *Araucana* as "sacada / de la verdad, cortada a su medida" or as "taken from the truth, cut to its measure") (1.3.5–6), culminate in an apostrophe to the

[72] Cf. Ralph Hexter, "Sidonian Dido," in *Innovations of Antiquity*, ed. idem and Daniel Selden (New York: Routledge, 1992), 332–84, at 341–42.

royal reader that nevertheless insists on the episode's being not simply pleasurable, but useful as well:

> Y pues de aquí al presidio yo no hallo
> cosa que sea de gusto ni contento,
> sin dejar de picar siempre al caballo,
> ni del tiempo perder sólo un momento,
> no pudiendo eximirme ni escusallo
> por ser *historia* y *agradable* el cuento,
> quiero gastar en él, si no os enfada,
> este rato y sazón desocupada. (32.49.1–8)

> And since there is nothing interesting or pleasing between here and the fort, I would like to use my response to the soldiers to fill this empty occasion, as long as it does not annoy you. I cannot refuse to recount a story that is so *pleasing* as well as *historical*, continuing to spur my horse all the while and thus not losing a single moment.

Interwoven with such claims to the digression's unpremeditated and recreational nature are powerful suggestions as to its actual significance. The first appears near the beginning of the passage, when, agreeing to the soldiers' request for Dido's history, the narrator states that "[. . .] también quiero / daros aquí *razón de mí* primero" (32.47.8), which is to say, "I also want to provide you first of all with *my own razón,*" ostensibly referring to his own *rationale* or *motive* for telling the story, i.e., the restoration of Dido's good name, but doing so in a phrase that hints strongly at self-justification. Given the emotional intensity the passage subsequently exhibits, together with the narrator's practice of alluding to his own experience while representing that of his characters, the reader has every reason to suspect that *razón de mí* refers as much to the narrator as to Dido and that the restoration of her honor is a surrogate for his own, maligned in the nearly fatal misunderstanding that occurred during the latter part of the poet's time in Chile. The incident, in which the young, aristocratic Ercilla, until a few years earlier a member of the royal household, was publicly seized and almost executed on the spot, is mentioned twice in the closing cantos of the *Araucana*, first in a passage that notes the damage done by "la voz y fama pública" ("word-of-mouth and public reputation") (36.33.6), his own unforgettable encounter with the Blatant Beast, then in lines that refer to the unjust detention he suffered, "tan sin culpa molestado" ("so inconvenienced without guilt") (37.70.6). The from all appearances deeply held sense of shame and indignation at having been wrongly convicted is previewed here in lines that refer to "una vida casta, una fee pura / de *la fama y voz pública* ofendida" ("a chaste life, a pure faith, offended by *word-of-mouth and public fame*") (32.48.1–2), and that complain of how "[. . .] una falsa opinión que tanto dura / no se puede mudar tan de corrida, / ni del rudo común, mal informado, / arrancar un error tan arraigado" ("a false opinion that lasts so long cannot be altered so quickly, nor can an error so ingrown among misinformed, coarse people be uprooted") (32.48.1–8). A second and equally revealing play on words comes a few lines later, in the reference to Dido's story as a place where "os pueda *recrear* y *recrearme*" ("I might *entertain* both you [i.e., Philip] and *myself*") (32.50.8), on the one hand rehearsing the topos of the restorative pause from labor, on the other clearly voicing his desire, twenty years after the fact, to redress the wrong he had suffered by re-creating not only himself, but therewith the previously unblemished bond between monarch and servant. The closing lines of the introduction reiterate these themes, emphasizing how the *verdad* or truth of Dido's *historia* will lead to "honor restituida" ("restored honor") for an "inculpable vida" ("blameless life"), a life that a "ficción impertinente" or impertinent fiction had inadvertently condemned ("inadvertidamente condenado") (32.52.1–32.53.4).[73]

The truth about Dido that Ercilla's narrator is determined to assert is a direct challenge to rather than a *renovatio* of Virgil. It stems from Hellenistic accounts of the heroine that predate the *Aeneid* by more than three hundred years and survive into the early modern era via the Augustan historian Pompeius Trogus, whose *Historiae Philippicae* is reprised by Justin, widely read in the Middle Ages and Renaissance and especially popular in Spain, where a vernacular version of his work appeared in 1540.[74] Justin's account, a scant one hundred lines, describes

---

[73] While the details of Ercilla's encounter with battlefield justice are unclear, the incident appears to have stemmed from a potentially violent dispute over protocol between the poet and another aristocratic soldier during ceremonies led by the Spanish commander, García Hurtado de Mendoza. Ercilla's references to the event in Cantos 36 and 37 date the matter as occurring several months after the scenes discussed below. A contemporaneous account by Mariño de Lobera (*Crónica*, chap. 11) describes the context for how quickly the situation escalated into a capital offense as one of Spanish anxiety over the potential for revolt among soldiers, a situation they had just overcome in Peru two years earlier. Ercilla was precipitously sentenced to public beheading (36.33.4 and 37.70.4) and only reprieved at the last moment through the intercession of friends, his penalty commuted to banishment to Peru the following year, where he served a brief detention (37.70.5) before returning to Spain. That the affair continued to trouble him: "[. . .] el agravio, más fresco cada día, / me estimulaba siempre y me roía" ("the insult, fresher each day, was always inciting and gnawing at me") (36.36.7–8), is evident in these passages from Part III of the poem, which appeared some 30 years after the event. Cf. Medina, *Vida*, 77 ff.; commentary has long associated the *Araucana*'s lack of a celebrated leader or unifying hero to this incident; cf. Nicolopulos, "Reading," 235 ff.

[74] The earliest references to Dido are associated with the 4th-c. Greek historian Timaeus's history of Sicily, known principally through the 2nd-c. Polybius, in turn preserved in the work of the Macedonian rhetorician Polyaenus (fl. 150 CE). Justin's epitome of Trogus was popular in Spain in part because of its attention to Spain's fabled past; cf. María Rosa Lida de Malkiel, *Dido en la literatura española* (London: Tamesis, 1974), 59; Trogus is translated into Spanish by Jorge de Bustamante in 1540 (some fifteen years be-

the plot adopted by Virgil to the point of Carthage's success as a thriving metropolis, when the earlier tradition tells of Dido's being forced to marry the African
king Hiarbas or face the destruction of the city. Unwilling to break her vow to
Sychaeus but determined to protect Carthage, she kills herself instead, thereby
safeguarding both and establishing herself as an archetype of chastity.[75] Writers
contemporaneous with the Punic Wars were the first to devise a connection between Aeneas and Dido. They did so for the same reason that Virgil would two
centuries later, in order to explain the animosity between Carthage and Rome,
and they even anticipated the *Aeneid* in having Dido die of love for the Trojan
prince. This complex and contradictory prehistory of Virgil's heroine was familiar to ancient critics, who also identified various literary models for her including
Homer's Helen, Briseis, and Polyxena, as well as women in Euripides, Apollonius, and Catullus. The formidable difficulties of Homeric interpretation, well
known from Hellenistic scholarship, which recognized a deliberate frustration of

---

fore Hernández de Velasco's *Aeneid* in 1555); into English by Arthur Golding in 1564, as
Justins Histories from Trogus; cf. Rafael González Cañal, "Dido y Eneas en la Poesía Española del Siglo de Oro," *Criticón* 44 (1988): 25–54, at 26; for additional discussion of the
issues raised here, see Hexter's examination of what he terms "the overdetermined net-
work of possible associations and reflections" related to Dido ("Sidonian Dido," 332–84);
cf. Colin Burrow's exploration of the ambiguities of *pietas* in the Dido episode, which he
views as reflecting Virgil's complex imitation of the Homeric hero (*Epic Romance: Homer
to Milton* [Oxford: Oxford University Press, 1993], 38–51).

[75] According to Justin, the beautiful Elissa, daughter of the king of Tyre, married her
uncle Acherbas, a high priest whose great wealth led to his murder at the hands of Dido's
avaricious brother Pygmalion, when he succeeded to the throne. After an elaborate ruse involving dumping what appeared to be her fortune into the sea, Dido fled with her supporters, eventually arriving in Africa, where she offered to buy as much land as a single cowhide
would encompass. When the natives agreed, she had the hide cut into narrow strips and
laid end to end, acquiring the land where Carthage was founded and quickly flourished. A
neighboring king, Iarbas, attracted by the city's prosperity, threatened the leading citizens
with war unless they arranged for Dido to marry him. Afraid to convey the demand to their
chaste queen, the citizens devised their own charade, telling Dido that Iarbas was insisting
that they themselves come to his country to help educate his subjects, a task for which they
were unwilling to leave their homes and families. When Dido chastised them for refusing
to consider the well-being of the city before their own, they revealed the truth of the matter and the queen was caught in her own logic. Having built a great pyre, ostensibly to offer
sacrifices to placate the spirit of her dead spouse, Dido then killed herself instead, claiming
that she was going to join a husband as the citizens had demanded. Justin notes in closing
that Carthage was founded 72 years before Rome: *Justin: Epitome of the Philippic History of
Pompeius Trogus*, trans. J. C. Yardley (Atlanta: Scholars Press, 1994), secs. 18.3–18.9; his-
torians typically date the fall of Troy at 1183 BCE and the founding of Carthage circa 814,
some seventy years before Rome's traditional date of origin of 753. Given these dates, which
were widely agreed upon during late antiquity and the Middle Ages, the confluence of Aeneas and Dido was clearly excluded.

univocal readings in the *Iliad* and *Odyssey*, offered a clear precedent for such complexity.[76] Additionally, many educated Romans still read Greek during Virgil's lifetime, offering them ancillary access to the era's vibrant literary polyvalency. A significant pleasure of these early readers of the *Aeneid*, long since lost to all but a few classicists, must surely have been their recognition of how masterfully Virgil had interwoven competing strands of Dido's histories with the varied tales of Aeneas, adapting both to the enrichment of his own design.[77] Here as elsewhere a crucial component of Virgil's appropriation was his deliberate complication of key issues, most notably the origin of Aeneas' and Dido's erotic involvement, acknowledging Dido's fabled chastity even as he undermined it and entangling the intentions of both protagonists with those of the gods. Ovid is one of many subsequent authors unwilling to resolve the rich ambivalence of Virgil's character, referencing two portraits of the heroine: one, the sentimental, prolix lover of Aeneas in *Heroides* 7, vacillating between resignation and anger at being abandoned while bearing his child (133–135); the other no more than a footnote on betrayal in the condensed version of the *Aeneid* in the *Metamorphoses* (14.78–81). Part of what makes such ambivalence appealing as well as sustainable, beyond its adumbration of psychological complexity, is the deliberate ambiguity of Virgil's text.

With the end of antiquity and the demise of the gods Dido's fortunes shifted once again. The beautiful, chaste heroine of Justin persisted primarily in the ecclesiastical tradition inaugurated by Tertullian and Jerome, from whom it passed to Dante, Petrarch, Boccaccio, and Chaucer, and thence to many others, including Castiglione and Boscán.[78] A competing tradition presented the heroine as a victim of Fortune, captured in the pithy chiasmus of Ausonius's fourth-century epigram, widely anthologized in the Renaissance:

---

[76] The third-century Naevius is frequently identified as first to assert a connection between Aeneas and Dido, which Ennius and Varro maintain. Some have suggested that Naevius modeled his account on Apollonius' Hypsipyle and Jason; Varro's account has Dido die for love of Aeneas; cf. Lida de Malkiel, *Dido*, 57 n. 1. On the problems that Virgil and his contemporaries encountered in reading Homer, an activity they found "fraught with difficulty at every step," see Hexter, "Sidonian Dido," 335–36 and 364 n. 21.

[77] See Sergio Casali, "The Development of the Aeneas Legend," in *Companion*, ed. Farrell and Putnam, 37–51.

[78] Petrarch also relies on Justin and Jerome to refute Virgil's version of Dido in his *Africa*; Boccaccio's *De casibus virorum illustrium*, translated in the mid-fourteenth century by Pero López de Ayala, and his *De claris mulieribus* are among the important sources of the story for Spain. Dido appears in Chaucer's *Legende of Goode Women* as a heroine of classical antiquity, with no reference to Aeneas, and Chaucer's disciple Lydgate narrates Justin's version of events in his *Fall of Princes* (cf. Lida de Malkiel, *Dido*, 62, 82). Many Renaissance authors refer to Dido as a paragon of virtue, among them Ariosto, whose defense of her follows his remark that all poets exaggerate to flatter their benefactors, requiring that one invert what they say to discover the truth (35.27.5–8).

Infelix Dido, nulli bene nupta marito,
hoc pereunte fugis, hoc fugiente peris.

Ah! Luckless Dido, unhappy in both husbands: this one, dying, caused thy
flight; that one, fleeing, caused thy death.[79]

Commentators occasionally addressed the issue of conflicting versions of the
heroine. Servius complained of Virgil's anachronistic juxtaposition of historical
eras, and Macrobius explicitly distinguished between the *Aeneid*'s artful rendition of Dido and the truthful, though artless, account of the heroine offered by
earlier sources. Sidney, discussing the relative merits of poetry and history in the
Apology, will make a similar distinction, asserting that for purposes of "use and
learning" one should prefer "[. . .] the feigned Aeneas in Virgil than the right
Aeneas in Dares Phrygius."[80] An emphasis on Dido's betrayal is characteristic of
medieval accounts of the Trojan war, a key source of information on the subject
even after the recovery of authentic Homeric texts beginning with Petrarch. As
revealed by Sidney's remark, the absence of the gods in these accounts had an
even more dramatic impact on Aeneas than it did on Dido, with both Dictys and
Dares, the linchpins of the genre,[81] depicting his departure from Troy not as a
sacred mission to preserve the *penates* and found a new city, but as an act of civic
betrayal whose only purpose was to save his own skin. According to this tradition it was Aeneas' anxiety over the exposure of his cowardice that prompted his
leaving Carthage, not a god-inspired return to a mission that most medieval narratives completely ignored. While only a corrupt textual tradition combined with
a counter-classical sensibility could have proven so durable, the *Aeneid*'s own ambiguity surrounding its hero's final hours in Troy abetted such speculation, from

---

[79] English translation is from *Ausonius*, trans. E. H. Warmington, 2 vols. (Cambridge, MA: Harvard University Press, 1967), Appendix VIII, 2:289. Ausonius'
epigrams, popular in Siglo de Oro Spain, were printed in the 15th c. together with a Latin
version of the 10th-c. *Greek Anthology* (cf. Lida de Malkiel, *Dido*, 65). One of the early
Spanish translations of the distich is by Luis Zapata, a contemporary of Ercilla's who was
also an epic poet (*Carlos Famoso*, 1566) and also spent time in the Americas; Zapata's version of Ausonius's couplet is found in his *Miscelánea*, where he construes it as:
>Dido, con ningún marido
>de dos nunca bien casada;
>muerto uno, huyes, y ido
>otro, mueres con su espada.

Dido, well-married with neither of two husbands; one dead, you flee, and the other
gone, you die by your own sword (quoted in González Cañal, "Dido," 48).

[80] Cf. *An Apology for Poetry*, ed. Geoffrey Shepherd (Manchester: Manchester University Press, 1973), 110.

[81] See Sarah Spence, "*Felix Casus*: The Dares and Dictys Legends of Aeneas," in
Companion, ed. Farrell and Putnam, 133–46.

the circumstances in which he lost track of his wife to his disguising himself and his men in Greek armor. The worst possible interpretation is given the former by Ovid's Dido, who voices the distrust apparent in her Virgilian counterpart's final speech (*Aen.* 4.597–599), accusing Aeneas of lying about the death of Creusa, who, "occidit a duro sola relicta viro" ("perished, left behind by her unfeeling lord") (*Her.* 7.84). The precise nature of the latter, which Aeneas and his companions recount with some defensiveness at Dido's banquet, is still capable of generating discussion over the degree to which the maneuver was an offensive or defensive strategy. The issue is anticipated near the beginning of the *Aeneid* when Aeneas and Achates come upon Carthage's temple of Juno emblazoned with scenes of Troy's final battle (1.453 ff.), an encounter that prompts the hero's famous remark that "sunt lacrimae rerum et mentem mortalia tangunt" (1.462). While the phrase is generally construed along the lines of "here, too, there are tears for misfortune and mortal sorrows touch the heart," and while the temple decorations are understood by modern readers as illustrating Aeneas' heroic past, the medieval anti-Homeric tradition, in keeping with its view of him as a traitor, interpreted the words to signify not that the Carthaginians, like other civilized people, sympathized with hardship, but rather that Aeneas was distraught upon discovering his cowardice, i.e., his hiding in enemy armor, exposed to all.[82] Once again the mis-reading was likely emboldened by an ambiguity in the description a few lines later: "se quoque principibus *permixtum* adgnovit Achivis" (1.488), which, while usually translated similarly to "himself, too, in close *combat* with the Achaean chiefs, he recognized," has been parsed recently by those who note that it literally says nothing of combat, signifying only that Aeneas is "thoroughly *mixed in* with the Achaean chiefs," which might just as well reflect his attempt to pass undetected among them. The latter would certainly appear more plausible than having the decorations of the temple of Juno, fierce enemy of Venus and all things Trojan, celebrate the heroism of Aeneas.[83] Aeneas' treachery is associated with Dido's first appearance on the Iberian peninsula in two thirteenth-century

---

[82] Cf. Lida de Malkiel, *Dido*, 9.

[83] The donning of Greek armor by the Trojans, even as a purely offensive maneuver, is potentially less than heroic, as evidenced by the remark of one of Aeneas' companions: "dolus an virtus, quis in hoste requirat?" ("whether deceit or valor, who would ask in warfare?") (2.390). At Dido's banquet Aeneas seems to fear mixed reviews of the strategy since he defends himself so emphatically: "Iliaci cineres et flamma extrema meorum, / testor in occasu vestro nec tela nec ullas / vitavisse vices Danaum et, si fata fuissent, / ut caderem meruisse manu" ("O ashes of Ilium! O funeral flames of my kin! I call you to witness that in your doom I shunned not the Danaan weapons nor their answering blows, and had the fates willed my fall, I had earned it by my hand!") (2.431–434). Tertullian is another who identifies Aeneas and Antenor as traitors since they abandoned their companions while Troy was burning (*Ad nationes* 2.9 [PL 1. 598–599]); cf. Hexter, who characterizes Aeneas as a poor reader of what he sees depicted on the temple doors ("Sidonian Dido," 354–57).

texts, Rodrigo el Toledano's *Historia Romanorum*, which depicts the hero's cowardly escape from Carthage, and the *Castigos y documentos del Rey don Sancho*, which describes Dido's suicide as a reaction to her shame at having married a traitor. Both works are appropriated for the slightly later Alfonsine histories, the principal medieval source on Dido in Spain, which offer both versions of the heroine.[84] These secular medieval narrations, in contrast to the ecclesiastical tradition, reveal little interest in Dido's chastity, a theme that, after reemerging in the fifteenth century in works such as the *Crónica troyana*, peaks in the second half of the following one, possibly with Ercilla.[85]

Unlike earlier portraits, the *Aeneid*'s depiction of the association between Aeneas and Dido goes far beyond a retrospective determinism regarding the Punic Wars. The fact that Virgil has Venus introduce the heroine suggests the direction of her fate, and given the goddess's bias it is not surprising that her brief

---

[84] Two additional medieval works on the Trojan epic cycle deriving from Dictys and Dares are Benoît de Sainte-Maure's *Roman de Troie* and a work that borrows freely from it, the *Historiae destructionis Troiae* of Guido de Colonna. The former, via the *Historia troyana polimétrica* and Leomarte's *Sumas de historia troyana*, represents an additional source in Spain for a chaste Dido, subsequently incorporated into Mena's *Laberinto de Fortuna* and *Coplas contra los pecados mortales*; cf. Lida de Malkiel, *Dido*, 70–72. There are accounts of Dido in both the *Primera Crónica General* and the *General Estoria*, which comprise the Alfonsine histories. The former presents both versions of the heroine (chaps. 51–55; 56–57); the *General Estoria*, by contrast, portrays the heroic, solitary Dido, founder of Carthage; neither text is concerned with Dido's chastity; cf. Rina Walthaus, "La fortuna de Dido en la literatura española medieval (Desde las crónicas alfonsíes a la tragedia renacentista de Juan Cirne)," in *Actas del III Congreso de la Asociación Hispánica de Literatura Medieval (Salamanca, 1989)*, ed. María Isabel Toro Pascua (Salamanca: Biblioteca Española del Siglo XV, 1994), 2: 1171–81, here 1172–74. Judith Miller Ortiz explains the Alfonsine histories' incorporation of both versions of Dido as a response to changing concepts of history and literature exemplified in the decline of epic and the growth of didacticism: "The Two Faces of Dido: Classical Images and Medieval Reinterpretation," *Romance Quarterly* 33 (1986): 421–30.

[85] The Virgilian version of Dido and Aeneas is widely represented in Siglo de Oro literature, inspiring at least six *romances*. The topic typically focuses personal honor and chastity, largely ignored by the Middle Ages, while continuing the medieval attitude that minimized Aeneas' mission in favor of the love story. Garcilaso's *Copla V* consists of a free translation of the closing couplet of Ovid's *Heroides* 7; Lope de Vega's epistle, "Alcina a Rugero," referencing Ariosto, echoes Ovid's letter more fully. Góngora, by contrast, treats the story as a burlesque in his *décima* "Musas, si la pluma mía" (cf. González Cañal, "Dido," 38). Among dramatic works on the theme are Juan Cruz Varela's *Dido* (1536), the first Argentine tragedy, and Juan Cirne's *Tragedia de los amores* from the 1550s. Walthaus identifies the apogee of Siglo de Oro defenses of Dido with Ercilla ("La Fortuna," 1180). Alonso López Pinciano, author of the earliest substantial poetics in Spain, the Aristotelian *Philosophia Antigua Poética* (1596), and Francisco Cascales, author of the *Tablas poéticas* (1617), both cite Virgil's Dido as an example of poetic license.

remarks offer little to tempt her son from his purpose, never referring to Dido's beauty, to the cleverness by which she kept her husband's wealth, nor to her skillful purchase of land for the city. Noting that Dido and her followers had made it to Africa with her husband's wealth, she plays down personal agency, stating simply: "dux femina facti" ("the leader of the action was a woman") (1.364). At this point in the narrative, prior to recognizing the benefits of an erotic attachment between the two protagonists, Venus catalogues the distasteful issues associated with the queen, including the "secret horror" (1.356) of her family and the fact that her brother was "blinded by the lust of gold" (1.349), "grasping" (1.363), "monstrous in crime" (1.347), and the victim of *furor* (1.348). As the plot progresses, the narrator, by contrast, provides a more attractive portrait, enhancing Dido's Justin-inspired individuality even as he makes her a pawn of larger forces. He compares her beauty to the gods, transmutes her Punic guile into political wisdom, and, while having her succumb to sexual desire maliciously implanted by Venus, emphasizes her conjugal loyalty, which he casts in terms of the virtue of *pudor* and the importance of *fama*, self-respect and public reputation. His intimate depiction of Dido's struggle with her emotions, borrowing heavily from Apollonius, assures her genuine pathos, and although finally sacrificed to Aeneas' mission, it is a mission dictated by Destiny as shaped by the animosity between goddesses. When Dido and Aeneas finally come face to face, long after Venus has left the scene, they do so not only thematically, as Virgilian characters, but also structurally and, as it were, self-consciously, as textual traditions. Upon discovering that the strangers at her court are Trojans, Dido exclaims, "quis genus Aeneadum, quis Troiae nesciat [. . .]?" ("who could be ignorant of the race of Aeneas' people, who of Troy's town?") (1.565). When she meets the hero himself she is amazed, recalling her own youthful memories of stories of Troy and of Venus's having a child by Anchises, as though she can scarcely believe she is meeting a footnote to a marvelous tale of gods and heroes, a reaction possibly shared by Virgil's early readers. Once brought up to date on Aeneas' recent past—on the post-Homeric Aeneas-as-envisioned-by-Virgil, that is—she recognizes a similarity between them, proclaiming, "me quoque per multos similis fortuna labores / iactatam hac demum voluit consistere terra" ("Me, too, has a like fortune driven through many toils, and willed that at last I should find rest in this land") (1.628–629). By the time Virgil's revision of her own history is complete, their similarities will go far beyond what Dido can see, which, limited as it is includes the fact that not only are they both children of royal parents, were previously married, and have lost their spouses, but both have had to flee their homelands and make perilous journeys by sea, becoming exemplary leaders in the process. Were she visionary the unhappy queen would also see, as will readers of the *Aeneid*, that, however differently, both she and Aeneas colonize new lands, establish law-abiding cities, and oversee the transplantation of their respective cultures into new worlds. She would see as well that with each other they both experience their first emotional attachment since being widowed, a development

that forces both into ineluctable choices between public and private spheres, between duty and desire. Ercilla, while condemning Virgil for the liberties taken
with Dido's history, finds these passages as irresistible as most subsequent readers. Beyond adopting Virgilian names for queen and spouse, Ercilla's portrait of
Dido highlights conjugal loyalty, a concern with honor, and exceptional administrative skill, all emphases of Virgil. Even those Virgilian elements that Ercilla
rejects in his defense, notably Dido's unrequited love and the articulate, deadly
struggle it entails, he embraces elsewhere, such imagery generating many of the
intertexts already discussed.[86]

The *Araucana*'s account of Dido follows Justin in all key respects. Ercilla
enlarges upon details the ancient text only mentions, however, and introduces
new elements in order to construct a story that is more realistic, immediate, and
suspenseful. Most important, his innovations provide the plot with a moral and
legal rationale consistent with the *Araucana*'s treatment of the same key themes.
The defense focuses in particular on Dido's emotions, with numerous descriptions echoing earlier passages involving the Araucan heroines, e.g., "soltó con
doloroso y fiero llanto / de lágrimas un flujo en large vena" ("a great flood of tears
poured forth with a sorrowful, fierce cry") (32.57.2–3); and: "¡Ay!, que de tibia fe
y amor procede / no acabar de matarme el sentimiento" ("Oh, what tepid loyalty
and love I must have since this feeling doesn't kill me") (32.59.3–4).[87] The episode is particularly expansive on Dido's anger, offering her a nine-octave speech
in which she condemns Pygmalion, beginning with his transgressions against
the bonds of *hermandad* or brotherhood (32.61.2) and of family (32.62.2), like
Glaura's cousin (28.16.7–8), then moves on to his "sed de riquezas insaciable"
("insatiable thirst for riches") (32.61.5), "impiedad y furia insana" ("impiety and
insane madness") (32.61.7), and "inorme intento y desatino" ("enormous intention and folly") (32.63.1), all of which leave him "ciego de codicia" ("blind with
greed") (32.64.3). The jeremiad culminates in a clamor of epithets: "[. . .] traidor
[. . .] tirano, / perverso, atroz, sacrílego, homicida" ("traitor, tyrant, perverse,
atrocious, sacrilegious, murderous") (23.65.2–3). Being thought an accomplice
in the death of her husband is a primary concern for Dido (32.65.3–4), introducing the theme of honor long before the appearance of Iarbas. The narrator has
the heroine explore her predicament in detail, noting that if she flees Pygmalion

---

[86] Ercilla's Virgilian intertexts frequently reveal the same lines from the *Aeneid* adapted to multiple locations. They include, with regard to Guacolda: *Ar.* 13.48.4,
13.49.3, 14.1.8, and 14.3.4, for which see *Aen.* 1.688 and 4.66–69; for the Vision of Beauty: *Ar.* 18.66.4 and 18.71.5–6; cf. *Aen.* 1.659–660, 1.668, 1.713, 4.1–2, 4.68, 4.101, and
4.474–475; these last-cited passages are also appropriated for scenes involving Tegualda
(20.58.7–8, 20.61.5–6, and 20.62.4), as well as for scenes referencing the feelings of the
narrator (22.1.5–8), discussed above.

[87] With regard to Guacolda, see 13.47.7–8, 13.48.3, and 13.57.1; for Tegualda:
20.31.7–8, 20.32.5–8, and 20.76.1–2; for Lauca, see 32.36.1–2 and 32.39.1–4.

will pursue her; if she dies he will gain control of her wealth; and if she remains as she is she will be seen as content with events if not complicit in them, each of these alternatives destroying her *fama* and *opinión* (32.66.1–8). Her lament at this point: "¿Qué medio he de buscar a mal tan fuerte [. . .] " ("what remedy must I seek for an evil so great?") (32.67.1) echoes Tegualda quite closely ("¿Qué consuelo ha de haber a mal tan fuerte?" — "what consolation can there be for an evil so great?") (20.73.5), leading to a rationale for suicide reminiscent of earlier passages in the poem: "¡Ay!, que si es malo desear la muerte, / es peor el temerla, si conviene; / que no es pena el morir a los cuitados / sino fin de las penas y cuidados" ("Ah, if it is evil to long for death, it is worse to fear it if it fits, for dying is no burden to those afflicted, but an end to their troubles and cares") (cf. Ecclesiasticus 41:3–4) (32.67.5–8). The planning and execution of the scheme by which Dido escapes with Sychaeus' wealth dominates the episode, growing from Justin's twenty-three lines into twenty-five octaves, enhancing the suspense of the story. Emphasized once again are Pygmalion's "bárbara impaciencia" (32.85.5), "tiranía" (32.86.1; cf. 32.79.8), "impetu" ("impetuosity or violence") (32.86.2) and "furia *acelerada*" ("*violent* fury") (32.85.2), the last an unusual qualifier applied elsewhere to the Araucans and, notably, to the officer who sentenced Ercilla in his judicial ordeal.[88] Dido, by contrast, is the image of stoic fortitude, noting with regard to the dangers of the ocean voyage she is about to undertake: "[. . .] que están todos los bienes / sujetos a peligros y vaivenes" ("that all worldly goods are subject to dangers and fluctuations") (32.88.7–8). After a canto break and brief exordium presenting Pygmalion as someone whom greed has deterred from "la carrera de virtud fragosa" ("the rough road of virtue") (33.1.2.), ten octaves focus on Dido's accomplishments in Africa. The feint with the bull hide occurs as in Justin and Virgil, with Ercilla noting that although the people on whom it was perpetrated "[. . .] a la prudencia / de la Reina sagaz y aviso estraño, / le quisieron poner nombre de engaño" ("were inclined to call the prudence and rare precaution of the wise queen deception") (33.8.7–8), she compensated them well, "dejándolos contentos y pagados" ("leaving them paid and happy") (33.9.2). In contrast to the *Aeneid*, which refers only once to the queen's administrative skill ("iura dabat legesque viris" — "laws and ordinances she gave to her people") (1.507), Ercilla's text swells the praise of this quality into six octaves describing how "la prudente Reina" ("the prudent queen") (33.10.3) corrected "las faltas y defectos / al orden de vivir perjudiciales" ("the faults and defects prejudicial to

---

[88] In addition to its primary sense of acceleration, *acelerado* is used occasionally by Ercilla to signify violence: in three instances this usage concerns Araucan fighters (9.74.2), (29.32.2), and (29.53.2), the latter two both regarding the notably violent Tucapelo; a fourth instance, cited here, involves Pygmalion; the term's final usage is with regard to the young officer, ostensibly García Hurtado de Mendoza, a "mozo capitán acelerado" ("violent young captain") (37.70.2) who condemned Ercilla; cf. Lerner, *Araucana*, 241 n. 38 and 865 n. 130.

an orderly life") (33.10. 1–2), establishing institutions so that "[. . .] el pueblo en *razón* se mantuviese / y en paz y orden política viviese" ("the people might maintain themselves in *reason* and live in peace and order") (33.11.7–8). Such is her success that the city attracts many new citizens, who come to consider her a "milagro de natura" ("miracle of nature") (33.15.5) and a goddess (33.15.2). Her praise concludes with a list of virtues that no heroine since antiquity has ever combined, a recitation counter-balancing Pygmalion's evils recorded earlier: "fue rica, fue hermosa, fue castísima, / sabia, sagaz, constante y prudentísima" ("she was wealthy, beautiful, most chaste, she was wise, astute, loyal, and most prudent") (33.16.7–8).

The ruse involving Iarbas, Dido, and what Ercilla calls the Carthaginian senate occupies the next twenty octaves. Ercilla transfers the Virgilian attribute of amorous *furor* from Dido to the African king, correcting Virgil and reassigning the failure of continence to men, with whom he has consistently associated it. Dido's response to the ploy of the senate, which feigns resistance to Iarbas's supposed demand for help in educating his people, offers the first of the episode's two significant intertexts with Virgil, both based on Aeneas' speech of encouragement to his men after their shipwreck on the African coast. Having Dido deliver a variation on this address not only enhances her stature, but again corrects the *Aeneid*, returning the harangue, as it were, to its logically prior source. The speech is introduced with a reference to the queen as: "con alegre rostro y grave risa, / aunque sentía en el ánimo otra cosa" ("with cheerful countenance and grave smile, although she was feeling something different in her spirit") (33.27.2–3), lines that mimic Aeneas' similar dissemblance of optimism (*Aen.* 1.208–209).[89] The verses that follow expand her Justinic counterpart's exhortation to civic duty into a lecture on citizenship:

> Es a todos común, a todos llano,
> que debe (como miembro y parte unida)
> poner por su ciudad el ciudadano
> no sólo su descanso, mas la vida,
> y por *razón* y por derecho humano
> de justa deuda natural debida,
> a posponer el hombre está obligado
> por el sosiego público el privado. (33.29.1–8)

> It is common to everyone and applies to all that the citizen (as a member and united part) must risk not only his tranquility but also his life for his city, and obligated both by *reason* and by the just and natural debt of human law, man must postpone his private tranquility for that of the public.

---

[89] Cf.: "Talia voce refert, curisque ingentibus aeger / spem voltu simulat, premit altum corde dolorem" ("So spake his tongue; while sick with weighty cares he feigns hope on his face, and deep in his heart stifles the anguish") (*Aen.* 1.208–209).

She concludes by declaring that she would gladly avert the threat with her own life if it were possible (33.30.1–2). Realizing that she "en el armado lazo había caido" ("had fallen into the trap that was set") (33.31.3), the senate reveals the demand for marriage, reminding the queen that if she persists in "el casto infru-tuoso presupuesto" ("the barren cause of chastity") (33.36.2) she will be putting her own well-being ahead of the city's. Resigned, Dido asks for the same three-month interval found in Justin, expressing herself in terms very similar to Teg-ualda: "Que es mostrar liviandad y demás deso, / falto a la obligación y fe que debo / si del intento casto y voto espreso / a la primera persuasión me muevo" ("since it will show frivolity and, more than this, my failure in the obligation and loyalty that I owe if I deviate from my chaste intentions and explicit vow at first persua-sion") (33.39.1–4).[90] Such a delay is also desirable, "que el libertado *vulgo* maldi-ciente / aun quiere calumniar lo que es honesto" ("since the brazen, slanderous *masses* calumniate even what is virtuous") (33.40.5–6). Within a few octaves an-other close imitation of Virgil appears, in this instance of the opening line of Ae-neas' speech: "O socii (neque enim ignari sumus ante malorum)" ("O Comrades, for ere this we have not been ignorant of evils") (1.198 ff.), which is closely mod-eled by Ercilla's Dido: "¡Oh fieles compañeros, que contino / en todos los trabajos lo mostrastes [. . .]" ("Oh loyal companions, who continually have proved it in all your undertakings") (33.45.1–2).[91] Finally revealing her resolution to die, Dido tells the citizens not to mourn, "que una breve fatiga y muerte honrada, / ase-gura la vida y la eterniza" ("since a brief struggle and honorable death assure both life and eternity") (33.50.3–4). Expressing the pagan view of suicide that Ercilla himself has just repudiated in the scene with Lauca, she adds that, "no os debe de pesar si Dido muere, / pues vive el que se mata cuanto quiere" ("it shouldn't grieve you if Dido dies, since he who kills himself lives as long as he desires") (33.50.8). The narrator emphasizes, once again, that, "Éste es el cierto y verdadero cuento" ("this is the certain, true story") (33.54.1) that Virgil falsified "por dar a sus ficio-nes ornamento" ("in order to give his fiction ornamentation") (33.54.5), and the episode closes with a chiasmic crescendo of assonance and consonance that simul-taneously alludes to 1 Corinthians while overgoing Ausonius:

pudiéndose casar y no quemarse,
antes quemarse quiso que casarse. (33.54.7–8)

being able to marry and not burn, she preferred to burn rather than marry.[92]

---

[90] See 68–74, 79–80, supra.

[91] Aeneas' speech to his comrades is modeled on Odysseus' to his companions after Circe has warned him of the Sirens (*Od.* 12.154 ff.).

[92] Cf. 1 Cor. 7:9: "quod si non se continent nubant melius est enim nubere quam uri" ("But if they cannot contain, let them marry: for it is better to marry than to burn") (King James version); the Revised Standard translation makes the association between

It comes as no surprise that the three versions of Dido discussed here are determined primarily by their historical-cultural contexts. Justin's references to Tyrian wealth and his emphasis on the beautiful protagonist's cleverness, a positive trait to later biographers, belies the discomfort of his Greek sources with their Asiatic neighbors, whom they stereotype as full of Punic guile, starting with the queen and extending through the citizenry, as reflected in the parallel plots of their respective deceptions. In the *Aeneid*'s subordination of Dido's story to the plot of Augustan epic, by contrast, her beauty, intelligence, and cleverness embody the Homeric motif of erotic distractions to epic goals, presented in a way that grants the female genuine sympathy while reflecting unflatteringly on the hero and his project of nation-building. In contrast to Justin, Ercilla uses his version of the heroine to help refute a cultural stereotype of the Amerindians as lawless barbarians, even as his sympathetic portraits help establish the contrary cliche of noble savages. To the extent that Virgil enhances Dido's virtues, Ercilla absorbs them; the rest of the *Aeneid*'s portrait he ignores. His protestations notwithstanding, Ercilla's broader goals in the defense are not so different from Virgil's. Both authors use the story of Dido to counterpoint the heroic narratives that frame it; both juxtapose love to war and private to public good. In Virgil the eros-epos conflict is the heart of the tale, however, while in Ercilla, who foregrounds this opposition in each of the episodes already discussed, attention now shifts to the defense of individual honor that Virgil has sacrificed for personal gain, transgressing the "honestos límites" ("honorable limits") (28.12.4) of authorship, much as the behavior of Glaura's cousin exceeded the limits of *vergüenza* or shame. The focus of Dido's defense is thus quite distinct from Virgil, offering another example of feminine virtue in keeping with Ercilla's ongoing defense of women, yet imbuing this instance of the topic with an especially personal fervor in which Dido becomes the archetype par excellence of the Araucan women as well as an emblem of the poet's own unjust defamation.[93]

---

the flames of damnation and those of passion explicit: "But if they cannot exercise self-control, they should marry. For it is better to marry than to be aflame with passion"). Lida de Malkiel identifies this as Ercilla's only significant departure from Justin, noting that it reflects the New Testament's approval of remarriage after the death of a spouse (see 1 Cor. 7:39 and Rom. 7:2; cf. *Dido*, 131); Lupher argues that Ercilla takes the conceit from Tertullian's *Exhortation to Christianity: Romans*, 307.

[93] Dido as heroic colonist had a special place in the hearts of New World explorers, who identified with her skillful colonization and development of Carthage. In addition to Luis Zapata, noted earlier (102–3 n. 79, supra), Gabriel Lasso de la Vega, author of another early epic on the Spanish in Mexico, *Cortés Valeroso* (1588), pursued the Dido theme in two works: *La honra de Dido restaurada* (1587) and *Manojuelo de romances* of 1601. Fernández de Oviedo, the official *Cronista* of the Indies, includes a defense of Dido in his *Quincuagenas*, composed on the island of Hispaniola in the 1550s. These works are among those discussed by Roland Greene (*Post-Petrarchism*, 131–33, 149–58). While the Spanish may be alone in developing the defense of Dido into a genre, they are far from

Ercilla's defense of Dido is sometimes discussed in terms of a confusion of life and art, either admiringly noted as an example of passion bringing literature to life or gently derided as an instance of the naivete regarding genres still prevalent in the early modern era, a confusion parodied in Don Quijote's defense of Queen Madásima from the Amadís novels and largely resolved with the help of the Cinquecento debates. Distinctions between history and poetry have less to do with Dido's fate than the rise of humanism, however, whose revival of classical culture assembled a corpus of texts it promulgated at the expense of other, primarily medieval ones. While class played a role in the process, as popular traditions were suppressed in favor of authorized texts, its manifestation here reveals more about Ercilla than it does about socio-literary dynamics. The young soldier and his companions are presented as an unschooled, boorish *vulgo*, in contrast to the aristocratic poet, whose education and courtly ethics enable him to discern the truth among the competing narratives of the Carthaginian queen. It is the poet's distaste for the disparagement of women, however, combined with an emphasis on honor, particularly his own public honor or *fama* so unjustly defamed, that drives his rejection of the Virgilian Dido, not erudition or the confusion of history and fiction, a deliberate obfuscation he and many others, both before and after, rightfully attribute to Virgil. Ercilla's humanist education, on the other hand, prevents his following in the footsteps of those who accept the *Aeneid*'s plot while misreading its hero, and it also familiarizes him with Justin's history. The result is a paradox where Virgil, a central author in the humanist revival, is associated with popular taste easily swayed by the *Aeneid*'s salacious tale, while the Aeneas-free Dido, an archetype of chastity associated with medieval traditions, is championed by the educated, courtly narrator.[94] Today, by contrast, with humanist canonization long since accomplished and Ercilla's combat on behalf of the queen long since lost, the conundrum is even more pronounced, specialists alone being now familiar with Dido's earlier unsullied existence, while readers who know of her at all do so primarily through Virgil's indelible portrait (if not Purcell's opera).[95]

---

exercising a monopoly on the subject during this era. In addition to the English authors referred to earlier, Lodovico Dolce and Giambattista Giraldi are among the Cinquecento writers basing tragedies on the figure; cf. Lida de Malkiel, *Dido*, 69–70, 106.

[94] John Watkins argues that Renaissance debates over the humanist defense of poetry are inseparable from debates over Aeneas' abandonment of Dido, with those who question poetry's didactic value defending Dido or parodying events in Carthage, while their opponents not only endorse Aeneas' behavior but imitate his sacrifice in their own relationships to literary tradition, the epic hero's rejection of female sensuality thus becoming a topos of epic poets distinguishing themselves from suspect literary influences, primarily lyric: "Specter of Dido," esp. 4–5.

[95] On which see William Fitzgerald, "Vergil in Music," in *Companion*, ed. Farrell and Putnam, 341–52, at 342, 346–48.

Ercilla's defense of Dido begins as a clarification of the historical record combined with a welcome distraction for weary soldiers returning to camp. Refuting Virgil's portrayal of the Carthaginian queen soon grows into a full-throated rehearsal of the *Araucana*'s key themes, her experience providing the perfect opportunity to recapitulate the virtues of a just and civil society, of fortitude and self-control, conjugal loyalty, chastity, and, in particular, of personal integrity and honor. Emphasis on the latter results in the clearest depiction yet of Ercilla's own identity, going beyond the authorizing function of Virgilian *imitatio* to the assertion of his own authority and beyond his courtly defense of women to a ringing endorsement of Dido's devotion to husband and homeland, a testimonial that echoes his own to Philip II and Spain. These verses also allow Ercilla to present not only an alternative to Dido's story, but the melancholy suggestion of a different version of his own, not just a personal one in which his own *vida casta* and *fe pura* receive the acknowledgment they merit, but a broader one encompassing the Spanish presence in the New World and the suggestion of an alternative conquest. If the encounter with Cariolán offered a vision of native resistance overcome by humane treatment and mutual respect, Dido's history in Africa provides a concrete example of similar mien, a conquest in which settlement is based on mutually beneficial terms rather than inhuman brutality driven by craven self-interest and greed. The result is a *renovatio* not only of the classical tradition and of personal honor and reputation, but also of New World exploration and colonization, Ercilla's *razón de mí* a *cri du coeur* that resonates long after the episode has ended.

The righteous indignation of Dido's defense is rapidly lost in the octaves that follow, which detail, well into Canto 34, the capture and execution of Caupolicán. These scenes depict the protagonists of the Araucan wars at their worst, with the ferocious Indian leader, now bound in chains and publicly humiliated by his wife, the unlikely mouthpiece for a rational resolution of hostilities, echoing much of the poem's previous moralizing in such platitudes as: "[. . .] la ira / es en el poderoso impertinente" ("rage in the powerful is impertinent") (34.9.5–6), and "[. . .] a muchos vences en vencerte, / *frena* el ímpetu y cólera dañosa" ("you conquer many in conquering yourself, *rein in* your impetuousness and harmful anger") (34.11.1–2). While earlier examples of such paradoxical enunciations of virtue by the Araucan women were highly effective, the result here is grotesque, reflecting the deeply conflicted narration of what is to come. Caupolicán appeals for his life in a schizoid mix of Christian moralizing and grandiose threat, the latter exemplified in his famous response to any hope the Spanish may have had about ending the Araucan resistance by decapitating it: "No pienses que aunque muera aquí a tus manos, / ha de faltar cabeza en el Estado, / que luego habrá otros mil Caupolicanos" ("Don't think that if I die here at your hands the State will lack a leader, for there will instantly be a thousand other Caupolicáns") (34.10.1–3). When his offer to convert his people to Christianity and live in peace with the Spanish fails to beguile his captors, who condemn him to death by impalement combined with being shot by archers, he announces his conversion to Christianity and asks for baptism (a transformation as incredible as that of Tasso's Clorinda). This last request being not only granted but also enhanced by a summary catechism, a scene described as provoking a combination of pity and great contentment among the Spanish, ostensibly justified in their behavior (34.18.5–6), Caupolicán's final moments go some way toward resurrecting his dignity, an unexpectedly Christ-like figure: "Descalzo, destocado, a pie, desnudo" ("barefoot, bareheaded, on foot, unclothed") (34.20.1), who remains stoically impassive throughout the torturous execution: "No la muerte y el término excesivo / causó en su gran semblante diferencia" ("Neither his death nor the excessive measures caused any alteration in his stately countenance") (34.17.5–6). This final performance reinforces his ferocious reputation among his own people, who watch the proceedings in stupefied silence and dare not disrespect him even in death, his *fama*, ironically, intact to the end, unlike Ercilla's or Don García's.[96] The mix of revulsion and admiration not only for the emasculated Araucan leader but also for the inhumanly cruel Spanish erupts in an apostrophe, added to the second edition of Part III, which appeared within a year of the first, in which the poet assures Philip II that he was not present at the "barbaric" scene ("deste bárbaro caso") (34.31.3) and would have stopped it had he been. Not surprisingly, the brutal punishment has the opposite effect of what the Spanish desired: "antes de aquella injuria provocada / a la cruel satisfación aspira, / llena de nueva rabia y mayor ira" ("rather provoked by that injury it [the Araucan people] aspires to cruel satisfaction, filled with new hate and greater rage") (34.35.6–8), and the Indians soon gather to choose a new leader. The meeting quickly descends into chaos as various warriors boast of their prowess, however, replaying the dissension that threatened a similar convocation at the poem's start.

This unflattering view of the Araucans as incapable of self-government turns out to be the last the reader will have of them, as the poet abruptly breaks away from the scene to insert a two-and-a-half-canto recitation of an exploratory expedition he joined, which made its way south of the Araucan state across the formidable Andes, eventually reaching the gulf of Ancud half-dead from exposure.[97] Once again the account conjoins admiration with disillusion. The determination that drives the men across mountains that appear like a geological manifestation of Caupolicán's death threat: "[. . .] una sierra y otra sierra, / y una espesura y otra y otras ciento") ("one mountain range after another, and one dense forest and then another and then a hundred more") (35.17.3–4), as though the entire Southern Cone were rising up to resist the Spanish conquest, is nothing short of heroic. In the words of Don García they reach an "otro nuevo

---

[96] Cf. Padrón on the execution's complex inversion of gender roles in the context of the Spanish project in Chile ("Love American Style," 563, 575–76).

[97] The account, which begins at 34.44 and ends at 36.43, was added to the poem beginning with the 1597 Madrid edition; cf. Lerner, *Araucana*, 908 n. 62.

mondo" ("another new world") (35.6.1), a place, he assures them, "donde podrán mejor sin estrecharse / vuestros ánimos grandes ensancharse" ("where you will be able, without constricting yourselves, to better stretch your great spirits") (35.7.7–8), the image effectively materializing earlier uses of the conceit as a narrative space for refreshing the weary poet and reader. Once the tribes of the region have restored them through generous gifts of food and other assistance, however, the motivation for the Spanish accomplishment is revealed once again to be *interés* or self-interest (35.1–3), and any pretense of heroism is undercut by the narrator's remarkably frank declaration:

> Pero luego nosotros, destruyendo
> todo lo que tocamos de pasada,
> con la usada insolencia el paso abriendo
> les dimos lugar ancho y ancha entrada (36.14.1–4)

> But with our usual insolence, destroying everything we touch in passing, we immediately opened the way for these qualities [greed, evil, theft, and injustice, cited in the previous octave], offering them wide entry and ample space.

The final effect of the expedition: "plantó aquí la cudicia su estandarte / con más seguridad que en otra parte" ("greed planted its standard more securely here than elsewhere") (36.14.7–8). In contrast to this negative view of the Spanish, the people they encounter in the Chiloe archipelago are depicted as an innocent, Edenic race entirely free of such moral failures (36.3–10):

> La sincera bondad y la caricia
> de la sencilla gente destas tierras
> daban bien a entender que la cudicia
> aún no había penetrado aquellas sierras;
> ni la maldad, el robo y la injusticia [. . .] (36.13.1–5)

> The sincere goodness and charity of the simple people of these lands made it clear that greed had not yet penetrated those mountains, nor evil, theft, and injustice.

The idealization is reciprocal, with the natives addressing the fair-skinned, fair-haired, bearded strangers (*blancos, rubios, barbados*) (36.16.3) as "hombres o dioses rústicos" ("men or rural gods") (36.4.1). The narrator indulges his curiosity about these new people and their customs, making notes on habitat, diet, and behavior (35.19.1–2). Thinking of the importance of recording the Spanish presence in the area, he carefully carves his name and the date on a tree (35.29.1–8). For the brief period of the expedition the interaction between the two groups has been a courteous one (exploitation will come soon enough), and the encounter becomes, in stark contrast to the sordidness of the preceding events, a brief sojourn in a bucolic paradise.

The return of the Spanish to La Imperial is the setting for the festivities at which the altercation arises leading to Ercilla's judicial problems. After briefly relating the aspects of the case, noted earlier, the narrator ends Canto 36 and opens Canto 37, the last of the poem, which presents in sixty-five uninspired octaves a defense of Philip's annexation of Portugal. The case provides an opportunity to rehearse not only themes of just war and proper governance, on which the passage focuses, but also to highlight one last time the rational control of the emotions, since the death of King Sebastião in North Africa, the source of the succession dispute with Spain, is described as that of "un mozo ardiente, / movido sin razón" ("an ardent youth, impelled without reason [i.e., needlessly risking his own life]") (37.37.8). In ten concluding octaves the narrator returns to the theme of his arduous poetic undertaking now drawing to a close, reviewing his service to Philip both before and after the years he spent in the New World:

> ¡Cuántas tierras corrí, cuántas naciones
> hacia al helado norte atravesando,
> y en las bajas antárticas regiones
> el antípoda ignoto conquistando!
> Climas pasé, mudé constelaciones
> golfos innavegables navegando,
> estendiendo, Señor, vuestra corona
> hasta casi la austral frígida zona. (37.66.1–8)

> So many lands I traveled, crossing so many nations toward the icy north and conquering the unknown antipodes in the lower antarctic regions! I passed through climates, changed constellations navigating innavigable gulfs, extending your domain, my Lord, almost to the southern frozen zone.

The final lines invoking the image of the poet's vessel now brought to shore are disconsolate, alluding to the adverse fortune that leaves him far from his desired port (37.71.7–8), cornered by utmost misery (37.73.2), and bemoaning "el poco fruto que he sacado" ("the little benefit I have gained") (37.76.5). Having continued to serve on occasion as an emissary of the king during the years he worked on the *Araucana*, made royal inspector of books, and with the poem held in high esteem, there's good reason to believe the stance is largely rhetorical, an act of personal debasement before God and king. After years of witnessing the vagaries of royal power, however, a weariness with the courtliness of the court, the object of such derision in the *Faerie Queene*, may well be evident in this most courtly of poets, who brings the *Araucana* to an end looking forward to the merciful God of heaven, "que nunca su clemencia usó de arte" ("whose clemency was never artful [i.e., disingenuous]") (37.75.5).

The implications of narrative are harder to contain than those of deliberative rhetoric, and truth is one of the most surprising consequences of fiction.

Richard W. McCabe,
Spenser's Monstrous Regiment (5)

III. Shifting Strategies: Idealism and *Realpolitik* in Early Modern England

1. Courtiers, Humanists, and Reformers

In shifting focus from the Southern Cone of the Americas to the dramatically different topography of faery land and its analogues, it is worth pausing to recall how close the worlds of Ercilla and Spenser sometimes came, both during and after the first half of the sixteenth century, when the interests of Spain and England intermittently overlapped. In 1548 a fifteen-year-old Ercilla accompanied Prince Philip, only twenty-one himself at the time, on a state visit to Emperor Maximilian in Brussels. The entourage returned to Spain in 1551 via Trent, where the Council had just resumed after several years' suspension and was in the process of addressing some of its most critical issues.[1] Two years after Spenser's birth, in 1554, Ercilla was with the court in London for Philip's marriage to Mary, where part of the festivities included the staging of a chivalric joust between Spanish and English courtiers. Among the latter, and making one of their first public appearances since the execution of their father the year before, were the three Dudley sons, including Robert, earl of Leicester, Spenser's future patron.[2] It was during the court's stay in London that word reached it of the rebellion by soldiers in Peru, prompting the decision to send reinforcements, Ercilla receiving permission to join them. Three years later the Dudleys

---

[1] Suspended since 1547, the Council resumed in 1551 under Julius III, the eleventh through fourteenth sessions meeting in Trent from May through December. The meetings were crucial ones, affirming the Eucharist and refuting "the execrable errors and schisms which the enemy has in these our troubled times disseminated regarding the doctrine," establishing reforms for bishops and ecclesiastical courts, and expounding on the sacraments of penance and extreme unction (*Canons and Decrees*, trans. and ed. Schroeder, 72). In a splendid irony that life alone could create, the Council entertained Philip and the royal entourage with performances based on scenes from Ariosto (Medina, *Vida*, 28).

[2] The inclusion of the Dudleys in the jousts, an early step in the reversal of the family's fortunes, was due, in part, to Philip himself, who supported their participation as part of his effort to gain English support for the marriage; see Richard McCoy, *The Rites of Knighthood* (Berkeley: University of California Press, 1989), 31–32.

fought alongside the Spanish at San Quentin. Spenser's first published work, an anonymous translation of Petrarch, appeared in 1569, the same year as Part 1 of the *Araucana*. By the publication of *The Shepherds' Calendar* in 1579 relations between the two countries had deteriorated, exacerbated by Spain's occupation of the Low Countries, and by 1580 Spenser was on his way to residency in Ireland and already at work on his magnum opus, in which Philip, far from his days as royal consort, has become the enemy of Gloriana, Book 1's "proud Paynim king" (12.18.8). During these years the combination of resentment and condemnation of Spain's success in the New World manifest in the spread of the Black Legend, accelerated by the translation of Bartolomé de Las Casas's *Brevísima Relación* in 1583, and in fact it was the envy of New English settlers in Ireland that precipitated the first English version of the *Araucana*, evidence not only of the politicization of hermeneutics in the era of early modern globalization, but also of the fluidity of ideological association at the heart of the process. This translation, composed of the first sixteen cantos of the poem (through the opening of Part II), was by the Elizabethan statesman George Carew, intimately involved in Irish affairs from the 1590s and made president of Munster in 1600. Carew's translation, completed as early as the last decade of the century, is functional rather than literary, conveying the essentials of the Spanish military campaign against the Araucans, with particular attention to its early reversals. Unexpected is the degree to which the work evokes a parallel between the Araucans and the Irish and thus between the respective efforts by the Spanish and English to contain them, positing potential lessons to be learned from Spain's experience even as it promulgates anti-Spanish propaganda and indulges the cliche of linking the Irish with New World savages.[3] By 1619 a second translation of the *Araucana* had been generated by a similar conjunction of envy and indignation, this one including all but the last four cantos of the poem into Dutch. The context, in contrast to Carew, was the bitter Dutch revolt against Spanish occupation, and the corresponding associations, for some readers at least, were completely altered, now mapping a parallel between the calamity of the *Conquista* and events in the Low Countries and identifying the Dutch with the natives of Chile and Peru, who, during three embassies sent by the United Provinces between 1620 and 1640, were invited to participate with the Dutch in a joint *reconquista* of America.[4]

---

[3] *The Historie of "Aravcana". Written in Verse by Don Alonso de Ercilla. Translated out of the Spanishe into Englishe Prose allmost to the Ende of the 16: Canto,* ed. Frank Pierce (Manchester: Manchester University Press, 1964); cf. Pierce, *Alonso de Ercilla y Zuñiga,* 8, 25. Cf. Fuchs on epic as a "traveling genre" and on the *Araucana* as an example of the complexities of rhetorical production in "vexed political arenas" ("Traveling Epic," 384 ff.).

[4] Cf. Benjamin Schmidt, who notes that Willem of Orange's *Apologia* (1581) legitimized the American analogy, leading to the Dutch West India Company's efforts to enlist American natives in an alliance against Spain, envisioning "a cataclysmic uprising in America ignited by the Peruvians and fueled by soldiers of the Dutch Reformed

Enriching the context of such polymorphously perverse affiliations is the mix of admiration and distaste with which Spain was viewed as continuing the Reconquest proper on the Iberian peninsula against the Moriscos, which persisted side by side with the widespread cliche both in political pamphleteering and popular literature conflating Spanish and Moors. The era's confessional conflicts took full advantage of the potential for identity politics, and just as efforts were made to unify contending powers, particularly in joint offensives against the Turks, other schemes exploited these divisions, English religious reformers eliding anti-Catholicism with anti-Spanish attitudes and the all-too-real fear of Spanish interference in Ireland, while the conflation of Turks and Moors suggested more intimate contamination.[5] There is no evidence that Spenser was familiar with Carew's translation of the *Araucana*. The two men were surely acquainted, however, since Spenser was Deputy Clerk of Council in Munster from 1584 and succeeded to the clerkship itself in 1589, during a period in which Ireland played an increasingly significant role in England's image of itself.

While Ercilla and Spenser both were shaped in large part by the *translatio studii* of classical antiquity and early modern Italy, Spenser, unlike most of those inspired by these movements, who turned decisively away from the Middle Ages, was at pains to preserve substantial components of England's medieval heritage, literary and linguistic, which he saw as expressing an essential religious and national identity. In contrast to the humanist canon, English native tradition was built on the genres of satire, complaint, and allegorical eclogue, components of a heritage headed by Chaucer, whom many in Tudor society considered a Protestant forerunner. As the new Italianate poetry, associated most closely in England with the works of Sir Thomas Wyatt and Henry Howard, earl of Surrey, gained influence among Tudor authors, this older, popular tradition persisted, achieving a degree of canonization during the Edwardian era that was reversed during the reign of Mary, which saw the presentation of Wyatt and Surrey as poets of courtly love in *Tottel's Miscellany* of 1557, the mid-century's most important collection of

---

Church." The effort, fueled in part by admiration for the warlike portrait of the Araucans drawn by Ercilla and conveyed by Isaac Iansz Byl's translation, failed conclusively when the Dutch, initially welcomed, revealed their corollary interest in gold. Byl's translation represents the first known reference in print to Ercilla's supposed anti-Spanish and pro-Indian sympathies ("Exotic Allies: The Dutch-Chilean Encounter and the [Failed] Conquest of America," *Renaissance Quarterly* 52 [1999]: 440–73).

[5] Lara Vila i Tomás notes that in spite of the exoticism of the *Araucana*'s American matter the poem never stopped being a reflection of the conflict between East and West occurring at that moment in Europe ("Épica y imperio: Imitación virgiliano y propaganda política en la épica española del siglo XVI", [Ph.D. diss., Universitat Autònoma de Barcelona, 2001]).

verse.[6] In spite of the her identification as a Protestant, Elizabeth's rise to power did not include a revival of the reforming aesthetic, since her secular inclinations, together with a growing distrust of reformers and anxiety over the social unrest with which their predecessors were associated, insured that their poetry remained out of favor. An underlying association between the courtly aesthetic and Catholicism persisted, while the older tradition continued to exert a special attraction for religious reformers, who conflated ideas of pure poetry with pure faith and appreciated not only the ideological contrast such verse offered to the *maniera ariotesca* but also its appeal to a less educated, uncourtly audience. The archaic language of this tradition held similar connotations for Spenser. In contrast to Ercilla, Spenser also drew enthusiastically on medieval romance, which provides the *Faerie Queene* with key motifs as well as with the quest structure of each book. As discussed above, such literature in Spain was identified with the *Amadís* novels, attacked for their outlandish fantasies, Horace's *aegri somnia*, as well as their immorality. The chivalric heritage appropriated by Spenser, by contrast, was that of the Franco-Burgundian tradition, the Arthurian material of which supplied him with legends of national origin, scarcely less fantastic, together with the basis for a militant Protestant chivalry, while popular medieval romances offered tales of love and adventure. Renewed interest in the Franco-Burgundian matter, which provided a literary model for the relationship between sovereign and courtier, underlay a revival of chivalry by the Tudors in the late fifteenth century. This multifaceted renewal, enacted in processions, masques, jousts, and other performances, particularly those related to Elizabeth's Accession Day, ritualized the central tension in Tudor politics between honor and obedience, represented by the rights of knighthood on the one hand and those of royalty on the other. Chivalry enacted a compromise between these forces, symbolized in the knight's balance of deference and aggression, which remained largely intact until the Essex rebellion at the century's close.[7]

The relations Ercilla and Spenser envisioned themselves enjoying with their monarchs, the one unswervingly devoted, if dis-located, the other a "reluctant royalist," in Willy Maley's words, were central to their choices of historical epic on the one hand and "historicall fiction" on the other.[8] Having distinguished between the pleasing variety of historical examples and the stridency of philosophical precepts in the "Letter to Ralegh," a difference he associates with the attention span of readers, Spenser proceeds to identify his method with a

---

[6] And cf. *Richard Tottel's Songes and Sonettes: The Elizabethan Version*, ed. Paul A. Marquis, MRTS 338 (Tempe: ACMRS, 2007).

[7] Cf. Guy, *Tudor England*, 423–26; cf. McCoy, *Rites of Knighthood*, esp. 2–5.

[8] See Willy Maley, "How Milton and Some Contemporaries Read Spenser's *View*," in *Representing Ireland: Literature and the Origins of Conflict, 1534–1660*, ed. Brendan Bradshaw, Andrew Hadfield, and idem (Cambridge: Cambridge University Press, 1993), 191–208, at 201.

third way, one in which such examples are "clowdily enwrapped in Allegoricall deuices" (757), which he fears may prove unpleasant for their excessive oblique-ness. He attributes the need for this approach to current usage, where "[. . .] all things [are] accounted by their showes, and nothing esteemed of, that is not delightfull and pleasing to commune sence" (757). As has long been recognized, equally important, given the realities of Elizabethan politics, was the need for discretion and the plausible deniability his procedure made possible, a virtue fre-quently noted by E. K. in *The Shepherds' Calendar.*[9] An illuminating contrast to Spenser's guidelines in the "Letter" for reading his poem is found in the first of the commendatory verses accompanying the work, a sonnet by none other than Ralegh himself. Rather than dwell on the schema of moral virtues or epic gene-alogy, Ralegh's encomium, after noting that the spirit of Homer grieves at being upstaged, concentrates on the poem's imagined impact on Petrarch, whom he envisions as devastated upon seeing the Graces of love and virtue abandon their vigil at Laura's tomb to attend the Faerie Queene. The image cuts to the chase, as it were, exposing the inescapable conflation of literary and political dynam-ics in the Tudor context. It also reveals stark differences between Spanish and English Petrarchism, with the fact of a female monarch who encouraged a cult of unattainable chastity transforming the absent object of desire from an ethe-real Laura to an equally idealized Cynthia in Ralegh's verses or to Gloriana in Spenser's, while the frustrated lover was all too often a Ralegh or an Essex.[10] Enriching such associations was the English Petrarch's affiliation with Chaucer and the medieval proto-Protestant tradition, whose reading of the *Canzoniere*'s verses about historical events and figures, especially those criticizing the papacy, encouraged reformers to view the Italian poet as a Protestant prophet. Repre-senting a fundamental dissonance with the spirit of iconoclasm, by contrast, was the inherent idolatry of Petarchan efforts to "render presence" with regard to the absent object of desire, an undertaking the reformers were bent on annulling in the religious sphere. The distinction between image and essence at the heart of iconoclasm can be seen as a logical extension of humanist textual criticism, in

---

[9] With so much attention devoted to Spenser's own directions for reading his poem, it is important to note that in the first edition of the work, in 1590, the "Letter" appeared at the rear of the volume, between the end of the text and the commendatory verses, and that in the 1596 and folio 1609 editions it did not appear not at all. In the folio 1611 edition of the collected works the "Letter" reappeared, again at the volume's close, and it was only in the eighteenth century that the "Letter" began to precede the text and to exert the influ-ence with which it is currently associated; cf. Darryl J. Gless, *Interpretation and Theology in Spenser* (Cambridge: Cambridge University Press, 1994), 48.

[10] Cf. Louis Montrose, "The Elizabethan Subject and the Spenserian Text," in *Lit-erary Theory / Renaissance Texts*, ed. Patricia Parker and David Quint (Baltimore: Johns Hopkins University Press, 1986), 303–40, at 319–23); Greene, *Post-Petrarchism*, 131–32; and Colombí-Monguió, *Petrarquismo.*

which the attention to language highlights the difference between sign and sig-nified. A similar thrust propels the humanist exegesis of scripture, where the goal of correct reading underlines the distinction between text and message. For its part, the focus of reformers on inward feelings rather than outward forms and on the individual as the recipient of grace and the starting point in a personal discovery of justification by faith offered an alternative to the Petrarchan dis-course of self and subjectivity.[11] Additionally, Protestantism's emphasis on inter-pretation saw rhetoric as a tool for decoding as well as encoding speech and thus as important to readers as well as producers of verbal art. This expanded role for rhetoric corresponds to the alternation of deliberative and epideictic modalities that cycles through oratory's history, and Spenser's allegory reflects, in part, the same cycle, as well as the precarious *rapprochement* in England between religious sincerity and the sophistication of courtly aesthetics.

The development of the new poetry in England reveals both similarities to and differences from corresponding Spanish developments. As there had been earlier in Spain, there was a pervasive sense of cultural belatedness among Eng-lish humanists. In contrast to Spain, where the vernacular developed hand in hand with early humanist scholarship, in England frustration was expressed not only over what was seen as the backwardness of poetry but over prose as well, with calls for the improvement of both persisting throughout the century. The poets most responsible for introducing the new verse forms into English, Wyatt and Surrey, resemble Boscán and Garcilaso in their efforts to develop a courtly, aristo-cratic literary voice based largely on the *Canzoniere*, and while the similarities are largely formal, the cultural polyvalencies that undergird both developments are striking.[12] Wyatt, who introduced the rhyming pentameter sonnet into English, resided in Spain from 1537 until 1539 as Henry VIII's ambassador to Charles V.

---

[11] Cf. David Norbrook's discussion of the reformers' attacks on natural signs, among which the Eucharist was a primary target (*Poetry and Politics in the English Reformation* [London: Routledge, 1984], 33–36). Linda Gregerson discusses the concomitant strate-gies adopted by Christian poets to distinguish their works from idols (*The Reformation of the Subject: Spenser, Milton, and the English Protestant Epic* [Cambridge: Cambridge Uni-versity Press, 1995], 3–4); Greenblatt argues that the emphasis on Protestant in contrast to Catholic interiority is misleading, since the church had focused on the inner life of the individual over a period of centuries (*Renaissance Self-Fashioning*, 99); cf. Burke, *Fortunes of the Courtier*, 108.

[12] These calls are frequently identified with Thomas Elyot, who in *The Boke named the Gouernour* (1531) encouraged his countrymen to undertake the cultural translation already accomplished by the French, Italians, and Germans (the Spanish notably absent); and with *Tottel's Miscellany* (1557), whose preface urged English poets "to purge that swinelike grossenesse" characteristic of their previous efforts. In *The Scolemaster* (1570), by contrast, Roger Ascham complained of those who "[. . .] follow rather the Gothes in Ryming, than the Greeks in trew versifying." Wyatt's and Surrey's works were known primarily through *Tottel's Miscellany* (see Marquis, *Tottel's Songes and Sonettes*). By the end

Surrey, in addition to his sonnet translations and experiments with verse forms, translated Books 2 and 4 of the *Aeneid*, refining the unrhymed iambic pentameter of blank verse in the process.[13] Wyatt's and Surrey's efforts to establish a poetic discourse based on courtly life, later codified in Puttenham's *The Arte of English Poesie* (1589), were at the heart of a vernacular, national humanism that, while multi-cultural in its roots, superseded the international, Latin humanism of Sir Thomas More, William Grocyn, and Thomas Linacre.

Concurrent with the intermittent but steady progress in England of courtly poetics over native prosody, courtly discourse gained dominance over the discourse of civic humanism. This development, as noted earlier, was a broad one, arising from the centralization of power in the new monarchies. In England, the shift from political to literary discourse reinforced the identification of poetry with pleasure rather than duty, a difference reflected in the majority of Elizabethan poets describing themselves as amateurs and their writing of verse as youthful frivolity, eventually superseded by a return to public service as adults.[14] While this contrast of pleasure and utility reflects the *delectare-docere* distinction and ultimately suggests the venerable oppositions of philosophy to rhetoric and poetry, the underlying moralism of which emerges full-throated by the end of the cinquecento debates over epic and romance, the contrast of amateur and professional, a distinction that almost always mirrored that of nobility and commoner, emerges squarely from the milieu of Castiglione's *Courtier* with its emphasis on *sprezzatura* and the avoidance of anything demonstrably labor-intensive. The discourse of the reformers, by contrast, by turns deliberative, epideictic, and prophetic, contrasted with that of both humanism and courtliness, opposing what has been described as the latter's culture of performance with its own culture of sincerity.[15] Elements of secular humanism offered a potential link between courtiers and reformers, as well as generally between Catholics and Protestants, both of whom emphasized the textuality of scripture, as manifest in authors as diverse as Erasmus and William Tyndale. One of the only areas in which these competing ideologies coincided was in their opposition to popular culture: in the case of reformers, in spite of their adoption of popular verse traditions; for humanism, in spite of its popularization of the New Learning, particularly by Peter Ramus; for courtly culture, which opposed the popular by definition, in spite of the emphasis it placed on vernacular in contrast to Latinate learning.

A clear indication of the crossover appeal and ultimate triumph of courtliness by the mid-1500s was the translation of *Il Cortegiano* by Sir Thomas Hoby,

---

of the century Boscán and Garcilaso were highly esteemed among Elizabethans, being featured as positive examples in Abraham Fraunce's *The Arkadian Rhetorike* (1588).

[13] Braund, "Foreignizing Translations," 460–62.

[14] Cf. Richard Helgerson, *Self-Crowned Laureates: Spenser, Jonson, Milton, and the Literary System* (Berkeley: University of California Press, 1983), 22–26, 37, 48.

[15] Cf. Burke, *Fortunes*, 109.

one of a circle of pre-Elizabethan Protestant intellectuals at Cambridge, who in the preface to his work joined those calling for the improvement of the English vernacular through the study of classical languages, so that "we alone of the worlde maye not bee styll counted barbarous in oure tungue, as in time out of minde we have been in our maners."[16] Although Hoby is believed to have completed the translation by 1555, publication of it was delayed until 1561, several years into the reign of Elizabeth, at which point it was printed with a letter of dedication to Lord Henry Hastings, earl of Huntingdon, a well-known Puritan supporter of preachers. Two passages in Hoby's letter are especially noteworthy. The first is the identification of the *Cortegiano* with Cicero's *Orator*, revealing the degree to which, at this stage in Castiglione's English reception, he was seen as proposing a vision of the active life based on Ciceronian idealism and Neoplatonism. The second, a reference to the readers of the work, of whom Hoby voices a desire "[. . .] to fill their minde with the morall vertues, and their body with civyll conditions [. . .]" (9), not only offers an unexpected homology with Spenser's stated purpose in the *Faerie Queene*, but exhibits the extent to which, as it had in the *Orator*, the ideal civic life was believed to rest on moral virtue, itself the prerequisite of accomplished oratory. Assisted by the imprimatur of figures like Sir John Cheke and Roger Ascham, Hoby's translation was well received, even among Christian humanists who were aesthetically and morally more conservative, desirous of enhancing the vernacular with classical languages, on the one hand, yet already wary of the threat posed by Italian morals, on the other, a concern that within a few years would dominate all others. At this point in its reception, however, the *Cortegiano* provided a true bond between Italian humanists and religious reformers, reassured by Castiglione's appeal to Aristotle's *Ethics* in making magnanimity the foundation of *sprezzatura*, as well as appreciative of the *Cortegiano*'s emphasis on self-dependence and self-assertion.[17]

---

[16] Citations of Hoby's work are from Walter A. Raleigh, ed., *The Book of the Courtier*, trans. Sir Thomas Hoby (New York: AMS Press, 1967). For more on the circle of Protestant intellectuals at Cambridge, which included William Cecil, Roger Ascham, and Sir John Cheke, see Burke, *Fortunes*, 64.

[17] Hoby, who spent time in Italy in 1549–1550 and again in 1554, was entertained in Siena by Diego Hurtado de Mendoza, the Spanish luminary; cf. Raleigh, *Courtier*, "Introduction," xxxii, lxiv. The *Ethics* describes the desire for honor as the quality of magnanimity (4.3).

2. From the Corruption of *Cortegianía* to Christian Civility

After its apotheosis in rituals of courtly magnificence that characterized much of the Elizabethan era, *cortegianía* fell from grace in the closing years of the century.[18] Some have argued that the period preceding this development was one in which the suppression of civic humanism resulted in a net gain for English poetry, with the rules of courtly aesthetics providing direction for a new poetics, while the playfulness of courtly irony ensured poetry an audience more accustomed to religious earnestness.[19] To the extent that the monopolization of power forced the sublimation of political action, resulting in strategies of indirection constituting tropic structures per se, the same might be posited for other early modern societies beside England. The *Cortegiano* itself embraces the potential for such an impact when its rules for courtly demeanor are extended to writing. Garcilaso explicitly linked the two in praising Boscán's translation of Castiglione for its lack of *afectación*, originally employed as a behavioral trait. In Elizabethan England, by contrast, where the tradition of pre-courtly, popular verse was linked with opposition to official policy, the melding of courtly and literary aesthetics took a more complex path and assumed political significance it lacked in Spain and Italy.

Part of Hoby's justification for translating *Il Cortegiano* had been to counter distortions of it by those who were familiar only with fragments of the text. Even with better knowledge of the work, its reception changed substantially during its sixteenth-century migration north. On the one hand it was filtered through the same didactic utilitarianism that humanism had been, the subtleties of its artful exchanges increasingly reduced to rules of etiquette. On the other hand the ethical implications of its ideals were exaggerated, revealing themselves to readers like Harvey and Sidney as capable of inspiring virtuous behavior, while others, Spenser eventually included, saw them as threatening moral corruption. The gradual dominance of this darker view was driven by the corruption associated with Elizabeth's final decade in power, and, specifically, by changing perceptions of *sprezzatura* and *dissimulazione*, the former increasingly viewed as it was by Sidney's biographer, Fulke Greville, who referred to it as "that hypocritical figure Ironia," simultaneously damning as wanton deceit rhetorical or performative modes that ventured beyond the literal; the latter now being seen as a principal rather than subsidiary attribute of the courtier and equated with deception designed to maintain the favor of the prince, in contrast to its original role as an aesthetic component of behavior that skirted disagreement through artful indirection. This shift in perception was exacerbated by confessional conflict,

---

[18] Cf. Norbrook, *Poetry and Politics*, 31; Burke notes that the term *cortegianía* emerged as part of the institutionalization of Castiglione's concepts (*Fortunes*, 31).

[19] Javitch, *Poetry*, 107.

resulting in the *Cortegiano*'s appearance on the Tridentine Index of 1564 and the Catholic Index of 1590.[20] An expurgated edition of the text was published in 1584; with the exception of a few years in the 1590s this was the only version of the work recognized by the Catholic church until 1966. Similar injunctions extended to Spain, which saw no edition of the *Courtier* between 1573 and 1873. Prior to its northern progression and the ensuing translations, commentaries, and imitations, Castiglione's text had emphasized the balancing of viewpoints and sublimation of competitiveness. While at times largely formal, the autonomy of its speakers was at other times entirely genuine, resulting in *aporia* rather than unequivocal conclusions. These qualities were lost in the work's northern *translatio*, which transformed not only its content but its form, suppressing its originally dialogic quality.

The emphasis on the utilitarian and ethical aspects of courtliness were articulated in a particularly English fashion by Harvey and Sidney. Harvey, an admirer of Machiavelli, whose focus on the *realpolitik* of how the prince maintained power explored the obverse of Castiglione's emphasis on the demeanor necessary to serve such a figure, was associated with the articulation of a pragmatic humanism and, in particular, with the effort to distinguish rhetorical production from its moral foundation. This approach viewed flattery as practical rather than performative and courtly speech as a spur to action, reflecting the influence of Ramus, whose pedagogical focus inspired his reduction of rhetoric from the welter of stylistic refinements with which it had become identified to a system of universally applicable interpretive strategies.[21] Sidney's significance for English letters has similarities to Garcilaso's for Spain. Both men, in addition to their stature as preeminent poets, were viewed as ideal embodiments of courtiership combined with soldiery, and Sidney's death in 1586, shortly before his thirty-second birthday, from a minor wound suffered in an inconsequential skirmish between English forces and the Duke of Alba, recalls the death of Garcilaso, who perished at the age of thirty-five after being injured in an attack on a insignificant watchtower while traveling as part of the bodyguard of Charles V. Like Harvey, Sidney was associated with the Leicester faction: sober, practical nationalists with moderate Puritan sympathies. In the 1580s he authored the best-known poetics of the period, *An Apologie for Poetrie*, in an atmosphere of increasingly moralistic discourse, evident earlier elsewhere in attacks on romance. The *Apologie* foregrounds the tensions among courtliness, humanism, and Protestantism, the first acknowledged through its association with Surrey, one of the

[20] Cf. Burke, *Fortunes*, 109.
[21] Cf. Grafton and Jardine, *From Humanism to the Humanities*, 189. Hubert Languet, a close friend of Sidney's, was personally acquainted with Ramus; Abraham Fraunce, who resided at Leicester House during the same period as Spenser in the 1570s, in the early 1580s authored the *Shepeardes Logike*, a work suggesting a combination of Ramism with Spenser's allegorical pastorals; cf. Geoffrey Shepherd, "Introduction," in *Apology*, 34.

only poets Sidney refers to with admiration, the didacticism of the second and the moralism of the third evolving, via Neoplatonism, into a vision of poetry as a spur to virtue. The humanist pedigree of Sidney's poetics is particularly clear in its engagement with rhetoric, which, in contrast to scholasticism's emphasis on logic, saw the expression of ideas as inextricably bound to their content. While the same perspective spurred Spenser's view of the specificity of history as more persuasive than the abstract principles of philosophy, Sidney, distrusting the restrictions that particularity imposed on history, transformed the opposition. What emerged in its place was a Neoplatonic celebration of poetry for the access it offered, through the imitation of nature unfettered by particularity, to the universal design of reason in human affairs, which neither history nor philosophy could attain. Sidney's argument has been taken as evidence of his familiarity with Amyot's foreword to his translation of Plutarch's *Lives* (1559), which argued that history was preferable to moral philosophy for instructing the reader in virtue, Sidney ostensibly substituting poetry for history. A more straightforward and more likely explanation may stem from his familiarity with Amyot's earlier preface to his translation of the *Aethiopica*, discussed above, which sought to ameliorate the unpleasant specificity of history's *ab ovo* methodology by combining it with probable fiction or *contes fabuleux*.[22] The conflation of poetic virtuosity with virtue per se and the consequent shift from courtliness as enabling good verse to good poetry as inspiring good action reflects, in part, the beginning of the courtier's fall from grace. Sidney's response was to rescue poetry from its detractors by imbuing it with a mission, countering the moralism of Puritans like Stephen Gosson, whose attack on the perceived depravity of English drama was the original stimulus for Sidney's treatise.[23] The *Apologie* also inscribes a radical break with Petrarchan self-absorption while reflecting the need that was felt in the wake of the Counter-Reformation for a comprehensive Protestant theory of art. Influenced by Italian writers on painting and architecture, Sidney refined his vision of poetry's access to the universal into the concept of a poem's "fore-conceit" or guiding Idea. The thesis is invoked by Spenser in his "Letter

---

[22] Cf. Anthony Miller, "Sidney's *Apology for Poetry* and Plutarch's *Moralia*," *English Literary Renaissance* 17 (1987): 259–76. Sir Thomas North translated Amyot's translation of Plutarch's *Lives*, including the interesting "Aux lecteurs," into English in 1579. Amyot derived his conflation of history and *contes fabuleux* from Strabo's analysis of poetic invention; see 17 ff., *supra*; Amyot's text is reprinted in Appendix B. On the appeal that Platonism held for many Puritans due to its emphasis on purity, internality, and the directness of the individual path to divine truth, see Guy, *Tudor England*, 413.

[23] Gosson's work, *The Schoole of Abuse* (1579), was dedicated to Sidney; for contextualization of Gosson and Sidney, see Clare Carroll, "Humanism and English Literature in the Fifteenth and Sixteenth Centuries," in *The Cambridge Companion to Renaissance Humanism*, ed. Jill Kraye (Cambridge: Cambridge University Press, 1996), 246–68, at 257–59.

to Ralegh," where he describes an image in the artist's mind that regulates all aspects of his work, enabling the creation of a second or "other nature," in imitation of the work of God.[24]

Sidney's ambivalence toward courtliness, a milieu in which, unlike those of humanism or Protestantism, women played more key roles, is echoed in the passive-aggressive posture Leicester's party maintained with the monarchy. Among the group's domestic policy disappointments were the pace of religious reform, which led to anti-Catholic rhetoric being used against Elizabeth herself, and the queen's posture toward marriage, which after resisting for many years she considered with the duke of Alençon. In foreign affairs the apocalyptic world-view of Puritanism encouraged militant policies, from the Low Countries, where the tepidness of official support for their Continental co-religionists was especially galling, to relations with Spain, whose Catholicism made it a constant object of distrust by this point in the century.[25] Political and religious moderates, by contrast, usually identified with Leicester's chief rival at court, William Cecil, were likely to emphasize the uniqueness of the Church of England, which they saw not only as a compromise between Catholicism and Protestantism, but also, given the distinction it made between English Protestants and their foreign counterparts, as an impediment to any meddlesome common cause between the two. Such considerations colluded in a particularly frustrating manner with regard to Ireland, where a combination of the shifting priorities of successive Tudor governments and fiscal limitations that often proved more significant than political ones resulted in repeated changes in policy. Disagreements over how best to control the island typically pitted Leicester's faction against Cecil's moderates, with the former focusing on the morality of the situation, on the one hand, which it viewed as hopelessly depraved, and on its practical prospects, on the other, with the island seen as ripe for colonization. For those advocating increased intervention, the overlap of religious, political, and economic concerns eventually made common cause, with the island's perceived pastoralism identifying it as a natural target for reformers, who saw the degenerate Irish as requiring a reformation equal to that of Catholicism. Given the Calvinist conflation of idleness and immorality, plans to address these issues most often included the reorganization of the island's clan-based social structure into stable agrarian communities. In most instances, these plans either motivated or were absorbed into resettlement programs linked to schemes for English-owned plantations, which in turn encouraged the seizure of monastic property under the guise of reform. The influence of Machiavelli, whose appeal was especially strong among radical

---

[24] Sidney's concept of the "fore-conceit" draws on Giovanni Paolo Lomazzo's *Trattato dell'arte della pittura, scultura et architetettura* (1584–1585) and *Idea del tempio della pintura* (1590), as well as on Federico Zuccaro's *L'Idea de pittori, scultori et architetti*; cf. Shepherd, "Introduction," in *Apologie*, 64–65.

[25] Cf. Norbrook, *Poetry and Politics*, 82.

Protestants, is apparent in the theorizing over the Irish problem, most notably in terms of the "innovative" solutions demanded by those who argued that Elizabeth's Viceroy on the island, the Lord Deputy, needed unlimited power in order to bring the natives under control.[26]

As the ideological struggles played out from mid-century onward, Ireland assumed ever greater importance in the English psyche, becoming, even more than the New World had for Spain, the site of competing versions of national identity, with early English inhabitants of the Pale, or Old English, seen as supporting the native Irish, in contrast to more recent arrivals, or New English, whose ranks were swelled by the limited prospects for many in the younger generation at home.[27] In some ways the situation resembled that of the Spanish, who experienced similar conflicts between early arrivals in the Americas, including the *conquistadores*, who became known as *veteranos*, and more recent arrivals or *chapetones*, including Ercilla. In the case of Ireland, frequent charges of Gaelic-Old English sympathy were often justified, with divisions between the two groups diminished by oppressive English policies and the unifying thrust of post-Tridentine Catholicism. On several occasions, anxiety over the papacy's support for Irish rebels and over Spanish-Irish collusion were also well founded, notable instances of such assistance including the 1570 Ridolfi plot; Gregory XIII's 1578 financing of an aborted invasion of Ireland by Thomas Stukley, which resulted in the imprisonment and subsequent massacre at Smerwick of some thousand Italian and Spanish soldiers by troops under the command of Ralegh, acting on the orders of Lord Grey de Wilton; and Philip II's covert aid to James Fitzmaurice Fitzgerald in the second Desmond revolt of 1579. By the end of the 1580s Leicester's partisans despaired over the recall from Ireland of a number of Lord Deputies, among them Sir Henry Sidney, father of Philip, who was twice brought

---

[26] Cf. Willy Maley, *Salvaging Spenser* (New York: St. Martin's Press, 1997), 114–17; Andrew Hadfield, *Edmund Spenser's Irish Experience: Wilde Fruit and Salvage Soyl* (Oxford: Clarendon Press, 1997), 37–46, 74; Nicholas Canny, "Identity Formation in Ireland: The Emergence of the Anglo-Irish," in *Colonial Identity in the Atlantic World, 1500–1800*, ed. idem and Anthony Pagden (Princeton: Princeton University Press, 1987), 159–212, at 166–68; McCabe, *Spenser's Monstrous Regiment*, 216–18. Moors remaining in Andalucía were severely persecuted from the mid-1560s to the 1580s; during this period the majority were driven from their property, which was seized by others; cf. Lynch, *Spain*, 1: 229–32.

[27] Cf. Ciaran Brady, "Spenser's Irish Crisis: Humanism and Experience in the 1590s," *Past and Present* 111 (1986): 17–49; Nicholas Canny, "Edmund Spenser and the Development of an Anglo-Irish Identity," *Yearbook of English Studies* 19 (1983): 1–19; idem, "Identity Formation," and idem, "Debate: Spenser's Irish Crisis: Humanism and Experience in the 1590s," *Past and Present* 120 (1988): 201–15; cf. Andrew Hadfield and Willy Maley, "Irish Representations and English Alternatives," in *Representing Ireland*, 1–23. McCabe identifies the matter of Ireland in the *Faerie Queene* more as an issue of intertext than context or subtext: *Spenser's Monstrous Regiment*, ix.

back, and Grey, his successor, whom Spenser served as secretary and alludes to in Book 5 of the *Faerie Queene*.[28] On the continent matters frequently fared no better from the Leicester perspective. Reflecting the importance she attached to his advice, the queen had made William Cecil Lord Burghley in 1572 and had also favored his son Robert with a position on the Privy Council, limiting Leicester's influence. Leicester himself fell into disgrace after accepting an appointment from Essex, in charge of English forces on the continent, without Elizabeth's permission. By 1586 Sidney was dead, Leicester's death followed in 1588, Ralegh was out of honor after failing to seek approval from the queen to marry Elizabeth Throckmorton, and the temperamental Essex, who now headed those opposed to Cecil, would soon come to grief. The Anglican Church, meanwhile, maintained its hold on mainstream Protestantism against the apocalyptic visions of the Puritans.

Dissatisfaction with the court toward the century's end was not limited to partisans of the Earl of Leicester. A growing number of Elizabethans saw the government as dominated by intrigue and bribery, which made the condemnation of life at court or its juxtaposition to the tranquility of life elsewhere all the more appealing. While criticism of the courtier often functioned as a surrogate for such misgivings, courtliness in England was also associated with Catholicism as well as with a maleficent caricature of Italy, seen by some as the principal agent corrupting not only English manners, as in the image of the Italian fop that flourished in the period's drama, but also English morals.[29] Such is the context for two works with potential significance for Spenser, both of which pay homage to Castiglione while departing sharply from the *Cortegiano*, beginning with their titles, which eschew any mention of the previously keynoted figure in favor of descriptions of their content, illuminating for what they reveal about changing perceptions of the topic. The first is Stefano Guazzo's *La Civil Conversazione* (1574), three books of which were translated into English in 1581 by George Pettie, author of *Petite Pallace of Pettie his Pleasure*, who, like Greville, had joined in the criticism of *sprezzatura*.[30] Guazzo's work, modeled broadly on Castiglione's, is also a dialogue in four parts, but until the final section utilizes

---

[28] Cf. Guy, *Tudor England*, 227, 285–86, 331–41; on the Smerwick massacre and Grey's "hysterical reaction" to threats of Catholic conspiracy, see Steven G. Ellis, *Tudor Ireland* (London: Longman, 1985), 282; as McCabe notes, Grey's recall was prompted in part by accusations of graft made by Elizabeth's courtiers, against whom the Lord Deputy attempts to turn the accusation (*Spenser's Monstrous Regiment*, 88 ff.).

[29] Italian tales were often associated with a threat to English morals; William Paynter published an admiring translation of such works in his *Palace of Pleasure* in 1566, which included an early version of the Romeo and Juliet story; Thomas Drant's preface to the translation of Horace's *Ars poetica* (1567) complains of the story's tawdriness (Raleigh, *Courtier*, "Introduction," l-lvii).

[30] Cf. Burke, *Fortunes*, 109.

only two speakers, with the second little more than a sounding board for the first. More important, rather than explore the behavioral subtleties of courtly life, the discussion focuses on the individual in relationship to civil society. In keeping with its less sophisticated milieu, Guazzo's language is less elevated than Castiglione's, utilizing folk wisdom and proverbs; reflecting an increased sensitivity to religious dogma, it incorporates many references to scripture. Guazzo's text reveals the extent to which perceptions of the court and of courtliness had changed in Italy itself, where, while not the fount of corruption imagined by many in England, *cortegianía* was increasingly viewed as hypocritical and dishonest. The second work, *A Discourse of Civill Life* by Lodowick Bryskett, composed in the early 1580s but not published until 1606, inscribes an even sharper turn from courtliness to a pragmatic, Protestant view of "civill felicitie," revealing the degree to which this shift coalesced, in the English imagination, against the backdrop of "this barbarous country of Ireland" (5).[31] Bryskett, a close friend of Philip Sidney who accompanied him on his European tour of the early 1570s, was one of many in Spenser's generation who became deeply involved in Irish affairs, holding a series of positions on the island in which he was either assisted or followed by Spenser, with whom he became acquainted as early as 1577. The figure of Thestylis in Spenser's *Colin Clouts Come Home Again* (1595) is generally associated with Bryskett, by this time Spenser's neighbor at Kilcolman, who was similarly driven from the Irish property he occupied by the Munster rebellion in 1598. Part of the attention the *Discourse* has attracted stems from its offering one of the first references to the *Faerie Queene*, parts of which Spenser was circulating among acquaintances in the early 1580s.

Much of Bryskett's text represents a translation of Giovambattista Giraldi's "Tre dialoghi della vita civile" of 1565, which was structured as a trio of dialogues about citizenship that took place during a three-day journey made by friends traveling from Rome to Marseille to escape the plague.[32] Also paying tribute to while differentiating itself from Castiglione, Giraldi's work, unlike Guazzo's, is still focused on maintaining the favor of the prince. *Dissimulazione* is stressed as essential to the task, as is *grazia*, but both of these qualities are now viewed, in contrast to Castiglione, as means to an end rather than as aesthetically

---

[31] Citations from Bryskett's work are from Thomas E. Wright, ed., *A Discourse of Civill Life, by Lodovico Bryskett* (Northridge: San Fernando Valley State College Renaissance Editions, 1970).

[32] Giraldi was an early defender of the *Orlando Furioso*, arguing that Ariosto's modern romanzo was just as admirable as ancient epic; cf. Daniel Javitch, *Proclaiming a Classic: The Canonization of* Orlando Furioso (Princeton: Princeton University Press, 1991), 22–25; the text discussed here was known in English as the "Discourse on what Befits a Young Nobleman"; it comprised the second part of Giraldi's *De gli hecatommithi*, more familiar for tales that provide the plots for numerous Elizabethan literary works, including Shakespeare's *Othello* and *Measure for Measure*; cf. Burke, *Fortunes*, 121.

desirable in their own right. Bryskett, who substitutes his own acquaintances for
the original characters and dedicates the work to Lord Grey, concocts a mix of
Giraldi and Castiglione, describing a cottage near Dublin where he has come to
avoid a contagion affecting the city and to reflect upon having recently resigned
his position in local government. Here he is visited by friends, including Spenser,
who encourage his return to public service, lauding the active over the contem-
plative life. The reference to the *Faerie Queene* is brief but revealing, made as
Bryskett introduces Spenser to the others with a reference to his ongoing work,
which the character Spenser then explains he is writing:

> [. . .] to represent all the moral vertues, assigning to every vertue, a knight
> to be the patron and defender of the same: in whose actions and feates of
> armes and chivalry, the operations of that vertue, whereof he is the pro-
> tector, are to be expressed, and the vices and unruly appetites that oppose
> themselves against the same, to be beaten down and overcome [. . .] (22)

The assembled group ask Spenser to elaborate, but he demurs. Bryskett's humanist patrimony is evident in his familiarity with Giraldi and in the attention he
gives to the broader context of "the Ethick part of Morall Philosophie" (24),
which forms the backdrop for the *Discourse*'s reflection on civic man. The utilitarian inflection this perspective has now assumed is clear from the preface, which
notes the difficulty of working with ancient texts and praises the Italians, Guazzo
and Giraldi among them, for the accessibility they provide to such sources. His
own adaptation, Bryskett claims, will insure that Giraldi's work is accessible to
English audiences "with the lesse labor and cost" (6) than that required of either
the Italians or the ancients.[33] The preface goes on to define Bryskett's goal as
"[. . .] to discourse upon the morall vertues, yet not omitting the intellectual,
to the end to frame a gentleman fit for civill conversation, and to set him in the
direct way that leadeth him to his civill felicitie" (6). Less there be any doubt as
to the relationship between moral philosophy and Christian doctrine, the former is identified as "but the hand-maide of the doctrine of Grace" (6), which the
author has pursued to enhance his knowledge of "the duties of a Christian man"
(15). A final clarification specifies "civill felicitie" as that "active or practicke

---

[33] The topic is a familiar one among vernacular humanists, e.g., the observation
of the Marquis of Santillana, an early patron of humanist projects with a limited facility for classical languages, upon requesting that his son, a student at Salamanca in the
mid-1440s, undertake a vernacular translation of Pier Candido Decembrio's Latin version of the *Iliad*: "E pues no podemos aver aquella que queremos, queramos aquella que
podemos. E si careçemos de las formas, seamos contentos de las materias" ("If we can't
have what we desire, let us desire what we can have. And if we lack the forms, let us content ourselves with the matter"); the Marquis's remarks are cited in Guillermo Serés, *La
traducción en Italia y España durante el siglo XV: La "Iliada en Romance" y su contexto cultural*
(Salamanca: Ediciones Universidad de Salamanca, 1997), 20–21.

felicite, consisting in vertuous actions, and reducing of a man's passions under the rule of reason" (19). Bryskett's remarks are notable for the degree to which they collect a variety of the themes encountered thus far. His pride in providing vernacular accessibility to classical texts contrasts sharply with Boscán's deprecatory remarks made fifty years earlier about those who "andar *romanzando* libros" ("go about making romance versions of books") (6).[34] Boscán, it will be recalled, articulated a singular ambivalence, denigrating the lack of scholarly skill this activity reflected while claiming that his own pursuits were anything but scholarly, relying instead on courtly *jüizio* rather than rules or sustained effort. No such ambivalence troubles Bryskett, whose *desprecio* is now directed not at scholarly but rather at courtly demeanor, all traces of earlier Tudor poets' shared sense of the *sprezzatura* of their vocation now supplanted by a *realpolitik* informed by reformed religion. The difference reveals the degree to which *civiltà* was altered from an aesthetic of manners articulated by a few with the requisite *ingegno* and *giudicio* into a civilizing project for Ireland promoted not only by Bryskett, Richard Beacon (*Solon his Follie*, 1594), William Herbert (*Croftus sive de Hibernia Liber*, c.1591), and Spenser in the *View* (1598; pub. 1633), but by political and religious figures generally, together with settlers and plantation owners, actual and aspirant.[35] Key strains in humanist, Neoplatonic, and Reformation thought coalesced in this project, in which the subjugation of the irascible and concupiscent to the rational offered rationale for social policy. Bryskett's remarks on framing a gentleman "fit for civill conversation" not only echo Hoby's earlier ones in his preface to the *Courtyer* regarding filling the minds of his readers with moral virtues "[. . .]and their body with civyll conditions," but also prefigure Spenser's comments in the "Letter to Ralegh" on the fashioning of "a gentleman or noble person in vertuous and gentle discipline." This synopsis of the *Faerie Queene* is notable, in turn, for the transformation it has undergone since its articulation some ten years earlier at Bryskett's salon, an interval in which the poet's absorption in the literary figuration of virtue and discipline has been overtaken by their implementation in society, now focused on the latter of the two terms. Neither Guazzo's nor Bryskett's work is conceivable without *Il Cortegiano*, but these later writers see the dream of *cortegianía* as hopelessly idealistic and the court itself as corrupt. To them, *sprezzatura* is affectation and *mediocrità* is disingenuous; *cortegianía* is opposed to rather than the apex of *civiltà*, and *grazia*, rather than a courtly attribute, is God's gift to man.

---

[34] See 27, supra.

[35] Cf. Palmer on the significance of "civil conversation" in early modern European social thought: *Language and Conquest*, 115.

3. The Treacherous Kingdom of Language

The confluence of themes being discussed here is apparent from the period of
Spenser's first published work, poetry translations contributed anonymously to
Jan van der Noot's *Theatre for Voluptuous Worldlings* in 1569. The *Theatre* exemplifies the contrast of cultural parallels and hybrids driven by a mix of humanism,
Petrarchism, courtliness, and reformation fervor. Van der Noot, a Dutch Calvinist
refugee living in London who had authored previous bilingual religious tracts in
Dutch and French, engaged the teenaged Spenser, fresh from the Merchant Tay-
lors' School, for English versions of the poems he placed at the start of his text to
attract "voluptuous worldlings," who would then be proselytized by the tract that
followed. These verses were a French version of Petrarch's canzone 323, by Clé-
ment Marot, and Joachim du Bellay's *Antiquitez de Rome* and *Songe*, all apocalyptic ruminations on human vanity and the transitoriness of happiness lending
themselves to a reformist, anti-Catholic interpretation.[36] Marot, a contemporary of
Surrey and Wyatt, had served as a page to Francis I before going on to experiment
with Italian verse forms in French, a *translatio* of the new poetry completed by
his successors, Ronsard and du Bellay. Spenser's version of Marot's Petrarch held
similar significance, representing the earliest translation of the Italian poet's canzone into English. 1569 also saw Spenser enter Cambridge, where he soon became
friends with Harvey, pursued literary theory with Harvey and Sidney, and became
a beneficiary of Leicester, Sidney's uncle. By the 1579 publication of *The Shepherds'
Calendar*, also anonymously (his authorship was acknowledged only in the 1611
folio edition of his works), the young poet had made a concerted attempt to shape
both the course of English verse and his own public image. The *Calendar* makes
clear that Spenser shares Sidney's view of Protestant art as an undertaking in which
the traditional components of *delectare*, *docere*, and *movere* are a trio in which the
first is a vehicle for the second and spur to the third. Unlike Sidney, in the *Calendar* Spenser rejects the prevailing mode of courtly discourse for an archaic dialect
that, while still utilizing Petrarchan elements, combines them with monarchical
imagery and pastoral motifs favored by the Edwardians. The result is provocative,
complex, and indicative of an author whose gravity and self-consciousness distinguished him from his contemporaries.

---

[36] Cf. Norbrook, *Poetry and Politics*, 78; Spenser published revised versions of his
early Petrarch and du Bellay translations in the 1591 volume, *Complaints: containing sun-
drie small Poemes of the Worlds Vanitie*. McCabe explores du Bellay's critique of imperial Rome as an indirect critique of Philip II (*Spenser's Monstrous Regiment*, 25). On the
notable role of English translators in the conquest of Ireland, a group that includes Bryskett, discussed above, and Barnaby Googe and Sir John Harington, discussed below, see
Palmer, *Language and Conquest*, 111; cf. the role of Irish poets as translators during the
conflict (193).

Spenser's correspondence with Harvey from this period reveals that together with Sidney, these three, frustrated by "balde Rymers," had discussed plans for reforming English meter not according to courtly models, but in keeping with humanist-inspired classical ones, much as Ronsard and du Bellay had accomplished earlier. "Why a God's name may not we, as else the Greeks, have the Kingdom of our own language," Spenser asks, "[. . .] and measure our accents by the sound, reserving the quantity to the verse?"[37] In contrast to the French Alexandrine, the attempt proved impractical, and Spenser, paradoxically, turned to a dialect of English whose strongest associations were medieval. Spenser's *Amoretti* and *Epithalamion*, sonnet sequences composed while he worked on the *Faerie Queene* and published in 1595, one year before the second installment of his romance-epic, reveal him to be a master of the courtly Petrarchan lyric he rejected for his magnum opus. Commemorating the poet's courtship of and marriage to Elizabeth Boyle, the verses are crucial forerunners to Shakespeare and offer a dramatic contrast in style, structure, and content to the world of Protestant chivalric romance in which he was otherwise immersed. Sonnet 80 from the *Amoretti*, often cited for its reflection on the poet's epic project, expresses the need for refreshment in terms that recall similar sentiments expressed on numerous occasions by Ercilla:

> After so long a race as I have run
> Through faery land, which those six books compile,
> Give leave to rest me (being half foredone),
> And gather to myself new breath awhile.
> Then, as a steed refreshed after toil,
> Out of my prison I will break anew,
> And stoutly will that second work assoil
> With strong endeavour and attention due.
> Till then, give leave to me in pleasant mew
> To sport my Muse and sing my love's sweet praise
> The contemplation of whose heavenly hue
> My spirit to an higher pitch will raise:
> But let her praises yet be low and mean,
> Fit for the handmaid of the Faery Queene.[38]

---

[37] Spenser's remark is cited in Richard Helgerson, "Barbarous Tongues: The Ideology of Poetic Form in Renaissance England," in *Edmund Spenser*, ed. Andrew Hadfield (London: Longman, 1996), 23–29, at 23–25.

[38] *Edmund Spenser: Selected Shorter Poems*, ed. Douglas Brooks-Davies (London: Longman, 1995), 279–80; 1595 also saw the publication of *Colin Clouts Come Home Again*, an allegorical pastoral based on Spenser's 1589 trip to court with Ralegh, who introduced him to the queen. In 1596, in addition to Books 4–6 of the *Faerie Queene*, Spenser also published the *Fowre Hymnes* and the *Prothalamion*, commemorating the betrothal of the earl of Worcester's daughters.

Spenser's repeated rejection of this courtly speech for the "studied barbarity" of language associated with Middle English is complex.[39] On the one hand, it reflects the reformers' frustrations with the policies of the court and their disavowal of the sophisticated, ironic posture that courtliness projected. On the other, it attempts to recapture an edenic era of religious and national purity such language both describes and was thought to enunciate, a divinatory *langue* accessible beneath the secular *parole*. In his "Dedicatory Epistle" to Harvey that precedes the *Calendar*, E. K. notes Cicero's endorsement of older, venerated language, but praises the work at hand for its use of "[. . .] such good and natural English words as have been long time out of use," arguing that their absence "is the only cause that our mother tongue (which truly of itself is both full enough for prose and stately enough for verse) hath long time been counted most bare and barren of both" (21).[40] The distinction echoes, in part, disputes over the *renovatio* of English a generation earlier between those who would ennoble it via the classical languages and others who favored an emphasis on its Anglo-Saxon heritage. Both arguments were informed by humanism, but the latter was especially appealing to the nationalism of Protestant intellectuals, exemplified by John Cheke, who, in spite of his classical erudition and facility with Greek, pushed for Saxon rather than classical cognates, claiming that "[. . .] our own tung shold be written cleane and pure, unmixt and unmangled with borrowing of other tunges" (12). The failure of this view to carry the day is apparent as E. K. proceeds in the *Calendar*, condemning the "[. . .] borrowing here of the French, there of the Italian, everywhere of the Latin [. . .] So now they have made our English tongue a gallimaufry or hodge-podge of all other speeches" (20–21), his polemic inscribing nativist resistance to Castiglionian imitation while promoting the *Calendar*'s author as the genuine article and redeeming alternative.[41] Spenser's efforts to equate the archaic, Chaucerian dialect with pure Englishness, linguistic and ethnic, a project the *Faerie Queene* promotes through the legends of Prince Arthur and his book of "British Moniments," was challenged by facts on the ground as well as by an increasingly sophisticated contemporary

---

[39] The phrase is once again Maley's (*Salvaging Spenser*, 6); cf. Javitch, *Poetry*, 55–56.

[40] Text for the Dedicatory Epistle is from *Selected Shorter Poems*, ed. Brooks-Davies, 18–25.

[41] E. K. goes on in his "Dedicatory Epistle" to note how critics of his approach, "[. . .] if they happen to hear an old word, albeit very natural and significant, cry out straightaway that we speak no English, but gibberish" (20–21), a preview of Ben Jonson's observation, regarding the language of the *Faerie Queene*, that "Spenser, in affecting the Ancients writ no Language" (*Timber*, 1478–79). For more on the Cambridge intellectuals referred to here, which included William Cecil and Roger Ascham, see Burke, *Fortunes*, 64 ff. A Ciceronian encouragement of borrowing words from other languages, especially Latin, was associated with "university writers" such as George Pettie; cf. Raleigh, *Courtier*, "Introduction," lvii.

understanding of their historical origins. Elizabethan Ireland comprised an actual linguistic "gallimaufry" if ever there was one, with Latin the language of the learned, Gaelic Irish that of bards and peasants, Middle English spoken by Catholic descendants of the island's twelfth-century colonists, and Early Modern English by post-Reformation Protestant planters. While E. K. fretted over the encroachment of an international, courtly sophistication, the crucial distinction and more acute danger, as Irenius makes clear in the *View*, was that between identity-affirming Anglo-Saxon English words and contamination-threatening Anglicized-Gaelic ones.[42] Efforts to designate the former as the "undefyled" source of Chaucerian speech were as problematic as those to avoid the latter in the everyday life of the Pale. Archaic English was inescapably associated via the Old English peasantry with Ireland, a contaminated source by definition, undermining the ease with which the two cultures were ideally contrasted by political and religious ideologues across a Manichean divide of barbarism and civility. The danger, initially a linguistic one to purity, eventually turns upon itself, becoming within the *Faerie Queene* a threat to the stability of meaning itself. The linking of linguistic and political identities characteristic of early modern nation-states, exemplified by Nebrija in Spain and du Bellay in France, was similarly vexed when it came to efforts by Spenser to indemnify the English as Britons rather than Saxons or Celts, leading him to highly politicized exercises in comparative ethnology alongside those in etymology.[43]

In the closing decades of the century, the frustration of reformers with courtly *dissimulazione* finds a correlative in linguistic duplicity. The associated dangers are thematized in the *Faerie Queene*, which constantly draws attention to the alertness required to distinguish between appearance and reality. Sorcerers concoct the most dramatic deceptions, namely Archimago's Duessa, who threatens the quest of the Redcross knight, and Acrasia's bower, which threatens Guyon's. Duplicity is not only a problem for the *Faerie Queene*'s characters, however, but also poses risks for the poem's readers in the doublings, substitutions,

---

[42] On imitative *contaminatio*, see Thomas Greene, *The Light in Troy: Imitation and Discovery in Renaissance Poetry* (New Haven: Yale University Press, 1982), esp. 39–40; on transformation/degeneration as an Elizabethan preoccupation, see Palmer, *Language and Conquest*, 98–99.

[43] McCabe, *Spenser's Monstrous Regiment*, 142, 160–61, 177–96; cf. Maley, *Salvaging Spenser*, 35–36; Hadfield, *Wilde Fruit*, 3, 11; Palmer notes that "without the knowledge that would have licensed opinions about semantic adequacy or cognitive range, the English judged Irish not as a language but as an index of difference in a context of polarised conflict" (*Language and Conquest*, 91); and cf. the early sixteenth-century Irish author Seathrún Céitinn's (*Foras Feasa ar Éirinn*) rejection of Spenser's false etymologies (105–6). Cf. Dorothy Stephens, "Spenser's Language(s): Linguistic Theory and Poetic Diction," in *The Oxford Handbook of Edmund Spenser*, ed. Richard A. McCabe (Oxford: Oxford University Press, 2010), 367–84.

and interchanges of images, characters, and episodes, and in the endless linguistic repetition of its phrases, words, morphemes, and phonemes. As a matter of plot, such echoing produces alternative and potentially false resolutions, complicating interpretation, as Spenser acknowledges in the "Letter to Ralegh." In terms of language, the continuous punning wordplay, establishing myriad interconnections between words diversely used and located, enhances narrative cohesion while simultaneously accentuating a slippage between the literal and metaphorical. The result is a tension between stability and dissolution, between centripetal and centrifugal forces that pervades the first four books of the poem, in particular, on every level, from the plot, where the distinction between appearance and reality is fraught with danger, to the language, where linguistic integrity is eventually challenged by a mutability arising from the polysemy inherent in speech itself. Complicating such considerations is the degree to which the poet's language becomes a vehicle for aestheticizing/anesthetizing violence, exacerbating a fundamental instability in speech that threatens to revert to the generative chaos of an Adonis's garden of words, transforming language from the ultimate stability with which Spenser and his colleagues had hoped to imbue it to a site of ultimate peril, leading to fundamental changes in the narrative in Books 5 and 6.

In contrast to such linguistic concerns, the threat of uncontrolled proliferation was more commonly associated during the sixteenth century with religious and literary matters. Tridentine fears of schism drove efforts to control the text of the scriptures as well as their exegesis, the Council issuing decrees in 1546 to reaffirm the canonicity of the Vulgate and "to check unbridled spirits (*petulantia ingenia*)," lest anyone "[. . .] relying on his own judgement [. . .] presume to interpret them [the Holy Scriptures]." In language that variously recalls attacks on romance as well as Spenser's own struggles with the control of speech, the Council went on to condemn such liberties, "[. . .] wishing to repress that boldness (*temeritas*) whereby the words and sentences of the Holy Scriptures are turned and twisted to all kinds of profane uses," including "to things scurrilous, fabulous, vain, to flatteries, detractions [. . .] and defamatory libels [. . .]."[44] While championing freedom of access to God's word and the individual reading of scripture, the Reformation had similar concerns, as exemplified in the ban on Tyndale's New Testament only one year after its publication. All sides in the religious disputes were alert to the hazards of print technology, which, while essential to their goals, was felt to threaten them if not strictly controlled.[45] The *Faerie Queene* begins and ends by depicting such concerns, first in Redcross's killing of Errour, which results in a spewing forth of texts, and finally in images of a resurgent Blatant Beast that refuses to be silenced. Such anxieties had an analogue in fears of civic disorder, which Sidney and Spenser attempted to counter

---

[44] Citations are from the Fourth Session of the Council: *Canons and Decrees*, 18, 20.

[45] Cf. Christopher Haigh, *English Reformations: Religion, Politics, and Society under the Tudors* (Oxford: Oxford University Press, 1993), 57, and Guy, *Tudor England*, 292, 416–17.

by imbuing what they saw as the natural order of the Elizabethan social hierarchy with Neoplatonic harmony. As the discussion of Book 6 will argue, such
natural-order arguments were fundamentally at odds with the spirit of the iconoclastic attack on natural signs. If Archimago and Acrasia's *dissimulazione* makes
them agents of idolatry, encouraging the poem's characters to take signs for reality, Spenser's archaic dialect mounted a closely related counter-effort directed at
the poem's readers, designed to reveal a natural bond between words and their
meanings. Etymology lay at the heart of the project. The increasingly frail border
between etymologies and puns, by contrast, undermined this effort, becoming
instead a source of uncertainty and insecurity.[46]

4. Allegory and *imitatio*:
Tropes of Difference, Strategies of Similitude

Earlier in the century, as the conflation of ecclesiastical and literary issues got
underway in earnest in the Italian debates, defenders of the *Furioso* began resort-
ing to allegoresis as a defense against precisely the sort of accusations of profanity
and scurrility the Tridentine decrees enumerated, and by the mid-1550s the poem
was regularly published with such interpretations attached to each of its cantos.
Tasso went further, and having composed the neo-Aristotelian *Discorsi dell'arte
poetica* in the 1560s (first published in 1587; revised as the *Discorsi del poema heroico*
in 1594/5), authored his own "Allegoria del poema" a decade later as he was fin-
ishing the *Liberata*. The humanist erudition and theoretical sophistication of the
Discorsi far outshone that of the "Allegoria," but it was the latter that proved more
reassuring in the long run against threats of ethical impropriety, and when the
Liberata began to be published in 1581 the "Allegoria" was regularly included.
This sixteenth-century turn to allegory represented a retreat for humanism, which
eschewed the medieval, occult associations of allegoresis in favor of a textual analysis focused on grammar, literal meaning, and the recovery of authorial intention.[47]
Such basic philology, recuperating Hellenistic practice, required a degree of disin-
terestedness, however, and whenever this element was lacking, from antiquity on,
the agenda of readers took precedence over those of authors, from Stoic rationaliza-
tions of mythology and patristic reconciliations of classical antiquity, to medieval

---

[46] Cf. Andrew Hadfield, *Literature, Politics, and National Identity: Reformation to
Renaissance* (Cambridge: Cambridge University Press, 1994), 137–38; Hadfield also discusses the pun as "the harbinger of uncertainty and insecurity" that threatens etymology's
epistemological principle (*Wilde Fruit*, 99–111); cf. Stephens, "Spenser's Language(s)."
[47] Cf. Brian Cummings, "Protestant Allegory," in *Companion to Allegory*, ed. Copeland and Struck, 177–90.

"moralizations" of Ovid.[48] Allegoresis was no more appealing to religious reformers, who, while equally focused on intention, associated such multilevel interpretations with an idolatry that Protestant exegesis was meant to undermine. This applied in particular to the Scriptures, which reformers viewed as fundamentally rhetorical constructions designed to persuade that, while divinely inspired, were nonetheless susceptible to the same interpretive methods as secular works from antiquity. Tyndale exemplifies their perspective in *The Obedience of a Christian Man* (1527), arguing that the meaning of scripture is literal and reducing allegory to no more than a device for heightening the effect of the text on the reader.[49] As resistance to what were perceived to be the deceptive subtleties of courtly speech increased, tropes as such became potential targets of criticism, as seen in Greville's attack on irony. Demands for "plain speech," meanwhile, however in sync with a humanist focus on "literal" meaning, were at odds with the need that was felt by reformers in particular to encode potentially controversial speech. Further complicating matters was the need to make sure that, once engaged, such codes could be unlocked, an issue that was far from straightforward, as Spenser's expressed desire regarding "auoyding of gealous opinions and miscontructions" in the "Letter to Ralegh" makes clear.

Allegory's systematization as an interpretive device was associated with Dante, whose *Letter to Can Grande* articulated a four-part schema distinguishing among the literal, allegorical, moral, and anagogic registers of a "polysemous" text.[50] Dante did not define the terms, offering instead an illustration of their application to Psalm 114, which revealed that in contrast to literal or historical meaning, the latter three categories designated increasingly elevated (Christian) significance leading to an ultimate, all-embracive spirituality. In fact these three terms were grouped together by Dante and later writers to contrast the allegorical or mystical to the literal. Dante's *Convivio* distinguished between an allegory of the Holy Scriptures or theologians and an allegory of the poets, the first describing biblical text where language was either literal or symbolic, with some passages simply historical while others had additional meaning, the second applied to poetry, whose use of language was by nature more than literal. The significance

---

[48] Cf. H.-I. Marrou, *A History of Education in Antiquity* (Milwaukee: University of Wisconsin Press, 1956), 165–68; Edward Watts, "Education: Speaking, Thinking, and Socializing," in *Oxford Handbook of Late Antiquity*, ed. Scott F. Johnson, Oxford: Oxford University Press, 2012), 437–66. Javitch discusses the resistance to allegoresis among neo-Aristotelian critics in Cinquecento Italy (*Proclaiming a Classic*, 144); cf. Craig Kallendorf, "Philology, the Reader, and the *Nachleben* of Classical Texts," *Modern Philology* (1994): 137–56, at 138.

[49] Cf. Greenblatt, *Renaissance Self-Fashioning*, 102; cf. John King, *Spenser's Poetry and the Reformation Tradition* (Princeton: Princeton University Press, 1990), 77–78.

[50] The classic method: see J. C. Hendrickson, "Exegesis," in *Oxford Dictionary of the Middle Ages*, ed. R. Bjork, 4 vols. (Oxford: Oxford University Press, 2010), 2: 597–99, at 598.

of the distinction was for the *Commedia*, which Dante associated with Scriptural rather than poetic allegory, identifying much of its narrative as no more (or less) than literal description of what lay ahead for the soul after death, while other passages encoded the additional degrees of meaning just noted. The boldness of Dante's affiliation as well as a suggestion of his distinction is apparent as the *Faerie Queene* gets underway, with Spenser describing his project of moral fashioning as a mix of allegory and "*historicall* fiction," i.e., legends meant both literally and symbolically.[51] Tasso's "Allegoria," by contrast, maintained the simpler binary opposition between the literal, which it described as imitation, or the image of human action, and allegory, characterized as "[. . .] mysterious symbols, which can fully be understood only by connoisseurs of the nature of things."[52] Departing from both Tasso and Spenser, Sir John Harington, a godson of Elizabeth and favorite among her courtiers, reverted to Dante's four-part system in his widely read translation of the *Furioso*, copying the schema directly from Ariosto's Italian editors. Harington preceded the translation, which he completed in 1591, with a "Briefe Apologie of Poetrie." His remarks began by echoing Sidney in more than his title, then parted unmistakably from the prior work's lofty Neoplatonism to make distinctions among literal, moral, and allegorical meanings that he detailed in an elaborately wrought passage designed to affiliate Ariosto's poem with the gravity of political and moral philosophy:

> First of all for the litterall sence (as it were the utmost barke or ryne) they set downe, in manner of an historie, the acts and notable exploits of some persons worthy memorie; then in the same fiction, as a second rine and somewhat more fine as it were nearer to the pith and marrow, they place the Morall sence, profitable for the active life of man, approving vertuous actions and condemning the contrarie. Manie times also under the selfesame words they comprehend some true understanding of Naturall Philosophie or somtimes of politike governement and now and then of divinitie, and these same sences that comprehend so excellent knowledge we call the Allegorie [. . .] [53]

---

[51] Cf. Charles S. Singleton, *Dante's Commedia: Elements of Structure* (Baltimore: Johns Hopkins University Press, 1977), 13–15, 87–92. The distinction also suggests the medieval conception of God's two books, Holy Scripture on the one hand, the world on the other, both viewed as texts with literal or visible as well as symbolic or inner meaning.

[52] English translation of Tasso is by Lawrence Rhu, *Tasso's Narrative Theory*, 155.

[53] Citations are from *Orlando Furioso*, trans. John Harington, ed. Robert McNutty (Oxford: Oxford University Press, 1972); in practice Harington usually added a fourth category, "Allusion," which he described in another prefatory paratext as "[. . .] of fictions to be applied to some things done or written of in times past, as also where it may be applied without offense to the time present." For more on Harington's use of materials authored by Italian editors of Ariosto, cf. Javitch, *Proclaiming a Classic*, 137–39; on his "frankly pornographic" passages, cf. Townsend Rich, *Harington and Ariosto: A Study in*

As it had been in Italy, such posturing was a preemptive effort to shield the work from accusations of frivolity and immorality characteristic of attacks on romance. The tension between probity and licentiousness in Harington's project, notorious for its quasi-pornographic renditions of Ariostan ribaldry, reflected the even more intense strain in England between the morals of the court and Protestant reformers. The appeal of such a defense as Puritan attacks on poetry and drama accelerated, in conjunction with the spread of Italophobia and the decline of *cortegianía*, can well be imagined.

Although Spenser briefly describes Tasso's use of allegory in the "Letter to Ralegh," his own poem recalls the medieval English tradition of pastoral eclogue more than it does Tasso or Harington. Two works in this tradition, *The Shippe of Safegarde* (1569) by Barnaby Googe and Stephen Bateman's *The Travayled Pylgrime* (1569), appeared shortly before the *Faerie Queene*, both texts employing allegory as a vehicle for Protestant polemics combined with the quest motif of medieval romance.[54] The *Faerie Queene* dramatically expands the scope of these earlier projects while displaying a similar imitative strategy, one that draws on multiple models, ancient, medieval, and early modern, native and imported, the separate identities of which are maintained and even accentuated rather than being subsumed in a newly unified product. Spenser's approach to these two components of *imitatio*, the first a matter of a single or multiple models, the second the degree to which a model was acknowledged or disguised, offers further insight into his break not only with courtly aesthetics but also with humanist practice. From antiquity onward servile following had been contrasted to more sophisticated appropriation in the oppositions of *mimesis* to *zelos* and *imitatio* to *aemulatio*. As the second term of these pairs reveals, the issue was more than one of narrative skill, focusing instead on an author's efforts to equal or surpass a predecessor while advertising or concealing the associated text. Renaissance discussions of the matter often divided imitation

---

Elizabethan Verse Translation (New Haven: Yale University Press, 1940), 57. Harington served as an undertaker in the Munster plantation and returned to Ireland with the second earl of Essex in 1599 (Palmer, *Language and Conquest*, 47); he presented a copy of his translation of Ariosto to Hugh O'Neill, earl of Tyrone, on the occasion of his truce with Essex: cf. Hadfield, *Wilde Fruit*, 47, and Palmer, *Language and Conquest*, 143.

[54] Richard Helgerson explores the impact of Tasso's "Allegoria" on the "Letter" as well as on changes Spenser made to the *Faerie Queene* between 1580 and 1590: "Tasso on Spenser: The Politics of Chivalric Romance," *Yearbook of English Studies* 21 (1991): 153–67; Rhu argues that Spenser had not read the *Discorsi* before publishing the 1590 *Faerie Queene* (*Tasso*, 10). Googe is part of the group of Cambridge graduates who, like Spenser, make their careers in Ireland, eventually becoming Provost-Marshal of Connacht (Palmer, *Language and Conquest*, 111); in addition to *The Shippe of Safegarde* Googe authored "Ecloges, Epytaphes, and Sonnettes" (1563), one of the poems of which, "Cupido Conquered," directly influenced Spenser's "Court of Cupid" in Book 6 of the *Faerie Queene*; cf. Maley, *Salvaging Spenser*, 15–16.

into three classes, as did Bartolomeo Ricci, a learned defender of Ariosto (discussed by Ascham in his *Scholemaster*), who spoke of *sequi, imitari*, and *aemulari* (to follow, to imitate, to emulate), and Daniel Barbero, a member of Bembo's circle, who used *accostarsi, aguagliarli*, and *superargli* to indicate following in the footsteps of, overtaking, and (sur)passing an antecessor.[55] Whatever an author's position on the issue, narrative theory had regularly championed the careful integration of such material. In contrast to simple aping or copying, transformative imitation was frequently associated with metaphors of digestion, the best known being that of Seneca, who compared the process to the making of honey by bees, an image that simultaneously addressed the issue of a single versus multiple models. Either aspect of Seneca's simile could be emphasized: Macrobius focused on the arrangement of varied materials, Petrarch on the process of creative reformulation. In contrast to such an approach, Googe, Bateman, and Spenser, practicing what has been called "Elizabethan syncretism," went out of their way to preserve the identities of their sources, paying homage to rather than disguising them. The result is a juxtaposition of epic, romance, and English vernacular traditions compounded in direct contravention of humanist *imitatio* precisely to emphasize the newly reformed status of the product it constitutes.[56] Nothing could be further from a courtly understanding of literary *imitatio*, of which Canossa remarks, taking Virgil as a guide, that "le cose tolte da Omero o da qualche altro stiano tanto bene in Virgilio che più presto paiono illustrate chi imitate" ("things taken from Homer or from whatever other [author] stand so well in Virgil that they seem rather enhanced than copied") (1.39). This spirit informs *cortegianía* as a whole, which strives above all else, in its emphasis on the effortless grace of *sprezzatura* and the avoidance of undue attention, or *affectazione*, for flawless integration, whether of the skills and attitudes comprising the self or of the varied components of narrative art, its ultimate goal the seamless

---

[55] The contrast of imitation and emulation is found in Dionysius of Halicarnassus and Longinus; cf. Greene, *Light in Troy*, 58–60, 78–81; Ricci's discussion is from his *de Imitatione* (1541); Barbero's from the *Trattati* (1547), 2.450; both are cited by G. W. Pigman, who notes the probable inspiration of Ricci's schema in Erasmus: "Versions of Imitation in the Renaissance," *Renaissance Quarterly* 33 (1980): 1–32, at 3–4 and 26 n. 35; cf. Carroll, "Humanism," 255. Present-day scholars have generated their own classifications of *imitatio*: Pigman makes a tripartite classification of transformative, dissimulative, and eristic ("Versions," 2–3); Greene adopts the quartet of sacramental, eclectic, heuristic, and dialectical (*Light in Troy*, 38–45); the most succinct of recent discussions of Renaissance *imitatio*, including the ancient, early modern, and contemporary authors mentioned here, is that of Nicolopulos (*Poetics*, 43–58).

[56] Cf. Seneca, *Epistulae morales* 84. 3–8; Macrobius, *Saturnalia*, 1.4, 1.8; and Petrarch, *Familiares*, 1.8.23, 22.2.20–21, and 23.19.15; Lucretius had used the apian image prior to Seneca (*De Rerum Natura*, 3.11–12). On "Elizabethan syncretism," see King, *Spenser's Poetry*, 185–87. Thomas Greene describes Spenser's *imitatio* as sacramental: *The Descent from Heaven: A Study in Epic Continuity* (New Haven: Yale University Press, 1963), 303.

blending of art and life. Spenser and the art of the *Faerie Queene*, by contrast, call attention to themselves at every opportunity.

Like etymology and paronomasia, allegory and *imitatio* are forces both for stability and instability in the *Faerie Queene*. Allegory promotes the former through its function as the primary route to meaning and as the structural principle underlying the poem's generic, thematic, and linguistic components and procedures; it accentuates the latter as meanings multiply and the need for interpretation expands, producing a paratactic reading whose forays into mimetic realism are repeatedly cut short. Spenser's imitative strategy enhances stability as a stylistic imprimatur; it threatens dissolution as literary models, linguistic, characterological, and narrative, resist integration, verging on autonomy. The poem's application of these rhetorical and structural devices is most pronounced in Books 1 and 2, where Spenser's pursuit of a new variety of Protestant epic is most enthusiastic. As has often been noted, the optimism of these opening books declines as the poem advances, starting with an increased emphasis on the *entrelacement* of romance narrative in Books 3 and 4, whose complex allegorical structures are abandoned for allegory *tout court* in Book 5, and culminating with the Greek-romance-inspired adventure story at the heart of Book 6. The resulting narrative is both elucidating and contradictory; progressive in its commitment to vernacular culture, to a new aesthetics, and to questioning of the monarchy; conservative in its rejection of courtly discourse, in its efforts to revive an archaic dialect, and in its project of restoring the connection between the monarchy and its legendary roots; confident, initially, in its challenge to literary and political assumptions; resigned, eventually, as it relinquishes its own ambitious outline. These tensions account, in part, for the hybrid quality of Spenser's poem. Its hybridity reflects, as well, the identities of the poet and other English in Ireland, whether Old and suspended between Gaelic culture and the *patria*, or New and caught between the *patria* as it existed and as they envision its future through the lens of apocalyptic Protestantism.

A striking manifestation of the hybrid quality of both the *Araucana* and *Faerie Queene* is the degree to which Ercilla's account of the epic conflict between native Americans and the Spanish and Spenser's allegorized bricolage of romance, epic, and reformist doctrine end up emphasizing so many of the same key themes: the contrast of love and violence, the struggle among the irascible, concupiscent, and rational faculties, the focus on types of love, on lust and greed, and on the qualities of temperance, shame, and honor. Ercilla examines these issues as part of a *renovatio* of classical epic, Petrarchism, and courtly discourse, with the last applied to the first to effect a real-life lesson in gallantry and the courtly defense of female virtue. Spenser, embarked on nothing less than the *transformatio* of these traditions through reformed religion, relies on many of the same key images. The abandoned woman is among the most important, appearing alongside that of the night raid early in Spenser's poem. The bridle appears soon after, evoked by the Palmer as a remedy to Phedon's anger and Pyrochles's burning ire.

Fire and bridle are joined again in the sexual desire of Malecasta, who, in a gen-der-inverted rendition of Dido's banquet for Aeneas, falls in love with Britomart and suffers, as Dido did, from love as a wound, a poison, and a flame. Apparent even in such brief descriptions is the fact that, in contrast to the *Araucana*'s use of these motifs, where they resonate in harmony with the *translatio* of classical tradition—for even Ercilla's quarrel with Virgil over Dido is inter-cultural, a *desafío* between gallants—Spenser's appropriation of this material is conducted in a context where the stakes are higher, where questions about the canon are as likely theological as literary, and where, given the fallen nature of the world, the results are almost always demonic parodies, renditions of topoi whose ves-tiges of pagan glory, irrepressible remainders of a cultural translation, are now seen as contaminated, if not by the absence of religion then by its perversion in the Roman Church. The image of the bridle reflects with special resonance the differences between Ercilla's text and Spenser's, between the mid- and late six-teenth century, and between the Iberian peninsula together with the Peruvian-Chilean littoral and the British Isles. In both poems the bridle is a symbol of restraint on sexual desire. Within a few years of the *Faerie Queene*'s publication, however, the bridle had migrated from the politicized aesthetics of faery land to the aestheticized politics of Spenser's *View of the Present State of Ireland*, where, contrasted to the Machiavellian image of the sword as a choice of solutions to the Irish problem, it is dismissed, its alternative being seen as the only effective avenue of social change.

[. . .] whenas this our poet hath been much travailed and thoroughly read, how could it be (as that worthy orator said) but that walking in the sun, although for other cause he walked, yet needs he mought be sunburnt; and having the sound of those ancient poets still ringing in his ears he mought needs, in singing, hit out some of their tunes.

E. K., Dedicatory Epistle to
The Shepherds' Calendar

IV. Spenser and the Pursuit of Virtue, Personal and Political

1. The quest for poetic legitimacy

Dido and Aeneas are only the most prominent of a beguiling web of literary allusions that inaugurate the Legend of Holiness. Increasing in number and subtlety, these intertexts soon threaten to entrap the reader, who, much like Redcross and Una in the Wandering Wood, will require the assistance of a higher power in order to extricate themselves successfully. In the case of the knight and lady, that power is figured in Arthur, image of heaven's authority and benevolent grace; in the case of the reader, the authority is the poet's, whose verses will ultimately encode the proper relationship between these alluring but ultimately misleading literary traditions and Spenser's newly reformed epic, inscribing a textual parody of salvation through grace. Here in the early pages of the poem the abandoned woman appears in a series of figures with notable similarities, for all their differences, to the women of Arauco: Una awakens at Archimago's to discover that Redcross has left her behind; a few stanzas later Duessa-Fidessa appears as a grieving widow, searching, like Tegualda, for the corpse of her beloved and telling a tale with numerous parallels to those of Glaura and Lauca. Soon another widow, Amavia, acts on the longing for death brought on by loss of the beloved, overgoing Lauca and her comrades. The night raid is encountered in these lines as well, transformed at Archimago's from an assault by earthly opponents to one by a sorcerer and his unearthly acolytes sent to undermine faith and impede the hero's progress. Two other venerable images are also featured here, the ancient forest and its analogue, the catalogue of trees, both epic in genealogy but associated more often with romance by the early modern era. Among the key themes in these early scenes: the deceptiveness of appearance, the initial focus on forking paths and the *errare-errore* conceit soon shifting to the complexities of perception and self-knowledge, especially with regard to erotic desire. Stoic virtues are repeatedly demoted as Redcross's quest proceeds, most visibly in the dungeon of the House of Pride. Their reformed alternatives—faith, hope, and charity—are introduced shortly afterwards at the House of Holiness. Along the way

Christianized versions of classical topoi, among them a notable instance of the epic simile of the dawn discussed above, begin to infiltrate their demonic parodies, inaugurating Spenser's *reconquista* of literary tradition. The process develops as a matter of genre, juxtaposing first Virgil and then Ariosto and Tasso to Spenser, emphasizing differences between epic and romance. As attention turns to reformed theology, Tasso becomes an increasingly important interlocutor, with Spenser pursuing a number of issues that Tasso introduced, exploring their internalization by characters. Spenser's dual-level *mimesis*, one part a neo-Aristotelian realism of event, the other an adumbration of personal psychology, facilitates the shift from external to internal worlds, from plot to perception. As it will be throughout the poem, a principal threat here is that of mistaking initial responses to danger, especially rational responses, as sufficient. By the end of Book 1 a number of theses can be established. Among the most important is the polyvalency of the literary topoi, which are revealed to have affiliations with both the epic and romance traditions, a genealogy complicating their ideological affiliations and thus any effort to mount an effective response to their perennial appeal. Spenser exploits this multiplicity for a series of intratextual repetitions that begin by interrogating genre but end by focusing on canon. A high degree of literary self-consciousness accumulates in the process, aftermath of a cultural saturation that eventually extends to the characters themselves, who constantly verge on the edge of a self-awareness suggesting a tertiary level of epic beyond the familiar distinctions of oral and written. The lesson to be learned at this stage in the poem: neither Stoic virtue nor Catholic reason, opposed to emotion, is enough. The edification of heroic poetry is similarly insufficient, and in fact the opposition of epic and romance, of Virgil vs. Ariosto and Tasso, is only a trap if not properly contextualized, focusing on genre when the conflict is canonical, that is, absorbed by plot when the crux is motivation.

The proem to Book 2, with its anxious evocation of Horace's *aegri somnia*, briefly shifts attention from the contrast of romance with epic to its differences with history and to concerns of verisimilitude and plausibility. The search for temperance is an emotional one, however, and soon gives rise to the image of the bridle as a remedy to Phedon's anger and Pyrochles's burning ire, as well as to the triad of the concupiscent, irascible, and rational faculties in the encounter with Amavia. Guyon's quest is notably gendered, as Britomart's will be in Book 3, temperance being figured largely through men, chastity through women. Among the key themes in these cantos: the sexualization of self-control, with shame identified as crucial to its acquisition, part of the ongoing internalization of the poem's search for virtue that continues the shift seen in the *Araucana* from epic *kleos* to Christian goodness. Among the lessons to be learned: the importance of anger, whose function, when properly associated with reason, is essential to the control of concupiscence. Guyon's story begins as chivalric adventure, still set in the enveloping woods of romance. It ends in an epic garden of delight, whose utter destruction is part of the inescapable logic of Spenser's reform. As the focus shifts from male to female in the Legend of Chastity, the imagery of woodland paths gives way to that of weaving and interweaving, figuring an emphasis on the *entrelacement* of romance that will continue in the Legend of Friendship. The instability of appearance persists here as a central concern, now focused on semblance and dissemblance and conjoined with gender in scenes that feature cross-dressing, transgendering, and the mistaken identities that ensue. A central goal of Britomart's quest is the differentiation between good and bad types of erotic desire, the first envisioned as conjugal harmony, the latter as the institutionalized lust of the castles of Malecasta and Malbecco. In spite of successive examples of virtuous alternatives, images of illicit love and of in-temperance continue to appear, enacting a central lesson both here and elsewhere in the poem, namely, the difficulty of attaining the quests in any lasting fashion, a pattern clearly emerging, instead, of their lessons repeatedly being forgotten and of the need to relearn them again and again. This repetition is structured as the persistence of intertexts, remainders of a *translatio* of pagan antiquity and un-reformed Christianity that endure "under erasure." It is figured as the contamination of imagery that continues to infect Spenser's narrative, on the one hand humanizing the efforts of the knights as their struggles for virtue ebb and flow and must be constantly re-engaged, in contrast to the implausibility of rote lessons learned by Tasso's characters, on the other offering early indications of a loss of narrative confidence that will ultimately prove conclusive. These concerns continue in the Legend of Friendship, where the imagery turns to gardens, Venus, and to a golden age of virtue. Here, as well, inter- and intratextual parodies provide a crucial mechanism for an ongoing critique of Ariosto and Tasso that extends to Apollonius, Ovid, Petrarch, and Castiglione, pastoral joining romance as a target of reform. Once again the characters' self-consciousness threatens to break through, as though their archetypes might get the best of them. Among the lessons to be learned, continued from Book 3, is the virtue of conjugal love, embodied in the Garden of Adonis. Among the dangers that persist, the difficulty of distinguishing between virtuous and base passion.

The Legends of Justice and Courtesy introduce fundamental changes to the imagery and themes of the previous quests. Book 5 temporarily leaves the world of romance for what is often seen as a thinly disguised critique of Tudor foreign policy, particularly as regards Ireland, a move that seems like nothing so much as a shift from multi-layered, Dantean allegory to a simpler historical version of the device. The Legend of Courtesy returns to themes of honor and shame, enacted here in a pastoral setting where virtue derives authority from proximity to the natural world and distance from the court. Applied to the book's titular virtue the association is deeply paradoxical, as are efforts to establish a bond between innate nobility and the social hierarchy, both of these an endorsement of natural signs fundamentally at odds with the iconoclastic impulse of reformist thought. A major threat in these final scenes of the poem is the familiar one of dissimulation, now both linguistic and political, enacted, on the one hand, in Calidore's reversal of the *rota Virgilii*, motivated problematically by a desire for Pastorella rather than for the virtues of bucolic life, and, on the other, by the ensuing breakdown between the autochthonous semantics of a natural language and the social realm, signaling a further retreat from the poem's original goals as well as the failure of efforts to recuperate England's soul through its archaic language, a vision overtaken by events on the ground, particularly in Ireland.[1] On Mt. Acidale the poet himself intrudes in double guise, Colin on the one hand, Coridon on the other, his presence disturbing narrative mimesis just as the clumsy shepherd upsets the magic circle of poetic creation. At this point the return of *entrelacement* threatens narrative progress, and the role of fortune supersedes individual effort, marking the abandonment of verisimilitude and a final turn to tales of fortuitous rescues and miraculous identities. Book 6 enacts a final deterioration of relations among the courtly, humanist, and reformers' worlds, humanism's contribution here being the revival of Greek romance, a literature enshrining an escape from reality. The final moral of these pages: efforts at virtue will always be forgotten and frequently come to naught, an utter discouragement figured in the Blatant Beast, last seen freely terrorizing the kingdom of speech.

2. Intertextual Forests and the Figuring of Grace

Virgilian epic provides a pattern for personal and literary identity that Ercilla and Spenser both emulate and challenge. Ercilla's emulation is most apparent in the *Araucana*'s celebration of Spanish imperial glory, in the *gravitas* with which he imbues events, and in the bond he asserts between public events and private integrity. His challenge to Virgil is most explicit in his defense of Dido, asserting a bond between the Araucan heroines and the Carthaginian queen, along with the juxtaposition of the abandoned woman and epic ideology. Beyond affirming his emulation of the *rota Virgilii*, Spenser's publication of the *Faerie Queene* reveals numerous analogues with the *Aeneid*,[2] key examples of which appear within the opening lines of the Legend of Holiness. Inscribed here as well is a fundamental challenge to the Latin poet, structured once again around Dido's abandonment, which once again assumes metafictional significance, transcending the issue of epos and eros to illuminate fundamental differences between Protestantism and the Roman Church, on the one hand, and between the reformers and partisans of the New Learning on the other. The first arises from a Pelagian indifference to God's grace and the justification by faith inherent in the interpretation

---

[1] Cf. Palmer on Spenser's "[. . .] coming to the dark realisation that language and meaning were not coextensive [. . .]": *Language and Conquest*, 106–7.

[2] See Hardie, "Spenser's Vergil"; Colin Burrow, "Spenser and Classical Traditions," in *Cambridge Companion to Spenser*, ed. Hadfield, 217–36, esp. 218–25; Syrithe Pugh, "Spenser and Classical Literature," in *Oxford Handbook*, ed. McCabe, 503–19.

of Aeneas' departure from Carthage as the victory of reason over emotion. This same Fulgentian reading (*Cont. Verg.* 16) gives rise to the second, forming as it does a central exhibit in the humanist celebration of epic as the supreme distillation of ancient wisdom, a role rightly reserved to Scripture. Defenders of Aeneas' victory saw Ariosto's Astolfo as his opposite, as someone dehumanized by lust. The *Faerie Queene*'s initial foray into the forest of literary models is structured around this contrast, framed on one end by allusions to Aeneas and Dido and on the other by those to their romance-epic analogues, Ariosto's Ruggiero and Alcina and Tasso's Rinaldo and Armida. Subservient to both as the poem begins is the mix of millenarian Protestantism and Arthurian chivalry that will come to dominate it.

The Virgilian motifs of the *Faerie Queene*'s opening lines have frequently been studied.[3] The discussion that follows suggests that, as was shown for the *Araucana*, expanding the analysis of these motifs to include their *dispositio* as well as *elocutio* reveals a structural dialogue with the *Aeneid* in addition to a thematic one. Individual analogues in this exchange are frequently minor. The exuberance with which they proliferate and their resonance as a whole, by contrast, are a powerful reminder of the fecundity with which imaginations saturated in the classical tradition generate secondary and tertiary echoes alongside primary ones. The beginning of the Legend of Holiness features an often-analyzed image of the catalogue of trees. Spenser's combination of this image with a second, that of the ancient forest or *antiqua silva* discussed earlier with regard to the *Araucana*, has been less frequently discussed. Following antiquity, the combination developed in contrasting directions that cinquecento theorists eventually associated with the opposition of epic and romance, the former linking it with the underworld journey, the latter employing it as a landscape of desire. The Wandering Wood recalls both these branches, and in its environs both traditions are shown to be inadequate. As one would expect, these topoi are fundamentally altered in the Spenserian context, the catabasis transformed from a topographic itinerary to a psychomachic one, its Virgilian identity as the tragic intersection of four types of desire refocused on sexual lust, foregrounding an issue that not only belies the individual's capacity for moral virtue, but that generates much of the *Faerie Queene*'s remaining action.

The grove where Redcross and Una seek shelter from the storm and where, rather than reenacting the amorous climax of Dido and Aeneas, they encounter Errour, is no sooner entered than a catalogue of twenty trees and their epithets

---

[3] See, inter alia, James Nohrnberg, *The Analogy of "The Faerie Queene"* (Princeton: Princeton University Press, 1976), 137–39; Gless, *Interpretation and Theology*, 57–61; Watkins, *Specter*, 91 ff.; Jennifer C. Vaught, "Spenser's Dialogic Voice in Book 1 of *The Faerie Queene*," *Studies in English Literature 1500–1900* 41 (2001): 71–89; Pugh, *Spenser and Ovid*, 42–76; and Hardie, "Spenser's Vergil"; Burrow, "Classical Traditions"; Pugh, "Classical Literature."

takes up half of the eighth stanza and all of the ninth. Given the speed with which the reader has been "thrusteth into the middest," as Spenser will say in the "Letter to Ralegh," this rhetorical flourish presents an unexpected and initially inexplicable delay.[4] The loci classici of this imagery, which momentarily suggests a *locus amoenus*, are found in the *Iliad*'s description of the Greeks as climbing to a remote, high forest in order to fell "high-crested oaks" for the funeral pyre of Patroclus (*Il.* 23.118), and in the *Odyssey*'s passing reference to Persephone's Grove with its miniature catalogue of "tall, black poplars" and "willows whose fruit dies young" (*Od.* 10.510), Homer thus condensing in a few brief lines what his successors will develop in two distinct directions. On the one hand subsequent use of the catalogue is associated with Virgil's modest version of it as a site where the Trojans gather wood for the funeral of Misenus (*Aen.* 6.180–182), which overgoes Homer by listing five species of trees. Ovid is the source of another tradition, envisioning the music of Orpheus as attracting an arboretum of twenty-six species to a barren hilltop (*Met.* 10.86–106). While the significance to Spenser of both versions of the catalog, together with their subsequent imitations, is well acknowledged, the importance of a fundamental difference between the two, reflected in the presence or absence of the corresponding *antiqua silva*, has been less frequently explored. The ancient forest is traditionally identified with isolation, great height, and light-blocking density, on the one hand, and with attributes of sacredness and purity on the other.[5] Its conjunction with the catalogue is notable in epic, where cutting down such old-growth trees, properly executed, is a ritual of purification, while improperly pursued it invites pollution. Virgil speaks of the "silvam immensam" or "boundless forest" (*Aen.* 6.186) as a place where "[. . .] pinguem dives opacat / ramus humum" ("the rich bough overshades the fruitful ground") (6.195–196). Following the *Aeneid*, the catalogue-ancient-forest combination appears in two key texts. In Lucan's *Pharsalia*, the original demonic parody, a blasphemous Caesar, obsessed with the siege of Massila, destroys "Lucus [. . .] longo numquam violatus ab aevo" (" [. . .] a wood, unfelled for countless generations") (3.399) that includes a catalogue of five species (3.440–442); in Statius's *Thebaid* the Seven construct a propitiatory pyre from "veteres incaedua ferro / silva comas" ("a wood that axe has never shorn of its ancient boughs") (6.90–91), a forest "[. . .] largae qua non opulentior umbrae / Argolicos inter saltusque educta Lycaeos / extulerat super astra caput" ("than

---

[4] On *dilatio* as an element of romance structure related to rhetorical *amplificatio*, see Patricia Parker, *Inescapable Romance* (Princeton: Princeton University Press, 1979), esp. 7–8, 58–60; for a recent analysis of Spenser's catalogue of trees that identifies it as Ovidian in origin, see Pugh, *Spenser and Ovid*, 45 ff.

[5] Ercilla characteristically modifies this imagery to conform with his New World surroundings, classical images of towering trees transmuted into the tangled undergrowth of the Andean foothills: "[. . .] una selva espesa / de matorrales y árboles cerrados" ("a compact forest of thickets and dense trees") (23.30.5–6); see 84 supra.

which no woods in Argos or Arcadia was taller or richer in shade") (6.91–92), where the species enumerated increases to twelve.[6] In the epic tradition the purification of funeral rites precedes climactic events, inspired by those for Patroclus that precede the attack on Troy. In Virgil, cleansing the pollution associated with Misenus makes it possible for the hero to enter the underworld, while in Statius the pyre precedes the attack on Thebes. In Lucan, who characteristically subverts heroic triumphalism, the significance of the episode is precisely the opposite, the destruction of the forest an act of sacrilege preceding an early tactical failure in Caesar's brutal campaign. Ovid's use of the catalogue, which inaugurates the development of this imagery associated with romance, makes no reference to old growth or the cutting of trees. Here the motif is a background for Orpheus's songs of illicit desire (*Met.* 10.152–154), an association continued by Ariosto, who locates his eight-species catalogue at the heart of the romance setting on Alcina's island (*O.F.* 6.21–24), and by Chaucer in the *Parliament of Fowls* (176–182), where the forest is the setting for the colloquy on love. The fact that both branches of the topos are inspired by Homer is early evidence of the innate erotic potential of epic argued in the pages that follow.

While the texts just noted emphasize an epic-romance opposition, others blur the distinction. Dante's *Inferno* opens with another protagonist lost in the woods, in this case a "selva selvaggia ed aspra e forte" ("savage forest, dense and difficult") (1.5). Here too the forest, now *sans* catalogue, precedes the pilgrim's epic journey through the underworld, but the theme of desire is never far from the heart of the *Commedia* as a whole.[7] Boccaccio's sequel to Statius transforms his predecessor's dark foreboding into the determinedly upbeat *Teseida*, where epic figures enact a courtly romance and royal marriage in a *selva vecchia* or "venerable forest" (*Teseida* 11.18.3) of eighteen species (11.22–24) that "[. . .] toccava con le cime il cielo" ("touched the heavens with its brow") (11.19.1). Displaying the complex synthesis that makes his work so pivotal to the Cinquecento debates, Tasso acknowledges the split personality of the ancient forest-catalogue combination in separate passages, associating the former with the epic funeral

---

[6] English translation of Lucan is by P. F. Widdows (Bloomington: Indiana University Press, 1988); translation of Statius is by D. H. Mozley (Cambridge, MA: Harvard University Press, 1928).

[7] Another forest appears in the *Inferno*'s Seventh Circle, the *selva dolorosa* (14.10) of suicides and squanderers, whose tormented Pier della Vigna provides an indirect link between Spenser's imagery here and the Fradubio episode in Canto 2. The Seventh Circle is also home to Capaneus, one of the Seven who attack Thebes, who appears shortly after the night raid in the *Thebaid* (10.738 ff.), and to the Harpies, who pollute the food of Aeneas' men (*Aen.* 3.225–228). In Apollonius the Harpies enact this punishment on the man who cuts down an ancient oak in spite of the pleas of a Hamadryad who resides within it (*Arg.* 2.476–481), providing another link between this imagery and Spenser's Fradubio.

of Dudone, in Canto 3, which speaks of "un bosco / sorge d'ombre" ("a dark
and waving wood") (3.56.7–8) composed of eleven species (3.75–76), and then
later of "[. . .] alta foresta, / foltissima di piante antiche, orrende" ("a lofty forest
[. . .] grown thick with ancient waving trees") (13.2.2–3), and finally of "l'antica
alta foresta" ("the deep and ancient forest") (18.17. 3) and "le piante antiche e
folte / en quelle solitudini selvagge" ("the thick and ancient trees in those savage solitudes") (18.22.6–7), this final locale envisioned as a place of diabolical
enchantment and the site of the climactic subordination of romance desire to
Counter-Reformation values, the dynamic that drives so much of Jerusalem's
epic liberation.

   Spenser establishes a web of structural and semantic intertexts with these
works. Like his epic predecessors, he associates the catalogue with the ancient
forest, which he identifies, on the one hand, by the height of the "loftie trees"
(1.7.4), the density "that heauen's light did hide" (1.7.5), and the sense of isolation, locating the cave "Amid the thickest wood" (1.11.7), and, on the other, by
the relationship between the forest and subsequent events. In Virgil, the appearance of the forest precedes Aeneas' journey through the underworld; Lucan, true
to form, inverts the topos, the journey made not by the protagonist to the world
below, but rather one from the underworld to the land of the living, creating the
vision of a hell-on-earth. Statius' battle of Thebes suggests Lucan's transformative pessimism; Dante, by contrast, elaborates the motif of the journey into a
full-fledged narrative. Tasso's forest alludes to the underworld journey at each of
its appearances, the funeral of Dudone followed by a description of the infernal
invocation called by the devil; the enchanted forest a site whose diabolical perils
must be physically as well as psychologically traversed.[8] Tasso's treatment of the
matter is especially significant for Spenser, who associates events at Archimago's
with the catabasis by means of several key images, most notable, a reference to
the gates of ivory and horn (*Aen.* 6.892–896), the initial invocation of underworld powers, a rite transferred from Virgil's Sibyl to Archimago via Lucan's
Erictho and Tasso's Ismen, and the journey itself, made here along a route that
mingles Ovidian and Virgilian descriptions of the underworld, the former most
apparent in the description of the house of Morpheus, source of the river Lethe
(*Met.* 11.592). Also noteworthy is the motif of the sorcerer threatening a lethar-
gic demonic authority with an "unmentionable name," one that remains unspeci-
fied in Lucan (6.744–745) and Tasso (13.10.2–8) but is identified by Archimago's
spirit helper as that of Hecate (1.43.1–3).[9] While the catabasis has a Christian

---

   [8] Cf. the convocation called by Lucifer, *G. L.* 4.1–17; Tasso's description of the forests's eventual felling maintains much of the heritage of infernal imagery: e.g., the gates
of hell, references to the Cocytus and to Pluto, and the nightly horrors, "che rassembra
infernal" ("that seem as if from Hell") (13.3.5); cf. *G. L.* 13.6–10 and 13.25.7–8.
   [9] In her translation of Lucan Braund notes the various identifications suggested for
the "unmentionable name," from Demiurgus or Creator to Hermes, Osiris, and Typhon/

counterpart in the Harrowing of Hell, in works prior to Spenser the underworld journey is both a trial and a source of knowledge. Even in pagan texts the challenge exceeds martial prowess, requiring the hero to suppress his fight-or-flight response in order to follow wiser counsel. Odysseus is instructed how to withstand terrifying hordes of spirits in order to gain the prophetic insight of Tiresias (*Od.* 11.28–185); the Sibyl assures Aeneas that the diabolical beasts he wants to attack are not what they appear, but rather, "sine corpore vitas" ("bodiless lives") that move about "sub imagine formae" ("under a hollow semblance of form") (*Aen.* 6.292–293); Dante's pilgrim faints from fear at what he sees and must be constantly reassured. Tasso and Spenser both offer Christian interpretations of the appearance-reality distinction: Rinaldo, like his literary predecessors, must brave similarly threatening visions, trusting Goffredo's instructions rather than his own perceptions; discarding the analogue to priestly advice, Spenser concentrates on the same dynamic, emphasizing the calamity that results when Redcross attempts to make the distinction on his own.

While these aspects of the *Faerie Queene*'s relationship to its epic predecessors stress structural parallels, the theme of erotic desire is never far from this portion of the epic plot. Circe instructs Odysseus on Hadean protocol; the funeral games for Anchises are the only distraction between Aeneas' departure from Carthage and his trip to Avernus, where, their roles fittingly inverted, Dido shuns him in the *lugentes campi*. The centrality of desire to these episodes of the *Gerusalemme Liberata* and the *Faerie Queene* results in numerous parallels between the two. Especially noteworthy is Tasso's description of the forest, even before Ismen's curse, as a gathering place for witches, who come here with their lovers for "i profani conviti e l'empie nozze" ("profane feasts and impious nuptials") (13.4.8).[10] After the first attempts to cut the forest down are thwarted by indistinct fears and strange forebodings (13.18), Tancredi, "lui che solo è fievole in amore" ("whose only weakness is love") (13.46.3), manages to distinguish between the appearance and reality of the initial threats, only to succumb to a vision of his beloved Clorinda. It is left to Rinaldo to finally succeed where Tancredi has failed, his victory made possible by the fact that "[. . .] fede il pensier nega / a quel che 'l senso gli offeria per vero" ("[his] reason is refusing faith in

Seti (*Civil War*, 285–86); in his translation of Tasso Anthony M. Esolen argues that the name is that of Jesus (*Jerusalem Delivered* [Baltimore: Johns Hopkins University Press, 2000], note to 13.10). The unmentionable-name motif is also appropriated by Ercilla, whose sorcerer, Fitón, in a similar scene, explicitly calls on Demogorgon, among other infernal deities (*Ar.* 23.80.5); Fitón, who has a great deal in common with the earlier models referred to here, responds to the motif of delay by threatening the spirit world with his own power (23.82.4–8); cf. Nicolopulos, *Prophecy*, 182–240.

[10] Text for Tasso is from *Gerusalemme Liberata*, ed. Lanfranco Caretti (Turin: Giulio Einaudi, 1971); English translation of Tasso, unless otherwise noted, is that of Ralph Nash, *Jerusalem Delivered* (Detroit: Wayne State University Press, 1987).

what his sense would proffer him as truth") (18. 25.1–2).[11] Spenser's focus on the process through which the Christian individual acquires moral virtue, in contrast to the *Liberata*'s emphasis on doctrinal rectitude, requires that he explore an interiority that Tasso no more than suggests, and he rewrites the *catabasis* as a challenge that Redcross fails, as an entering into hell in which the protagonist becomes trapped. It also requires that the challenge of the underworld journey, which functions in epic to certify the hero for a climactic trial, be transformed into an episode that drives the narrative, precipitating events to come.

As Archimago's machinations unfold, elements of the night-raid motif begin to percolate through the imagery of the underworld journey. The initial association is cursory: Redcross is "drowned in deadly sleepe" (1.36.6) when approached by the enemy, Spenser's phrase capturing each element of Virgil's "somno vinoque sepultam" (*Aen.* 2.265), from liquid imagery to fatal rest. The battle that ensues threatens Redcross's eternal life rather than his mortal one, and thus the erotic subtext of Virgil and Statius, where the potential for sexual lust combines with greed to sully the heroic enterprise, is elevated by Spenser from a complicating factor to the crux of the story, identifying it as the greatest threat to the knight's success. Once underway, the attack unfolds in *mise-en-abîme* fashion, initiated by a sexually charged dream that brings the knight to the edge of climax, at which point he wakes to discover himself within the dream and with Una's phantom double at his side:

> In this great passion of unwonted lust,
> Or wonted feare of doing ought amis,
> He started up, as seeming to mistrust
> Some secret ill, or hidden foe of his (1.49.1–4).

The description of sexual desire as unfamiliar and the heightened concern over comportment suggest adolescence, and embarrassment appears to motivate the anger that follows, a response foretelling the violence that Guyon will indulge at the Bower: "All cleane dismayd to see so vncouth sight, / And halfe enraged at her shameless guise, / He thought haue slaine her in his fierce despight" (1.50.1–3). Redcross's fury at Una's incontinence precipitates his questioning of her, a scene that hints at projection rather than his own "sufferance wise" (1.50.4). In the background is Dido's and Aeneas' meeting in the cave, Virgil's "conscius

---

[11] Nash's translation of "pensier" as "reason" captures the underlying significance of the scene, in contrast to Esolen's more literal "his thoughts"; Rinaldo's success in the forest explicitly Christianizes key components in the images being discussed here: he approaches the forest via a variation on the simile for the dawn referred to earlier; there's a pleasant breeze and "a dewey mist from the lap of lovely dawn" (18.15.7–8), further identified as "La rugiada del ciel," or "dew of Heaven") (18.16.1), echoed by Spenser as Redcross and Una encounter the rainstorm (1.6.6–7).

Aether conubiis" ("Heaven, the witness to their bridal") (*Aen.* 4.167–168) echoed in Spenser's "Hymen iō Hymen" (1.48.8). Juno, enemy of Aeneas, oversaw the Virgilian nuptials; in Redcross's perception, Venus, whose eroticism obstructs the quest for holiness, masterminds the Spenserian ones.

If the first canto concludes with an adumbration of the night raid, the second opens with a stanza-long simile for the dawn that functions to confirm it. As a device for accentuating a break in the narrative the simile is unexceptional. Notably medieval in its references to "the Northerne wagoner" with "his seuen-fold teme" and to "chearefull Chaunticlere" (2.1.1–6), it introduces Archimago's next attack on Redcross, which consists of revealing to him what appears to be Una in bed with another man. Jealousy now succeeds where lust had failed, and the voyeuristic revelation drives the knight once more into murderous rage, restrained in this instance by the sorcerer, whose subterfuge would be unmasked if the attack were allowed to proceed.[12] Redcross returns to his room, and after a second, decidedly more classical simile for the dawn, i.e., "[. . .] Hesperus in highest skie / Had spent his lampe, and brought forth dawning light" (2.6.7), he flees the hermitage. The following verse presents yet another simile for the same sunrise, the third in seven stanzas. Once again the reader is confronted with a procedure that, like the catalogue of trees, appears unwieldy, even in the context of frequent repetition, until the simile is discovered to be the pivotal one of the epic tradition, Spenser's version of which combines Homer's epithet, "rosy-fin-gered," not used by Virgil, with Virgil's description of Tithonus's bed as saffron, an adjective Homer uses instead to describe Dawn's robe:

> Now when the rosy-fingred Morning faire,
> Weary of aged Tithones saffron bed,
> Had spred her purple robe through dewey aire,
> And the high hils Titan discouered [. . .] (2.7.1–4).[13]

Ercilla, it will be recalled, employed the simile after his version of the night raid with Guacolda and Lautaro. His use of it imitated Virgil's, and Virgil's Homer, both of whom introduced the figure between their versions of the Doloneia and the resumption of intense fighting.[14] The opening stanzas of the *Faerie Queene*'s second canto, with their emphatic repetition of the simile, suggest the same construction. These verses simultaneously reference Virgil's only other use of the

---

[12] Cf. the narrator in the *Parliament of Fowls*, who, hearing groans coming from Venus's temple, says, "[. . .] wel espied I thenne / That al the cause of sorwes that they drie / Cometh of the bittre goddesse Jalousye" (250–252); jealousy is also central to Tasso's adaptation of this material, aroused by Armida in Goffredo's soldiers, "embroiled with one another and each man jealous in himself" (*G.L.* 10.60.6).

[13] Hamilton remarks on the incorporation of Ovid's *purpurae Aurorae* (*Met.* 3.184) in his note to *Faerie Queene* 2.7.1–3.

[14] See 57 ff., above.

image, which appears in a description of the morning on which Dido discovers her abandonment by Aeneas. Confirming this second parallel, no sooner has Spenser's simile concluded than

> The royall virgin shooke off drowsy-hed,
> And rising forth out of her baser bowre,
> Lookt for her knight, who far away was fled,
> And for her Dwarfe, that wont to wait each houre;
> Then gan she waile and weepe, to see that woefull stowre. (2.7.5–9)

Strengthening the correspondence with Virgil is the alarm with which the male protagonists flee their surroundings: Aeneas, rushing to launch the Trojan ships after his true dream-vision from Mercury; Redcross, of whom it is said that, after witnessing the false dream of Archimago, "Then vp he rose, and clad him hastily; / The Dwarfe him brought his steed: so both away do fly" (2.6.9).

Departing Archimago's in self-righteous jealousy, Redcross, in an intratextual parody characteristic of the poem, comes face to face with a personification of himself in the pagan knight Sansfoy. Redcross's victory over the knight, like that over Errour, is solely martial and therefore of limited value in his quest for Holiness, forcing him, as through repetition-compulsion, to reenact his earlier behavior. Sansfoy had been accompanied by Una's demonic counterpart disguised as the beautiful Fidessa. Again there is a mix of Virgilian and Ariostan models, with Sansfoy dying as a chivalric Turnus and Fidessa fleeing in feigned fear until Redcross catches up to her, at which point, drawing on the same motif of the damsel-in-distress utilized by Ercilla's Tegualda, she, "[. . .] turning backe with ruefull countenaunce, / Cride, Mercy mercy Sir vouchsafe to show / On silly Dame, subject to hard mischaunce, / And to your mighty will [. . .]" (2.21.2–4).[15] Assured of his benign intentions, Fidessa is asked to tell her story, a cynical parody of those told by Ercilla's heroines regarding the sole daughter of a king who betroths her to a handsome prince killed shortly thereafter, transforming her into the abandoned-woman-as-widow searching for the corpse of her spouse. In describing her sorrow, Fidessa associates herself with Dido via Virgil's well-known simile (*Aen.* 4.68–73) of the stricken hind (2.24.6–9).[16] As if to reassure

---

[15] Additional references to the *Aeneid* in these lines include the simile comparing the combat between Redcross and Sansfoy to two rams (2.16.1–2), recalling Virgil's simile of Aeneas and Turnus as two bulls (*Aen.* 12.717–719), and the battle-ending blow cleaving Sansfoy's head, which references the death of Pandarus (in a blow, paradoxically for present purposes, delivered by Turnus) (*Aen.* 9.754–755); cf. Ercilla's use of the image at *Ar.* 25.31.2–4; for Tegualda, see 67 ff., supra.

[16] See 52, n. 14, supra. Spenser and Ercilla employ a number of the same romance conceits in these scenes. Redcross is struck by Fidessa's rich attire (2.21.5): cf. the similar reaction of the *Araucana*'s narrator to the dress of Glaura (28.3.7–8) and Lauca (32.32.4); it is said of Redcross that Fidessa's story "Did much emmoue his stout heroïcke

her of romance rather than epic intentions, Redcross, "in great passion all this while" (2.26.5), disassociates himself from his Virgilian model by articulating his sympathy in the very same terms that Dido used to describe the obduracy of Aeneas: "[. . .] Faire Lady hart of flint would rew / The vndeserued woes and sorrowes, which ye shew" (2.26–29). At this point the narrative begins to repeat itself, with the knight and lady traveling together until, beset by the heat of the sun rather than rain, they seek shelter, once again, under trees.[17] Again the site mixes the attractions of a *locus amoenus* with intimations of foreboding, and again the Virgilian model is subverted, not, in this case, by imagery of the militant Protestant knight, but rather by a brief incursion into Petrarchan discourse as Redcross and Fidessa distract themselves, and then by the Ariostan Fradubio, whose warning plaint, although unnerving to the knight, has no more effect on him than did its model on Ruggiero. The Fradubio episode brings the *Faerie Queene*'s initial foray into these classical motifs full circle, not only through its focus on sexual content, but also by means of its subtext regarding the *auri sacra fames* (*Aen.* 3.57) or lust for gold that links the three main literary models here: the death of Polydorus at the hands of the king of Thrace, the deaths of Nisus and Euryalus, and the death of Sychaeus, murdered by Pygmalion.

The opening cantos of the *Faerie Queene* are marked by a density of intertexts that threaten to entrap the reader while drawing attention to their own complex affiliations, impeding forward progress while signaling an important series of Virgilian revisions and the poem's first group of demonic parodies. Spenser controls what is frequently structured as a generic competition through the deployment of imagery identified with Virgilian epic, on the one hand, and with romance or romance-epic on the other. Each of these motifs, not only the catalogue of trees, the ancient forest, and the underworld journey, but also the abandoned woman and the night raid, while originally epic in affiliation, has either established or potential significance in romance. Even in antiquity the forest, so central to the later landscape of Arthurian chivalry, is associated, as is the catalogue, not only with Virgilian catabasis, but also, via Ovid, with Orpheus, who makes his own underworld

---

heart" (2.21.6): cf. the effects of Tegualda and Glaura on Ercilla's narrator (20.35.1) and (28.5.6–7); Ercilla's Araucan heroines are frequently the daughters of Araucan leaders and engaged to promising youths; Tegualda's beloved is killed shortly after their marriage rather than before, as in Fidessa's case (*Ar.* 20.37.1–20.75.8); Lauca's admirable young spouse is similarly killed (32.34.7–8). Tegualda, it will be recalled, was also searching for the body of her beloved (20.31.5).

[17] Cf.: "[. . .] sed duris genuit te cautibus horrens Caucasus" ("but rugged Caucasus on his flinty rocks begat thee") (4.366–367). Fidessa feigns shamefastness as they proceed (2.27.6); cf. the dissimulations of Tasso's Armida in the Christian camp, once her petition has been granted, with its many echoes of the issues raised both here and earlier (*G. L.* 4.87.5–8).

journey, driven by love.[18] The abandoned woman is enacted as convincingly by
chivalric damsels as classical heroines, while the night raid's subliminal eroticism,
elevated to primacy, transforms the episode into a romantic encounter. Each of
these variations is evidence of the degree to which the questioning of heroic values,
rather than characteristic of a secondary epic tradition, is located fully within the
primary one, where it is consistently figured, beginning with Homer, in terms of
conflict between the epic and erotic. Spenser takes advantage of the inherent polyvalency of these images to repeat them as intratextual variations. These variations,
in turn, expose contrasting ideologies, none of which, at this early point in the
poem, is acceptable: ancient models, if virtuous, are either pagan or, if Christian-
ized, Pelagian; chivalric ones, especially via Ariosto, are at best irreverent. Emphasizing this multiplicity are the multiple models for Spenser's protagonists, who
enact a series of roles. Redcross plays Aeneas, but also Ruggiero-Rinaldo. As the
one true Church Una cannot be divided and is therefore doubled: a noble Dido, on
the one hand; her *doppelgängers*, Duessa-Fidessa, as Alcina-Armida on the other,
these figures, recalling the tradition of bifurcated heroines, as neatly opposed as
the commentarists envisioned Astolfo and Aeneas to be: the abandoned woman,
on one side, the seductive sorceress abandoning a succession of male lovers on the
other. The polyvalency of this imagery derives from Virgil himself, who exploited
its erotic potential for his critique of epic triumphalism. In the opening pages of the
Faerie Queene, by contrast, the erotic itself becomes the target, interrogated by the
quest for Christian holiness.[19]

Spenser's *imitatio* proceeds from two perspectives, one the external realm of
plot components, the other an internal stance contributing to the proto-psychological quality of key passages. This combination endows the protagonists with
a quality of literary self-consciousness, as though subliminally aware of their
textual heritage. In interactions with Una, Redcross appears at times to inten-
tionally imitate his Trojan predecessor. The poem's opening storm and seeking
of shelter establishes the association; subsequent less obvious correspondences
extend it. At Archimago's hermitage the evil dream leads Redcross to envision
Venus leading Una to his bed, suggesting that he sees himself as Aeneas, whose

[18] See Brumble, *Myths*, 248–53.

[19] Tasso's version of the night raid segues from the original pair of marauders, Clorinda and Argante (*G. L.* 12.9 ff.), to the unrequited mixed-religion couple, Clorinda and
Tancredi (*G. L.* 13.51 ff.). Splitting the erotic component of the night raid along enemy
lines allows Tasso to thematize the control of desire through its destruction, a denouement in keeping with the *Liberata*'s more programmatic treatment of issues. In the process Tancredi is transformed into a male version of the abandoned woman who voices
many of the associated sentiments discussed above (*G. L.* 12.75.1–8), an excess of grief
identified with feminine infirmity and criticized as an intemperance that must be bridled
(12 88.3–8). The denouement is a pathetic scene in which Tancredi kills Clorinda, the
emotional equivalent of Nisus killing Euryalus.

goddess-mother oversaw the encounter between her son and the queen of Carthage; Archimago seems similarly aware of the literary context, which he takes advantage of to ensnare his victim. Redcross's subsequent abandonment of Una, which the simile of the dawn and Una's outcry associate with Dido, extends the parallel; shortly thereafter comes the knight's victory over Sansfoy, whose death alludes so clearly to that of Turnus. The Virgilian references are poised to repeat themselves when Redcross and Fidessa seek shelter from the sun. Here, however, parallels with the *Aeneid* are rejected, most importantly, by Redcross himself, who explicitly disavows Fidessa's implicit identification of him with the Trojan hero, then by the "courting dalliaunce" (1.2.14.1) the knight initiates, and, finally, by the Fradubio motif which interrupts Redcross's incipient Petrarchan persona, providing an early indication of how little courtly *grazia* will have to do with true grace. While these variations on traditional imagery highlight a dynamic of Virgilian emulation, Spenser's underlying contention, like Ercilla's, is with canon rather than genre, his parodic variations interrogating canonical logic while highlighting what is truly at stake for reformed religion.

3. Platonic Visions and the Gendering of Continence

Canto 3 opens with a paean of devotion to female beauty wronged reminiscent of the *Araucana*, in which Spenser's narrator speaks of the "fast fealtie" he owes "vnto all woman kind" (3.1.7). Tensions persist, however, between such characteristically courtly expressions and the frequent marginalization of women by humanism together with their demonization by the reformers. Redcross passes through Lucifera's House of Pride, a hotbed of courtly vanity whose dungeon is filled with classical heroes enshrined by humanist pedagogy, figures whose ignorance of true religion reduces their Stoic virtues to the house's nominal transgression. Imprisoned alongside them are examples of female notoriety, including Semiramis and Cleopatra, emblems of a fatal eroticism prefiguring Acrasia's appearance at the Bower of Bliss. Classical topoi continue to proliferate in these cantos, together with a bewildering multiplicity of characters and plots inscribing the potential for moral error, each of these elements increasingly confronted with properly reformed versions of themselves. Redcross's combat with a second pagan knight, Sansjoy, is introduced by yet another simile for the dawn, whose echo of biblical imagery in the description of the sun as "a bridegroom leaving his chamber" (Psalms 19:4) offers a further integration of Christian and classical imagery:

And *Phoebus* fresh, as bridegroome to his mate,
Came dauncing forth, shaking his deawie haire:
And hurld his glistring beames through gloomy aire. (5.2.1–5).[20]

Upon leaving Lucifera's palace, Redcross and Duessa/Fidessa are found once
again in another demonic *locus amoenus* where they resume their earlier dalliance interrupted by Fradubio. On this occasion the peril of the encounter is
made explicit, and the post-coitally incapacitated knight is defeated by Orgoglio,
precipitating the first appearance of the poem's perennial hero, Prince Arthur.
Arthur's introduction concludes by recounting how he fell in love with a vision of
the Faery Queene that came to him in a dream: "Me seemed, by my side a roy-
all Mayd / Her daintie limbes full softly down did lay" (9.13.5–8), a nominally
chaste version of Redcross's lustful nightmare at Archimago's: "Then seemed him
his Lady by him lay" (1.47.8), the near quotation suggesting how difficult it will
be in the verses ahead to distinguish between good and bad erotic passion.[21]
At the heart of the book the knight enters the House of Holiness and learns
the Christian virtues of faith, hope, and charity, destined to supplant those of
the classical world. Having sought forgiveness for his sins, Redcross's instruc-
tion culminates in his ascension—accompanied by the hermit Contemplation, a
Christian Archimago—of a peak symbolically combining the Mount of Olives,
Mount Sinai, and Parnassus, which offers a panorama not of the *piccolo mondo* of
epics such as Ariosto's, Tasso's, and Ercilla's, but of the city of God's chosen, the
New Hierusalem. The knight's experience here contrasts instructively with that of
the *Araucana*'s narrator during the vision of Spanish beauty. Both passages are
strongly Platonic, referencing the soul's ascension to the realm of truth, recalled
in subsequent encounters with beauty. The *Araucana*'s narrator, describing his
awakening to true love and stressing the moral strength demanded of honor,
focuses on the interplay of the concupiscent, irascible, and rational parts of the
soul. While Spenser will emphasize these qualities in the legends of Temperance and Chastity, his inspiration at this point in the poem comes from Plato's
description of the newly initiated soul's beatific sensations. A blissful Redcross
would remain on the mount forever were it not for the hermit's insistence that
the route to paradise lies through the active life and the completion of his quest.

---

[20] Cf. Hamilton's note at *Faerie Queene* 5.2.3–5; on the earlier, classical simile at
2.7.1–4, see 157, supra; an additional version of the simile appears prior to Redcross's
defeat of the dragon in Canto 11 (11.51.2–5). Redcross's battle with Sansjoy, the brother
of Sansfoy, features various Virgilian motifs, e.g., the pagan knight's temporary rescue by
a protecting cloud, in imitation of Aeneas (*Aen.* 5.810) and Hector (*Il.* 20.444).

[21] Hamilton makes a distinction between the "immediate satisfaction" sought by
the lustful false-Una of Redcross's dream and the future love promised by the chaste
Faerie Queene; his citation of C. S. Lewis's "double obscurity" in these lines acknowledges the argument's limited persuasiveness (note to *Faerie Queene* 9.14.1–8).

Accepting his destiny as the future Saint George, Redcross captures and impris-
ons Archimago and defeats the dragon that has usurped the kingdom of Una's
parents. The Legend of Holiness closes with the betrothal of the two, a celebration of the conjugal state that assumes such importance in Spenser's vision.

The optimism engendered by the victories of Redcross and Arthur persists
into Book 2, informing the Proem's identification with New World exploration.
The link stems as well from the poet's anxiety regarding the credibility of faery-
land, which he worries some readers may identify with the "aboundance of an idle
braine" rather than with recent discoveries of the Amazon, Peru, and Virginia,
a conceit less notable for what it reveals about the provisional quality attached to
transatlantic reality than for its echo of Horace's *aegri somnia* and Petrarch's *sogno
d'infermi* and thus of the early modern attacks on romance, contrasted by Amyot
and now by Spenser with history and by the cinquecento debates with epic. The
Legend of Holiness acknowledged the epic-romance opposition through its juxtaposition of canonical imagery associated with each. At the start of the Legend
of Temperance, by contrast, the poet engages with history, claiming to write
a "famous antique" (2.1.2) version of it founded on "iust memory" (2.1.5), an
assertion that affiliates him with accounts of imperial expansion such as Ercilla's
while figuring himself an explorer of the spiritual realm. Given the emphasis in
the "Letter to Ralegh" on the pleasing variety of history's examples in contrast
to philosophy's rules, it comes as no surprise how deftly the narrative not only
reverts from issues of genre to indulge in multiple storylines, but how the first
of these stories, notwithstanding the proem's concern with credibility, enacts a
parody of the basic romance plot, the rescue of a damsel in distress. The hero here
is Archimago, who has escaped imprisonment (setting a pattern for the Blatant
Beast later in the narrative), and the maiden Duessa, the two of them joining
forces to simultaneously take revenge on Redcross and distract the poem's next
knight, Sir Guyon, from his quest. The trap they set nearly succeeds, with the
sorcerer, said "to weave a web of wicked guile" (1.8.4) (an early example of the
imagery of weaving associated with the *entrelacement* of romance), impersonating
a squire who seeks Guyon's help to punish a grievous example of intemperance,
the rape of Duessa, his supposed mistress.[22] Like Redcross before him, Guyon
has begun his quest already possessing substantial aspects of the virtue he seeks
to acquire. Like his predecessor he must discover the true nature of this virtue,
which in Spenserian terms means locating its source within himself rather than
simply learning new rules. The subject of shame, which dominates the account of
Duessa's violation, offers ideal access to these issues while also proving central to
the quest for temperance. The term is first used to condemn the assault on Duessa
and describe her response; it recurs nine times in the next twenty cantos, most
notably in reference to Archimago, whose *raison d'être* is described as turning the

---

[22] Cf. Eugène Vinaver, *Form and Meaning in Medieval Romance* (Leeds: Modern
Humanities Research Association, 1966), 7–10.

fame of knights to shame, a conceit that reveals the degree to which the two are conceived as opposites, reflecting the epic contrast of *kleos* and *aidos*. In narrowly avoiding combat with each other, Redcross and Guyon acknowledge their escape from shame (1.27.2–1.28.5). Chastity and "honour virginall" (1.10.8), targets of the alleged attack on Duessa, are noted as qualities whose loss occasions shame.

As events proceed, the underlying concern with temperance and chastity is increasingly sexualized, reflecting a heightened sensitivity to gender magnified on the one hand by Puritan mores and on the other by Elizabethan England's attitude toward its maiden queen. The progression is part of the broader sexualization of self-control that characterizes the Christianizing of classical concepts, including, as events go on to reveal, the Platonic bridle of shame and continence. As noted earlier, *aidos* or shame originally encompassed ideas of modesty and self-respect, whereas *sophrosyne* or continence combined those of temperance, modesty, and chastity. While the sexual aspect of chastity was subsequently singled out for special attention in concepts of *pudor*, *pudicitia*, and *continentia*, in Spenser the components of continence, activating previously subliminal associations, have been gendered, with temperance now a predominantly male concern, as confirmed by Guyon's quest, while chastity, the quest of Britomart in Book 3, is predominantly female. Here in Book 2 attention is soon directed by Duessa's damsel-in-distress and by the story told by Amavia, another abandoned woman whom Guyon encounters in the wake of Archimago's failed plot, to the related Platonic distinctions among the concupiscent, irascible, and rational faculties. The proper integration of these three, i.e., the subservience of the first to the second, in turn submissive to the third, will be the goal of Guyon, who, having internalized the hierarchy, will face Acrasia and the Bower of Bliss. The inspired eroticism of the Bower, conjoined with Guyon's violent repudiation of it, have inspired impassioned responses from readers, including an influential study discerning a deconstructive disjunction between the two. However discordant the scene, its logic is inescapable, rooted in a Platonic conception of self-control and carefully constructed throughout the book, an object lesson, on the one hand, on just how seductive the path of error, imaged here in the epic garden of delight, can be, and on the other of the harshness required to counter it effectively.[23]

In addition to foreshadowing the climax of his quest, the story that Amavia tells Guyon before she kills herself offers a succinct inversion of the romance plot that Archimago and Duessa had tried to trick him into believing. Here, instead of the hapless female ravished by a miscreant male, it is Amavia's husband, Sir Mordant, first ravished by Acrasia and then killed by her when Amavia manages to rescue him from the Bower, having "[. . .] him recured to a better will, / Purged from drugs of foule intemperance" (1.54.8). Amavia's suicidal grief for

---

[23] Cf. Greenblatt, *Renaissance Self-Fashioning*, 157–92; for an opposing reading, see Watkins, *Specter of Dido*; for recent analysis of the Bower episode that takes issue with Greenblatt, see Pugh, *Spenser and Ovid*, 81–115.

her husband recalls Ercilla's heroines and, specifically, one of their models noted earlier, Xenophon's Panthea, who, after risking her life to retrieve the body of her husband from the battlefield, killed herself as Xenophon's narrator attempted to console her. In the Spenserian context not only is Amavia's suicide un-Christian, but her Stoic self-absorption is also heretical, as Lucifera's dungeon made clear, and it comes as no surprise to find her repeatedly identified with Dido.[24] Guyon's incipient understanding of temperance is displayed shortly after the Amavia episode, when he reassures Phedon, a battered victim of Furor, that "all your hurts may soone through temperance be eased" (4.33.9). Like a teacher with a promising student, the Palmer expands upon this in familiar Platonic terms:

> Then gan the Palmer thus, Most wretched man,
> That to affections does the *bridle* lend;
> In their beginning they are weake and wan,
> But soone through suff'rance grow to fearefull end [. . .] (4.34.1–4)

Besting Pyrochles, emblem of irascibility, in combat a few stanzas later, Guyon notes, "That hasty wroth, and heedlesse hazardrie / Do breede repentaunce late, and lasting infamie" (5.13.8–9), a lesson he exemplifies by resisting the urge to kill him. He proceeds to deliver a homily on shame and temperance worthy of the Palmer himself, the conclusion of which proves his newfound insight in how clearly it shifts the focus from shame as an external attribute, i.e., as the absence of *kleos* or public honor to a matter of internal sensibility:

> Losse is no shame, nor to be less then foe,
> but to be lesser, then himselfe, doth marre
> Both loosers lot, and victours prayse alsoe.
> Vaine others ouerthrowes, who selfe doth ouerthrowe. (5.15.6–9)

In spite of such eloquence if not because of it (rhetorical sophistication being a notoriously weak link in the wisdom of pagan antiquity), subsequent events reveal Guyon's understanding of temperance to have been largely confined to anger and pride, whereas his confrontation with Acrasia will prove concupiscence the more insidious opponent.

The crucial relationship between irascibility and concupiscence is made explicit at the opening of Canto 6, where the poet reflects on the effort to summon Cymochles, Pyrochles's brother and the emblem of concupiscence, to Pyrochles' assistance. Echoing Redcross's earlier dalliance with Duessa (1.9.7.2),

---

[24] Cf. the imagery of the wounded hind (1.38.6) and the operatic resilience with which Amavia thrice appears to succumb to death only to revive and extend her plaint (1.46.3); Watkins sees Spenser as appropriating both Didos available in the Renaissance, Amavia representing "a chaste Dido who liberates the hero from her concupiscent counterpart [Acrasia]" (*Specter of Dido*, 125).

Cymochles is discovered at the bower of Acrasia, where he must be shamed into re-arming, his masculinity paradoxically relinquished in an act that supposedly confirms it. His departure from the garden, foreshadowing Guyon's rousting of Verdant, simultaneously enacts the traditional treatment of the topos while exposing its ineffectiveness. The lesson applies especially to Ariosto and Tasso, who in spite of Christianizing pagan themes had left these paradisiacal topographies intact in the wake of the errant hero's rescue, ignorant, from Spenser's perspective, of their true threat and of the need to destroy them, a concern he now elucidates in a stanza revealing the heart of Guyon's challenge:

> A harder lesson, to learne Continence
> In ioyous pleasure, then in grieuous paine:
> For sweetnesse doth allure the weaker sence
> So strongly, that vneathes it can refraine
> From that, which feeble nature couets faine;
> But griefe and wrath, that be her enemies,
> And foes of life, she better can restraine. (6.1.1–7)

Not only is sensual pleasure more difficult to resist than wrath, but as the *Republic* figures it, in opposition to Stoic *apatheia*, the high-spirited part of the soul or its capacity for righteous anger, *ho thymos*, allies with reason in subduing the irrational or appetitive part, *hē epithymetikos* (*Rep.* 4.439d-440b).[25] This Platonic paradigm, unexplored by Ercilla, whose imagery recalls the *Phaedrus* and the Neoplatonism of Castiglione, was embraced explicitly by Tasso, whose "Allegory" states that "[. . .] the rational faculty must not exclude the irascible from action (for the Stoics were much deceived in this regard) and must not usurp its functions (since such an usurpation would be counter to natural justice) but must become its attendant and minister" (161). Having figured the alliance of the two in Rinaldo's cutting down of the tree that appeared inhabited by Armida, thereby breaking the spell that protected the enchanted wood (*G. L.* 18.37), Tasso went on to lay out the precise nature of their relationship in a passage notable for its militarization of the issue, stating with regard to anger:

> It exists in the soul the way soldiers exist in human society. Just as it is their duty to fight against enemies in obedience to princes who have the art and knowledge of command, so the irascible faculty, as the robust and martial

---

[25] In Homer ὁ θυμός sometimes corresponds to the Latin *anima* as a more generalized sense of the soul; at other times it signifies anger, as in that which Achilles finally relinquishes (*Il.* 19.66) (Achilles's famous initial anger is ἡ μῆνις). The conception of θυμός as a kind of righteous indignation is distinctly Platonic; cf. Paul Shorey, *Republic I* (Cambridge, MA: Harvard University Press, 1930), 398 n. c; cf. *Laws* 731b-c, which confirms the thesis. Aristotle concurs in describing anger as less difficult to control than pleasure (*Nicomachean Ethics*, 2.4.1105a).

part of the soul, is obliged to arm itself on behalf of reason against the concupiscent faculties and, with that vehemence and ferocity characteristic of
itself, to beat back and drive away everything that can be an impediment
to happiness. (160)[26]

While Guyon's experience in the Legend of Temperance has shown wrath to be
increasingly important, Spenser's take on wrath's relationship to lust, as expected,
goes beyond Tasso's programmatic treatment of the topic not only in the degree
to which he explores Guyon's internal experience, but more significantly in his
shifting the locale for their climactic confrontation from the enchanted wood
of romance to epic's erotic bower, a more appropriate because more seductive
and thus more dangerous topography in light of cinquecento attacks on romance
and the humanist celebration of epic. The intimate association between the two
emotions becomes explicit when the imagery of fire and wounds traditionally
evoked by erotic passion is employed by Pyrochles to complain of his "inly flam-
ing syde" (6.44.3) and of the fire that "burnes in mine entrails bright" (6.50.4).
Having failed to quench this Furor-born conflagration in the waters of Idle
Lake, it is Archimago who, searching his "secret wounds" (6.51.3) and "hidden
fire" (6.51.5), will finally bring Pyrochles relief. Not being based on the proper
subordination of irascibility to reason, however, the cure is only temporary, and
Pyrochles returns in Canto 8, once again "inflam'd with rage" (8.12.1), for a final
showdown with Arthur.

While Guyon's quest will ultimately focus on the erotic component of concupiscence, his preparatory adventures enact a lust for wealth as well as an excessive pursuit of pleasure more broadly, the former bringing him into contact with
Mammon, the latter with Phaedria, a figure devoted to frivolity and "loose dalliaunce" (6.8.1) whose lair on Idle Lake offers a less sexualized version of Acrasia's
bower. Idleness itself is a signal evil, associated with both Acrasia and Phaedria
via Cymochles, whose "idle mind" (5.28.5) at the Bower of Bliss is mirrored in
the "idle dreme" (6.27.2) that later seduces him on Phaedria's wandering island,
a replay of his earlier experience in terms of sensuality more generally, both of
these episodes being narrative foreplay to Guyon's climactic appearance at the
Bower. The depiction of Mammon's cave enacts the motif of the underworld
journey as a series of temptations focused on greed and an excessive desire for
reputation or honor for its own sake. Having successfully resisted these, Guyon

---

[26] These passages in Tasso's "Allegory" have special resonance with the works of
Guazzo and Bryskett, discussed above, as well as with Spenser's *View*. Following the
citation here, the "Allegory" momentarily suggests a more politic solution to discord, only
to reject it (161); displaying his characteristic mix of religious and political dogma, Tasso
goes on in terms that presage some aspects of Spenser's natural order arguments in Book
6 (161–62). For additional discussion of the "ireful" and concupiscent powers in the *Liberata*, represented by Tancredi and Rinaldo, see Helgerson, "Tasso on Spenser," 224–25.

is led to the garden of Proserpine, a *locus eremus* whose catalogue of five funereal trees (7.52.1–5) parodies not only its model, the *Odyssey*'s depiction of Persephone's grove, discussed above, but also the catalogue of virtuous trees associated with the Wandering Wood. If the former figures Guyon as an Odysseus, the silver stool and tree of golden apples at the heart of Proserpine's grove envision him an Aeneas, and, via the association with Paris and Helen, as a metonym for classical epic (7.55.9). Concluding the catabasis is a Dantean scene in which Guyon is shown the suffering figures of Tantalus and Pontius Pilate, after which he is banished by Mammon to the upper world, reaching which, like Dante's pilgrim, he faints. Having been saved by "th'exceeding grace / of highest God" (8.1.5–6) in the guise of Arthur, Guyon and the prince undergo a Platonic initiation at Alma's castle or the House of Temperance, at the heart of which each man is drawn to a maiden embodying his particular genius. The prince chooses Prays-desire, the knight Shamefastnesse, two figures, as seen earlier, derived from Petrarch's "Desio-sol-d'onore" ("desire for honor") and "Timor-d'infamia" ("fear of infamy"), of which Elyot remarks in the *Governour*: "By shamfastnes, as it were with a *bridell*, they rule as well theyr dedes as their appetites. And desire of prayse addeth to a sharpe spurre to their disposition towarde lernyng and vertue" (1.9) (emphasis added). Book 2 closes with their newfound insights translated into action, Arthur defeating Maleger and the enemies of temperance with heaven's help in the guise of his squire, of whom the poet remarks that "had not grace thee blest, thou shouldest not suruiue" (11.30.9), Guyon proceeding to his confrontation with Acrasia.[27]

Guyon's destruction of the Bower of Bliss is not only the spectacular climax of the Legend of Temperance, but also a striking repudiation by Spenser of prior treatments of the epic garden of delight. The episode's violent end is foreshadowed in scenes on the bower's gate, the description of which forms a central part of the episode's inspired sensuality. While the subject of these illustrations is said to be "the famous history / Of *Iason* and *Medea*" (12.44.4), Spenser's lines more prominently recall corresponding scenes by Ariosto and Tasso. The *Liberata* describes Rinaldo's rescuers as entering Armida's palace through gates that depict two sets of couples, Hercules with Iole and Antony with Cleopatra (*Lib.* 16.3.1–16.7.8), while the *Furioso*, although not mentioning gates, sustains the motif by describing Ruggiero's lavish welcome at Alcina's as including "[. . .] chie, cantando, dire / d'amor sapesse gaudi e passioni" ("he who, singing, knew how to tell of love's joys and ecstasies") (*O. F.* 7.19.6) and by mentioning King Ninus, Antony and Cleopatra, and Jove and Ganymede. Tasso's gates continue the ecphrastic tradition of Homer and Virgil. While focusing on notorious love affairs, the descriptions in Tasso and Ariosto both reference the shield of Aeneas via Antony and Cleopatra and, by extension, the battle of Actium and heart

---

[27] As did Book 1, Book 2 repeatedly distinguishes Christian grace from the courtly variety, e.g.: 1.9.9, 4.21.1, and 7.50.2.

of Vulcan's handiwork.[28] Ariosto's three references are presented as narratorial commentary rather than as seen by Ruggiero, their negative connotations part of the *Furioso*'s familiar use of dramatic irony.[29] The *Liberata*'s ecphrasis, by contrast, is problematic, for while its reference to love affairs in which the males die inglorious deaths may be intended as irony, these images, in full view of all who enter Armida's realm, serve as poor advertisements of the charms that lie ahead. This is especially true in the case of Hercules, whose love for Iole results in the magic robe sent by his wife to eradicate his passion, a robe that, similar to the one sent by Medea to Creusa (noted by Spenser in this same passage) (12.45.9), ends up setting him alight and consuming him from within, a scene illustrated by the same canonical imagery of erotic furor encountered throughout the present discussion, with the notable difference that here the flames are actually fatal: "caecaque medullis / tabe liquefactis tollens" ("his very marrow melts with the hidden, deadly fire") (*Met.* 9.174–175). In contrast to Tasso's mixed message, the presence of Jason and Medea on the gates of the Bower of Bliss illustrates another of Spenser's corrections of the *Liberata*, resolving as it does the competing demands of narrative logic and authorial commentary. From the point of view of the epic hero gone astray the legend of the golden fleece offers the allure of heroic exploits enabled by love. Guyon's ultimate destruction of the garden and of these very illustrations, on the other hand, enacts Spenser's necessary rejection not only of what he considers the misplaced tolerance inscribed by Ariosto's and Tasso's treatments of this epic motif, but more pointedly of the intemperance at the heart of Virgil's depiction of the love of Dido and Aeneas, for which Jason and Medea provided a key model.[30] As a prologue to the climax of Book 2 the reference to Apollonius has additional significance in light of the central role played by shame in Medea's falling in love, the suppression of her *aidos* setting the stage for all that follows. It is this same sense of self-respect that, once suppressed, results in the abandonment of their missions not only by Ruggiero and

---

[28] Cf. Brumble, *Myths*, 11–12.

[29] King Ninus, a wealthy Assyrian monarch, married Semiramis, one of the emblems of eroticism encountered by Redcross in the dungeon of the House of Pride; after Ninus's death, Semiramis became renowned, on the one hand, for her prowess as a warrior and as the ruler most responsible for the magnificence of Babylon, suggesting similarities with Dido and Carthage, and on the other for her unnatural attraction for her son, who according to some sources had her killed. See Brumble, *Myths*, 307–9.

[30] Antonius and Cleopatra are earlier relegated to Lucifera's dungeon (I.5.49.9; I.5.50.7). While the legend of the golden fleece has a complex, ambiguous character exploited by Apollonius, Jason is nonetheless a heroic figure rather than a tragic one, like Antony; unlike Hercules, his accomplishments are made possible by love, however excessive this love is deemed, as in the case of Comus, for whom Jason and Medea represent a surrender to "voluptatum desiderium" (cf. *Var.* 2. 351); see Brumble, *Myths*, 186–89. On Jason and Medea as models for Aeneas and Dido, asserted as early as Macrobius, see Hexter, "Sidonian Dido," 339–40.

Rinaldo, who must be shamed into leaving the bowers of Alcina and Armida, but also by Redcross, who had to be rescued by Arthur after his dalliance with Duessa.

After a brief flirtation in its opening lines with cinquecento mantras contrasting romance to history and epic, Book 2 has been seen to return to a pattern of multiple characters and storylines inscribing a variety of allusions to the humanist patrimony of pagan antiquity, literary and philosophical, topoi increasingly confronted with properly reformed versions of themselves. As is true for each of the faery knights, the core of Guyon's quest for a specific virtue revolves around his thoroughly personalized encounter with it, a series of experiences facilitating its internalization. In the case of temperance the quality best suited to this task is found to be shame, whose internalization most clearly distinguished Christian culture from the epic values of *aidos* and *kleos*, externalized, public versions of shame and honor. Internalized here as well by the knight, and more significantly, is the Platonic paradigm of wrath not suppressed but subservient to reason, with which it allies to control concupiscence, a lesson that once learned equips him for his showdown with Acrasia, the violence of which, however unexpected, is logically required. Just as important as the thoroughness of Guyon's lessons in virtue in these cantos are Spenser's painstaking corrections of Ariosto and Tasso, whose narratives he repeatedly invokes in order to revise their seductive but erroneous plots. Acrasia's bower proves the ideal locale for the most important revision of all, in which Spenser establishes not only the supremacy of Christianity over the pagan world or that of Christian grace over the courtly variety, both of which had been asserted by the *Liberata*, but that of the properly reformed, Protestant epic over its humanist-inspired, Renaissance counterparts, whether that of Ariosto, according to his many devoted followers, or that of Tasso, painstakingly rewritten to meet the rigors of the strictest religious critique.

4. From Temperance to Chastity

A central element of the shift from a predominantly male context in the Legend of Temperance to a predominantly female one in the Legend of Chastity is a transition from scenes populated primarily by men, who play the most virtuous roles opposite female villains, to the reverse. Accompanying this is a difference in narrative structure, now less a matter of episodes that feature the knightly protagonist progressing however haltingly toward his goal than a group of loosely parallel storylines, related as often by motif as plot, which explore details of the highlighted moral virtue instead of its acquisition. These changes, which persist into the Legend of Friendship and result in a proliferation of characters and in more women overall, have often been associated with a move from epic to romance based on the increasing importance in these scenes of *entrelacement*. The sense of generic shift is reinforced by the circular structure of Book 3, which, unlike the ultimately linear plots of the first two books, contrasts settings of tainted erotic desire at its start and finish, Malecasta's Castle Joyeous and the House of Busirane, with the edenic Garden of Adonis at its center. The result is a contrast of centripetal and centrifugal forces, characters and storylines driving the narrative outward in multiple directions, imagery and rhetoric directing attention back to the same key themes. The association with romance is strengthened by an increase in medieval motifs related to allegorical masques, medieval gardens, and courts of love, which now supplant the classical garden of delight. Spenser's focus on chastity rather than temperance directs attention from control of the passions to types of erotic desire, with much of the action now institutionalized, either ideally in the traditions of conjugal love and marriage or parodically in a courtly culture corrupted by lust. Three leading women, in addition to Britomart, the book's protagonist, associate the highlighted virtue with different contexts: Amoret, united with Scudamour in Book 4, with love in marriage; her sister, Belphoebe, a Diana-like huntress whose brilliant virginity, emblematic of Elizabeth, is dedicated to an ideal future spouse, with chaste premarital love; and Florimell, a shadowy figure glimpsed most often in flight from pursuit, with chastity constantly under threat. Amidst these idealized figures counter-models continue to intrude, in part because of the tenacity of malevolence and of the remedial quality of virtue's attainment, in part, one increasingly suspects, because moral virtues show up so well against their opposites and because accounts of moral failure have such appeal for poet and reader alike. Male versions of uncontrolled passion are enacted here by the Foster, Proteus, and Busirane, as well as by the satyrs, who eventually become the companions of Hellenore, one of two key female figures of lust, along with Malecasta. Hovering in the background are numerous icons of sexual depravity that continue to emphasize themes of shame and continence.

Books 1 and 2 made clear that a key aspect of Spenser's fashioning of the moral virtues is the degree to which he individualizes their arduous acquisition, a process repeatedly interrupted by the distractions of erotic desire. In light of the sharp differentiation in the Legend of Friendship between chaste love and lustful passion, the first characterized by loyalty to spouse and devotion to virtue, the second by immediate gratification, one would expect their respective emotions to be equally dissimilar. It soon becomes apparent, however, that in spite of the effort to segregate these types of desire by associating the first with self-denial, coldness, and melancholy and the second with erotic heat, suggestions of the latter repeatedly infiltrate the former, resulting in disconcertingly similar descriptions being applied to both. The effect of this contamination is complex, on the one hand dulling the transparency of Spenser's didacticism through the creation of doubt, on the other humanizing the Knight of Chastity through imagery that endows her with a degree of nuance characteristically missing in the poem's project of moral improvement. Intertexts once again define the process, with the *Argonautica* and the *Phaedrus* continuing to play key roles, the latter inspiring additional Platonic imagery via its descriptions of metempsychosis and the divinity of love. Ecphrasis returns as a favored narrative device, and a number of motifs discussed above make reappearances, including those of the *piccolo mondo* vignette and the simile of the dawn. Once again the reformation of genre is a primary concern, but while Tasso was the focus of this effort in Book 2 and his presence in Book 3 is never far from view, the prominence in these cantos of highly advertised allusions to the *Furioso* signals Ariosto as the primary interlocutor in this portion of Spenser's reforming dialogue, reinforcing the sense of generic shift.

Three key episodes in the Legend of Chastity reflect the return of complex intertextuality as well as a newfound emphasis on intratextual voices and images: Malecasta's falling in love with Britomart, a parody of Fiordispina's falling for Bradamante in the *Furioso*; Britomart's falling in love with Artegall, which replays central aspects of Malecasta's experience; and the banquet at which Hellenore falls in love with Paridell, which echoes both of these while shifting Spenser's revisionary focus from romance to epic. The first two episodes rework a series of images from Apollonius, Virgil, Ovid, Apuleius, and Ariosto. The third presents a multi-dimensional re-enactment of Dido's banquet for Aeneas with characters simultaneously enacting multiple roles. The complexity of these devices, not only advertised inter- and intratexts but also those discernible only under erasure, the irrepressible remainders of cultural *translatio*, increasingly dominate and at times overwhelm the intended lessons of these cantos, offering an early warning, perhaps, of a pending failure of confidence, manifest here as a softening of thematic and structural clarity, that will characterize the poem's close. Intimations of such misgivings appear in the Legend of Chastity's opening stanzas, where, parroting the previous book's meeting between Redcross and Guyon, Guyon and Britomart mistake each other for rivals and, unlike the earlier scene where friend-on-friend combat was narrowly avoided, proceed to an exchange of blows in which Guyon is unseated. The narrator emphasizes Guyon's sense of shame, adding how much more ashamed he'd be if he knew his opponent was a woman. As if such a beginning weren't inauspicious enough for the Knight of Temperance, the verses go on to recount how, from all appearances oblivious to the philosophy he'd previously articulated on the control of anger and significance of internal versus external foes, he picks himself up "full of disdainefull wrath" (1.9.1) to continue the fight, still trapped as it were in the Legend of Temperance. The Palmer and Prince Arthur intervene to prevent a repeat of Guyon's humiliation, counseling him with familiar refrains regarding the restraint of his "reuenging rage" (1.11.2) and advising him "His wrathful will with reason to asswage" (1.11.4). Sensing the lack of persuasiveness of these arguments for his client, Arthur mollifies the knight's wounded pride by playing down Britomart's skill and stressing the role of a page who supposedly saddled his horse improperly, and Guyon, like a remedial student, is forced to repeat the lessons of the previous book. The narrator remarks neither on Guyon's recidivism nor on Arthur's facilitating lie, stating perfunctorily of the knight and Britomart: "Thus reconcilement was betweene them knit, / Through goodly temperance, and affection chaste" (1.12.1–2).

At this point lust makes an early and dramatic appearance in the guise of the Foster pursuing Florimell, whom Guyon and Arthur pursue in turn. After their departure, Britomart comes upon Redcross fighting Malecasta's knights, defenders of the Castle Joyeous whose official policy of infidelity forces those they defeat to renounce their ladies in favor of the castle's sovereign, while those by whom they are defeated win her attentions, this lose-lose treatment of faithful love being an institutionalized version of the Bower of Bliss and an early attack on the court as the site of moral corruption. Tapestries depicting the myth of Venus and Adonis line the castle's hall, their images of sensual indulgence, wounding, and transformation presaging what is to come while replaying, cartoon-like, the encounter with Acrasia, whose role Malecasta assumes as the narrator describes how "She caused them [Britomart and Redcross] to be led in curteous wize / Into a bowre [. . .]" (1.42.3–4). Here Redcross, the persistent slow learner, threatens to repeat his earlier defeat by Duessa by disarming in the company of a beautiful female companion. The castle's knights arrive, disarmed themselves and described as "curteous and gent" (1.44.4) and "traynd in all ciuilitee" (1.44.6), completing the scene as a parodic *convivio* or Castiglionian soiree. The odd-person-out in this setting is Britomart, who, transgendered by the armor she refuses to remove, becomes the object of Malecasta's *seriatim* lust, at which point all the cliches of sexual passion make their appearances: fire in the entrails, poison in the veins, and grievous wounding, culminating in the description of the castle's shameless doyen as "Giuing the bridle to her wanton will" (1.50.1–3), an image contrasted with that of chaste desire, which "[. . .] does alwayes bring forth bounteous deeds, / And in each gentle hart desire of honour breeds" (1.49.8–9). While key elements of this imagery link Malecasta to Dido, even more prominent is the allusion to Ariosto's story of Bradamante and Fiordispina, a model for Spenser's cross-dressing adventure embedded within the *Furioso*'s primary story of true love between Bradamante and Ruggiero. Ariosto's tale addresses the same themes of love, lust, shame, and unnatural attraction from an entirely different point of view, depicting love as no more than a fervent emotional attachment, lust as a natural if discomfiting affect of healthy vigor, shame as a result of superficially diminished self-worth, and unnatural attraction as a physiological puzzle, his version of events an anti-Platonic, Petrarchan farce where pleasure is deemed the highest good and unfulfilled desire turns on issues of human plumbing rather than existential angst. Far from such bawdy positivism, festivities at the Castle Joyeous portray the confluence of irrational desire and courtly immorality. While surprised, like Bradamante, at finding herself the object of attraction, Britomart, unlike her Ariostan counterpart, decides to keep her disguise a secret, a decision that prolongs the confusion but allows Spenser to pursue the attraction into Britomart's bedroom. Here Malecasta's dramatic appearance recalls the *Argonautica*'s depiction of the youthful Medea discussed above, Spenser's reference not only capturing the similarity of situation, but going further, as did Ercilla's allusion to the same scene, to highlight the quality of shame at its heart.[31] The awkwardness of the scene is exacerbated by Britomart's mistaking Malecasta's motive as love rather than lust and dissembling her own lack of attraction since she considers it discourteous to despise "a gentle harts request" (1.55.4). The explanation, like that of her refusal to disarm, is more credible as plot than character, once again allowing the action to be prolonged. Eventually responding with Spenserian outrage rather than Ariostan bemusal, the British maid fights her way out of the castle, the scene—"Where feeling one close couched by her side, / She lightly lept out of her filed bed, / And to her weapon ran, in minde to gride / The loathed leachour" (1.62.1–4)—replaying yet again the motif of the nocturnal visitor who slips unseen and uninvited into a sleeper's bed, bringing to life not only Redcross's nightmare at Archimago's but Arthur's dream of the Faery Queene and suggesting that, while the ultimate parody of mutual love may be sexual assault, encountered more often in Spenser is something less brutal but similarly self-absorbed. The episode's denouement inverts the dynamic of the Bower of Bliss, with the innocent victim now freeing herself. Britomart's escape comes not without injury, however, one that, as has often been noted, literalizes the wound of love while foreshadowing the wounded lady in Cupid's masque, with which the Legend of Chastity will end.

The Malecasta episode is both parodic and proleptic, correcting Ariosto's moral insouciance via themes and motifs that in characteristically Spenserian fashion are soon revisited as objects of parody. Leaving the Castle Joyeous, Britomart reveals that she is secretly in love and experiencing emotions quite similar to those just attributed to Malecasta, as seen in references to her "sighing softly," to her "hart-thrilling throbs," and to the fact that "As if she had a feuer fit, did quake, / And euery daintie limbe with horrour shake" (2.5.1–5). As these images reveal, any attempt to differentiate Britomart's sensations from Malecasta's will be a challenge, in part because of the shared lexicon of erotic passion, in part because of the archetypal scenes from which this terminology is derived, whose powerful overtones continually intrude into their translated contexts. Britomart became aware of her love for Artegall after looking into Merlin's "glassie globe" (2.21.1), a prophetic sphere that personalizes epic's *piccolo mondo* motif by revealing, instead of world events, as in Ariosto and Ercilla, whatever most pertains

---

[31] The scene in Apollonius describes how Medea, whose "heart is trembling" (*Ar.* 3.638), decided to go to Jason, and "rising from her bed opened the door of her chamber, bare-footed [. . .]" (3.645–646); Spenser describes how Malecasta, "whose engrieued spright / Could find no rest in such perplexed plight" decided to go to Britomart and "Lightly arose out of her wearie bed [. . .] Then panting soft, and trembling euerie ioynt, / Her fearfull feete towards the bowre she moued" (1.59.4–1.60.2); regarding the scene's focus on shame, see 74 n. 36, supra.

to the individual petitioner.[32] The maid's response to the vision has been a mix of attraction, confusion, and anxiety. Considering that she shares her experience with no one and doesn't realize it reveals the future, her subsequent feelings of withdrawal, sorrow, and even images of death are plausible ones, contributing to a contrast between images of lustful heat and those of frigidity, the latter culminating in the scene with her nurse, Glauce, who, finding her distraught and unable to sleep after her vision, brings her back to bed, where: "[. . .] euery trembling ioynt, and euery vaine / She softly felt, and rubbed busily, / To doe *the frosen cold* away to fly" (2.34.5) (emphasis added). While such language contrasts dramatically with cliches of erotic heat, blurring the distinction is a disconcerting similarity the scene begins to develop with the poem's prior depictions of seductresses with their lovers. Glauce's consolation of Britomart, described as "And her faire deawy eies with kisses deare / She oft did bath, and oft againe did dry" (2.34.6–7), is disturbingly close to the depiction of Acrasia and Verdant, which says of the sorceress: "And oft inclining downe with kisses light, / For feare of waking him, his lips bedewd, / And through his humid eyes did sucke his spright" (II.12.73.5–7), as well as to the scene of Venus and Adonis in the tapestries of the Castle Joyeous, which says of the goddess: "And her soft arme lay vnderneath his hed, / And with ambrosiall kisses bathe his eyes" (1.36.3–4). Augmenting these associations is a rapid return to the canonical imagery of passion with its motifs of wounding, poison, and fire now encountered in references to "bleeding bowels" (2.39.2), "poysnous gore" (2.39.4), "my flame" (2.43.4), and "hart-burning brame" (2.52.4). Just as significant as these images and intratextual echoes are the intertexts that crowd the shadows of the scene, leaving a trail of textual traces extending to Virgil, Ovid, Apuleius, and Ariosto.

It has long been recognized that the nurse-with-the-troubled-charge conceit is modeled on Virgil's *Ciris*, an epyllion that tells the story of Scylla. In both Virgil and Spenser the aged companion is awakened when the distraught young woman is unable to sleep; in both the nurse brings her back to bed, where she finally elicits the cause of her unhappiness. Virgil's story recounts Scylla's betrayal of her father and city because of her passion for Minos. A sub-plot identifies the nurse as the mother of Britomartis, a figure of Diana-like chastity, who leaps to her death to escape Minos' pursuit (294–304). Spenser's episode also draws on Ovid's story of Scylla and Myrrha, and Ovid and Virgil both allude to

---

[32] Merlin represents an additional, important example of competing literary traditions discussed above with regard to Dido and Aeneas, Spenser's figure derived from Geoffrey of Monmouth's anti-Irish Ambrosius Merlinus, in contrast to the later Merlinus Calidonius or Sylvestris, supposedly born in Scotland in the time of King Arthur and one of four Irish prophets held in high esteem. Merlinus Calidonius foresaw no successful conquest of Ireland by England, only ongoing strife. Christopher Highley explores Spenser's appropriation of these traditions in *Shakespeare, Spenser, and the Crisis in Ireland* (Cambridge: Cambridge University Press, 1997), 19–20.

Apollonius' depiction of Medea.[33] In the *Faerie Queene* the scene develops with
Britomart referring enigmatically to her secret love by claiming that, "[. . .] no
vsuall fire, no vsuall rage / It is, O Nurse, which on my life doth feed" (2.37.3–4).
Recalling earlier instances where Spenser's characters begin to exhibit something
like literary self-consciousness, Glauce responds as though aware of her Virgilian pedigree with its tales of unnatural passion, and when Britomart finally tells
her the truth she exclaims with relief that the situation is only natural, indicating
"No guilt in you, but in the tyranny of love" (2.40. 9). Revealing just how substantial this self-consciousness is, the prolix old woman proceeds to describe how
she'd feared something much worse, a "filthy lust, contrarie unto kind" (2.40.4),
offering detailed synopses of three examples of such perversion in the persons
of Myrrha, Pasiphae, and Biblis.[34] While the maladroitness of the digression as
part of her effort to comfort the young woman, inept to the point of comical, is
explained, on the one hand, by the plot of the *Ciris*, in which the nurse learns
that her young charge suffers from a passion for her father, like Myrrha, and on
the other by the lessons these ancient exempla are meant to reinforce, there's a
growing sense in these verses of the fascination such stories have always exerted
beginning in antiquity, an appeal that threatens to override their effectiveness
as negative examples. Even more surprising than Glauce's disquisition is Britomart's response, which proceeds in close imitation of Ariosto's Fiordispina, who
had herself referred to Semiramis, Myrrha, and Pasiphae and is the inspiration
for Britomart's now fretting that, however unnatural the desires of these figures,
they at least had the satisfaction of them, unlike her own situation, which "Can
haue no end, nor hope of my desire, / But feed on shadowes, whiles I die for
food" (2.44.2–3).[35] However un-ironic Spenser intends the statement, the echo

---

[33] The *Ciris* recounts how Scylla falls in love with Minos, who has besieged her
father's kingdom, leading her to cut a lock of his magically protective hair as he sleeps to
present to Minos, who recoils at her betrayal and abandons her. Scylla's passion quotes
Dido's: cf. esp.: "Quae simul ac venis hausit sitientibus ignem / et validum penitus concepit in ossa furorem" ("Soon as she drank the fire into her thirsty veins, and caught deep
within her marrow the potent frenzy") (163–164); and: "infelix virgo tota bacchatur in
urbe" ("the luckless maid raves through the city") (167); translation is by H. Rushton
Fairclough, *Virgil: Aeneid 7–12; The Minor Poems* (Cambridge, MA: Harvard University Press, 1918). Ovid's story of Scylla has no nurse and no fraught decision regarding
betrayal, but focuses instead on Scylla's rage at being abandoned by Minos (*Met.* 8.1 ff.).
Ovid's angry Scylla recalls angry Dido, accusing Minos of cruelty and suggesting he was
mothered by the Armenian tigress, just as Dido applies the image of mothering by the
Hyrcanian tigress to Aeneas (*Aen.* 4.367). See Brumble, *Myths*, 305–7.

[34] See Brumble, *Myths*, 232–33, 261–62, 57–58 respectively.

[35] Two intertexts-within-intertexts are worth noting here: in the *Ciris*, Carme fears
that Scylla is actually another Myrrha (*Ciris* 237–238); Ovid's Scylla claims that her
experience of Minos' cruelty has made her realize what drove Minos' wife, Pasiphae, to
her assignation with the bull, and her hesitation at the door of her father's bedroom (*Met.*

of Ariostan flippancy is strikingly dissonant. As if aware of how perilously close his heroine's flirtations with these paragons of perversity, ancient and early modern, have come, Spenser quickly concludes Canto 2 and opens Canto 3 with a stanza designed to establish, once and for all, the distinction between the Platonically inspired divine fire of love and the demonic flames of lust. While adroitly associating this difference with broader themes of beauty and virtue, the use of "same" for "similar" in the stanza's central line ineluctably suggests the very confusion it seeks to clarify:

> Most sacred fire, that burnest mightily
> In liuing brests, ykindled first aboue,
> Emongst th'eternall spheres and lamping sky,
> And thence pourd into men, which men call Loue;
> Not that *same*, which doth base affections moue
> In brutish minds, and filthy lust inflame,
> But that sweet fit, that doth true beautie loue,
> And choseth vertue for his dearest Dame,
> Whence spring all noble deeds and neuer dying fame. (3.1.1–9)

With Britomart's love and future happiness established by Merlin's revelation of her role as the matriarch of British royalty, the theme of chaste love is revisited, once again in terms of an Ariostan intertext, in this case the story of Angelica and Medoro, now cast in terms of Arthur's page, Timias, and Belphoebe.[36] Once again Spenser introduces the intertext in order to exploit its potential as a teachable moment, as well as for the opportunity it allows for an indirect commentary on the meeting between Dido and Aeneas, to which the scene in the *Furioso* alludes. Ariosto's tale offers a comic inversion of convention in which the poem's unattainable focus of desire, a Christian princess, develops a consuming passion

---

10.369–377) recalls Apollonius' indecisive young Medea (esp. *Ar.* 3.645 ff.). With regard to the other two women mentioned in this context, Semiramis, noted earlier as one of the female prisoners at the House of Pride (I.5.50.3), developed a passion for her son, who, according to some sources, killed her; Biblis, mentioned by Glauce, had a sexual relationship with her brother. Among the many shared intertextual details in these stories note, in addition to scenes recalling Dido's falling in love, depictions of her anger at rejection, and the young Medea's hesitancy, the motif of the indecisive young woman's feet: in the *Ciris*: Scylla's "tender feet" (169) and "marble-cold feet" (256); in Ovid's story of Myrrha, her "stumbling feet" (*Met.* 10.452); in Apollonius, Medea's bare feet (*Argonautica* 4.646); and cf. Malecasta's "fearful feete" (III.1.60.2) as she goes to Britomart's room a few cantos earlier.

[36] Gently mocked by Merlin, Britomart is compared to Aurora in yet another variation on the dawn simile discussed above, one that, in addition to associating the color of early morning with shame, recalls other elements in these scenes, including the presence of Aurora, Tithonus, and the description of Tithonus's bed as *frosen*, echoing the *frosen cold* that Britomart had earlier felt (3.20.1–9); see 157, supra.

for a common Moslem soldier. As if the attraction weren't sufficiently taboo, the female is the aggressor, first nursing back to health, then offering her virginity to an initially passive male whom she dominates as thoroughly as a benevolent Acrasia. Nothing could be further from the Legend of Chastity than Ariosto's typical endorsement of sexuality in this supremely ironic tale. The *Faerie Queene*'s couple are both Christian, but maintain the *Furioso*'s emphasis on different social classes; unlike Ariosto, Spenser normalizes the role of instigator to the male, although one who blends Petrarchan fetishization with Christian self-renunciation. A good Platonist, Timias does his best to exert rational control over the concupiscent: "Long while he stroue in his courageous brest, / With reason dew the passion to subdew, / And loue for to dislodge out of his nest" (5.44.1–3); unsuccessful, he languishes in suicidal despair. Oblivious to his efforts, his unrequited love is not even noted by the chastely oblivious Belphoebe, much less reciprocated, until fourteen cantos later and well into the Legend of Friendship, where the object of his desire condescends to the titular virtue while Timias persists in imitating Orlando by carving her name on trees. Timias' love is chaste and therefore akin to Britomart's, their similarities most prominent in shared imagery of self-doubt and withdrawal instead of erotic heat. Belphoebe presents a thoroughly reformed object of romance attraction and an emblem of Christian courtliness, an example of God's "heauenly grace" (5.52.2) and someone "curteous and kind, / Tempred with grace, and goodly modesty" (5.55.2–3).

The ideological and structural center of the Legend of Chastity is occupied by the Garden of Adonis, which rewrites the tragic myth of Venus's infatuation as a triumph of conjugal happiness set in a hybrid *locus amoenus* of classical and Christian motifs. The garden is a literal and figurative hothouse, the source from which all life is said to emanate and return in thousand-year cycles, recalling the soliloquies of Anchises in the underworld and Socrates in the *Phaedrus*; its heart is an allegory of female fecundity in which Adonis enacts a Christian paradox of never-ending mortality, living in bliss with his goddess-lover, the two of them a fundamental principle of perpetual regeneration.[37] Cupid and Psyche are also resident here, and the conceit of Amoret, "th'ensample of true loue" (6.52.4), being brought to the garden by Venus to be raised alongside their daughter offers a sequel to and Christian reconciliation of the underlying tensions of Apuleius' story of the couple, with Spenser looking beyond the initial, tortuous stages of their relationship to a subsequent marriage in which they live in "stedfast loue and happy state" (6.50.6), much as Maffeo Vegio envisioned Aeneas and Livinia

---

[37] Later in the *Phaedrus* Socrates refers disparagingly to the Ἀδώνιδος κήπους or Garden of Adonis, which had come to designate a horticultural forcing-bed, in his belittling of the recently invented technique of writing (276b). Hamilton notes that etymological confusion led to the association of Adonis with Eden and thus of forcing-beds with paradisiacal settings (note to *Faerie Queene* 6.30.1).

in his thirteenth book of the *Aeneid*.[38] The hybrid qualities of Spenser's garden and of the Legend of Chastity in general make a fitting backdrop for allusions to *The Golden Ass*, an archetype of hybridity, beginning with its allegorizing of the troubled relationship between eros and the soul, or *psyche*, envisioned by the *Phaedrus*. Numerous details in Spenser's scenes recall Apuleius, including fears of unnatural love, the dangers of socially mismatched attraction (as when Venus instructs her son to infect Psyche with the lust for someone of low social standing, a directive he ignores but that Shakespeare will exploit in *A Midsummer Night's Dream*), and excessive lust, erotic and monetary, which lures Psyche's sisters to their deaths. Both sisters, meanwhile, have been married to much older husbands, a motif that returns shortly afterwards in the Malbecco episode. Indeed, in spite of its normative conclusion celebrating the institution of marriage and family, Apuleius' tale is replete with undertones ranging from the kind of irony and ecumenical humor associated with Ariosto to such deeply disturbing echoes of archetypal perversity as Cupid's coming to Psyche only in the protective shroud of darkness, reminiscent of Myrrha, who goes to her father similarly disguised, and even more notable the fact that, according to Ovid, the offspring of this cursed incestuous union is none other than Adonis himself (*Met.* 10.298–599, 708–739). Echoing such grotesque irony is a troubling antithetical principle at the heart of the Garden of Adonis's landscape of ideal beauty and eternal regeneration, a principle whose description recalls the Nile's "fertile slime" (I.1.21.3) and Errour's "fruitfull cursed spawne" (I.1.22.6) in Book 1, while suggesting aspects of the two "Cantos of Mutabilitie" in Book 7 (VII.6.26.6):

> For in the wide wombe of the world there lyes,
> In hatefull darknesse and in deepe horrore,
> An huge eternall *Chaos*, which supplyes
> The substances of natures fruitfull progenyes (6.36.9).

The Garden of Adonis is a fragile center that cannot hold, an effort at pastoral withdrawal not from history, to which it is traditionally opposed, but from the romance maelstrom that precedes and follows it, whose barely suppressed remainders threaten constantly to commandeer the plot. The juxtaposition of the two is brought to a climax at the end of the following canto with the misogynistic Squire of Dame's tale, Book 3's final advertised intertext with Ariosto. In the *Furioso*, the story of the fruitless search to find an instance of female chastity offers a sexually positive comic digression in spite of its transgressive plot, the Ariostan narrator not only introducing it with an elaborate apology for the aspersion it casts on women, but concluding it with a rejoinder by an audience member who retorts that men are not only more unchaste than women, but worse

---

[38] See Maffeo Vegio, *Short Epics*, ed. and trans. C. J. Putnam (Cambridge, MA: Harvard University Press, 2004), 2–41, at 28–37.

characters in general (*O.F.* 23.4–85). Spenser's version has no such analogue, of course, and absent such jocularity comes off as petulant and embittered.

Book 3's juxtaposition of chaste and unchaste characters takes on epic proportions at the castle of Malbecco. Like much of the imagery just discussed, the castle is Ariostan in inspiration (*O.F.* 32.65 ff.). Yet in spite of this affiliation and repeated references to courtliness, together with the presence of a compulsive Petrarchan lover, Paridell, and a Boccaccian plot involving a suspicious old husband whose amorous young wife, Hellenore, ends up seduced by a guest, the principal inspiration of the episode is earlier, as the names of the protagonists suggest. The setting is a banquet reminiscent of Dido's, where the hostess falls in love with the guest who is asked to tell his life story. Complicating the *imitatio* is the fact that Aeneas' role is played by Paridell, who, reinforcing the link between ancient Troy and Britain established by the earlier reference to London as Troynouvant, traces his genealogy to Parius, a son of Paris and Oenone, who appears to have usurped the role traditionally ascribed to Aeneas, shepherding Ilium's *penates* to a new home following its defeat (9.36.7–9). Dido's role at the banquet, on the other hand, is played not only by Hellenore, "this second Hellene" (10.13.1), who, while she "[. . .] shewed her selfe in all a gentle curteous Dame" (9.26.9), responds enthusiastically to Paridell's sexual overtures, but simultaneously by Britomart, who, having unwittingly sought shelter at the castle, waxes nostalgic at Paridell's mention of the fall of Troy and asks him to recount what happened to Aeneas on the night the city was overrun. This duplication of characters results in the poem's most bewildering overlay of literary references yet, with Paridell's name suggesting Paris while he plays Aeneas, while Hellenore impersonates not only Helen, but also Dido, whom Britomart plays as well. The result, for the female role, is both versions of the Carthaginian queen being presented side by side, the paragon of chastity envisioned by Justin as well as Virgil's passionate lover, neither of them aware of their own or the other's literary identity, insights that would surely short-circuit the plot. Paridell, by contrast, appears fully aware of his own complex heritage, impersonating Virgil's version of Aeneas who has an affair with his hostess, while recounting, in response to Britomart, the history of the other, pre-Virgilian Aeneas who had no connection to Carthage or to Dido at all. The preface to Britomart's question about the Trojan hero: "[. . .] sith that men sayne / He was not in the Cities wofull fyre / Consum'd, but did *him selfe* to safetie retyre" (9.40.7–9), is a pointed one, its failure to mention the *penates*, his father, Iulus, or any other survivors taken with him to safety suggesting the anti-Homeric tradition with its alternative motivation for Aeneas' departure from Troy.[39] The fact that the insinuation comes from the character with the most significant claim to Trojan genealogy, via Geoffrey of Monmouth's enabling mythology of Brutus, is additionally noteworthy,

---

[39] Cf. Sergio Cascali, "The Development of the Aeneas Legend," in *Companion*, ed. Farrell and Putnam, 37–51.

evidence of Spenser's willingness to go beyond a critique of the *Aeneid*'s eroticism to question, albeit indirectly, Aeneas' heroic status itself. While substantiating most of Aeneas' traditional exploits, Paridell's three-stanza reply does so in a markedly anti-heroic manner, emphasizing how he "[. . .] through fatall errour long was led / Full many yeares, and weetlesse wandered" (9.41.4–5), and noting the many setbacks that he "Escaped hardly" (9.42.9), before spending half its last stanza attributing the founding of Rome and its subsequent early glory to Iulus (9.43.5–9). Spenser's construction of these shadowy parallel lineages, Brutus, Aeneas, and Paris being all descended from a common great-grandfather, Assaracs (II.10.9.7), allows him to offer alternative explanations for the *Aeneid*'s imperial significance in general, while emphasizing in particular, in contrast to the womanizing Paridell-Aeneas, the alternative, chaste Aeneas, unsullied by his dalliance in Carthage, corresponding to chaste Dido, a more appropriate model for Britomart than Virgil's suicidal lover. By the same token, Paridell's assumption of this alternative role avoids exposing his true identity as an unfaithful lover, which would risk frightening away his current conquest, Hellenore-Dido. With Aeneas' history complete, a Boccaccian modality reasserts itself. Sexual desire is consummated, and Hellenore, yet another abandoned woman in the wake of Paridell's lust, is eventually adopted by the satyrs, in whose organized debauchery she becomes a willing participant. The Legend of Chastity closes with a return to the pageantry of love at the House of Busirane and to another set of tapestries depicting a litany of love's vagaries among the ancient gods. In spite of Britomart's rescue of Amoret, the episode is decidedly pessimistic, focusing on a demonic parody of Petrarch's *Trionfi* that features a parade of negative emotions associated with erotic attraction, the rear of which features Reproach, Repentance, and Shame, bringing the book to a close on the same key themes with which it began. The sense of stasis is reinforced by the fact that the stories of Britomart and Artegall, Belphoebe and Timias, Amoret and Scudamour, and Florimell and Marinell are all continued in Book 4.

The effort in Book 3 to champion an idealized Platonic vision of chaste love over debased erotic passion is systematically undermined by a failure to segregate their respective imagery, with descriptions of the former consistently contaminated by the latter. A greater obstacle to the effective championing of virtue in these cantos is posed by the repeated invocation of icons of sexual impropriety whose histories threaten to generate more curiosity than moral outrage. In Books 1 and 2 the persistence of counter-examples and negative imagery as well as the duplication of characters and storylines was seen to manifest the remedial nature of virtue's acquisition. Here, by contrast, there's a growing sense of the subversive appeal such tales of moral failure exert on poet and reader alike. The result is a dilution of the poem's message, on the one hand, but a humanizing of its characters, on the other, a process that in one form or another will continue to characterize the depiction of the struggle between the appetitive and rational parts of the soul. While much of the inspiration in these verses comes from Ariosto, on whom Spenser focuses most of his revisionary fervor, by the end of the book Virgilian epic has proven just as important a target in the guise of one of its most indelible emblems, Dido's banquet. Earlier in the poem the intensity of intertexts suggested a writerly atmosphere so saturated in classical culture that it generated a degree of literary self-consciousness among key characters. Here Spenser's practice of envisioning the personal achievement of moral virtue as an internal one is applied to literary topoi, whose effective reformation is similarly undertaken from inside out. If the Wandering Wood evoked a forest of intertexts, the Legend of Chastity suggests that literary allusion is by its nature akin to romance, the simplest appeal to an external text diverting attention, however briefly, from narrative unity, while multiple, interrelated references, as in the passages just discussed, with their seemingly endless tangential associations, inscribe the very conceit of "di qua di là" ("here and there") and "di su di giù" ("now this way now that") variety. Apparent in any such consideration involving Spenser is the love of story-telling per se, one that permeates his moral program at every step, allowing him, ideally, to have his reforming cake and eat it too. These ultimately competing but often complementary forces are manifest here in his re-envisioning of the tragedy of Britomartis as comedy, the maiden who had to die in order to protect her chastity now incarnated as the chaste warrior maid who overcomes all challengers in order to assure her future happiness with Artegall.

5. Courtesy and the Failure of Pastoral Escape

Much that is new in the 1596 *Faerie Queene* is familiar. The Legend of Friendship is a thematic and structural continuation of Book 3 that pursues a further categorization of good and bad erotic passion; at its heart is another Edenic garden featuring another encounter with Venus, as well as another nostalgic paean about a long-lost age of virtue and honor. The shift from pastoral tranquility at the heart of Book 3 to the romance maelstrom in the rest of the book is repeated more sharply in the contrast between the romance intricacies of Books 3 and 4 and the comparatively straightforward structure of Book 5, whose Legend of Justice has long been associated more closely than other parts of Spenser's poem with events in his lifetime. Allegory continues to be the dominant mode in Book 5, but, rather than a Dantean sense of allegory as encoding a multi-layered, polysemous world, the poet reverts here to a simpler, historical version of the device. An equally dramatic contrast characterizes the transition from Book 5 to Book 6, which returns temporarily to earlier romance modalities in the guise of Sir Calidore and the Legend of Courtesy only to be commandeered by an extended adventure story inspired by Greek romance, a digression with erotic pastoral once again at its heart. Calidore's quest reprises the themes of honor, shame, temperance, and grace, with courtesy's new prominence taking two different forms, one associating it with the court, the other with civil society. The first, a key example of Spenser's etymological determinism, is closely related to the ethical determinism that soon emerges in the natural predisposition to and inevitable recognition of courtesy, both of these manifesting a retreat from the poem's ambitious moral program. The book's highlighted virtue is once again explored in terms of its opposite, crudeness and brutality, in starkest terms, but also a parodic version that is only skin-deep, a matter of show rather than essence and associated with the affectations of courtly life in contrast to an innate courtesy that emanates from the heart or the soul. This emphasis on natural courtesy leads seamlessly to reflections on natural order and the social hierarchy, best captured in these cantos by the unfailing ability of social superiors to recognize each other in the most disparate circumstances. Expanded to language, such reasoning suggests the existence of natural signs, which in turn has ramifications for Spenser's narrative process, both directly, via semiotics, and obliquely, via the contradictions not only between such theories and the spirit of Protestant iconoclasm but more pointedly between the ostensible beneficence of such a language as the vehicle for a program of "vertuous and gentle discipline" and its actual function, increasingly revealed as that of mystifying the violence associated with virtue's attainment, whether directly, in a progression that culminates in Book 5, or casually, as in the slaughter of the shepherds that terminates Calidore's pastoral idyll.[40] Not surprisingly, the determination that emerges to distinguish between good and bad courtesy and thus between inner and outer, motivation and behavior, encounters problems reminiscent of those associated with earlier attempts to differentiate between good and bad erotic passion, with the division often difficult to discern, much less define. Returning to prominence as part of the process is the issue of dissimulation, an ever-present danger in the 1590 *Faerie Queene*, which typically figured it as the perilous instability of appearance, of things frequently not being what they seem. Here the problem is more complex, persisting, on the one hand, in a variant where, rather than bad things always coming from what appears to be good, the reverse also occurs, with unexpectedly courteous behavior enacted by a series of apparently unexceptional figures (although most of these are later revealed to come from elevated social origins), and on the other in a more intricate challenge, namely, the identification of a good type of dissemblance, one restricted to personal relations rather than politics and justified by the benevolence of its purpose. Numerous difficulties beset the process. Natural courtesy is frequently associated not only with qualities of goodness and bravery but also with comeliness and hidden nobility, motifs that Pastorella is only the most prominent to embody, that reduce it to a supporting role for cultural norms. Equally problematic is the identification of language as a vehicle for courteous dissimulation, with the poem's initial substitution of courtly by archaic speech, designed in part to avert this very process, now called into question by the

---

[40] Cf. Palmer, *Language and Conquest*, 118, 122; cf. McCabe, *Spenser's Monstrous Regiment*, 230–33.

championing of a variety of verbal courtesy capable not only of curing the wounds of injured honor but of avoiding violence in the resolution of conflict, a principal rationale of Castiglionian eloquence. Spenser's obsession with an autochthonous semantics was always as much political as aesthetic, rejecting Tudor policy along with the rhetoric in which it was articulated as *dissimulazione*, in particular, declined from the apex of courtly virtue to its nadir as a strategy of deceit and self-advancement. Here at the end of the poem his linguistic maneuver appears more than ever a flagrant grab for verbal power, an effort by one whose ideology had failed to dominate the political realm to wrest control of the semantic one. Dissimulation, in fact, is seen to link the civic and linguistic realms in these cantos, with the difference between persuasiveness and seduction increasingly important but ever more difficult to establish. The inherent instabilities and potential contradictions of these issues play out both narrowly and broadly, with a series of incidents exposing Calidore's questionable dissembling to gain the love of Pastorella, a project in which he personifies some of the worst characteristics of *cortegianía* condemned elsewhere in the poem, while the quest itself is eventually abandoned for the knight's sojourn among the shepherds. This pastoral interlude begins as a retreat from epic and the active life and ends as an escapist adventure subversive not only of Calidore's obedience to Gloriana but also of the poem's moral program; it concludes with scarcely enough time to acknowledge the knight's initial goal before the book and, as it turned out, the poem comes to an end. These structural disjunctions are mirrored thematically in the exaggerated role played by fortune, a quality that minimizes rational control of the emotions along with causation while threatening to upstage divine grace as the *deus ex machina* ensuring the protagonist's success. The growing sense of retrenchment on all fronts is mirrored in the rhetoric of Book 6, which exhibits a marked reduction in wordplay, especially in the poem's earlier, effusive punning. Capping these changes is the intrusion of Spenser himself into the scene on Mt. Acidale. If the attack of the brigands that comes a few stanzas later denies the possibility of pastoral escape from history, a retreat that was driven by the corruption of life at court, Calidore's casual destruction of Colin's contented piping suggests a far greater loss, one of poetic invention as an effective response to and shaper of the enframing world, a diminution perhaps reflected in the elimination of allegory altogether from this section of the poem, both the moral-anagogical and historical varieties being abandoned for simple narrative. What's left in the wake of these thematic, structural, and ultimately spiritual lacunae is difficult to gauge; certainly aporia threatens. After its temporary suppression it is the Blatant Beast that dominates speech, not the poet, who, far from having a kingdom of language he can call his own, appears resigned to the slander directed not only at political allies but also at himself and his poem. Such pessimism reflects the further deterioration of relations among courtliness, humanism, and the reformers as the sixteenth century comes to a close. In earlier books the three maintained an uneasy *convivencia*. Here, by contrast, humanism's contribution is ironically most evident in the access it facilitates to the *Aethiopica*, whose reactionary ideology replaces Reformation faith. In the *Araucana* Greek romance was seen not only to structure the reunion of Glaura and Cariolán, but also to inspire Ercilla's figuring himself an heroic Orlando. In drawing on the same material Spenser will be seen to assume an even more dramatic persona.

After the dispirited close of Book 5, with its depiction of a harried Artegall returning to Gloriana's Court, Book 6 opens with an unexpectedly lighthearted apostrophe to "this delightfull land of Faery" (6 Pr. 1.1), whose "sweet variety" (6 Pr. 1.4) and promises of refreshment from the poet's "tedious trauell" (6 Pr. 1.7) invoke the *otium-negotium* distinction seen so frequently in Ercilla and in Spenser's Sonnet 80 from the *Amoretti*. The conceit has something of forced optimism about it here, and the proem goes on to suggest a complex relationship between Calidore's quest and the poet's own project, the two linked by the Parnassian Muses, identified as the guardians not only of "learnings threasures" (6 Pr. 2.3) but of "the sacred noursery / Of vertue" (6 Pr. 3.1) that lies hidden in a "silver bowre" (6. Pr. 3.3), a virtuous garden of delight and literary Garden of Adonis, whose prize specimen is a glorious hybrid incorporating three recurrent themes of the book and the poem:

> [. . .] the bloosme of comely courtesie,
> Which though it on a lowly stalke doe bowre,
> Yet brancheth forth in braue nobilitie,
> And spreds it selfe through all ciuilitie [. . .] (6 Pr. 4.2–5)

Almost immediately a less optimistic comparison is drawn between the present age and "plaine Antiquitie" (6 Pr. 4.7), whose "true curtesie" (6 Pr. 5.1) is said to have declined these days to "nought but forgerie, / Fashion'd to please the eies of them, that pas" (6 Pr. 5.3–4). The following adage, which claims that "vertues seat is deepe within the mynd, / And not in outward shows, but inward thoughts defynd" (6 Pr. 5.8–9), is meant to resolve these competing visions. Instead it exposes their inherent tension, the insolubility of which will deconstruct Calidore's rationale as the effort intensifies to distinguish between courtesy as a moral quality and its manifestation as a behavioral one.

The opening lines of Canto 1 establish the connection between the court and courtesy, defined here as the basis of "all goodly manners" (1.1.5) and "roote of ciuill conuersation" (1.1.6). Calidore is introduced as the embodiment of this virtue, with distinctions promptly introduced to distance him from any taint of the foppish courtier: his manners "were planted naturall" (1.2.4), and in spite of his "comely guize withal" (1.2.5) and "gracious speech" (1.2.6), which "did steale mens hearts away" (1.2.6), he was "full stout and tall" (1.2.7). Most important: "[. . .] he loathd leasing, and base flattery, / And loued simple truth and stedfast honesty" (1.3.8–9). These clarifications made, the perversion of courtesy is met at Briana's castle, another site, like Malecasta's, inspired by Ariosto's castle of

Pinabello. The resemblance between this adventure and Britomart's at the Castle
Joyeous, both of which feature the mistreatment of knights and their ladies, is
the first of numerous counter-examples whose replay of earlier scenes contributes
to an impending uneasiness. Calidore manages to dispatch the castle's evil war-
den, but in doing so becomes the target of an unruly mob and of the opprobrium
of Briana, who declares his killing of her seneschal shameful and threatens that
"[. . .] shame shal thee with shame requight" (1.25.9). The knight rejects the
charge, but the issue goes on to dominate their verbal encounter, appearing eight
times in five stanzas (1.24.8–1.28.9). Distancing Calidore from the violence of
Book 5 while recalling earlier examples of temperance, the knight restrains himself from slaying Crudor, lecturing him instead to compel a promise of future
compliance. The climax of Calidore's harangue: "In vaine he seeketh others to
suppresse, / Who hath not learnd him selfe first to subdew" (1.41.5–6), repeats
Guyon's to Pyrochles: "Vaine others ouerthrowes, who selfe doth ouerthrowe"
(5.15.6). As it did earlier, however, rhetoric merely masks the use of force, and
the effectiveness of such persuasion is only temporary. As if aware of the weakness of his argument, Calidore shifts momentarily to a vaguely scriptural mode:
"All flesh is frayle, and full of ficklenesse" (1.41.7) (cf. Isaiah 40:6, 1 Peter 1:24),
before segueing abruptly to a closing emphasis on luck: "Subiect to fortunes
chance, still chaunging new; / What haps to day to me, to morrow may to you"
(1.41.8–9). In contrast to Crudor, the effect of courtesy on Briana is of an entirely
different magnitude, made apparent when the "discourteous Dame with scorn-
full pryde" (1.30.4) is completely transformed by Calidore's treatment of her and,
born again to the virtues of courtesy, becomes a perfect hostess.

Canto 2 opens with what appears at first to be no more than a reprise of lessons from the previous scene. In praising courtesy, however, these lines deflect
the virtue from the realm of interpersonal relations to a clear focus on the dues
of social inferiors to their betters:

> What vertue is so fitting for a knight,
> Or for a Ladie, whom a knight should loue,
> As Curtesie, to beare themselues aright
> To all of each degree, as doth behoue?
> For whether they be placed high aboue,
> Or low beneath, yet ought they well to know
> Their good, that none them rightly may reproue
> Of rudenesse, for not yeelding what they owe:
> Great skill it is such duties timely to bestow. (2.1.1–9)

The following stanza attempts to ground both courtesy and class distinction in
nature, beginning with those who "[. . .] so goodly gratious are by kind, / That
euery action doth them much commend, / And in the eyes of men great lik-
ing find" (2.2.2–4). Attention then turns to all the rest, for whom such status,
"Though they enforce themselues, cannot attaine" (2.2.6), and the verse closes

with the ominous caveat that "[. . .] praise likewise deserue good thewes, enforst with paine" (2.2.1–9). The episode with Tristram explores these themes as a series of mysteries, beginning with the apparent violation of chivalric law in the youth's combat with the knight and continuing with the puzzling identities of the knight, the youth, and the lady. The focus finally turns to Tristram himself, "A goodly youth of amiable grace" [. . .] "tall and faire of face" (2.5.2–4), by all appearances an elegant woodman but identified by Calidore's own gentility as coming from noble origins. The role of *peripeteia* and *anagnorisis* in the solution of these mysteries presages Pastorella's story, while the attendant explanations defuse the threat to social norms, Tristram's gentility being confirmed by his recognition of Calidore's superiority.

Canto 3 opens with another passage portending events yet to come, in this case regarding the converse of inborn courtesy. The lesson, which soon plays out with Coridon, is an ostensibly straightforward one that baseness will also out, but its articulation here further elides issues of class and character:

> For seldome seene, a trotting Stalion get
> An ambling Colt, that is his proper owne:
> So seldome seene, that one in basenesse set
> Doth noble courage shew, with curteous manners met. (3.1.5–9)

With Calidore's departure in pursuit of the Blatant Beast, a series of episodes unfolds whose repetitions of earlier plots and themes reinforce misgivings of narrative as well as moral progress. Timias reappears from Books 3 and 4, once again injured and in need of rehabilitation. Rather than being cared for by Belphoebe, however, Timias and Serena, victims of the Blatant Beast, recuperate at the cottage of a hermit, a scenario once again recalling Ariosto's Medoro. Characteristically for Spenser, the episode not only repeats but foretells, offering numerous similarities with the bucolic setting where Calidore will later reside. The hermit offers a more pointed embodiment of courtesy's irrepressibility, his backstory of being a knight who exchanged his chivalric vows for religious ones, reinforcing the distinction between his current genuine courtliness: "entire affection and appearaunce plaine" (5.38.9), and the counterfeit variety of his earlier milieu: "forged showes, as fitter beene / For courting fooles, that curtesies would faine" (5.38.7–8). Such clarity is significantly undermined once it becomes clear that his experience at court is what enables him to properly diagnose the wounds inflicted by the Blatant Beast, while the rhetorical skills of that earlier life, "As he the art of words knew wondrous well" (6.6.2–3), are at the heart of his curative counseling. The hermit's initial advice recalls earlier lessons on temperance. By the end of his harangue his prescription is for the complete avoidance of the emotions rather than their control, guidance he expresses with a puritanical stridency whose invocation of the bridle disguises neither the echo of Stoic *apatheia* nor the broader desperation of these pages:

> Abstaine from pleasure, and restraine your will,
> Subdue desire, and *bridle* loose delight,
> Vse scanted diet, and forbeare your fill,
> Shun secresie, and talke in open sight:
> So shall you soone repaire your present euill plight. (6.14.5–9)

Prior to Calidore's reappearance, additional reenactments of earlier scenes magnify the sense of repetition in this portion of the poem not as variations on a theme, but as a reiteration of lessons as soon forgotten as learned. Following the episode at the hermitage there is another Court of Cupid, last encountered at the House of Busirane in Book 3. Much of this material was familiar even before Busirane from the Garden of Adonis and from the Venus and Adonis tapestries at Malecasta's castle. In the 1590 *Faerie Queene* such repetition became a vehicle for exploring multiple facets of complex issues in a constantly shifting mix of theme and character. A corollary lexical process, apparent from the earliest pages of the poem, enveloped the narrative in a web of intratextuality, the polyvalency of which suggested a trope of Garden-of-Adonis-like endless renewal. The growing reliance on circular structures of romance in Books 3 and 4 prefigured a softening of the confidence with which this program was pursued. Here in these final pages of the poem retrenchment proceeds: structural and character repetition becomes more literal.

Out of sight since Canto 3, Calidore's reappearance in Canto 9 on the heels of the Blatant Beast, presented in terms that explicitly reverse the *rota Virgilii*, inscribes a dramatic feint from epic purposefulness to pastoral self-absorption, one whose further transformation into an extended adventure story dramatically distances both reader and protagonist from the *Faerie Queene*'s primary plot. Although the dissonance is jarring, Spenser's moral agenda has a natural affinity for the obsession of Greek romance with chastity, noble lineage, and the importance of decorum, the last of these especially resonant with a focus on courtesy. A more problematic association between the two is created by the reactionary ideology of the "adventure novel of ordeal" as Bakhtin termed such narratives, on the one hand reinforcing social cliches, a function that Spenser embraces and indeed extends to the realm of ethnicity, on the other hand focusing on the role of fortune rather than individual accountability, a position completely at odds with his moral program.[41] In this scenario Meliboe replays the role of yet another courtly

---

[41] Merritt Y. Hughes has observed: "With Heliodorus Spenser can claim at least 'a certain like-mindedness' in moral purpose, a quality stressed in Underdowne's translation, which Spenser could have known. Heliodorus was a preacher, and his gospel was composed of commonplaces not unlike Spenser's *Twelve Morall Virtues*. Chastity, temperance, friendship, justice, and courtesy are all formal topics in his ethic. They are identified with the six moral virtues which Spenser actually allegorized, minus the first, holiness or courage, which he derived mainly from Christian and chivalrous sources [. . .] Heliodorus in a fashion infinitely less serious than Spenser tried to vulgarize the principles of an

hermit, who after participating in the life of the metropolis has retired to the pastoral margins of society from which he reflects on their juxtaposition. Calidore's
falling in love with Pastorella, by contrast, far from being the intensely emotional
experience of earlier love scenes, is a methodical, affectless affair inspired by the
natural superiority revealed in her "rare demeanure" (9.11.2), a quality that, as
with Tristram, the knight's own nobility enables him to recognize.

Calidore's role as a model of courtesy is fraught from the start, with the
knight repeatedly abandoning the "simple truth and stedfast honesty" (1.3.9)
originally attributed to him. Genuine courtesy, embodied by the hermit, is distinguished by its lack of dissimulation, a virtue the knight notoriously lacks.
Calidore's response to Meliboe's paean on pastoral life is as rhetorically sophisticated as any in the *Faerie Queene*, the imagery of its request "To rest my barcke,
which hath bene beaten late [. . .] In seas of troubles and of toylesome paine"
(9.31.4–6) repeated almost identically in the opening lines of the book's final
canto, where the narrator speaks of his poetic program: "[. . .] as a ship, that
through the Ocean wyde / [. . .] / Is met of many a counter winde and tyde"
(12.1.1–3). In Calidore's case such imagery is simply a subterfuge for his pursuit
of Pastorella, and it soon becomes apparent that his assumption of pastoral life
is not for restorative purposes at all but rather part of an orchestrated strategy
for gaining the object of his desire. Other instances of dissimulation constitute
a pattern of such behavior, beginning with the story he tells Priscilla's father to
prevent the disclosure of her dalliance with Aladine (2.43.3; 3.18.5). This continues with Coridon, a buffoonish foil borrowed from Greek romance from whom
he dissembles his interest in Pastorella, and extends to the rest of the shepherds,
all of whom he patronizes as part of his erotic campaign. In these scenes Calidore
employs the full arsenal of courtly resources, not only *dissimulazione*, but also
sprezzatura in the ease with which he appears to excel at pastoral life, *mediocrità*
in the skill with which he avoids arousing resentment among the shepherds, and
of course *grazia* in all his actions, their combined effect epitomizing the dangerous seductiveness of *cortegianía* so bitterly resented in political rather than personal relationships.

A different scale of dissonance is introduced with the Mt. Acidale episode,
much of which has a sense of déjà vu from yet another encounter with Venus
in another *locus amoenus*. Entirely unexpected, on the other hand, is the figure
of Colin, an analogue of Spenser himself, who describes the Graces in whose
midst he plays as Venus's handmaidens and the source of "all the complements of

---

eclectic ethic derived from classical and Christian sources[. . .]" (in *Variorum Edition* 6:
379); cf. Henry C. Aiman, "Spenser's Debt to Heliodorus in *The Faerie Queene*," *Emporia State Research Studies* 22 (1974): 5–18. See the earlier discussion of Heliodorus and
Jacques Amyot's preface to the French *Aethiopique* at 17 ff., supra.

curtesie" (10.23.6).[42] Colin's emphasis on the civil function of these figures: "They teach vs, how to each degree and kynde / We should our selues demeane, to low, to hie; / To friends, to foes, which skill men call Ciuility" (10.23.7–9), reiterates earlier links between courtesy and the social compact. Their association with the Parnassian Muses would also seem inevitable, a connection that Calidore's disruptive voyeurism confirms. Reminiscent of the "saluage nation" leering at Serena a few cantos earlier, the knight's intrusion is charged from the beginning, a further example of how little he possesses of genuine courtesy. His tardy apology is hardly in keeping with the gravity of his offense as a distraught Colin breaks his pipes, mourning as irretrievably lost a scene that unexpectedly links courtly *grazia* with the ineffable gift of poetic invention: "For being gone, none can them bring in place, / But whom they of them selues list so to grace" (10.20.3–4). The figure at the center of the circle is a multi-faceted one corroborating the association, Venus, certainly, but also "that iolly Shepheards lasse" (10.16.1), with intimations of the woman Spenser was to marry, as well as Elizabeth, all of these apt sources of love and inspiration. The transition between such themes and the rest of Calidore's story is dramatic, the brigand's attack on the shepherds and the taking of prisoners, including the heroine, being concluded only after dramatic rescue and the climactic recognition of Pastorella as the long lost daughter of a noble couple. These scenes, which recall the plot-heavy structure of Glaura's tale and their common antecedent in the *Aethiopica*, with its Bakhtinian "logic of random contingency," expose how sharply Spenser has strayed from his original goal, where, far from the arduous acquisition of moral virtue, he resorts to a Heliodoran presentation of character as entirely one-dimensional: virtue as a *fait accompli*, moral integrity as a device of pathetic enhancement for scenes of near-calamity whose outcome is never in doubt. It is only twenty stanzas before the close of Book 6 that Calidore, as though awakening from a dream or transfiguring spell, is ashamed to recall how long ago he abandoned his quest for the Blatant Beast. The pastoral adventure concludes as abruptly as it began, and while the closing cantos of the poem make some effort at reversing the emphasis on fortune and at establishing a degree of completion, the threat of the Blatant Beast remains an open one.[43]

---

[42] McCabe notes that the shock of encountering Colin Clout on Mt. Acidale is like having Virgil's Tityrus reappear in the sixth book of the *Aeneid* (*Spenser's Monstrous Regiment*, 233).

[43] Spenser's Pastorella and Tasso's Clorinda (*G. L.* 12.21 ff.) are both influenced by Heliodorus' Charikleia, discovered to be the rightful heir of the king and queen of Ethiopia despite her white skin, explained by her mother's having prayed to a painting of St. George; medieval folklore considered Ethiopia an ancient Christian kingdom ruled by Prester John, and thus the story dovetails nicely with the reformers' claim to authority via the primitive, Eastern church; cf. Hamilton, note to 1.5.5; cf. Ariosto (*O.F.* 33.100–112); Heliodorus's plot and the legend of St. George both derive from the myth of Andromeda,

The early modern era's progressive concentration of power in monarchical states and the concomitant restrictions on individual agency have been viewed by some as having encouraged elaborate codes of etiquette, the most celebrated of which was the *Cortegiano*. Others have seen this shift from political to aesthetic discourse as providing a conceptual framework for literary endeavor, the irony of courtly aesthetics informing an alternative to the earnestness of religious reformers. Spenser's *Faerie Queene* resides on the precarious border of these two realms, transfiguring political commentary and moral harangue into a fictional form that manages through most of the poem to prevent the absorption of one by the other. The project begins with the effusive energy of the Legends of Holiness and Temperance, which emerge against an ominous background of crystal-clear heroes and villains. With the introduction of romance circularity in the Legends of Chastity and Friendship, both the energy and the clarity of the narrative begin to recede, and in Book 5 the balance tilts precariously toward commentary, with sobering historical allegory and a bitter aftertaste of the Irish problem. Book 6 begins with an effort at retaining the structure and spirit of the poem's earliest books, but soon veers precipitously toward fantasy, relinquishing both connotative language and the distracting dissolution of romance for the denotative speech that characterizes the idyll of Calidore and Pastorella, a tale in which the protagonists have no more effect on their literary environments than most readers perceived themselves as having on their real-life ones.

If the exotic blossom of courtesy, nobility, and civility is deemed an inborn trait that the *vulgo* can at best perform their obeisance to but never embody, the rationale for love or poetry as spurs to virtue is limited to a select few, and the grounds for a general reformation, religious or political, is called into question. In such a climate, and with the ideals of civic humanism challenged on the one hand by Machiavellian conceptions of a *practick felicite* and on the other by Calvinist severity, it is a small step from the figural control by reason of the concupiscent and irascible components of the soul to Irenius in Spenser's *View*, a prime example of monologic dialogue, who, in response to Eudoxus's query as to how the "reformation" of the Irish can be accomplished, replies, "Even by the sword, for all the evills must first be cut away by a strong hand, before any good can bee planted" (93). When Eudoxus notes that he himself had just proposed a similar solution employing the image of a halter rather than a sword, Irenius makes clear that the two symbols represent fundamentally different approaches to the problem, and despite his efforts to obfuscate the distinction as one between royal and secular power and as a "cutting off" of "Those evils [. . .] and *not of the people which are evill*" (93) (emphasis added), the violence of his recommendation is clear. Irenius had already disparaged the image of the bridle at the start of the tract, doing so in a way that exposed its contiguity with Plato while revealing

---

another abandoned woman, whom Perseus rescues from the dragon. See Brumble, *Myths*, 265–67, 25–26.

how far the context had deteriorated from a vision of the individual soul as a charioteer attempting to master unruly passions through the bridle of shame and continence. In a passage recalling the trotting stallions and ambling colts of natural courtesy, the link between such imagery and the issue of discipline is maintained, but now the Irish have been demoted to equine rather than human status and the role of control is no longer that of the rational component of the soul but of the external force of English law, while the ultimate target is still concupiscence:

> But what bootes it to break a colte, and to let him straight run loose at ran-dome. So were these people at first well handled, and wisely brought to acknowledge allegiance to the Kings of England: but, being straight left unto themselves and their owne inordinate life and manners, they estsoones forgot what before they were taught, and so soone as they were out of sight, by themselves shook of their *bridles*, and begun to colte anew, more licen-tiously than before. (16) (emphasis added)

Setting out on their narratives from different starting points and toward different ends, Ercilla initially rejecting fiction for eyewitness history, Spenser choosing historical fiction over moral philosophy, both poets draw on a shared heritage of the *translatio studii* and on many of the same essential images from this tradition. Both feature two key figures arising from epic's underlying tension between epos and eros: the abandoned woman and the night raid. Traditionally, the first of these exposes the private cost of epic achievement and public glory; the second, its brutal underside. For Ercilla, who narrates his own involvement in a military campaign, these images become an unexpected conduit for a deeply-held sense of personal honor. For Spenser, whose purview encompasses the virtues of Prot-estant civility, these images from pagan antiquity, almost always associated with the danger of deception and sexual predation, have a seductive similarity to Dido and Aeneas, most notable in the case of Una abandoned by Redcross. Both poets incorporate the ancient forest, which Spenser combines with the catalogue of trees, both poems mirroring the original function of these motifs in introducing a transformative, albeit symbolic, catabasis. Both authors take advantage of the Virgilian variation on Homer's simile for the dawn, again maintaining the struc-tural integrity of the original image, in one instance juxtaposing the tranquility of early morning to a night of violence, in the other heralding the departure of the beloved. Throughout these appropriations Ercilla and Spenser both chal-lenge Virgilian authority and the literary canon, Ercilla condemning the sacri-fice of personal integrity for personal gain reflected in Virgil's fictionalization of Dido's history, Spenser rejecting epic's ethos, however retroactively Christian-ized by Ariosto and Tasso, for its Pelagian denial of grace. The early modern state represents a more immediate authority for both men. Ercilla celebrates Spanish empire while reminding his royal reader of a proximity based not only on the poet's youthful service in the royal household, but more importantly on their shared championing of *pietas* and *clemencia*. From a more conflicted mix of political partisanship, personal association, and religious faith, Spenser finesses a celebration of Elizabeth with an increasingly embittered critique of Tudor policies. Both poems foreground private authority in the issue of self-control, Ercilla addressing the issue in terms of continence and shame, with an emphasis on integrity; Spenser, before abandoning his program in Calidore's adventure with the shepherds, evoking these same values together with the distinctions among concupiscence, the irascible, and the rational, in which the control of sexuality, embodied in chastity, becomes the focus. Both authors invoke the Platonic image of the bridle as the emblem of this control.

The foregoing discussion has repeatedly emphasized the role of genre in these appropriations, focusing on the interplay of epic, lyric, and pastoral elegy. Ercilla found in epic an analogue to the dramatic events in which he was an actor in Chile and to the heroic spirit these events at times inspired. He found in lyric and pastoral elegy a solace for the failure of such idealism as well as a way of figuring the New World Other, whose representation became inextricably entwined with his own. For his part, Spenser imparted the matter and authority he drew from literary tradition to his poetic conquest of virtue and to his role in England's colonization of Ireland. In Book 6 he attempts to reassert the difference between these two, lost in Book 5, but the focus on dissimulation and on the difficulty of distinguishing persuasiveness from seduction only highlights the impossibility of separating the personal from the political. In the *Araucana*'s episode of Glaura and Cariolán, inspired like the tale of Calidore and Pastorella by the *Aethiopica*, Ercilla figures himself a magnanimous Orlando to Glaura and Cariolán's Isabella and Zerbino. At the climax of the *Faerie Queene*'s variation on this material, in the melancholy atmosphere of the briefly paradisal Mt. Acidale, Venus' favorite landscape, Spenser performs a similar transformation, identifying himself not only with Colin Clout, but in a moment of wistful ambiguity, with Adonis, an even more audacious impersonation.

Appendix A

Selected passages from Gregorio Hernández de Velasco's translation of the *Aeneid*. Text is from the 1557 edition manuscript at the Hispanic Society of America Library.

Titlepage:

LOS DOZE LIBROS
de la Eneida de VERGILIO
Principe de los Poetas Latinos.
Traduzida en octaua ri-
ma y verſo Ca-
ſtellano.

SVSTINE ET ABSTINE

[emblem]

NVLLA VIA INVIA VIRTVTI

Impreſſo en Toledo en caſa
de Iuan de Ayala.
Año. 1555.

Excerpts, with location in the original:

1.659 ff.:

y cõ los ricos dones
la triſte reyna ya furioſa abraſe,
Y dentro delos hueſſos y en las venas
Vn venenoſo y fiero ardor le emprẽda. (B₁ᵣ / 9ᵣ)

1.687 ff.:

Mientras a ti ella beſos dulces diere,
su pecho tu con punta de oro hiere. (B₁ᵥ / 9ᵥ)

1.712 ff.:

Y eſpecialmente la infeliçe reyna
Ala rauioſa peſte, que tan cerca
Tenia, triſtamente deſtinada,
No puede contentar la mal ſana alma:
Abraſaſe y consumeſe mirando. (B$_{1v}$ / 9$_v$)

4.26 ff.:

Mas ãtes plega a dios mill muertes mue
La třra ſe abra y dõde eſtay me hŭda, (ra
con fiero rayo Iupiter me hiera,
Y enel horrible infierno me confunda,
Do ay ſiẽpre horror, do ſiẽpre pſeuera
Noche tenebroſiſsima y profunda,
O ſancta caſtidad, q te haga vltraje,
Y q tu ley quebrante y omenage. (D$_{4v}$ / 28$_v$)

4.54 ff.:

Aqueſtas perſuaſiones inflamaron
El ya encendido pecho de la reyna
Con nueua llama de amoroſo fuego. (D$_{4v}$ / 28$_v$)

4.66 ff.:

En tanto vn lento y dulce fuego roe
L'alma y entrañas dela triſte reyna,
Y alla en el centro del mal ſano pecho
Crece vna occulta y venenoſa llaga.
Arde ſe toda la infelice Dido,
Y y furioſa y de juyzio agena,
Anda por toda la ciudad vagando. (D$_{4v}$ / 28$_v$)

4.101 ff.:

Ya no ay en Dido vena a qen no ẽciẽda
Vu fiero ardor inſano. ya ſe abraſa
En biuo fuego y amoroſa braſa. (D$_{5r}$ / 29$_r$)

4.167 ff.:

La reyna Dido y el Troyano Eneas,
Iũtos ſe entrarõ a vna meſma cueua.
La dioſa dela tierra la primera,
Y Iuno delas bodas preſidente,
Dierõ ſeñal del matrimonio inſauſto.

4.584 ff.:

> Ya la purpuera Aurora, el roxo lecho
> De ʃu Tithon dexando, de luz nueua
> Las tierras cerca y lexos eʃparzia:
> Quando la miʃerable reyna vido
> Deʃde vna alta atalaya; la luz clara (E$_{iiir}$ / 35$_r$)

9.189 ff.:

> Ves que deʃcuydo, y que ʃeguridad
> Tiene alos enemigos confiados?
> Mvy raras luzes mueʃtran claridad.
> Llenos de ʃueño y vino eʃtan echados
> ves como la nocturna eʃcuridad. (K$_{7v}$ / 79$_v$)

9.316 ff.:

> Y por la ʃombra dela eʃcura noche
> Al real enemigo van por muerte:
> Bien q primero la daran a muchos.
> Do ya llegados, veen a cada paʃʃo
> Cuerpos en vino y ʃueño ʃepultados,
> Tendidos por el prado y verde hierua. (L$_{1r}$ / 81$_r$)

Appendix B

L'Histoire Aethiopique d'Heliodore
Jacques Amyot, bishop of Auxerre (1513–1593)

[princeps 1547; following text transcribed from 1553
edition at NYPL; orthography modernized]

Le proême du Traducteur

Ainsi comme un certain grand philosophe admoneste sagement les nourrices, de ne conter indifféremment toutes sortes de fables à leurs petits enfants, de peur que leurs âmes de le commencement ne s'abreuvent de folie & ne prenent quelques vitieuse impression: aussi me semble il, que l'on pourrait avec bonne cause conseiller aux personnes déjà parvenues en âge de connaissance, de ne s'amuser à lire sans jugement toutes sortes de livres fabuleux: de peur que leurs entendements ne s'accoutument petit à petit à aimer mensonge, & à se paître de vanité, outre ce que le temps y est mal employé. Et pourrait à l'aventure cette raison être assez valable pour condamner tous écrits mensongers, & dont le sujet n'est point véritable, si ce n'était que l'imbecilité de nôtre nature ne peut porter, que l'entendement soit toujours tendu à lire matières graves, & sérieuse, non plus que le corps ne saurait sans intermission durer au travail d'oeuvres laborieuses. Au moyen de quoi il faut aucune fois que nôtre esprit est troublé de mesaventures, ou travaillé & recru de grave étude, user de quelque divertissement, pour le détourner de ses tristes pensées, ou bien de quelque rafraîchissement puis après le remettre plus allègre, & plus vif à la considération, ou action des choses d'importance. Et parce que la propre & naturelle délectation d'un bon entendement est toujours voir, oir, & apprendre quelque chose de nouveau, il n'y a point de doute, que l'histoire, à cause de la diversité des choses que y sont comprises, ne soit l'une des lectures que plus on doit chercher & élire pour le revivre: entendu en même temps que le profit est conjoint avec le plaisir. Mais toutes fois encores a il semblé à quelques hommes du bon jugement, que la vérite de celle était un petit trop austère pour suffisament délecter, à cause qu'elle doit réciter les choses nettement & simplement, ainsi comme elles sont avenues, & non pas en la sorte qu'elles seraient plus plaisantes à lire, ni ainsi comme nos courages (qui naturellement se passionnent en lisant, ou voyant les faits & fortunes d'autrui) le souhaitent, & le désirent. Et si ne lui peut on donner tant d'aide en richissement de langue, ni par tout artifice d'eloquence, qu'elle ait autant de force à récreer l'entendement de celui qui la lit, comme un conte fait à plaisir expressement pour délecter quand il est subtilement inventé, & ingénieusement deduit. Aussi n'est ce le but auquel elle est proprement adressée, ains la fin principale pour laquelle elle doit être écrite & lue, est par exemples du passé s'instruire aux affaires de l'avenir, là où ceux, qui pour suppléer au default de la vraie histoire, en cet endroit inventent & mettent par écrit des contes fabuleux en forme d'histoire, ne se proposent autre but principal, que la délectation. Mais tout ainsi comme en la portraiture les tableaux sont estimés les meilleurs, & plaisent plus aux yeux à ce connaissance, qui representent mieux la verité du naturel, aussi entre celles fictions, celles qui sont les moins eloignées de nature, & où il y a plus de vérisimilitude, sont celles qui plaisent le plus à ceux qui mesurent leur plaisir à la raison, & qui se délectent avec jugement: Parce que, suivant les préceptes du Poëte Horace, il faut que les choses feintes, pour délecter, soient aprochantes des véritables. Et si n'est pas besoin que toutes choses y soient feintes, attendu que cela n'est point permis aux Poëtes mêmes. Pour autant que l'artifice d'invention Poëtique, comme doctement a écrit Strabon, consiste en trois choses. Premierement en histoire, de laquelle la fin est vérité. À raison de quoi, il n'est point loisible aux Poëtes, quand ils parlent des choses qui sont en nature d'en écrire à leur plaisir autrement que la vérité n'est: parce que cela leur seroit imputé, non à licence, ou artifice: mais à ignorance. Secondement en ordre & disposition, dont la fin est l'expresion & la force d'atraer & retenir le lecteur. Tiercement en la fiction, dont la fin est l'établissement & la délectation, qui procéde de la noueauté des choses étranges, & pleines de merveilles. Par ainsi beaucoup moins se doit on permettre toutes choses et fictions que l'on veut déguiser du nom d'historiale vérité: ainsi il faut entrelacer si dextrement du vrai parmi du faux, en retenant toujours semblance de vérité, & si bien raporter le tout ensemble, qu'il n'y ait point de discordance du commencement au milieu, n'y du milieu à la fin. Et au contraire la plus grande partie des livres de cette sorte, qui ont anciennement étés écrits en nôtre langue, outre ce qu'il n'y a nulle érudition, nulle connaissance de l'antiquité, ne chose aucune (à brief parler) dont on peut tirer quelque utilité, encore sont ils le plus souvent si mal cousus & si éloignés de toute vraisemblabe apparence, qu'il semble que ce soient plutôt songes de quelque malade rêvant en fièvre chaude, qu'inventions d'aucun homme d'ésprit & de jugement. Et pour ce m'est il avis qu'ils ne sauroient avoir la grâce, ni la force de délecter le loisir d'un bon entendement: car ils ne sont point dignes de lui. C'est un certain signe que celui n'a point de sentiment des choses ingénieuses & gentiles, que se délecter des lourdes & grossières. Mais tout ainsi qu'entre les exercices du corp, que l'on prendre par ébattrement, les plus recommandables sont ceux qui, outre le plaisir que l'on en reçoit, adressent le corps, renforcent les membres & profitent à la santé: aussi entre les jeux & passe-temps de l'esprit les plus louables sont ceux qui, outre la réjouissance qu'ils nous aportent, servent encore à limer (par manière de dire) & affiner de plus en plus le jugement, de sorte que le plaisir n'est point du tout oiseux. Ce que j'espère que l'on pourra aucunement trouver en cette fabuleuse histoire des amours de Chariclea & Theagenes, en laquelle, outre l'ingénieuse fiction, il y a en quelques lieux de beaux discours tirés de la philosophie naturelle & Morale: force dits notables, & propos sentencieux: plusieurs belles harangues, où l'artifice d'éloquence est très bien enployé & par tout las passions humaines paintes au vif, avec si grand honnêteté, qui l'on n'en sauroit tirer occasion, ou exemple de mal faire. Parce que de toutes affections illicites, & mauvaises il a fait l'issue malheureuse: & au contraire des bonnes & honêtes, la fin désirables & heureuse. Mais pourtant la disposition en est si singulière: car il commence au milieu de son histoire, comme font les Poëtes Héroiques. Ce qui cause de prime face un grand ébahissement aux lecteurs, & leur engendre un passioné désir d'entendre le commencement: toutesfois il les tire se bien par l'ingénieuse liaison de son conte que l'on n'est point résolu de ce que l'on trouve tout au commencement du premier livre jusques à ce que l'on ait lu la fin du cinquième. Et quand on en est là venu, encore a l'on plus grande envie de voir la fin que l'on n'avait au parvenant d'en voir le commencement: de sorte que toujours l'entendement demeure suspens, jusques à ce que l'on vienne à la conclusion, laquelle laisse le lecteur satisfait, de la sorte que le sont ceux, qui à la fin viennent à jouir d'un bien ardemment désir, & longuement attendu. Toutesfois je ne me veux pas beaucoup amuser à la recommander: parce que (quand tout est dit) ce n'est qu'une fable, à laquelle encore défaut [défaille ?] (à mon jugement) l'une des deux perfections requise pour faire une chose belle, c'est la grandeur, à cause que les contes, même quant à la personne de Theagenes, auquel il ne fait exécuter nuls mémorables exploits d'armes, ne me semblent point assez riches, & ne mériteraient pas à l'aventure d'être lus, si ce n'était, ou pour divertir quelque ennui ou pour en avoir puis après l'entendement plus delivré & mieux dispos à faire & à lire autres choses meilleures, suivant le précepte du sage, qui dit, Qu'il faut jouer pour faire à bon escient, & non pas faire à bon escient pour jouer: C'est à dire: Que l'on doit user des choses des plaisir, pour être puis après plus apte à faire les choses d'importance, & non pas s'embesogner après une chose qui n'est que de plaisir, comme si c'était un affaire de consequence. Ce que je veux employer pour me servir de décharge & d'excuse envers les gens d'honneur auxquels j'ai voulu donner matière de réjouir leurs entendements travaillés d'affaires en lisant ce livre (au moins si tant il mérit de faveur que de venir en leurs mains) comme j'ai moi même adouci le travail d'autres meilleures & plus fructeuses traductions en le traduisant par intervalles aux heures extraordinaires. Mais au regard de ceux qui sont se parfaitement composés à la vertu qu'ils ne connaissent, ni ne reçoivent aucun autre plaisir, que le devoir, ou de ceux qui par une fièvre d'austerité intraitable ont le goût si corrumpu, qu'ils ne trouvent rien bon, & se déplaisent à eux mêmes, si d'aventure ils viennent à reprendre cette mienne entremise, je me contenterai de leur répondre, que ce livre n'a jamais être écrit, ne traduit pour eux: les uns parce qu'ils n'en ont que faire, les autres parce qu'ils ne le valent pas. Et quant à l'auteur de cette Histoire Aethiopique, on pense que ce soit celui Heliodore, duquel

Philostrate fait mention à al fin du second livre de ses Sophistes. Ce que l'on conjecture avec grande raison, tant pour la qualité de son style, que (sans point de doute), est un petit affété (ainsi que l'est ordinairement celui de ceux qui anciennement faisaient profession de Rhétorique & de Philosophie tout ensemble, que l'on appelait Sophistes) comme aussi pour ce que Philostrate le surnomme Arabe, & qu'Heliodore lui même a fin de son livre dit qu'il était Phoenicien, natif de la ville d'Emessa, laquelle est située confins de la Phoenecia, & de l'Arabie. A l'occasion de laquelle vicinité on estime que Philostrate l'appele Arabe. Et si c'est lui, il fut du temps même de Philostrate, lequel (comme témoigne Suidas) vécu sous l'Empereur Severus, & sous ses successeurs, jusque à Philipe, duquel temps au nôtre il y a plus de treize cents ans. Et néanmoins n'avait ce livre jamais été imprimé sinon depuis que la librairie du Roy Mathias de Hongrie fut détruite & saccagée, auquel sac il se trouvait un soldat allemand, qui mit la main dessus, pour ce qu'il le vit richement étoffé, & le vendit à celui qui depuis le fit imprimer en Allemagne, il y a quelques quatorze ou quinze ans. Combien qu'au parvenant il fut entre les mains d'aucuns particuliers, comme de Politian entre autres qui le cite en son livre de Miscellanes. Mais je n'ai point su qu'il ait jamais été traduit. À raison de quoi, si d'aventure mon jugement m'a trompé en restituant par conjecture aucuns lieux corrumpus, & vicieusement imprimés, les équitables lecteurs m'en devront plutôt excuser: tant parce que je n'ai pu recouvrer diversité d'exemplaires, pour les conférer, que pour autant que j'ai été le premier qui l'ai traduit, sans être du labeur d'aucun précédent aidé. D'une chose me puis je bien vanter, que je ne pense y avoir rien omis ni ajouté, ainsi comme les lecteurs le pourront trouver s'il leur plaît prendre le peine de le conferer.

Following Amyot's *proême* is the following:

> Au lecteur
> A mi lecteur, ne blâme de ce livre
> L'auteur premier, ni la solicitude
> Du translateur qui François le te livre,
> Pour recréer un peu la lassitude
> De ton esprit travaillé de l'êtude,
> Ou ennuyé de fortune adversaire:
> Car si tu dis, que tels songes écrire
> N'était besoin, ni de Graec les traduire,
> Encore est il à toi moins necessaire,
> Si tu ne veux les avoir, & les lire.

The following is from Amyot's prefatory matter to his translation of Plutarch's *Lives*:

Les Vies des Hommes Illustres de Plutarque, traduites du Grec par Amyot
Paris: Janet et Cotelle, 1818 (princeps 1559)

[. . .] Et si le fait avec plus de grace, d'efficace et de dexterité, que ne font les livres de philosophie morale, d'autant que les exemples sont plus aptes à esmouvoir et enseigner, que ne sont les arguments et les preuves de raisons, ny leurs imperieux preceptes, à cause qu'ilz sont particuliers, accompagnez de toutes leurs circonstances, là où les raisons et demonstrations sont generales, et tendent plus à fin de prouver, ou de donner à entendre, et les exemples à mettre en oeuvre et à executer: pource qu'ilz ne monstrent pas seulement comme il faut faire, mais aussi impriment affection de le vouloir faire, tant pour une inclination naturelle, que tous hommes ont à imiter, que pour la beauté de la vertu que a telle force, que par tout où elle se voit, elle se fait desirer et aimer. (xxv-xxvi)

Sir Thomas North's translation of the passage immediately above:

Plutarch's Lives of the Noble Grecians and Romans, Englished by Sir Thomas North
New York: AMS Press, 1967

[. . .] These things it doth with much greater grace, efficacie, and speede, than the bookes of morall Philosophie doe: forasmuch as examples are of more force to move and instruct, than are the arguments and proofes of reason, or their precise precepts, bicause examples be the very formes of our deeds, and accompanied with all circumstances. Whereas reasons and demonstrations are generall, and tend to the proofe of things, and to the beating of them into understanding: and examples tende to the shewing of them in practise and execution, bicause they doe not onely declare what is to be done, but also worke a desire to doe it, as well in respect of a certain nautrall inclination which al men have to follow examples, as also for the beautie of vertue, which is of such power, that wheresoever she is seene, she maketh her selfe to be loved and liked. (10-11)

BIBLIOGRAPHY

Primary Texts

Ariosto, Lodovico. *Orlando Furioso.* Ed. Santorre Debenedetti and Cesare Segre. Bologna: Carducci, 1960.

——. *Orlando Furioso di M. Lodovico Ariosto, dirigido al principe Don Philippo N. S. Traduzido en romance castellano por el S. Don Hieronimo de Urrea.* Venice: G. Giolito, 1553.

——. *Orlando Furioso.* Trans. Guido Waldman. Oxford: Oxford University Press, 1974.

Boscán, Juan. *Las obras de Boscán, y algunas de Garcilasso de la Vega, repartidas en quatro libros.* Envers: M. Nucio, 1597.

Bryskett, Lodowick. *A Discourse of Civil Life.* (London, 1606.) Ed. Thomas E. Wright. Northridge, CA: San Fernando State College Renaissance Editions, 1970.

Castiglione, Balthasar. *Il Cortegiano.* Ed. Carlo Cordié. Milan: Arnoldo Mondadori, 1960.

——. *The Book of the Courtier.* Trans. Sir Thomas Hoby. Ed. Walter A. Raleigh. New York: AMS Press, 1967.

——. *Los cuatros libros del cortesano.* Trans. Juan Boscán. Madrid: Librería de los Bibliógrafos, 1873.

Ercilla, Alonso de. *La Araucana de d. Alonso de Ercilla y Zuniga. Edicion del centenario, ilustrada con grabados, documentos, notas historicas y bibliograficas y una biografia del autor.* Ed. Jose Toribio Medina. 5 vols. Santiago de Chile: Imprenta Elzeviriana, 1910–1918.

——. *La Araucana.* Ed. Marcos A. Morínigo and Isaías Lerner. 2 vols. Madrid: Castalia, 1979.

——. *La Araucana.* Ed. Isaías Lerner. Madrid: Catedra, 1993.

——. *The Historie of "Aravcana". Written in Verse by Don Alonso de Ercilla. Translated out of the Spanishe into Englishe Prose allmost to the Ende of the 16: Canto.* Ed. Frank Pierce. Manchester: Manchester University Press, 1964.

Fulgentius, Fabius Planciades. *Fulgentius the Mythographer.* Trans. Leslie George Whitbread. Columbus: Ohio State University Press, 1971.

Garcilaso de la Vega. *Obra Poética y Textos en Prosa.* Ed. Bienvenido Morros. Barcelona: Crítica, 1995.

Guazzo, Stefano. *The civile conversation of M. Steeven Guazzo, the first three books translated by George Pettie, anno 1581, and the fourth by Barth. Young, anno 1586.* Ed. Edward Sullivan. New York: AMS Press, 1967.

Harington, Sir John. *Orlando Furioso, Translated in to English Heroical Verse.* Ed. Robert McNulty. Oxford: Clarendon Press, 1972.

Hernández de Velasco, Gregorio. *Los doze libros de la Eneida de Vergilio.* Antwerp: Bellero, 1557. Hispanic Society of America Library.

Justin. *Epitome of the Philippic History of Pompeius Trogus.* Trans. J.C. Yardley. Atlanta: Scholars Press, 1994.

Marquis, Paul A., ed. *Tottel's Songes and Sonettes: The Elizabethan Version.* MRTS 338. Tempe: ACMRS, 2007.

Mena, Juan de. *La "Ilíada" de Homero: edición crítica de las "Sumas de la Yliada de Homero."* Ed. T. González Rolán, María F. del Barrio Vega, and A. López Fonseca. Madrid: Ediciones Clásicas, 1996.

Petrarca, Francesco. *Petrarch's Lyric Poems: The Rime Sparse and Other Lyrics.* Trans. and ed. Robert M. Durling. Boston: Harvard University Press, 1967.

———. *Trionfi, Rime Estravaganti, Codice degli Abbozzi.* Ed. Vinicio Pacca and Laura Paolino. Milan: Mondadori, 1996.

———. *Lord Morley's Tryumphes of Fraunces Petrarcke: The First English Translation of the Trionfi.* Ed. D. D. Carnicelli. Cambridge, MA: Harvard University Press, 1971.

Rosales, Diego de. *Historia General de el Reino de Chile, Flandes Indiano.* 3 vols. Valparaiso: Mercurio, 1877–1878.

Sidney, Sir Philip. *An Apology for Poetry.* Ed. Geoffrey Shepherd. Manchester: Manchester University Press, 1973.

Spenser, Edmund. *The Faerie Queene.* Ed. A. C. Hamilton. London: Longman, 1977.

———. *Selected Shorter Poems.* Ed. Douglas Brooks-Davies. New York: Longman, 1995.

———. *Colin Clouts Come Home. Edmund Spenser's Poetry.* 3rd ed. New York: W. W. Norton, 1968.

———. *A View of the Present State of Ireland.* Ed. Andrew Hadfield and Willy Maley. Oxford: Blackwell, 1997.

———. *Works: A Variorum Edition.* Ed. E. A. Greenlaw, F. M. Padelford, C. G. Osgood, et al. 10 vols. Baltimore: Johns Hopkins University Press, 1932–1949.

Tasso, Torquato. *Discorsi dell'arte poetica e del poema eroico.* Ed. Luigi Poma. Rome: Laterza, 1964.

———. *Discourses on the Art of Poetry.* Trans. Lawrence F. Rhu. In *The Genesis of Tasso's Narrative Theory.* Detroit: Wayne State University Press, 1993.

———. *Gerusalemme Liberata.* Ed. Lanfranco Caretti. Turin: Einaudi, 1971.

———. *Gerusalemme Liberata.* Trans. Edward Fairfax. Philadelphia: C.G. Henderson & Co., 1855.

—. *Jerusalem Delivered*. Trans. and ed. Ralph Nash. Detroit: Wayne State University Press, 1987.
—. *Jerusalem Delivered*. Trans. and ed. Anthony M. Esolen. Baltimore: Johns Hopkins University Press, 2002.
Vega, Garcilaso de la. *Obra poética y textos en prosa*. Ed. Bienvenido Morros. Madrid: Crítica, 1995.
Vegio, Maffeo. *Short Epics*. Ed. and trans. Michael C. J. Putnam. Cambridge, MA: Harvard University Press, 2004.
Virgil. *Aeneid*. Ed. R. D. Williams. 2 vols. New York: St. Martin's Press, 1972.
—. *The Aeneid*. Trans. Robert Fitzgerald. New York: Random House, 1983.
—. *Georgics*. Ed. Richard F. Thomas. Cambridge: Cambridge University Press, 1988.

Secondary Texts

Abbott, Don Paul. *Rhetoric in the New World: Rhetorical Theory and Practice in Colonial Spanish America*. Columbia: University of South Carolina Press, 1996.
Adorno, Rolena. "Literary Production and Suppression: Reading and Writing about Amerindians in Colonial Spanish America." *Dispositio* 11 (1986): 1–25.
—. "Todorov y De Certeau: la alteridad y la contemplación del sujeto." *Revista de Crítica Literaria Latinoamericana* 17 (1991): 51–58.
—. "Reconsidering Colonial Discourse for Sixteenth- and Seventeenth-Century Spanish America." *Latin American Research Review* 28 (1993): 135–45.
Aiman, Henry C. "Spenser's Debt to Heliodorus in *The Faerie Queene*." *Emporia State Research Studies* 4 (1974): 5–18.
Albarracín Sarmiento, Carlos. "El poeta y su rey en *La Araucana*." *Filología* 21 (1986): 99–116.
Alexiou, Margaret. *The Ritual Lament in Greek Tradition*. Cambridge: Cambridge University Press, 1974.
Aquila, August J. *Alonso de Ercilla y Zúñiga: A Basic Bibliography*. London: Grant and Cutler, 1975.
Auerbach, Erich. "Philology and *Weltliteratur*." Trans. Maire and Edward Said. *Centennial Review* 13 (1969): 1–17.
—. *Literary Language and its Public in Late Latin Antiquity and in the Middle Ages*. Trans. Ralph Manheim. 2nd ed. Princeton: Princeton University Press, 1993.
Bakewell, Peter. "Conquest after the Conquest: The Rise of Spanish Domination in America." In *Spain, Europe, and the Atlantic World*, ed. Richard Kagan and Geoffrey Parker, 296–315. New York: Cambridge University Press, 1995.

Bakhtin, Mikhail. *The Dialogic Imagination.* Trans. Caryl Emerson and Michael Holquist. Ed. Michael Holquist. Austin: University of Texas Press, 1981.

Bataillon, Marcel. *Erasmo y España.* Mexico: Fondo de Cultura Económica, 1950.

Beardsley, Theodore S. Jr. *Hispano-Classical Translations Printed between 1482 and 1699.* Pittsburgh: Duquesne University Press, 1970.

———. "La Traduction des auteurs classiques en Espagne de 1488 a 1586, dans le domaine des belles-lettres." In *L'Humanisme dans les Lettres Espagnoles: XIXe Colloque international d'études humanistes, Tours, 5–17 juillet 1976,* 51–64. Paris: Librairie Philosophique J. Vrin, 1979.

———. "The Classics in Spain: The Sixteenth versus the Seventeenth Century." In *Studies in Honor of Gustavo Correa,* 11–27. Potomac, MD: Scripta Humanistica, 1986.

Bellamy, Elizabeth Jane. "*The Faerie Queene (1596).*" In *The Oxford Handbook of Edmund Spenser,* ed. Richard A. McCabe, 271–92. Oxford: Oxford University Press, 2010.

Benson, Pamela Joseph. "Praise and Defense of the Queen in the *Faerie Queene,* Book V." In *Edmund Spenser,* ed. Andrew Hadfield, 161–76. London: Longman, 1996.

Berger, Harry. *Revisionary Play: Studies in the Spenserian Dynamics.* Berkeley: University of California Press, 1988.

Bhabha, Homi K. *The Location of Culture.* London: Routledge, 1994.

Bialostosky, Don H. *Making Tales.* Chicago: University of Chicago Press, 1984.

Biow, Douglas. *"Mirabile Dictu": Representations of the Marvelous in Medieval and Renaissance Epic.* Ann Arbor: University of Michigan Press, 1996.

Bloom, Harold. "The Internalization of Quest Romance." In idem, *The Poetics of Influence,* 17–42. New Haven: Schwab, 1988.

Boone, Elizabeth Hill, and Walter D. Mignolo, eds. *Writing Without Words: Alternative Literacies in Mesoamerica and the Andes.* Durham, NC: Duke University Press, 1994.

Borris, Kenneth. "Allegory, Emblem, and Symbol." In *Handbook,* ed. McCabe, 437–61.

Bowra, C. M. *From Virgil to Milton.* London: Macmillan, (1945) 1967.

Bradshaw, Brendan. "Robe and Sword in the Conquest of Ireland." In *Law and Government under the Tudors,* ed. C. Cross, D. Loades, and J. J. Scarisbrick, 139–62. Cambridge: Cambridge University Press, 1988.

Brady, Ciarán. "Spenser's Irish Crisis: Humanism and Experience in the 1590s." *Past and Present* 111 (1986): 17–49.

Braudel, Fernand. *The Mediterranean and the Mediterranean World in the Age of Philip II.* 2 vols. New York: Harper, 1972.

Braund, Susanna Morton. "Mind the Gap: On Foreignizing Translations of the *Aeneid.*" In *A Companion to Vergil's* Aeneid *and its Tradition,* ed. Joseph

Farrell and Michael C. J. Putnam, 449–64. Oxford and Malden, MA: Wiley-Blackwell, 2010.

Brownlee, Kevin, and Marina Scordilis Brownlee, eds. *Romance: Generic Transformation from Chrétien de Troyes to Cervantes.* Hanover: University Press of New England, 1985.

Brumble, H. David. *Classical Myths and Legends in the Middle Ages and Renaissance.* Westport, CT: Greenwood Press, 1998.

Burke, Peter. *The Fortunes of the Courtier: The European Reception of Castiglione's Cortegiano.* Cambridge: Polity Press, 1995.

Burrow, Colin. *Epic Romance: Homer to Milton.* Oxford: Oxford University Press, 1993.

———. "Spenser and Classical Traditions." In *The Cambridge Companion to Spenser*, ed. Andrew Hadfield, 217–36. Cambridge: Cambridge University Press, 2001.

Camerlingo, Rosanna. *From the Courtly World to the Infinite Universe: Sir Philip Sidney's Two "Arcadias."* Alessandria: Orso, 1993.

Cañal, Rafael González. "Dido y Eneas en la poesía española del Siglo de Oro." *Criticon* 44 (1988): 23–54.

Canny, Nicholas. "Edmund Spenser and the Development of an Anglo-Irish Identity." *Yearbook of English Studies* 19 (1983): 1–19.

———. "Protestants, Planters and Apartheid in Early Modern Ireland." *Irish Historical Studies* 25 (1986): 105–15.

———. "Identity Formation in Ireland: The Emergence of the Anglo-Irish." In *Colonial Identity in the Atlantic World, 1500–1800*, ed. idem and Anthony Pagden, 159–212. Princeton: Princeton University Press, 1987.

———. "Introduction: Spenser and the Reform of Ireland." In *Spenser and Ireland: An Interdisciplinary Perspective*, ed. Patricia Coughlan, 9–24. Cork: Cork University Press, 1989.

———. *Making Ireland British: 1580–1650.* Oxford: Oxford University Press, 2001.

Canny, Nicholas, and Anthony Pagden, eds. *Colonial Identity in the Atlantic World, 1500–1800.* Princeton: Princeton University Press, 1987.

Cappello, Sergio. "*Histoire fabuleuse* e poetica del romanzo in Jacques Amyot." Università di Udine, 1999. [Forthcoming.]

Caravaggi, Giovanni. "Petrarch in Castile in the Fifteenth Century: The *Triumphete de Amor* by the Marquis of Santillana." In *Petrarch's "Triumphs": Allegory and Spectacle*, ed. Konrad Eisenbichler and Amilcare A. Iannucci, 291–306. Toronto: Dovehouse Editions, 1990.

Carne-Ross, Donald S. "The One and the Many." *Arion* n.s. 3 (1976): 146–219.

———. "The One and the Many: A Reading of the *Orlando Furioso*, Cantos 1 and 8." *Arion* 5 (1966): 195–234.

Carroll, Clare. "The Construction of Gender and the Cultural and Political Other in *The Faerie Queene* 5 and *A View of the Present State of Ireland*: The Critics, the Context, and the Case of Radigund." *Criticism* 32 (1990): 163–92.

———. "Humanism and English Literature in the Fifteenth and Sixteenth Centuries." In *The Cambridge Companion to Renaissance Humanism*, ed. Jill Kraye, 246–68. Cambridge: Cambridge University Press, 1996.

———. "Spenser and the Irish Language: The Sons of Milesio in *A View of the Present State of Ireland*, *The Faerie Queene*, Book V and the *Leabhar Gabhála*." In *Spenser in Ireland: 'The Faerie Queene,' 1596–1996*, spec. no. of *Irish University Review* 26 (1996): 281–90.

———. *The Orlando Furioso: A Stoic Comedy*. MRTS 174. Tempe: ACMRS, 1997.

———. *Circe's Cup: Cultural Transformations in Early Modern Writing about Ireland*. Cork: Cork University Press, 2001.

———, and Vincent P. Carey. "Factions and Fictions: Spenser's Reflections of and on Elizabethan Politics." In *Spenser's Life and the Subject of Biography*, ed. Judith H. Anderson, Donald Cheney, and David A. Richardson, 31–44. Amherst: University of Massachusetts Press, 1996.

Carron, Jean-Claude. "Imitation and Intertextuality in the Renaissance." *New Literary History* 19 (1988): 565–79.

Cascali, Sergio. "The Development of the Aeneas Legend." In *Companion*, ed. Farrell and Putnam, 37–51.

Cascardi, Anthony J. *Ideologies of History in the Spanish Golden Age*. University Park: Pennsylvania State University Press, 1997.

Castillo, Debra A. "Impossible Indian." *Chasqui: Revista de Literatura Latinoamericana* 35 (2006): 42–57.

Castillo Sandoval, Roberto. "'¿Una misma cosa con la vuestra?': Ercilla, Pedro de Oña y la Apropiación Post-Colonial de la Patria Araucana." *Revista Iberoamericana* 61 (1995): 231–47.

Cevallos, Francisco Javier. "Don Alonso de Ercilla and the American Indian: History and Myth." *Revista de Estudios Hispánicos* 23 (1989): 1–20.

Chevalier, Maxime. *L'Arioste en Espagne*. Bordeaux: Institut d'Etudes Ibériques et Ibéro-Américaines de l'Université de Bordeaux. 1966.

———. *Lectura y lectores en la España del Siglo XVI y XVII*. Madrid: Turner, 1976.

Coddou, Marcelo. "Nuevas consideraciones sobre el tema del amor en la obra de Ercilla." In *Homenaje a Ercilla*, ed. Luis Muñoz et al., 111–31. Concepción: Universidad de Concepción, Instituto Central de Lenguas, 1969.

Cohen, Walter. "The Discourses of Empire in the Renaissance." In *Cultural Authority in Golden Age Spain*, ed. Marina S. Brownlee and Hans Ulrich Gumbrecht, 270–76. Baltimore: Johns Hopkins University Press, 1995.

Colombí-Monguió, Alicia de. "Boscán frente a Navagero: el nacimiento de la conciencia humanista en la poesía española." *Nueva Revista de Filología Hispánica* 40 (1992): 143–68.

———. *Petrarquismo peruano: Diego Dávalos y la "Miscelánea Austral."* London: Tamesis, 1995.

Concha, Jaime. "*La Araucana*, epopea della controconquista." *Materiali Critici* 2 (1981): 93–128.

———. "El Otro Nuevo Mundo." In *Homenaje a Ercilla*, 31–82.

Conte, Gian Biagio. *The Rhetoric of Imitation*. Ithaca: Cornell University Press, 1986.

———. "On the Shoulders of Giants: Progress and Perspectives in Latin Studies." *Diogenes* 185 (1999): 27–33.

Corominas, Juan M. *Castiglione y "La Araucana": Estudio de una influencia*. Madrid: José Porrúa Terranzas, 1980.

Cox, Virginia. *The Renaissance Dialogue: Literary Dialogue in its Social and Political Contexts, Castiglione to Galileo*. Cambridge: Cambridge University Press, 1992.

Cruz, Anne J. "Spanish Petrarchism and the Poetics of Appropriation: Boscán and Garcilaso de la Vega." In *Renaissance Rereadings: Intertext and Context*, ed. Maryanne Cline Horowitz, and Wendy A. Furman, 80–96. Chicago: University of Illinois Press, 1988.

———. "The *Trionfi* in Spain: Petrarchist Poetics, Translation Theory, and the Castilian Vernacular in the Sixteenth Century." In *Petrarch's "Triumphs": Allegory and Spectacle*, ed. Eisenbichler and Iannucci, 307–24.

———. "Self-Fashioning in Spain: Garcilaso de la Vega." *Romanic Review* 83 (1992): 517–38.

———. "Arms Versus Letters: The Poetics of War and the Career of the Poet in Early Modern Spain." In *European Literary Careers: The Author From Antiquity to the Renaissance*, ed. Patrick Cheney, 186–205. Toronto: University of Toronto Press, 2002.

Cueva, Agustín. "El espejismo heroico de la conquista: Ensayo de interpretación de *La Araucana*." *Casa de las Americas* 110 (1978): 29–40.

Cummings, Brian. "Protestant Allegory." In *The Cambridge Companion to Allegory*, ed. Rita Copeland and Peter T. Struck, 177–90. Cambridge: Cambridge University Press, 2010.

Curtius, Ernst Robert. *European Literature and the Latin Middle Ages*. Trans. Willard R. Trask. Princeton: Bollingen, 1953.

Davies, Gareth A. "*La Araucana* and the Question of Ercilla's *Converso* Origins." In *Medieval and Renaissance Studies on Spain and Portugal in Honour of P. E. Russell*, ed. F. W. Hodcroft et al., 86–108. Oxford: Oxford University Press, 1981.

Davis, Elizabeth B. *Myth and Identity in the Epic of Imperial Spain*. Columbia: University of Missouri Press, 2000.

Di Camillo, Octavio. *El Humanismo Castellano del Siglo XV.* Valencia: Fernando Torres, 1976.

———. "Humanism in Spain." In *Renaissance Humanism, Foundations, Forms, and Legacy*, vol. 2: *Humanism Beyond Italy*, ed. Albert Rabil, Jr., 55–108. Philadelphia: University of Pennsylvania Press, 1988.

Durand, José. "El Chapetón Ercilla y la honra Araucana." *Filología* 10 (1964): 113–34.

Durling, Robert. *The Figure of the Poet in Renaissance Epic.* Boston: Harvard University Press, 1965.

———. "The Epic Ideal." In *The Old World: Discovery and Rebirth*, vol. 3 of *Literature and Western Civilization*, ed. David Daiches and Anthony Thorlby, 105–46. London: Aldus Books, 1974.

Einstein, Lewis. *The Italian Renaissance in England.* New York: Burt Franklin, 1902.

Elias, Norbert. *Norbert Elias on Civilization, Power, and Knowledge: Selected Writings*, ed. Stephen Mennell and Johan Goudsblom. Chicago: University of Chicago Press, 1998.

Elliot, J. H. *The Old World and the New: 1492–1650.* London: Cambridge University Press, 1970.

———. "Final Reflections: The Old World and the New Revisited." In *America in European Consciousness: 1493–1750*, ed. Karen Ordahl Kupperman, 391–408. Chapel Hill: University of North Carolina Press, 1995.

Ellis, Steven G. *Tudor Ireland: Crown, Community, and the Conflict of Cultures 1470–1603.* London: Longman, 1985.

Feeney, Denis. "How Virgil Did It." Review of Gian Carlo Conte, *The Poetry of Pathos: Studies in Virgilian Epic*, and Randall T. Ganibann, *Statius and Virgil: The "Thebaid" and the Reinterpretation of the "Aeneid."* *TLS* 15 February (2008): 26–27.

Ferguson, Margaret W. *Trials of Desire: Renaissance Defenses of Poetry.* New Haven: Yale University Press, 1983.

———. *Dido's Daughters: Literacy, Gender, and Empire in Early Modern England and France.* Chicago: University of Chicago Press, 2003.

Fletcher, Angus. *The Prophetic Moment: An Essay on Spenser.* Chicago: University of Chicago Press, 1971.

———. *Allegory: The Theory of a Symbolic Mode.* Ithaca: Cornell University Press, 1974.

Florit, Eugenio. "Los momentos líricos de *La Araucana.*" *Revista Iberoamericana* 33 (1967): 45–54.

Fogarty, Anne. "The Colonization of Language: Narrative Strategies in *A View of the Present State of Ireland* and *The Faerie Queene*, Book VI." In *Spenser and Ireland: An Interdisciplinary Perspective*, ed. Coughlan, 75–108.

Fowler, Don P. "First Thoughts on Closure: Problems and Prospects." *Materiali e Discussioni per l'Analisi dei Testi Classici* 22 (1989): 75–122.

———. "Second Thoughts on Closure." In *Classical Closure: Reading the End in Greek and Latin Literature*, ed. Deborah H. Roberts, Francis M. Dunn, and idem, 3–22. Princeton: Princeton University Press, 1997.

———. *Roman Constructions: Readings in Postmodern Latin*. Oxford: Oxford University Press, 2000.

Fowler, Elizabeth. *"A Vewe of the Presente State of Ireland* (1596, 1633)." In *Handbook*, ed. McCabe, 314–32.

Freccero, John. "The Fig Tree and the Laurel: Petrarch's Poetics." In *Literary Theory and Renaissance Texts*, ed. Patricia Parker and David Quint, 20–33. Baltimore: Johns Hopkins University Press, 1986.

Fuchs, Barbara. *Mimesis and Empire: The New World, Islam, and European Identity*. Cambridge: Cambridge University Press, 2001.

———. "Traveling Epic: Translating Ercilla's *La Araucana* in the Old World." *Journal of Medieval and Early Modern Studies* 36 (2006): 379–95.

Fumaroli, Mark. "Jacques Amyot and the Clerical Polemic Against the Chivalric Novel." *Renaissance Quarterly* 38 (1985): 22–40.

Futre Pinheiro, M. "The *Nachleben* of the Ancient Novel in Iberian Literature of the Sixteenth Century." In *The Novel in the Ancient World*, ed. Gareth Schmeling, 775–99. Leiden: Brill, 1996.

Gajardo Maldonado, Félix. "Alonso de Ercilla bajo censura militar." *Revista Chilena de Historia y Geografía* 161 (1994–1995): 7–38.

García-Macho, María Lourdes. *El léxico de la "Yliada de Homero en romance" traducida por Juan de Mena*. Madrid: Universidad Nacional de Educación a Distancia, 1998.

Geneste, Pierre. *Le Capitaine-Poète Aragonais Jerónimo de Urrea*. Paris: Ediciones Hispanoamericanas, 1978.

Gerli, Michael. "Elysium and the Cannibals: History and Humanism in Ercilla's *La Araucana*." In *Renaissance and Golden Age Essays in Honor of D. W. McPheeters*, ed. Bruno M. Damiani, 82–93. Potomac, MD: Scripta Humanistica, 1986.

Giamatti, A. Bartlett. *The Earthly Paradise and the Renaissance Epic*. Princeton: Princeton University Press, 1966.

Gibson, Charles. *Spain in America*. New York: Harper, 1967.

Gillingham, John. "The English Invasion of Ireland." In *Representing Ireland: Literature and Origins of Conflict, 1534–1660*, ed. Brendan Bradshaw, Andrew Hadfield, and Willy Maley, 24–42. Cambridge: Cambridge University Press, 1993.

Gless, Darryl J. *Interpretation and Theology in Spenser*. Cambridge: Cambridge University Press, 1994.

Goić, Cedomil. "Poética del Exordio en *La Araucana*." *Revista Chilena de Literatura* 1 (1970): 5–22.

————. "Poetización del espacio, espacios de la poesía." In *La cultura literaria en la América virreinal: concurrencias y diferencias*, ed. José Pascual Buxó, 13–24. México: UNAM, 1996.

Goldberg, Jonathan. *Endlesse Worke: Spenser and the Structure of Discourse*. Baltimore: Johns Hopkins University Press, 1981.

González Cañal, Rafael. "Dido y Eneas en la poesía española del Siglo de Oro." *Critícon* 44 (1988): 25–54.

González Echeverría, Roberto. *Isla a su vuelo fugitiva: ensayos críticos sobre literatura hispanoamericana*. Madrid: José Porrúa Turanzas, 1983.

Grafton, Anthony, and Lisa Jardine. *From Humanism to the Humanities*. Cambridge, MA: Harvard University Press, 1986.

Gregerson, Linda. "*The Faerie Queene* (1590)." In *Handbook*, ed. McCabe, 198–217.

Greenblatt, Stephen J. *Renaissance Self-Fashioning: From More to Shakespeare*. Chicago: University of Chicago Press, 1980.

————. *Shakespearean Negotiations: The Circulation of Social Energy in Renaissance England*. Berkeley: University of California Press, 1988.

Greene, Roland. *Post-Petrarchism: Origins and Innovations of the Western Lyric Sequence*. Princeton: Princeton University Press, 1991.

————. "Petrarchism among the Discourses of Imperialism." In *America in European Consciousness: 1493–1750*, ed. Kupperman, 130–66.

Greene, Thomas M. *The Descent from Heaven: A Study in Epic Continuity*. New Haven: Yale University Press, 1963.

————. "Petrarch and the Humanist Hermeneutic." In *Italian Literature: Roots and Branches. Essays in Honor of Thomas Goddard Bergin*, ed. Giose Rimanelli and Kenneth John Atchity, 201–24. New Haven: Yale University Press, 1976.

————. *The Light in Troy: Imitation and Discovery in Renaissance Poetry*. New Haven: Yale University Press, 1982.

Gregerson, Linda. *The Reformation of the Subject: Spenser, Milton, and the English Protestant Epic*. Cambridge: Cambridge University Press, 1995.

Gruzinski, Serge. *The Conquest of Mexico: The Incorporation of Indian Societies into the Western World, 16th-18th Centuries*. Trans. Eileen Corrigan. Cambridge: Polity Press, 1993.

Guy, John. *Tudor England*. Oxford: Oxford University Press, 1988.

Hadfield, Andrew. "Chariton and Scythian: Tudor Representations of Irish Origins." *Irish Historical Studies* 28 (1993): 390–408.

————. *Literature, Politics, and National Identity: Reformation to Renaissance*. Cambridge: Cambridge University Press, 1994.

————. *Edmund Spenser's Irish Experience: Wilde Fruit and Salvage Soyl*. Oxford: Clarendon Press, 1997.

————, ed. *Edmund Spenser*. London: Longman, 1996

———, ed. *The Cambridge Companion to Spenser*. Cambridge: Cambridge University Press, 2001.

———, and Willy Maley. "Irish Representations and English Alternatives." In *Representing Ireland: Literature and Origins of Conflict, 1534–1660*, ed. B. Bradshaw and eidem, 1–23.

Haigh, Christopher. *English Reformations: Religion, Politics, and Society under the Tudors*. Oxford: Oxford University Press, 1993.

Hamilton, A. C. *Essential Articles for the Study of Edmund Spenser*. Hamden, CT: Archon Books, 1974.

Hardie, Philip. "Spenser's Vergil: *The Faerie Queene* and the *Aeneid*." In *Companion*, ed. Farrell and Putnam, 173–85.

Helgerson, Richard. *Self-Crowned Laureates: Spenser, Jonson, Milton, and the Literary System*. Berkeley: University of California Press, 1983.

———. "Tasso on Spenser: The Politics of Chivalric Romance." *Yearbook of English Studies* 21 (1991): 153–67.

———. "Barbarous Tongues: The Ideology of Poetic Form in Renaissance England." In *Edmund Spenser*, ed. Hadfield, 23–29.

———. *A Sonnet from Carthage: Garcilaso de la Vega and the New Poetry of Sixteenth-Century Europe*. Philadelphia: University of Pennsylvania Press, 2007.

Henderson, John. "Exemploque Suo Mores Reget." *Hermathena* 164 (1998): 101–16.

Hendrickson, J. C. "Exegesis." In *Oxford Dictionary of the Middle Ages*, ed. R. Bjork, 2: 597–99. 4 vols. Oxford: Oxford University Press, 2010.

Hexter, Ralph. "Sidonian Dido." In *Innovations of Antiquity*, ed. idem and Daniel Selden, 332–84. New York: Routledge, 1992.

Hieatt, A. Kent. "The Alleged Early Modern Origin of the Self and History: Terminate or Regroup?" *Spenser Studies* 10 (1992): 1–35.

Highley, Christopher. *Shakespeare, Spenser, and the Crisis in Ireland*. Cambridge: Cambridge University Press, 1997.

Holst-Warhaft, Gail. *Dangerous Voices: Women's Laments and Greek Literature*. London: Routledge, 1992.

Hutcheon, Linda. *A Theory of Parody*. New York: Methuen, 1985.

Iglesias Feijoo, Luis. "Lectura de la *Egloga I*." In *Garcilaso: Actas de la IV Academia Literaria Renacentista*, 61–82. Salamanca: Ediciones Universidad de Salamanca, 1986.

Jameson, Fredric. "The Epic as Cliché, the Cliché as Epic." In *Fables of Aggression: Wyndham Lewis, the Modernist as Fascist*, 62–80. Berkeley: University of California Press, 1979.

———. "Magical Narratives: Romance as Genre." In idem, *The Political Unconscious: Narrative as a Socially Symbolic Act*, 103–50. Ithaca: Cornell University Press, 1981.

Javitch, Daniel. *Poetry and Courtliness in Renaissance England*. Princeton: Princeton University Press, 1978.

———. *"Cantus Interruptus* in the *Orlando Furioso." Modern Language Notes* 95 (1980): 66–80.

———. "Shifting Generic Boundaries in Late Renaissance Poetic Theory." In *Proceedings of the XIIth Congress of the International Comparative Literature Association*, 4: 463–68. Munich: Iudicium, 1990.

———. *Proclaiming a Classic: The Canonization of* Orlando Furioso. Princeton: Princeton University Press, 1991.

———. "The Shaping of Poetic Genealogies in the Late Renaissance." In *Comparative Literary History as Discourse*, ed. Mario J. Valdés et al., 265–38. Bern: P. Lang, 1992.

Johnson, W. R. "The Problem of the Counter-Classical Sensibility and Its Critics." *California Studies in Classical Antiquity* 3 (1970): 123–51.

Jones, R. O. *A Literary History of Spain: The Golden Age: Prose and Poetry*. New York: Barnes and Noble, 1971.

Kagan, Richard. "Clio and the Crown: Writing History in Habsburg Spain." In *Spain, Europe, and the Atlantic World*, ed. idem and Parker, 73–99.

Kallendorf, Craig. "Philology, the Reader, and the *Nachleben* of Classical Texts." *Modern Philology* 91 (1994): 137–56.

———. "Historicizing the 'Harvard School': Pessimistic Readings of the *Aeneid* in Italian Renaissance Scholarship." *Harvard Studies in Classical Philology* 99 (1999): 391–403.

———. "Representing the Other: Ercilla's *La Araucana*, Virgil's *Aeneid*, and the New World Encounter." *Comparative Literature Studies* 40 (2003): 394–414.

———. *The Other Virgil: "Pessimistic" Readings of the* Aeneid *in Early Modern Culture*. London: Oxford University Press, 2007.

———. "Vergil and Printed Books, 1500–1800." In *Companion*, ed. Farrell and Putnam, 234–50.

Kaske, Carol V. "Spenser and the Bible." In *Handbook*, ed. McCabe, 485–502.

Kennedy, William J. "Ariosto's Ironic Allegory." *Modern Language Notes* 88 (1973): 44–67.

King, Andrew. "Spenser, Chaucer, and Medieval Romance." In *Handbook*, ed. McCabe, 553–72.

King, John N. *Spenser's Poetry and the Reformation Tradition*. Princeton: Princeton University Press, 1990.

Knox, Dilwyn. *Ironia: Medieval and Renaissance Ideas of Irony*. Leiden: E. J. Brill, 1989.

———. *"Disciplina*: The Monastic and Clerical Origins of European Civility." In *Renaissance Society and Culture*, ed. John Monfasani and Ronald G. Musto, 107–35. New York: Italica Press, 1991.

Knox, Peter E. "Savagery in the *Aeneid* and Virgil's Ancient Commentators." *Classical Journal* 92 (1997): 225–33.

Komanecky, Peter M. "Epic and Pastoral in Garcilaso's Eclogues." *Modern Language Notes* 86 (1971): 154–66.

Krogh, Kevin. "Reading Spanish Colonial Literary Texts: The Example of *La Araucana*." *Journal of Iberian and Latin American Studies* 10 (2004): 35–43.

Kupperman, Karen Ordahl, ed. *America in European Consciousness: 1493–1750*. Chapel Hill: University of North Carolina Press, 1995.

Kushner, Eva. "Renaissance Dialogue and Subjectivity." In *Printed Voices: The Renaissance Culture of Dialogue*, ed. Dorothea Heitsch and Jean-François Vallée, 229–41. Toronto: University of Toronto Press, 2004.

Lagos, Ramona. "El incumplimiento de la programmación épica en *La Araucana*." *Cuadernos Americanos* 238 (1981): 157–91.

Laird, Andrew. "The *Aeneid* from the Aztecs to the Dark Virgin." In *Companion*, ed. Farrell and Putnam, 217–33.

Lanham, Richard. *A Handlist of Rhetorical Terms*. Berkeley: University of California Press, 1991.

Lapesa, Rafael. *La trayectoria poética de Garcilaso*. Madrid: Alianza, 1985.

Leonard, Irving. *Books of the Brave: Being an Account of Books and Men in the Spanish Conquest and Settlement of the Sixteenth-century New World*. Berkeley: University of California Press, 1949.

Lerner, Isaías. "Garcilaso en Ercilla." *Lexis* 2 (1978): 201–21.

——. "Pero Mexía en Alonso de Ercilla." *Bulletin of Hispanic Studies* 60 (1983): 129–34.

——. "Para los contextos ideológicos de *La Araucana*: Erasmo." In *Homenaje a Ana María Barrenechea*, ed. Lía Schwartz and idem, 261–70. Madrid: Castalia, 1984.

——. "Texto literario, documento histórico: *La Araucana*." In *Memoria 1987–1988*, 39–55. Ávila: Fundación Sánchez-Albornoz, 1988.

——. "Don Alonso de Ercilla y Zuñiga." In *Latin American Writers*, ed. Carlos A. Solé and María I. Abreu, 23–31. New York: Scribners, 1989.

——. "América y la poesía épica áurea: la versión de Ercilla." *Edad de Oro* 10 (1991): 125–39.

——. "Ercilla y la formación del discurso poético áureo." In *Busquemos otros montes y otros ríos: Estudios de literatura española del Siglo de Oro dedicados a Elias L. Rivers*, ed. Brian Dutton and Victoriano Roncero López, 155–66. Madrid: Castalia, 1992.

——. "Ercilla y Lucano." In *Hommage à Robert Jammes*, ed. F. Cerdan, 683–91. Toulouse: Presses Universitaires du Mirail, 1994.

——. "La colonización española y las lenguas indígenas de América." *Colonial Latin American Review* 6 (1997): 7–15.

——. "Entre Cervantes y Ercilla: *Quijote* 1.8–9." In *El comentario de textos*, ed. Inés Carrasco and Guadalupe Fernández Ariza, 207–20. Málaga: *Analecta Malacitana*, Universidad de Málaga, 1998.

———. "*La Araucana*: épica e imperio." In *Littérature et Politique en Espagne aux Siècles d'Or.* ed. J.P. Etienvre, Paris: Klincksieck, 1998.

———. "Felipe II y Alonso de Ercilla." *Edad de Oro* 18 (1999): 87–101.

———. "Persistencia de metáforas: Lucano, Ercilla, el romancero." In *Siglos Dorados: Homenaje a Augustin Redondo*, ed. Pierre Civil, 2: 765–74. Madrid: Castilla, 2004.

———. "Épica y lírica: un diálogo de géneros." In *El Canon poético en el siglo XVI*, 298–320. Seville: Universidad de Sevilla—Grupo PASO, 2008.

Lerzundi, Patricio C. *Romances basados en "La Araucana."* Madrid: Playor, 1978.

Lewis, Bernard. *Cultures in Conflict: Christians, Muslims, and Jews in the Age of Discovery.* New York: Oxford University Press, 1995.

Lida de Malkiel, Maria Rosa. *Juan de Mena, poeta del prerrenacimiento español.* Mexico, D.F.: Centro de Estudios Lingüísticos y Literarios, Colegio de Mexico, 1950, repr. 1984.

———. "Arthurian Literature in Spain and Portugal." In *Arthurian Literature in the Middle Ages: A Collaborative History*, ed. R. S. Loomis, 1: 406–18. Oxford: Clarendon Press, 1959.

———. *Dido en la literatura española.* London: Tamesis, 1974.

Lievsay, John L. *The Englishman's Italian Books,1550–1700.* Philadelphia: University of Pennsylvania Press, 1969.

Lim, Walter S. H. "Figuring Justice: Imperial Ideology and the Discourse of Colonialism in Book V of *The Faerie Queene* and *A View of the Present State of Ireland.*" *Renaissance and Reformation* 19 (1995): 45–67.

Lipking, Lawrence. *Abandoned Women and Poetic Tradition.* Chicago: University of Chicago Press, 1988.

Loomie, Albert J. *The Spanish Elizabethans.* New York: Fordham University Press, 1963.

Looney, Dennis. *Compromising the Classics: Romance Epic Narrative in the Italian Renaissance.* Detroit: Wayne State University Press, 1996.

———. "Marvelous Virgil in the Ferrarese Renaissance." In *Companion*, ed. Farrell and Putnam, 158–72.

Lozano-Renieblas, Isabel, and Juan Carlos Mercado, eds. *Silva: Studia philologica in honorem Isaías Lerner.* Madrid: Editorial Castalia, 2001.

Lupher, David A. *Romans in a New World: Classical Models in Sixteenth-Century Spanish America.* Ann Arbor: University of Michigan Press, 2003.

Lupton, Julia. "Home-making in Ireland: Virgil's Eclogue I and Book VI of *The Faerie Queene.*" *Spenser Studies* 8 (1990): 119–45.

Lynch, John. *Spain under the Habsburgs.* 2 vols. New York: New York University Press, 1981.

Lyne, R.O.A.M. "Virgil's *Aeneid*: Subversion by Intertextuality. Catullus 66.39–40 and Other Examples." *Greece and Rome* 41 (1994): 187–204.

MacCormack, S. G. *The Shadows of Poetry: Vergil in the Mind of Augustine.* Berkeley: University of California Press, 1998.

———. *On the Wings of Time: Rome, the Incas, Spain, and Peru*. Princeton: Princeton University Press, 2007.

Madrigal, Luis Íñigo. "Alonso de Ercilla y Zúñiga." In *Historia de la literatura hispanoamericana: época colonial*, ed. idem, 189–203.

———. ed. *Historia de la literatura hispanoamericana: época colonial*. Madrid: Catedra, 1982.

Maley, Willy. "How Milton and Some Contemporaries Read Spenser's *View*." In *Representing Ireland: Literature and the Origins of Conflict, 1534–1660*, ed. Bradshaw, Hadfield, and idem, 191–208.

A Spenser Chronology. London: Macmillan, 1994.

———. "Spenser's Irish English: Language and Identity in Early Modern Ireland." *Studies in Philology* 91 (1994): 417–31.

———. *Salvaging Spenser: Colonialism, Culture, and Identity*. New York: St. Martin's Press, 1997.

———. "Spenser's Languages: Writing in the Ruins of English." In *Companion to Spenser*, ed. Hadfield, 162–79.

Marinelli, Peter V. *Ariosto and Boiardo: The Origins of Orlando Furioso*. Columbia: University of Missouri Press, 1987.

Marrero-Fente, Raúl. "Épica, fantasma y lamento: la retórica del duelo in *La Araucana*." *Revista Iberoamericana* 73 (2007): 15–30.

Martindale, Charles. "Descent into Hell: Reading Ambiguity, or Virgil and the Critics." *Proceedings of the Virgil Society* 21 (1998): 111–50.

McCabe, Richard A. "Annotating Anonymity, or Putting a Gloss on *The Shepheardes Calender*." In *Ma(r)king the Text: The Presentation of Meaning on the Literary Page*, ed. Joe Bray, Miriam Handley, and Anne C. Henry, 35–54. Aldershot: Ashgate, 2000.

———. *Spenser's Monstrous Regiment: Elizabethan Ireland and the Poetics of Difference*. Oxford: Oxford University Press, 2002.

———. "Spenser and Ovid." Review of Syrithe Pugh, *Spenser and Ovid*. *Review of English Studies* 56 (2005): 786–87.

———. ed. *The Oxford Handbook of Edmund Spenser*. Oxford: Oxford University Press, 2010.

McCoy, Richard. *Sir Philip Sidney: Rebellion in Arcadia*. New Brunswick: Rutgers University Press, 1979.

———. *The Rites of Knighthood*. Berkeley: University of California Press, 1989.

McKeon, Richard. "Literary Criticism and the Concept of Imitation in Antiquity." *Modern Philology* 34 (1936): 1–36.

Medina, José Toribio. "Las Mujeres en *La Araucana* de Ercilla." *Hispania* (1928): 1–12.

———. *La Araucana de Don Alonso de Ercilla y Zuñiga*. 5 vols. Edición del Centenario. Mexico: Fondo de Cultura Económica, 1948.

———. *Vida de Ercilla*. Mexico: Fondo de Cultura Económica, 1948.

Mejías-López, William. "Alonso de Ercilla y los problemas de los indios chilenos: algunas prerrogativas legales presentes en *La Araucana*." *Bulletin of Hispanic Studies* 69 (1992): 1–10.

Melczer, William. "Ercilla's Divided Heroic Vision: A Reevaluation of the Epic Hero in *La Araucana*." *Hispania* 56 (1973): 218–20.

———. "Towards the Dignification of the Vulgar Tongues: Humanistic Translations into Italian and Spanish in the Renaissance." *Canadian Review of Comparative Literature* 8 (1981): 256–71.

Menéndez y Pelayo, Marcelino. *Historia de las ideas estéticas en España*. Madrid: CSIC, 1974 (orig. 1883–1891).

Mignolo, Walter D. "Cartas, crónicas y relaciones del descubrimiento y la conquista." In *Historia de la literatura hispanoamericana: época colonial*, ed. Madrigal, 57–116.

———. *The Darker Side of the Renaissance: Literacy, Territoriality, and Colonization*. Ann Arbor: University of Michigan Press, 1995.

Miller, David Lee. "Spenser's Poetics: The Poem's Two Bodies." In *Edmund Spenser*, ed. Hadfield, 85–111.

Montrose, Louis. "The Elizabethan Subject and the Spenserian Text." In *Literary Theory / Renaissance Texts*, ed. Patricia Parker and David Quint, 303–40. Baltimore: Johns Hopkins University Press, 1986.

———. "The Work of Gender and Sexuality in the Elizabethan Discourse of Discovery." In *Discourses of Sexuality from Aristotle to Aids*, ed. Domna C. Stanton, 138–84. Ann Arbor: University of Michigan Press, 1992.

Morgan, J. R. "Heliodoros." In *Novel*, ed. Schmeling, 417–56.

Morreale, Margherita. *Castiglione y Boscán: el ideal cortesano en el renacimiento español*. 2 vols. Madrid: Anejos del Boletín de la Real Academía Española, 1959.

Muñoz, Luis G. "Ercilla, protagonista de *La Araucana*." In *Homenaje a Ercilla*, 5–29.

Murrin, Michael. *The Veil of Allegory: Some Notes Toward a Theory of Allegorical Rhetoric in the English Renaissance*. Chicago: University of Chicago Press, 1969.

———. *History and Warfare in Renaissance Epic*. Chicago: University of Chicago Press, 1994.

———. "Renaissance Allegory from Petrarch to Spenser." In *Companion to Allegory*, ed. Copeland and Struck, 162–76.

Navarrete, Ignacio. *Orphans of Petrarch: Poetry and Theory in the Spanish Renaissance*. Berkeley: University of California Press, 1994.

Nelis, Damien P. "Apollonius and Virgil." In *A Companion to Apollonius Rhodius*, ed. T. D. Papanghelis and A. Rengakos, 237–59. Leiden: Brill, 2001.

Nicolopulos, James. *The Poetics of Empire in the Indies: Prophecy and Imitation in* La Araucana *and* Os Lusiádas. University Park: Pennsylvania State University Press, 2000.

————. "Pedro de Oña and Bernardo de Balbuena Read Ercilla's Fitón." *Latin American Literary Review* 26 (1998): 100–19.

————. "Reading and Responding to the Amorous Episodes of the *Araucana* in Colonial Peru." In *Ésta de Nuestra América Pupila: Estudios de Poesía Colonial,* ed. Georgina Sabat-Rivers, 227–43. Houston: Society for Renaissance and Baroque Hispanic Poetry, 1999.

Nohrnberg, James. *The Anatomy of the Faerie Queene.* Princeton: Princeton University Press, 1976.

Norbrook, David. *Poetry and Politics in the English Reformation.* London: Routledge and Kegan Paul, 1984.

Norton, Glyn P. *The Ideology of Language and Translation in Renaissance France and their Humanist Antecedents.* Geneva: Libraire Droz, 1984.

————. "*Fidus Interpres*: A Philological Contribution to the Philosophy of Translation in Renaissance France." In *Neo-Latin and the Vernacular in Renaissance France,* ed. Grahame Castor and Terence Cave, 227–51. Oxford: Clarendon Press, 1984.

O'Connor, John J. *Amadis de Gaule and its Influence on Elizabethan Literature.* New Brunswick, NJ: Rutgers University Press, 1970.

Ortiz, Judith Miller. "The Two Faces of Dido: Classical Images and Medieval Reinterpretation." *Romance Quarterly* 33 (1986): 421–30.

Padrón, Ricardo. "Love American Style: The Virgin Land and the Sodomitic Body in Ercilla's *Araucana*." *Revista de Estudios Hispánicos* 34 (2000): 561–84.

————. Review of Richard Helgerson, *A Sonnet from Carthage: Garcilaso de la Vega and the New Poetry of Sixteenth-Century Europe. Hispanic Review* 76 (2008): 99–102.

Pagden, Anthony. *Lords of All the World: Ideologies of Empire in Spain, Britain, and France: c. 1500–c. 1800.* New Haven: Yale University Press, 1995.

Palmer, Patricia. *Language and Conquest in Early Modern Ireland: English Renaissance Literature and Elizabethan Imperial Expansion.* Cambridge: Cambridge University Press, 2001.

Panofsky, Erwin. *Studies in Iconology: Humanistic Themes in the Art of the Renaissance.* New York: Oxford University Press, 1939.

Parker, Geoffrey. "David or Goliath? Philip II and his World in the 1580s." In *Spain, Europe, and the Atlantic World,* ed. Kagan and idem, 245–66.

Parker, Patricia A. *Inescapable Romance: Studies in the Poetics of a Mode.* Princeton: Princeton University Press, 1979.

————. *Literary Fat Ladies: Rhetoric, Gender, Property.* New York: Methuen, 1987.

————, and David Quint, eds. *Literary Theory / Renaissance Texts.* Baltimore: Johns Hopkins University Press, 1986.

Pastor, Beatriz. *Discursos narrativos de la conquista: mitificación y emergencia.* Hanover, NH: Ediciones del Norte, 1988.

Patterson, Annabel. *Reading Between the Lines.* London: Routledge, 1993.

Pavlock, Barbara. *Eros, Imitation, and the Epic Tradition.* Ithaca: Cornell University Press, 1990.

Perelmuter-Pérez, Rosa. "El paisaje idealizado en *La Araucana.*" *Hispanic Review* 54 (1986): 129–46.

———. "El desierto en *La Araucana.*" *Caliope* 4 (1998): 248–57.

Pierce, Frank. *La Poesía Epica del Siglo de Oro.* Madrid: Gredos, 1961.

———. *Alonso de Ercilla y Zúñiga.* Amsterdam: Rodopi, 1984.

Pigman, G. W. "Versions of Imitation in the Renaissance." *Renaissance Quarterly* 33 (1980): 1–32.

Piñero Ramírez, Pedro. "La épica hispanoamericana colonial." In *Historia de la literatura hispanoamericana: época colonial,* ed. Madrigal, 161–88.

Poggioli, Renato. *The Oaten Flute: Essays on Pastoral Poetry and the Pastoral Idea.* Boston: Harvard University Press, 1975.

Power, Henry. "The *Aeneid* in the Age of Milton." In *Companion,* ed. Farrell and Putnam, 186–202.

Prieto, Andrés I. "El Segundo Carlomagno: Las visiones proféticas de San Quintín y Lepanto en *La Araucana* de Ercilla." *Hispanófila* 140 (2004): 81–99.

Promís, José. *The Identity of Hispanoamerica: An Interpretation of Colonial Literature.* Trans. Alita Kelley and Alec E. Kelley. Tucson: University of Arizona Press, 1991.

Pugh, Syrithe. *Spenser and Ovid.* Aldershot: Ashgate Publishing, 2005.

———. "Spenser and Classical Literature." In *Handbook,* ed. McCabe, 503–19.

Quilligan, Maureen. *The Language of Allegory: Defining the Genre.* Ithaca: Cornell University Press, 1979.

———. *Milton's Spenser: The Politics of Reading.* Ithaca: Cornell University Press, 1983.

Quinn, David Beers. *The Elizabethans and the Irish.* Ithaca: Cornell University Press, 1990.

Quint, David. *Origin and Originality in Renaissance Literature: Versions of the Source.* New Haven: Yale University Press, 1983

———. *Epic and Empire: Politics and Generic Form from Virgil to Milton.* Princeton: Princeton University Press, 1993.

Quintero, María Cristina. "Translation and Imitation in the Development of Tragedy during the Spanish Renaissance." In *Renaissance Readings: Intertext and Context,* ed. Horowitz, Cruz, and Furman, 96–110.

Read, David. *Temperate Conquests: Spenser and the Spanish New World.* Detroit: Wayne State University Press, 2000.

Reichenberger, Arnold G. "Boscán and the Classics." *Comparative Literature* 3 (1951): 97–118.

Reynolds, L.D., and N.G. Wilson. *Scribes and Scholars: A Guide to the Transmission of Greek and Latin Literature.* Oxford: Clarendon Press, 1968.

Rhu, Lawrence F. *The Genesis of Tasso's Narrative Theory: English Translations of the Early Poetics and a Comparative Study of Their Significance.* Detroit: Wayne State University Press, 1993.

Rich, Townsend. *Harington and Ariosto: A Study in Elizabethan Verse Translation.* New Haven: Yale University Press, 1940.

Rico, Francisco. "El Destierro del Verso Agudo." In *Homenaje a José Manuel Blecua*, 525–51. Madrid: Gredos, 1983.

Rivers, Elias L. "Cervantes and the Question of Language." In *Cervantes and the Renaissance: Papers of the Pomona College Cervantes Symposium, Nov. 16–18, 1978*, ed. Michael D. McGaha, 23–33. Easton, PA: Juan de la Cuesta, 1978.

———. "El problema de los géneros neoclásicos y la poesía de Garcilaso." In *Academia Literaria Renacentista, IV: Garcilaso*, ed. Víctor García de la Concha, 49–60. Salamanca: Universidad de Salamanca, 1986.

Rosenmeyer, Thomas G. *The Green Cabinet: Theocritus and the European Pastoral Lyric.* Berkeley: University of California Press, 1969.

Rummel, Erika. *The Humanist-Scholastic Debate in the Renaissance and Reformation.* Cambridge, MA: Harvard University Press, 1995.

Said, Edward W. *Orientalism.* New York: Random House, 1978.

———. "The Problem of Textuality: Two Exemplary Positions." *Critical Inquiry* 4 (1978): 673–714.

———. *The World, the Text, and the Critic.* Cambridge, MA: Harvard University Press, 1983.

———. *Humanism and Democratic Criticism.* New York: Palgrave Macmillan, 2004.

Sandy, Gerald. "The Heritage of the Ancient Greek Novel in France and Britain." In *Novel*, ed. Schmeling, 735–73.

Schmidt, Benjamin. "Exotic Allies: The Dutch-Chilean Encounter and the (Failed) Conquest of America." *Renaissance Quarterly* 52 (1999): 440–73.

Schwartz, Lía. "Tradición literaria y heroínas indias en *La Araucana*." *Revista Iberoamericana* 38 (1972): 615–25.

———. "El diálogo en la cultura áurea: de los textos al género." *Insula* 542 (1992): 1–28.

———. "Fray Luis de Leon's Translations of Greek Texts and their Humanistic Context." *Allegorica* 17 (1996): 55–72.

Seem, Lauren Scancarelli. "The Limits of Chivalry: Tasso and the End of the *Aeneid*." *Comparative Literature* 42 (1990): 116–25.

Serés, Guillermo. *La traducción en Italia y España durante el siglo XV: La "Ilíada en Romance" y su contexto cultural.* Salamanca: Ediciones Universidad de Salamanca, 1997.

Shay, Jonathan. *Achilles in Vietnam: Combat Trauma and the Undoing of Character.* New York: Scribner, 1994.

Shepherd, Gregory. "Ercilla's Creative and Critical Conflicts: Balancing Oppositions in *La Araucana*." *Latin American Literary Review* 26 (1998): 120–33.

Simerka, Barbara. *Discourses of Empire: Counter-Epic Discourse in Early Modern Spain.* University Park: Pennsylvania State University Press, 2003.

———. Review of Patrick Cheney and Frederick A. de Armas, eds., *European Literary Careers: The Author from Antiquity to the Renaissance. Comparative Literature Studies* 43 (2006): 191–94.

Sitterson, Joseph C. Jr. "Allusive and Elusive Meanings: Reading Ariosto's Vergilian Ending." *Renaissance Quarterly* 45 (1992): 1–19.

Spence, Sarah. *"Felix Casus*: The Dares and Dictys Legends of Aeneas." In *Companion*, ed. Farrell and Putnam, 133–46.

Stephens, Dorothy. "Spenser's Language(s): Linguistic Theory and Poetic Diction." In *Handbook*, ed. McCabe, 367–84.

Strong, Roy C. *The Cult of Elizabeth: Elizabethan Portraiture and Pageantry.* London: Thames and Hudson, 1977.

Struever, Nancy S. *The Language of History in the Renaissance: Rhetoric and Historical Consciousness in Florentine Humanism.* Princeton: Princeton University Press, 1970.

Suzuki, Mihoko. *Metamorphoses of Helen: Authority, Difference, and the Epic.* Ithaca: Cornell University Press, 1989.

Terracini, Lore. *Lingua come problema nella letteratura dell'Cinquecento.* Turin: Stampatori, 1979.

Thomas, Henry. *Spanish and Portuguese Romances of Chivalry.* London: Cambridge University Press, 1920.

Thomas, Richard. F. "The 'Sacrifice' at the End of the *Georgics*, Aristaeus, and Vergilian Closure." *Classical Philology* 86 (1991): 211–18.

———. *Reading Virgil and his Texts: Studies in Intertextuality.* Ann Arbor: University of Michigan Press, 1999.

———. *Virgil and the Augustan Reception.* Cambridge: Cambridge University Press, 2001.

Triviños, Gilberto. "El mito del tiempo de los héroes de Valdivia, Vivar y Ercilla" *Revista Chilena de Literatura* 49 (1996): 5–26.

———. "Revisitando la literatura chilena: 'Sigue diciendo: cayeron / di más: volverán mañana'." *Atenea* 487 (2003): 133–33.

Vaught, Jennifer C. "Spenser's Dialogic Voice in Book 1 of *The Faerie Queene*." *Studies in English Literature 1500–1900* 41 (2001): 71–89.

Venuti, Lawrence. *The Translator's Invisibility: A History of Translation.* London: Routledge, 1995.

———. *The Scandals of Translation: Towards an Ethics of Difference.* London: Routledge, 1998.

Vila i Tomás, Lara. "Épica e imperio: Imitación virgiliana y propaganda política en la épica española del siglo XVI." Ph.D. diss., Universitat Autònoma de Barcelona, 2001.

———. "La Épica española del Renacimiento (1450–1605): propuestas para una revisión." *Boletín de la Real Academia Española* 83 (2003): 137–50.

Vilanova, Antonio. "Preceptistas españoles de los siglos XVI y XVII." In *Historia general de las literaturas hispánicas*, ed. D. Guillermo Díaz-Plaja, 3: 567–692. Barcelona: Barra, 1953.

———. *Las Fuentes y los temas del* Polifemo *de Góngora*. Madrid: CSIC, 1957.

Vološinov, V.N. *Marxism and the Philosophy of Language*. Trans. Ladislav Matejka and I. R. Titunik. Cambridge, MA: Harvard University Press, 1973.

Walthaus, Rina. "La fortuna de Dido en la literatura española medieval (Desde la crónicas alfonsíes a la tragedia renacentista de Juan Cirne)." In *Actas del III Congreso de la Asociación Hispánica de Literatura Medieval (Salamanca, 1989)*, ed. María Isabel Toro Pascua, 2: 1171–81. Salamanca: Biblioteca Española del Siglo XV, 1994.

Watkins, John. *The Specter of Dido: Spenser and Virgilian Epic*. New Haven: Yale University Press, 1995.

Williams, Raymond. *Marxism and Literature*. Oxford: Oxford University Press, 1977.

Wills, Garry. "Vergil and St. Augustine." In *Companion*, ed. Farrell and Putnam, 123–32.

Yates, Frances. *Astraea: The Imperial Theme in the Sixteenth Century*. London: Routledge and Kegan Paul, 1975.

Yndurain, Domingo. "La invención de una lengua clásica." *Edad de Oro* 1 (1982): 13–34.

Zamora, Margarita. "Historicity and Literariness: Problems in the Literary Criticism of Spanish American Colonial Texts." *Modern Language Notes* 102 (1987): 334–46.

Zuckerman, Michael. "Identity in British America: Unease in Eden." In *Colonial Identity in the Atlantic World, 1500–1800*, ed. Canny and Pagden, 115–57.

Index